Educational Leadership

perspectives
Educational Leadership

Academic Editor
Linda Orozco
Coastline College and University of California, Irvine

Bellevue • Boulder • Dubuque • Madison • St. Paul

Our mission at **Coursewise** is to help students make connections—linking theory to practice and the classroom to the outside world. Learners are motivated to synthesize ideas when course materials are placed in a context they recognize. By providing gateways to contemporary and enduring issues, **Coursewise** publications will expand students' awareness of and context for the course subject.

For more information on **Coursewise,** visit us at our web site: http://www.coursewise.com

To order an examination copy, contact: Houghton Mifflin Sixth Floor Media: 800-565-6247 (voice); 800-565-6236 (fax).

Coursewise Publishing Editorial Staff

Thomas Doran, ceo/publisher: Environmental Science/Geography/Journalism/Marketing/Speech
Edgar Laube, publisher: Political Science/Psychology/Sociology
Linda Meehan Avenarius, publisher: **Courselinks**™
Sue Pulvermacher-Alt, publisher: Education/Health/Gender Studies
Victoria Putman, publisher: Anthropology/Philosophy/Religion
Tom Romaniak, publisher: Business/Criminal Justice/Economics
Kathleen Schmitt, publishing assistant

Coursewise Publishing Production Staff

Lori A. Blosch, permissions coordinator
Mary Monner, production coordinator
Victoria Putman, production manager

Note: Readings in this book appear exactly as they were published.
Thus, inconsistencies in style and usage among the different
readings are likely.

Cover photo: Copyright © 1997 T. Teshigawara/Panoramic Images, Chicago, IL. All Rights Reserved.

Interior design and cover design by Jeff Storm

Copyright © 1999 by Coursewise Publishing, Inc. All Rights Reserved.

Library of Congress Catalog Card Number: 99-90062

ISBN 0-395-97214-0

No part of this publication may be reproduced, stored in a retrieval system, or transmitted,
in any form or by any means, electronic, mechanical, photocopying, recording, or otherwise,
without the prior written permission of the publisher.

Printed in the United States of America by Coursewise Publishing, Inc.
7 North Pinckney Street, Suite 346, Madison, WI 53703

10 9 8 7 6 5 4 3 2 1

from the Publisher

Sue Pulvermacher–Alt
Coursewise Publishing

*What makes a leader?**

Think of people that you know who are good leaders. How are they different from others? What makes them good leaders?

Since I joined the paid working world at the age of twelve, I've had the good fortune to work for several good leaders. Working on a neighbor's farm, I learned from my first boss that hard work can also be fun. During my teenage food-service career, a manager convinced me that I had the moxie to move from more solitary, kitchen work to the social, "out-front" job of waitress. In my first teaching job, the principal guided me through the challenging first year by checking in often, offering resources, and otherwise staying out of my way. When I joined the world of publishing (here in the upper Midwest), our president at that time openly admitted that his job was to "drive the snowplow and keep the roads clear" so we could get our jobs done.

Different people. Very different personalities. Different settings and different times. Why do I consider them all effective leaders? I now recognize some common traits. Each knew me well enough to provide the direction and motivation I needed. Each openly and frequently offered praise, which, in turn, gave me confidence to take on tasks I probably wouldn't have otherwise taken on. Each allowed me enough freedom to get the job done. Each had a great sense of humor and called upon it often. Each worked hard and expected me to do the same. My conclusion: Effective leaders make you *want* to follow.

Since you're reading this note, I assume that you want to be an effective leader. You're taking an important step by taking this class that focuses on leadership. The readings in this volume will help you to sort out the important issues surrounding effective leadership. In addition, the R.E.A.L web sites listed throughout the book and also at the **Courselinks**™ site have been chosen because they are particularly useful sites. You, however, need to be a leader and make this information your own. Read our annotations and decide if the site is worth visiting. Do the activities so you can get to know the site better. Search our **Courselinks** site by key topic and find the information you need to be a more informed and effective educational leader.

As publisher for this volume, I had the good fortune to work with Linda Orozco. Linda is both the Academic Editor of this volume and the editor of the **Courselinks** site for Educational Leadership. Linda's knowledge of the content, magnified by her professional passion, is capped

---

*1.05567 liquid quarts (oh yeah, that's a *liter;* you'll need to read on to find out what makes a *leader!*)

by her diligence to meet deadlines and get the job done right. She leads by her hard-working example. Take a look at her Academic Editor's Note. She's lived leadership and brings that experience to you.

We were helped by a top-notch Editorial Board. At **Coursewise** we're working hard to publish "connected learning" tools—connecting theory to practice and the college classroom to the outside world. Readings and web sites are selected with this goal in mind. Members of the Editorial Board offer critical feedback and pose interesting challenges. They know their content and are a web-savvy bunch. My thanks to Linda and the entire Editorial Board.

As you use our print and online resources and continue to build your understanding of educational leadership, I invite you to share your reactions to our materials. How'd we do in representing the subject of educational leadership? What worked and what didn't work in this *Perspectives: Educational Leadership* volume and the accompanying **Courselinks** site? I'd love to hear from you—as one aspiring leader to another.

Sue Pulvermacher-Alt, Publisher
suepa@coursewise.com

from the
Academic Editor

Linda Orozco
Coastline College and University of California, Irvine

Dr. Linda Orozco is Dean of Instruction at Coastline College in Southern California. She is also an adjunct professor at the University of California, Irvine, where she teaches educational leadership in the Ed.D. and M.A. programs. She received her Ph.D. in educational administration from the University of Minnesota. Dr. Orozco has over 20 years of experience in educational leadership, and her work has involved a variety of organizations, including K–12 schools, regional/county education agencies, private industry, and higher education. She is "web-mistress" for the California Association of Professors of Educational Administration (CAPEA), and also serves on a number of leadership journal review boards.

> "Let him that would move the world, first move himself."
> —Socrates

Twenty-five years ago, I began my professional career as a kindergarten teacher. Now, I serve as dean to over 100 faculty in higher education and also teach leadership to doctoral students at the University of California, Irvine. I continue to be fascinated with the theory, process, practice, and successful application of leadership.

My experience in leadership spans the country. Certainly, administrative experiences in local public schools and district offices provided a solid foundation for practicing the "art of leadership." But my experiences in leadership in more nontraditional educational settings provided an opportunity to fine-tune and examine the commonalties of the process.

An Apache reservation in the White Mountains of Arizona, a school for the deaf in Vancouver, and a women's prison in Tennessee all served as confirmation that successful leadership is critical to enhancing the teaching and learning process. Even at St. Michael's Catholic parish in St. Paul, Minnesota, I learned important lessons of leadership from faculty/nuns from the Sisters of St. Joseph. I've concluded that leadership is not an elusive, vague, and mysterious concept. It is clear and deliberate—even as it continues to be a fluid, evolving process in the world of education.

Perspectives: Educational Leadership is my examination of leadership from the inside out. What qualities are necessary for effective leadership? Are leaders born or created? What do successful leaders have to say about the art of leadership? How has the art of leadership changed over the years, and where is it going in the new millennium? The readings in this book address these and other questions.

This volume focuses on six major areas of leadership prevalent in educational organizations today. These are:

- Qualities of Effective Leaders
- Ethical Dimensions of Leadership
- Connecting: To People and Community
- Collaborating: Building Teams and Leadership Capacity
- Instruction: Learning and Leadership
- Change: To Understand, Respond and Influence

Each of these areas was selected for inclusion because of its importance in leadership development, organizational change, and reform.

In addition to the readings, the R.E.A.L. web sites cited in this volume and at the **Courselinks**™ web site for Educational Leadership expand on the topics encompassed within these six dimensions of leadership. The R.E.A.L. web sites provide current, immediately available resources for aspiring and current leaders who are seeking to understand and analyze the nature and process of leadership.

Editorial Board

We wish to thank the following instructors for their assistance. Their many suggestions not only contributed to the construction of this volume, but also to the ongoing development of our Educational Leadership web site.

Gerald (Jerry) Bass
University of North Dakota

Maenette K.P. Benham
Michigan State University

Maenette K. P. Benham, Ed.D., is an assistant professor in educational administration at Michigan State University. As a native Hawaiian scholar, her inquiry centers on the use of narrative to reveal issues and practices of school leadership, teaching and learning strategies that explore practitioner understanding and practice, the effects of educational policy and practice on native people, and the educational processes of building and sustaining social and cultural community capacity.

Rosalia D'Amico
University of New Orleans

Rosalia D'Amico, M.Ed., is assistant to the dean of academic services—World Wide Web and Internet Services at the University of New Orleans. Her areas of interest are technology in university administration, leadership in higher education, and university culture. She hopes to continue her studies and earn a Ph.D. in educational administration.

Michael England
Southwestern Adventist College

Dr. Michael England is an associate professor of education at Southwestern Adventist College, where he specializes in leadership in curriculum instruction. His areas of interest include integrating technology into teaching and infusing brain research into teaching and learning. Dr. England also enjoys the martial arts, running, and cycling.

Rick Ginsberg
Colorado State University

Bruce Kramer
University of St. Thomas

Ed Lind
University of Guam

Thelma Moore-Steward
California State University, Long Beach

Dennis T. Murphy
Long Island University, C.W. Post

Dr. Dennis Murphy is an associate professor of educational administration with Long Island University (NY) at its C.W. Post campus. His goal is to create a textbook-less, Internet-based set of resources for his educational administration students.

Fred Muskal
University of the Pacific

Fred Muskal earned his Ph.D. at the University of Chicago and is now professor of educational administration and foundations at the University of the Pacific. His interests include promoting upward mobility in low-income youth, multicultural education, higher education, instructional technology, and general education.

Maria Natera-Riles
National University, Sacramento

Maria Natera-Riles, Ed.D., is assistant professor and chair in the Educational Administration Programs at National University, Sacramento. She earned her Ed.D. in educational administration at the University of Southern California. Her areas of interest include educational technology and educating diverse learners. In addition to her work, Maria enjoys family, art, and friends.

V. Darlene Opfer
Georgia State University

J. Theodore Repa
New York University

J. Theodore Repa is an associate professor of educational administration and deputy director of the Metropolitan Center for Urban Education at New York University. He earned his Ph.D. in educational sociology and anthropology at Stanford University. His research interests include leadership, decision making, infusion of technology into schools, and the conditions necessary to promote equity in educational organizations.

Mimi Schuttloffel
The Catholic University of America

Mimi Schuttloffel is an assistant professor of educational administration and policy studies and director of the Catholic School Leadership Program at The Catholic University of America. Her work has been included in such publications as *Bulletin of Science, Technology & Society, International Journal of Educational Telecommunications,* and *Catholic Education Journal.* She received both her MA in school counseling and her Ph.D. in educational administration and research from the University of Tulsa. Her areas of specialization include educational leadership as it relates to institutional culture, policy studies, technology as an instrument of innovation and change in schools, and reflective practice.

Lynn Sullivan Taber
University of South Florida

WiseGuide Introduction

Question Authority

Critical Thinking and Bumper Stickers

The bumper sticker said: Question Authority. This is a simple directive that goes straight to the heart of critical thinking. The issue is not whether the authority is right or wrong; it's the questioning process that's important. Questioning helps you develop awareness and a clearer sense of what you think. That's critical thinking.

Critical thinking is a new label for an old approach to learning—that of challenging all ideas, hypotheses, and assumptions. In the physical and life sciences, systematic questioning and testing methods (known as the scientific method) help verify information, and objectivity is the benchmark on which all knowledge is pursued. In the social sciences, however, where the goal is to study people and their behavior, things get fuzzy. It's one thing for the chemistry experiment to work out as predicted, or for the petri dish to yield a certain result. It's quite another matter, however, in the social sciences, where the subject is ourselves. Objectivity is harder to achieve.

Although you'll hear critical thinking defined in many different ways, it really boils down to analyzing the ideas and messages that you receive. What are you being asked to think or believe? Does it make sense, objectively? Using the same facts and considerations, could you reasonably come up with a different conclusion? And, why does this matter in the first place? As the bumper sticker urged, question authority. Authority can be a textbook, a politician, a boss, a big sister, or an ad on television. Whatever the message, learning to question it appropriately is a habit that will serve you well for a lifetime. And in the meantime, thinking critically will certainly help you be course wise.

Getting Connected

This reader is a tool for connected learning. This means that the readings and other learning aids explained here will help you to link classroom theory to real-world issues. They will help you to think critically and to make long-lasting learning connections. Feedback from both instructors and students has helped us to develop some suggestions on how you can wisely use this connected learning tool.

WiseGuide Pedagogy

A wise reader is better able to be a critical reader. Therefore, we want to help you get wise about the articles in this reader. Each section of *Perspectives* has three tools to help you: the WiseGuide Intro, the WiseGuide Wrap-Up, and the Putting It in *Perspectives* review form.

WiseGuide Intro

In the WiseGuide Intro, the Academic Editor introduces the section, gives you an overview of the topics covered, and explains why particular articles were selected and what's important about them.

Also in the WiseGuide Intro, you'll find several key points or learning objectives that highlight the most important things to remember from this section. These will help you to focus your study of section topics.

At the end of the WiseGuide Intro, you'll find questions designed to stimulate critical thinking. Wise students will keep these questions in mind as they read an article (we repeat the questions at the start of the articles as a reminder). When you finish each article, check your understanding. Can you answer the questions? If not, go back and reread the article. The Academic Editor has written sample responses for many of the questions, and you'll find these online at the **Courselinks**™ site for this course. More about **Courselinks** in a minute. . . .

WiseGuide Wrap-Up

Be course wise and develop a thorough understanding of the topics covered in this course. The WiseGuide Wrap-Up at the end of each section will help you do just that with concluding comments or summary points that repeat what's most important to understand from the section you just read.

In addition, we try to get you wired up by providing a list of select Internet resources—what we call R.E.A.L. web sites because they're **R**elevant, **E**xciting, **A**pproved, and **L**inked. The information at these web sites will enhance your understanding of a topic. (Remember to use your Passport and start at http://www.courselinks.com so that if any of these sites have changed, you'll have the latest link.)

Putting It in *Perspectives* Review Form

At the end of the book is the Putting It in *Perspectives* review form. Your instructor may ask you to complete this form as an assignment or for extra credit. If nothing else, consider doing it on your own to help you critically think about the reading.

Prompts at the end of each article encourage you to complete this review form. Feel free to copy the form and use it as needed.

The Courselinks™ Site

The **Courselinks** Passport is your ticket to a wonderful world of integrated web resources designed to help you with your course work. These resources are found at the **Courselinks** site for your course area. This is where the readings in this book and the key topics of your course are linked to an exciting array of online learning tools. Here you will find carefully selected readings, web links, quizzes, worksheets, and more, tailored to your course and approved as connected learning tools. The ever-changing, always interesting **Courselinks** site features a number of carefully integrated resources designed to help you be course wise. These include:

- **R.E.A.L. Sites** At the core of a **Courselinks** site is the list of R.E.A.L. sites. This is a select group of web sites for studying, not surfing. Like the readings in this book, these sites have been selected, reviewed, and approved by the Academic Editor and the Editorial Board. The R.E.A.L. sites are arranged by topic and are annotated with short descriptions and key words to make them easier for you to use for reference or research. With R.E.A.L. sites, you're studying approved resources within seconds—and not wasting precious time surfing unproven sites.

- **Editor's Choice** Here you'll find updates on news related to your course, with links to the actual online sources. This is also where we'll tell you about changes to the site and about online events.

- **Course Overview** This is a general description of the typical course in this area of study. While your instructor will provide specific course objectives, this overview helps you place the course in a generic context and offers you an additional reference point.
- **www.orksheet** Focus your trip to a R.E.A.L. site with the www.orksheet. Each of the 10 to 15 questions will prompt you to take in the best that site has to offer. Use this tool for self-study, or if required, email it to your instructor.
- **Course Quiz** The questions on this self-scoring quiz are related to articles in the reader, information at R.E.A.L. sites, and other course topics, and will help you pinpoint areas you need to study. Only you will know your score—it's an easy, risk-free way to keep pace!
- **Topic Key** The Topic Key is a listing of the main topics in your course, and it correlates with the Topic Key that appears in this reader. This handy reference tool also links directly to those R.E.A.L. sites that are especially appropriate to each topic, bringing you integrated online resources within seconds!
- **Web Savvy Student Site** If you're new to the Internet or want to brush up, stop by the Web Savvy Student site. This unique supplement is a complete **Courselinks** site unto itself. Here, you'll find basic information on using the Internet, creating a web page, communicating on the web, and more. Quizzes and Web Savvy Worksheets test your web knowledge, and the R.E.A.L. sites listed here will further enhance your understanding of the web.
- **Student Lounge** Drop by the Student Lounge to chat with other students taking the same course or to learn more about careers in your major. You'll find links to resources for scholarships, financial aid, internships, professional associations, and jobs. Take a look around the Student Lounge and give us your feedback. We're open to remodeling the Lounge per your suggestions.

Building Better Perspectives!

Please tell us what you think of this *Perspectives* volume so we can improve the next one. Here's how you can help:

1. Visit our **Coursewise** site at: http://www.coursewise.com
2. Click on *Perspectives*. Then select the Building Better *Perspectives* Form for your book.
3. Forms and instructions for submission are available online.

Tell us what you think—did the readings and online materials help you make some learning connections? Were some materials more helpful than others? Thanks in advance for helping us build better *Perspectives*.

Student Internships

If you enjoy evaluating these articles or would like to help us evaluate the **Courselinks** site for this course, check out the **Coursewise** Student Internship Program. For more information, visit:

http://www.coursewise.com/intern.html

Brief Contents

section 1   Qualities of Effective Leaders   1

section 2   Ethical Dimensions of Leadership   51

section 3   Connecting: To People and Community   73

section 4   Collaborating: Building Teams and Leadership Capacity   106

section 5   Instruction: Learning and Leadership   132

section 6   Change: To Understand, Respond, and Influence   158

Contents

At **Coursewise**, we're publishing *connected learning tools*. That means that the book you are holding is only a part of this publication. You'll also want to harness the integrated resources that **Coursewise** has developed at the fun and highly useful **Courselinks**™ web site for *Perspectives: Educational Leadership*. If you purchased this book new, use the Passport that was shrink-wrapped to this volume to obtain site access. If you purchased a used copy of this book, then you need to buy a stand-alone Passport. If your bookstore doesn't stock Passports to **Courselinks** sites, visit http://www.courselinks.com for ordering information.

section 1

Qualities of Effective Leaders

WiseGuide Intro 1

1. **Toward a Critical Practice of Leadership,** William Foster. In J. Smyth (ed.), *Critical Perspectives on Educational Leadership,* New York: Falmer Press (1989).
   This reading examines two traditions of leadership research—the political/historical and bureaucratic/managerial models. It also discusses four distinguishing criteria for the definition and practice of leadership: Leadership must be critical, transformative, educative, and ethical. **3**

2. **The Problem with "Management": Perhaps It Starts with the Choice of Word,** John Mariotti. *Industry Week,* March 17, 1997.
   This is an analysis of the use of words and their meanings in defining jobs, roles, responsibilities, and potentials. Names and words create a picture in our mind—and this may be a desirable goal. **16**

3. **Teachers' Perceptions of Principals' Attributes,** Michael D. Richardson, Kenneth E. Lane, and Jackson L. Flanigan. *The Clearing House,* May/June 1996.
   A survey about the attributes of principals that was given to teachers revealed that teachers perceived the attributes of principals in a way similar to how employees perceive the attributes of their supervisors. The results showed that a principal's attributes are crucial to a school's success. **18**

4. **How Accountable Are You for Your Success?** Cassandra Hayes. *Black Enterprise,* July 1997.
   Being responsible and accountable enhances personal strengths and helps to advance careers. This reading provides a quiz for testing accountability. People who are not responsible exhibit such traits as playing the victim, tuning the situation out, or becoming upset. **21**

5. **The New Power Elite: Women, Jews, African Americans, Asian Americans, Latinos, Gays and Lesbians,** Richard L. Zweigenhaft and G. William Domhoff. *Mother Jones,* March/April 1998.
   This reading is a candid and revealing look at trends in leadership by various "minority" groups. Leader profiles and research information are included. **24**

6. **The Instructional Leader as Cultural Mediator,** Joseph Khazzaka. *The Clearing House,* January/February 1997.
   This reading suggests that the instructional leadership theory developed in the United States may not be applicable in other countries due to variances in culture. Teachers and school administrators play a role in helping foreign students to become bicultural. **28**

7. **What We Know About Leadership: Effectiveness and Personality,** Robert Hogan, Gordon J. Curphy, and Joyce Hogan. *American Psychologist,* vol. 49, no. 6, 1994.
   This reading defines leadership by answering nine questions, including: What is leadership? How do leaders build teams? and What about leadership in workforce 2000? **32**

8 **Before Looking for the Gas Pedal: A Call for Entrepreneurial Leadership in American Schools,** Kyle L. Peck. *Education,* Summer 1991.
According to Kyle Peck, the leadership that is needed is not the traditional leader/follower relationship, but a newer, more democratic type in which individuals are motivated and empowered. Rather than promoting their own ideas, successful leaders of educational reform efforts help teams of educators to create powerful, shared visions and provide the encouragement and support necessary to streamline the progress. **46**

WiseGuide Wrap-Up   50

section 2

Ethical Dimensions of Leadership

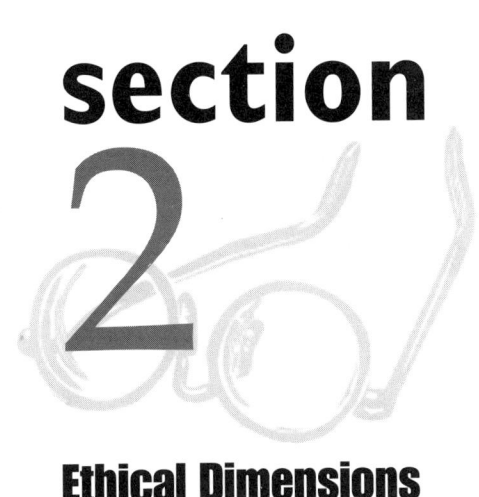

WiseGuide Intro   51

9 **Why Employees Love These Companies (100 Best Companies to Work for in America),** Ronald B. Lieber. *Fortune,* January 12, 1998.
Employees of such companies as Southwest Airlines, Mary Kay, Inc., and USAA cite the vision of their employers, the workplace atmosphere, and the physical work environment as reasons why they enjoy their jobs. Leaders who inspire their employees to succeed enjoy the psychological results. **53**

10 **Good Leaders Must First Be Good People,** Albert C. Yates. *Black Issues in Higher Education,* June 27, 1996.
Educationist Albert C. Yates believes that good leaders must be virtuous people who can be trusted to make the right choices for restoring optimism and spirit to the society. Leaders with intelligence, but not virtue, can lead society toward selfishness and cynicism. Virtue embodies all that is good and right in human life and is a combination of such values as commitment, integrity, compassion, truth, and competence. A major challenge facing education is to make students understand the relationship between leadership and the values that sustain a good democratic society. **56**

11 **Acting from the Center: Your Response to Today's Leadership Challenges Must Be Grounded in Personal Values,** E. Thomas Behr. *Management Review,* March 1998.
The new leadership power depends on the leader's personal values and convictions and his or her willingness to act on these values during a period of uncertainty. An organization is centered and balanced when employees, customers, and suppliers support the principles of the organization's leadership. **58**

12 **Where Leaders Come From,** Marshall Loeb. *Fortune,* September 19, 1994.
In this reading, scholar Warren Bennis describes seven attributes of successful leaders: business literacy, people skills, conceptual skills, a proven track record, taste, judgment, and character. Bennis believes that leaders are self-made. **63**

13 **Leadership: A Journey That Begins Within,** Aretha B. Pigford. *NASSP Bulletin,* January 1996.
According to Aretha Pigford, real leaders have a number of common characteristics. Leadership is based on mutual trust between leaders and their followers. Real leaders are willing to listen to everyone and to consider the effects of their decisions. They create a surplus of vision by supporting the development of other leaders. Real leaders also view discomfort as opportunities for growth and development. **66**

14 **Change Agent Skills: Creating Leadership for School Renewal,** Patricia A. Carrow-Moffett, *NASSP Bulletin,* April 1993.
This reading outlines and describes in detail six steps that can prove useful to leaders and managers who want to become effective change agents. The six-step process includes (1) identifying and speaking vision, (2) empowerment of self and others, (3) knowing one's values, (4) personal barriers and enhancers to change, (5) environmental barriers and enhancers to change, and (6) resisting the "change-back" phenomenon. **68**

WiseGuide Wrap-Up   72

section 3

Connecting: To People and Community

WiseGuide Intro 73

15 **Aristotle's Advice for Business Success (Interview with Business Philosopher Tom Morris),** Jennifer J. Laabs. *Workforce,* October 1997.
Business philosopher Tom Morris contends that Aristotle's views on what motivates people can help leaders to determine how they can direct workers toward the highest levels of excellence and satisfaction. Morris highlights four points that Aristotle made—namely, truth, beauty, goodness, and unity. **75**

16 **Creating Trust,** Karlene Kerfoot. *Nursing Economics,* January/February 1998.
According to Karlene Kerfoot, leaders must know how to communicate and demonstrate trust to create a high-performing environment for their organization. They must be willing to develop junior staff, to address their availability and accessibility, and to exhibit candor in talking with employees. **79**

17 **Paving the Road to TRUST,** Robert Glaser. *HR Focus,* January 1997.
This reading points out that trust is an important ingredient in the leadership of organizations. Without trust, the organization suffers from weak relationships, reduced innovation and risk-taking, and a poor decision-making process. To earn the trust of subordinates, leaders must close the gap between their intentions and their behavior, and must also have a high level of integrity and credibility. **82**

18 **The Art of Subservient Management,** Thom Davis. *Management Review,* May 1998.
Thom Davis believes that managers must realize that they have a responsibility to meet the needs of the people who work for them. An organization that institutes a supercilious managerial approach and persists in overlooking employees' welfare will not be able to survive in the twenty-first century. Managers need to acquire the characteristics that enable them to fully serve their constituents. **84**

19 **Building Community for Public Schools: Challenges and Strategies,** Sue van Slyke. *Phi Delta Kappan,* June 1997.
The Hattiesburg Area Educational Foundation (HAEF) of Hattiesburg, Mississippi, conducted interviews in its community to evaluate the educational foundation's efficiency. HAEF improved its public relations through a national project called "Public Conversations about the Public's Schools." **86**

20 **An Experiment in Democracy,** John F. Jennings. *Phi Delta Kappan,* June 1997.
John Jennings believes that public schools can regain public support and trust by conducting public dialogues, during which school officials and community members can develop solutions for the problems that public schools face. Public forums also initiate programs for school improvement. **90**

21 **Revitalizing the Ecosystem for Youth: A New Perspective for School Reform,** Michael Timpane and Rob Reich. *Phi Delta Kappan,* February 1997.
This reading stresses that school reforms and community development should be made from the perspective of the learners or students, and should also allow schools to be socially involved with other community agencies. **93**

22 **How Teamwork Transformed a Neighborhood,** Martie Thleen Lubetkin. *Educational Leadership,* April 1996.
The Pio Pico Elementary School in Santa Ana, California, galvanized parents, businesses, and social action groups to improve the conditions around the school to provide a healthy educational environment for the students. First, increased police surveillance eliminated criminal activities near the school. School officials then enlisted parents to help clean up and beautify the street. Additional community efforts included a holiday gift exchange sponsored by Korean-American entrepreneurs. **102**

WiseGuide Wrap-Up 105

section 4
Collaborating: Building Teams and Leadership Capacity

WiseGuide Intro   106

23. **Working Smarter Together,** Gordon A. Donaldson, Jr. *Educational Leadership,* October 1993.
    According to this reading, cooperation can bring about significant changes in a school system by encouraging creativity without wasting available resources. Teachers need to determine if their teaching efforts were successful in reaching students and at what cost to available resources. Teachers also should attempt to reexamine their purpose and their relationships with other staff members and the students to improve themselves.   108

24. **The Well-Managed SMT,** Milan Moravec, Odd Jan Johannessen, and Thor A. Hjelmas. *Management Review,* June 1998.
    More organizations are adopting the concept of self-managed teams (SMTs) as an employee empowerment strategy. SMTs foster a work environment that cultivates individual initiative and encourages people to become self-motivated.   113

25. **School Empowerment Through Self-Managing Teams: Leader Behavior in Developing Self-Managing Work Groups in Schools,** Paula M. Short. *Education,* Summer 1994.
    This reading focuses on leader behavior in developing self-managed teams. Paula Short highlights the advantages of self-managing teams for teachers, outlines an effective process for administrators to follow, and defines the term *unleader*.   116

26. **Creating a Climate for Change: Students, Teachers, Administrators Working Together,** Susan Benjamin and Jane Gard. *NASSP Bulletin,* April 1993.
    This reading describes how one school altered its organizational structure to allow for collaboration and shared leadership. In implementing the change, school officials challenged several previously held assumptions about the way things should be done.   124

27. **How to Build Leadership Capacity,** Linda Lambert. *Educational Leadership,* April 1998.
    Linda Lambert believes that school administrators can enhance their leadership qualities by rethinking the essence of leadership and capacity building. First, they must view leadership as a reciprocal learning process that promotes broad-based participation. True educational leaders recognize the potential and right of every individual to lead. They encourage leadership in others by evaluating the leadership capacity of staff and schools, fostering a culture of inquiry, developing and implementing initiatives for building leadership capacity, and creating policies for leadership capacity building.   127

WiseGuide Wrap-Up   131

section 5
Instruction: Learning and Leadership

WiseGuide Intro   132

28. **Instructional Leadership and Principal Visibility,** Beth Whitaker. *Clearing House,* January/February 1997.
    This reading looks at the role of principals in the instructional development of schools. To be effective, principals should play a variety of roles, such as resource provider, instructional resource, visible presence, and communicator.   134

29. **Leadership: Maintaining Vision in a Complex Arena,** Glen F. Ovard. *NASSP Bulletin,* February 1990.
    Providing leadership in instruction is a complex challenge. This reading highlights the reliance on values and principles as a fundamental process in facing this challenge.   137

30. **Collegiality: A New Way to Define Instructional Leadership,** Thomas R. Hoerr. *Phi Delta Kappan,* January 1996.
    School principals who are finding it difficult to cope with the many demands of their job should consider sharing the responsibility for instructional leadership with their teachers. This reading discusses steps for developing collegiality and for empowering teachers.   140

31. **In the Teachers' Own Words: Six Powerful Elements of Effective Staff Development,** Jo Blase and Joseph Blase. *International Electronic Journal for Leadership in Learning* (http://www.ucalgary.ca/~iejll), September 28, 1998.
This reading highlights six elements of effective staff development that lead to instructional enhancement for teachers. The findings are based on a recent national study. **143**

32. **Schools for All Seasons,** John I. Goodlad. *Phi Delta Kappan,* May 1998.
John Goodlad believes that a school for all seasons is one that is committed to preparing students for active participation in the human experience. It fosters an educational environment guided by caring and competent mentors and avoids the narrowing of focus that the utilitarian narrative of schooling requires. **149**

33. **Change and the School Administrator,** Marlow Ediger. *Education,* Summer 1998.
According to Marlow Ediger, change is a key concept in the school curriculum, as well as in society. School administrators need to evaluate the present curriculum to determine whether changes are needed. Students should experience the best in objectives, learning opportunities, and evaluation procedures. **151**

WiseGuide Wrap-Up **157**

section 6

Change: To Understand, Respond, and Influence

WiseGuide Intro **158**

34. **What I Learned in the Rainforest,** Tachi Kiuchi. *Technology Review,* November/December 1997.
According to Tachi Kiuchi, rainforests are more productive than any organization in the world, and organizations would be more productive and ecologically benign if they were managed and operated according to the principles of conserving the forest. Emulating the rainforest means following some basic paradigms. **160**

35. **A Good Case for Educational Change,** Caroline A. Sherritt and Margaret Basom. *Clearing House,* May/June 1996.
The information age demands workers who are flexible, able to keep pace with technology, self-directed, and knowledgeable about the world and cross-cultural communications. This reading points out that most policymakers have yet to realize this and persist in retaining the outdated education system. **162**

36. **Be a Model Leader of Change,** David M. Schneider and Charles Goldwasser. *Management Review,* March 1998.
This reading suggests that a leader must visualize change before it takes place. The leader must anticipate employee reactions, identify allies of the change, and keep the performance decline during the change transition to a minimum. **165**

37. **Breaking the Bonds of Dependency,** Michael Fullan. *Educational Leadership,* April 1998.
According to Michael Fullan, educational leaders must overcome dependency caused by work overload and vulnerability to instant solutions to achieve meaningful educational reform. In addition, school leaders must show emotional intelligence in helping teachers, parents, students, and others understand the goals of change. They must also display hope to inspire teachers in their quest for reform. **170**

38. **The Power of Reflection,** Michael Hammer and Steven A. Stanton. *Fortune,* November 24, 1997.
This reading suggests that many successful companies eventually fail because management does not reflect on the future. Such reflection requires eliminating preconceived notions and considering such areas as competition, customers, the validity of cherished customs, and possible new approaches. **174**

39 **A Systems Approach to School Reform,** Richard P. McAdams. *Phi Delta Kappan,* October 1997.
   Richard McAdams examines five factors that affect successful school reform: quality of leadership, local politics and governance, state and national politics, organizational characteristics, and change. The negative impact of any of these factors could hinder adequate school reform.   **179**

40 **Change as Collaborative Inquiry: A "Constructivist" Methodology for Reinventing Schools,** Tony Wagner. *Phi Delta Kappan,* March 1998.
   New educational standards that take into account how learning takes place and how organizations evolve have to be established if higher learning standards are to result. Tony Wagner recommends a collaborative approach to achieving high standards.   **186**

WiseGuide Wrap-Up   194

Index   195

Topic Key

This Topic Key is an important tool for learning. It will help you integrate this reader into your course studies. Listed below, in alphabetical order, are important topics covered in this volume. Below each topic you'll find the reading numbers and titles relating to that topic. Note that the Topic Key might not include every topic your instructor chooses to emphasize. If you don't find the topic you're looking for in the Topic Key, check the index or the online topic key at the Courselinks™ site.

Accountability
- 4 How Accountable Are You for Your Success?
- 25 School Empowerment Through Self-Managing Teams: Leader Behavior in Developing Self-Managing Work Groups in Schools
- 33 Change and the School Administrator
- 34 What I Learned in the Rainforest
- 40 Change as Collaborative Inquiry: A "Constructivist" Methodology for Reinventing Schools

Behavior
- 6 The Instructional Leader as Cultural Mediator
- 9 Why Employees Love These Companies (100 Best Companies to Work for in America)
- 14 Change Agent Skills: Creating Leadership for School Renewal
- 24 The Well-Managed SMT
- 28 Instructional Leadership and Principal Visibility
- 36 Be a Model Leader of Change
- 37 Breaking the Bonds of Dependency

Beliefs
- 11 Acting from the Center: Your Response to Today's Leadership Challenges Must Be Grounded in Personal Values
- 12 Where Leaders Come From
- 28 Instructional Leadership and Principal Visibility
- 37 Breaking the Bonds of Dependency
- 38 The Power of Reflection
- 39 A Systems Approach to School Reform

Change
- 1 Toward a Critical Practice of Leadership
- 3 Teachers' Perceptions of Principals' Attributes
- 8 Before Looking for the Gas Pedal: A Call for Entrepreneurial Leadership in American Schools
- 14 Change Agent Skills: Creating Leadership for School Renewal
- 19 Building Community for Public Schools: Challenges and Strategies
- 20 An Experiment in Democracy
- 21 Revitalizing the Ecosystem for Youth: A New Perspective for School Reform
- 22 How Teamwork Transformed a Neighborhood
- 23 Working Smarter Together
- 24 The Well-Managed SMT
- 26 Creating a Climate for Change: Students, Teachers, Administrators Working Together
- 32 Schools for All Seasons
- 33 Change and the School Administrator
- 34 What I Learned in the Rainforest
- 35 A Good Case for Educational Change
- 36 Be a Model Leader of Change
- 37 Breaking the Bonds of Dependency
- 38 The Power of Reflection
- 39 A Systems Approach to School Reform
- 40 Change as Collaborative Inquiry: A "Constructivist" Methodology for Reinventing Schools

Collaboration
- 21 Revitalizing the Ecosystem for Youth: A New Perspective for School Reform
- 22 How Teamwork Transformed a Neighborhood
- 23 Working Smarter Together
- 26 Creating a Climate for Change: Students, Teachers, Administrators Working Together
- 30 Collegiality: A New Way to Define Instructional Leadership
- 40 Change as Collaborative Inquiry: A "Constructivist" Methodology for Reinventing Schools

Communication
- 11 Acting from the Center: Your Response to Today's Leadership Challenges Must Be Grounded in Personal Values
- 16 Creating Trust
- 18 The Art of Subservient Management
- 26 Creating a Climate for Change: Students, Teachers, Administrators Working Together
- 28 Instructional Leadership and Principal Visibility
- 30 Collegiality: A New Way to Define Instructional Leadership
- 35 A Good Case for Educational Change
- 38 The Power of Reflection

Community
- 12 Where Leaders Come From
- 19 Building Community for Public Schools: Challenges and Strategies
- 21 Revitalizing the Ecosystem for Youth: A New Perspective for School Reform
- 22 How Teamwork Transformed a Neighborhood
- 26 Creating a Climate for Change: Students, Teachers, Administrators Working Together
- 27 How to Build Leadership Capacity
- 34 What I Learned in the Rainforest
- 35 A Good Case for Educational Change
- 40 Change as Collaborative Inquiry: A "Constructivist" Methodology for Reinventing Schools

Culture
- 4 How Accountable Are You for Your Success?
- 5 The New Power Elite: Women, Jews, African Americans, Asian Americans, Latinos, Gays and Lesbians
- 6 The Instructional Leader as Cultural Mediator

7 What We Know about Leadership: Effectiveness and Personality
30 Collegiality: A New Way to Define Instructional Leadership
34 What I Learned in the Rainforest
38 The Power of Reflection

Diversity
5 The New Power Elite: Women, Jews, African Americans, Asian Americans, Latinos, Gays and Lesbians
6 The Instructional Leader as Cultural Mediator
32 Schools for All Seasons
34 What I Learned in the Rainforest

Empowerment
12 Where Leaders Come From
13 Leadership: A Journey That Begins Within
14 Change Agent Skills: Creating Leadership for School Renewal
19 Building Community for Public Schools: Challenges and Strategies
22 How Teamwork Transformed a Neighborhood
23 Working Smarter Together
24 The Well-Managed SMT
25 School Empowerment Through Self-Managing Teams: Leader Behavior in Developing Self-Managing Work Groups in Schools
27 How to Build Leadership Capacity
30 Collegiality: A New Way to Define Instructional Leadership
40 Change as Collaborative Inquiry: A "Constructivist" Methodology for Reinventing Schools

Ethics
1 Toward a Critical Practice of Leadership
10 Good Leaders Must First Be Good People
15 Aristotle's Advice for Business Success (Interview with Business Philosopher Tom Morris)
39 A Systems Approach to School Reform

Goals
17 Paving the Road to TRUST
25 School Empowerment Through Self-Managing Teams: Leader Behavior in Developing Self-Managing Work Groups in Schools
32 Schools for All Seasons
36 Be a Model Leader of Change
40 Change as Collaborative Inquiry: A "Constructivist" Methodology for Reinventing Schools

Honesty
3 Teachers' Perceptions of Principals' Attributes
10 Good Leaders Must First Be Good People
15 Aristotle's Advice for Business Success (Interview with Business Philosopher Tom Morris)
20 An Experiment in Democracy

Human Relations
2 The Problem with "Management": Perhaps It Starts with the Choice of Word
4 How Accountable Are You for Your Success?
5 The New Power Elite: Women, Jews, African Americans, Asian Americans, Latinos, Gays and Lesbians
9 Why Employees Love These Companies (100 Best Companies to Work for in America)
12 Where Leaders Come From
14 Change Agent Skills: Creating Leadership for School Renewal
15 Aristotle's Advice for Business Success (Interview with Business Philosopher Tom Morris)
16 Creating Trust
17 Paving the Road to TRUST
18 The Art of Subservient Management
19 Building Community for Public Schools: Challenges and Strategies
24 The Well-Managed SMT
25 School Empowerment Through Self-Managing Teams: Leader Behavior in Developing Self-Managing Work Groups in Schools
28 Instructional Leadership and Principal Visibility
34 What I Learned in the Rainforest
36 Be a Model Leader of Change
37 Breaking the Bonds of Dependency
38 The Power of Reflection

Instructional Leadership
28 Instructional Leadership and Principal Visibility
30 Collegiality: A New Way to Define Instructional Leadership
32 Schools for All Seasons
33 Change and the School Administrator
35 A Good Case for Educational Change

Job Satisfaction
9 Why Employees Love These Companies (100 Best Companies to Work for in America)
15 Aristotle's Advice for Business Success (Interview with Business Philosopher Tom Morris)
33 Change and the School Administrator

Leadership Style
1 Toward a Critical Practice of Leadership
40 Change as Collaborative Inquiry: A "Constructivist" Methodology for Reinventing Schools

Management
2 The Problem with "Management": Perhaps It Starts with the Choice of Word
18 The Art of Subservient Management

Motivation
6 The Instructional Leader as Cultural Mediator
9 Why Employees Love These Companies (100 Best Companies to Work for in America)
15 Aristotle's Advice for Business Success (Interview with Business Philosopher Tom Morris)
23 Working Smarter Together
24 The Well-Managed SMT
25 School Empowerment Through Self-Managing Teams: Leader Behavior in Developing Self-Managing Work Groups in Schools
33 Change and the School Administrator
36 Be a Model Leader of Change

Topic Key **xxi**

Politics
- 19 Building Community for Public Schools: Challenges and Strategies
- 20 An Experiment in Democracy
- 29 Leadership: Maintaining Vision in a Complex Arena
- 39 A Systems Approach to School Reform

Power
- 5 The New Power Elite: Women, Jews, African Americans, Asian Americans Latinos, Gays and Lesbians
- 20 An Experiment in Democracy
- 24 The Well-Managed SMT
- 27 How to Build Leadership Capacity
- 39 A Systems Approach to School Reform

Reform
- 19 Building Community for Public Schools: Challenges and Strategies
- 20 An Experiment in Democracy
- 21 Revitalizing the Ecosystem for Youth: A New Perspective for School Reform
- 22 How Teamwork Transformed a Neighborhood
- 23 Working Smarter Together
- 24 The Well-Managed SMT
- 26 Creating a Climate for Change: Students, Teachers, Administrators Working Together
- 27 How to Build Leadership Capacity
- 35 A Good Case for Educational Change
- 36 Be a Model Leader of Change
- 37 Breaking the Bonds of Dependency
- 38 The Power of Reflection
- 39 A Systems Approach to School Reform

Responsibility
- 22 How Teamwork Transformed a Neighborhood
- 29 Leadership: Maintaining Vision in a Complex Arena
- 34 What I Learned in the Rainforest

Shared Leadership
- 13 Leadership: A Journey That Begins Within
- 26 Creating a Climate for Change: Students, Teachers, Administrators Working Together
- 27 How to Build Leadership Capacity

Success
- 4 How Accountable Are You for Your Success?
- 24 The Well-Managed SMT
- 29 Leadership: Maintaining Vision in a Complex Arena
- 37 Breaking the Bonds of Dependency

Team
- 7 What We Know about Leadership
- 8 Before Looking for the Gas Pedal: A Call for Entrepreneurial Leadership in American Schools
- 11 Acting from the Center: Your Response to Today's Leadership Challenges Must Be Grounded in Personal Values
- 22 How Teamwork Transformed a Neighborhood.
- 23 Working Smarter Together
- 24 The Well-Managed SMT
- 25 School Empowerment Through Self-Managing Teams: Leader Behavior in Developing Self-Managing Work Groups in Schools
- 26 Creating a Climate for Change: Students, Teachers, Administrators Working Together
- 27 How to Build Leadership Capacity
- 33 Change and the School Administrator
- 35 A Good Case for Educational Change

Trust
- 10 Good Leaders Must First Be Good People
- 12 Where Leaders Come From
- 13 Leadership: A Journey That Begins Within
- 16 Creating Trust
- 17 Paving the Road to TRUST
- 20 An Experiment in Democracy
- 27 How to Build Leadership Capacity
- 39 A Systems Approach to School Reform

Values
- 1 Toward a Critical Practice of Leadership
- 6 The Instructional Leader as Cultural Mediator
- 10 Good Leaders Must First Be Good People
- 11 Acting from the Center: Your Response to Today's Leadership Challenges Must Be Grounded in Personal Values
- 13 Leadership: A Journey That Begins Within
- 14 Change Agent Skills: Creating Leadership for School Renewal
- 17 Paving the Road to TRUST
- 29 Leadership: Maintaining Vision in a Complex Arena

Vision
- 2 The Problem with "Management": Perhaps It Starts with the Choice of Word
- 3 Teachers' Perceptions of Principals' Attributes
- 8 Before Looking for the Gas Pedal: A Call for Entrepreneurial Leadership in American Schools
- 9 Why Employees Love These Companies (100 Best Companies to Work for in America)
- 11 Acting from the Center: Your Response to Today's Leadership Challenges Must Be Grounded in Personal Values
- 12 Where Leaders Come From
- 13 Leadership: A Journey That Begins Within
- 14 Change Agent Skills: Creating Leadership for School Renewal
- 21 Revitalizing the Ecosystem for Youth: A New Perspective for School Reform
- 27 How to Build Leadership Capacity
- 29 Leadership: Maintaining Vision in a Complex Arena
- 32 Schools for All Seasons
- 36 Be a Model Leader of Change
- 37 Breaking the Bonds of Dependency
- 38 The Power of Reflection
- 39 A Systems Approach to School Reform

section 1

Qualities of Effective Leaders

Learning Objectives

- Describe the traditional perspectives of leadership and discuss the characteristics of a "new view" of leadership.
- Explain the difference between management and leadership, their impact within an organization, and the attributes of each.
- Summarize the major attributes of effective leaders and their influence within an organization.
- Analyze the leadership patterns of women and minorities; describe the impact of cultural competence.
- Identify the methods used to evaluate leadership effectiveness, including the important factors in leading innovation.

WiseGuide Intro

Who shall lead? This question has plagued humankind since the beginning of time. From nomadic tribes to Fortune 500 companies to national elections, the issue of leadership has been an important one. The search for the right leader requires a definition of leadership, usually by defining its qualities and skills.

Research on the concept of leadership is a relatively new process. Only since the 1940s have researchers been analyzing and studying leadership using scientific and formal methods. Leadership is a complex concept, one which has held the attention and fascination of those attempting to achieve it successfully. Knowing more about the qualities of effective leaders allows us to strive to achieve success in our own leadership endeavors.

The very process of identifying effective leadership prompts the question "Effective leadership in whose eyes?" Subordinates, peers, and supervisors all view successful leadership through different lenses. In schools and other organizations, effective leadership can also be judged by students, parents, the community, and government agencies. This complicates the process of dissecting and confirming the most important qualities of leadership. This section presents a collection of articles analyzing the qualities of effective leaders from a variety of sources.

In "Toward a Critical Practice of Leadership," Foster provides a comprehensive history of leadership research and contemporary practice. He supplies details about the essential elements of effective leadership. In his analysis, he describes the transitional nature of leadership over time.

Mariotti contrasts the concepts of management and leadership in his article "The Problem with 'Management'." His reflections on language use, definitions, and roles are insightful.

The specific attributes of leaders are revealed in "Teachers' Perceptions of Principals' Attributes." Richardson, Lane, and Flanigan compare the leadership attributes of business middle managers with those of school principals.

Reviewing one's own responsibility and accountability can be accomplished by taking the quiz provided by Hayes in "How Accountable Are You for Your Success" Her quiz identifies the key qualities of effective leadership.

Focusing on leadership by women and minorities is the article by Zweigenhaft and Domhoff, "The New Power Elite: Women, Jews, African Americans, Asian Americans, Latinos, Gays, and Lesbians." Their disturbing revelations regarding skin color and identity management provide other leaders with challenges and a "call to action" for all organizations in the pursuit of diversity.

1

Diversity and culture are further explored in "The Instructional Leader as Cultural Mediator," by Khazzaka. His explanations of locus of control, cultural mediation, and cultural competence are important for all leaders.

The many methods of evaluating leadership effectiveness are presented by Hogan, Curphy, and Hogan in "What We Know About Leadership: Effectiveness and Personality." Forecasting leadership, personality, and building teams are also discussed.

This section on the qualities of effective leaders concludes with Peck's "Before Looking for the Gas Pedal: A Call for Entrepreneurial Leadership in American Schools." Revisiting the management vs. leadership argument, Peck investigates organizational needs for innovation. His topics include vision, democracy, and empowerment.

Questions

Reading 1. What are the two traditions of leadership research, and how have they influenced current leadership practices and applications? What are the four criteria for defining and practicing the "new view" of leadership?

Reading 2. The use of action words to describe roles in organizations is suggested for what reason? What is conveyed with the use of the terms *management* and *leadership*, and which needs more presence in organizations?

Reading 3. What are the implications for principals in understanding teachers' expectations of their role? According to teachers, what are the top five attributes of effective educational leaders?

Reading 4. How is personal accountability in the workplace defined? What steps can a leader take to improve his or her accountability in the workplace?

Reading 5. Climbing the executive ranks in corporate America depends on what four factors for women and minorities? What qualities have women and minorities projected in order to secure top leadership positions in America?

Reading 6. What is cultural competence? What are the abilities necessary for an instructional leader to become skilled as a cultural mediator?

Reading 7. What is leadership? How do subordinates, peers, and supervisors evaluate leadership effectiveness? Managerial incompetence is associated with what characteristics?

Reading 8. What are the three sets of skills for leading innovation-stimulating environments? What are the characteristics of a good vision?

What are the two traditions of leadership research, and how have they influenced current leadership practices and applications? What are the four criteria for defining and practicing the "new view" of leadership?

Toward a Critical Practice of Leadership

William Foster

Leadership as a construct and a practice has considerable currency in contemporary thought. Whether one looks at academic disciplines, practical fields or the popular press, the term "leadership" figures prominently in the attempt to describe a particular set of relationships among people. There are undoubtedly a number of reasons for this position of significance given to the idea of leadership: these would certainly include the romanticized elements of leadership as well as the more realistic effect that "leaders" have on our social and natural world. Perhaps a good deal of interest in the concept can be traced to a certain malaise about our interactions with and within organizations and the routine and determined nature of life that organizations tend to impose. Facing an uncertain future where a mistake can have deadly and unknown ramifications, we ask that *somebody* be prescient enough to guide us. Whether the concern is with questions of a global nature or with questions of a more local character, and whether the concern is with improving an organization or improving chances of survival, it is clear that the idea of leadership meets some kind of modern need, a deep desire both to be in control of our circumstances and to alter them for the better.

But what exactly is meant by the term "leadership"? Like other such labels, the term covers a great deal and seems to mean whatever the user intends. It is, as Burns (1978) has noted, one of the most misunderstood concepts in our language, and the misunderstanding is a conceptual one. There remains, however, a sense that leadership *is* a real phenomenon, one that does make a difference. But before the term can be utilized meaningfully, it is necessary to try to tease out the various ways in which it has been used and to try to come to an agreement on its essential aspects.

To accomplish this, this reading examines, first, various contemporary accounts of leadership with a critical eye. It then proposes some alternative considerations which may be important to a more precise analysis of leadership. Finally, it attempts to examine the significance of leadership within the modern context.

The Two Traditions of Leadership Research

In contemporary usage there are essentially two different traditions which have informed social scientific definitions of leadership. One tradition comes from the political-historical disciplines; the other from business management and public administration.

The political-historical model of leadership has a long history and tends to focus on the role of significant individuals (from Machiavelli's Prince to modern presidents) in shaping the course of history. Leadership, in this sense, is largely the story of events and actions, of ideas, and of how individuals transformed their social milieux. The other major model of leadership is drawn from the sociology of organizations and the administration/management literature. Here leadership tends to mean the authority of office and is dependent on a variety of strategies designed for goal accomplishment. Neither approach, as we

Copyright 1989 Taylor & Francis. Reprinted with permission.

hope to show, is completely satisfactory to an understanding of the complexity of leadership. Yet both need to be analyzed in order to demonstrate the contemporary focus in leadership studies.

The Political-Historical Model

The study of leadership done through the lenses provided by this model is a study of power, politics and historical fact. Leaders are individuals who "make" history through their use of power and resources, and leadership is exemplified by familiar names: Gandhi, Churchill, Roosevelt and so on. Their stories, their history, tell us in a retrospective fashion what qualities, machinations and visions were of value in accomplishing a new and different social order.

This model of leadership, however, is not solely biographic, though it depends on biography for its sustenance. That an abstract and theoretical formulation of leadership can be derived through the study of individual biographies is demonstrated by James McGregor Burns' book (1978), *Leadership*. By analyzing the life stories of such individuals as Gandhi and Roosevelt, Mao Tse Tung and Lenin and Hitler, Burns arrives at the conclusion that there are essentially two basic types of leadership. These he labels "transactional" and "transformational."

Transactional leadership is largely based on exchange relationships between leader and follower. Much of political leadership is transactional; a series of exchanges between politician and voter is characteristic. In exchange for the voter's support, the leader adopts a program of promises designed for those particular groups. This type of leadership is representative of lay definitions of the term and is often what we think of when we consider politicians.

For schools, transactional leadership is seen in the superintendent's or governor's relationship with unions, with individual teachers and with parents. Concessions and negotiations need to be made, accommodations worked out, and a more or less popular support for the leader developed through the manipulation and interplay of various social forces.

Transformational leadership is cut from a different cloth entirely. Here Burns addresses what in the popular imagination might be termed "real leadership." Transformational leadership is the ability of an individual to envision a new social condition and to communicate this vision to followers. The leader here both inspires and transforms individual followers so that they too develop a new level of concern about their human condition and, sometimes, the condition of humanity at large. Gandhi, for Burns, is perhaps the exemplar of transformational leadership; his ideas and actions served to liberate minds as well as bodies.

Burns writes that transformational leadership requires that "leaders engage with followers, but from higher levels of morality; in the enmeshing of goals and values both leaders and followers are raised to more principled levels of judgment. . . . Much of this kind of elevating leadership asks *from* followers rather than merely promising them goods" (1978, p. 455). Leaders thus are essentially involved in the creation of *new* social realities, and their role is largely to convince followers that the current realities are not cast in concrete but can indeed be changed for the better.

Burns' work has been a significant advance in leadership studies. He has looked at the idea of leadership from a moral and value-driven basis, and has not accepted a view of leadership as simply a managerial tool. In his formulation history and politics become a driving force, shaped by individual action. In this way Burns' work rescues leadership from the more technocratic interpretations of the concept. His work, however, has not been without some criticism.

Tucker (1981), for one, has contended that Burns provides an inadequate distinction between the concept of leadership and that of simply wielding power. Burns suggests that these are two very different animals; leadership involves a moral dimension which requires that leaders elevate followers to new moral heights, whereas power wielding (demonstrated, for example, by Hitler) does not and, therefore, using Burns' definition, is not leadership at all. Tucker contests this distinction, suggesting that an evil leader is still a leader. Tucker provides an alternative formulation for leadership; leadership, simply put, is politics. What leaders do, for Tucker, is to "define the situation authoritatively . . . prescribe a course of group action . . . [and engage in a] mobilizing function . . ." (Tucker, 1981, pp. 18–19). Leaders, in this view, are not so much transformational as they are goalsetters and mobilizers. Clearly, this robs the concept of transformational leadership of a great deal of its power, and reduces the idea of leadership to the politics of group management.

Tucker's contribution is of value in pointing out the political and group dimensions of leadership; Burns' contribution is of value in stressing the moral and value base of leadership. Both, however, falter in their highly voluntaristic and individualistic treatment of the issue. Both continue to see leadership as residing in an individual, only to be brought out voluntarily by circumstances. While Burns does stress the fact that leadership occurs in a relationship between leader and led, he nevertheless tends to see leadership as something of a trait that certain individuals possess.

Such a view neglects two crucial aspects. First, leadership is always context bound. It always occurs within a social community and is perhaps less the result of "great" individuals than it is the result of human interactions and negotiations. Roosevelt and Churchill, to take two often cited examples, took advantage of what might be called a "corridor of belief" which already existed in followers. Each leader did not so much create a new and idiosyncratic universe so much as enter these corridors and open various doors. Leadership then is an entering into the currents of mainstream consciousness and changing it through a dialectical relationship.

It is also not particularly voluntaristic, where given individuals can volunteer for leadership roles and, by virtue of their charisma, achieve them by convincing others of the rightness of their ideas. Undoubtedly this occurs, but the more common path involves mutual negotiations and shared leadership roles. Leadership cannot occur without followership, and many times the two are exchangeable: leaders become followers and followers become leaders. The voluntaristic aspect of leadership found in the political-historical model tends to neglect the dialectical character of leadership. Leaders normally have to negotiate visions and ideas with potential followers, who may in turn become leaders themselves, renegotiating the particular agenda.

This genre of political and historical studies of leadership also tends to lack a critical focus. Even the leadership of a Gandhi or a Martin Luther King is seen more as a way of convincing followers to join a cause than as the trenchant social critique that it was. Certainly a major part of these individuals' appeal lay in personal magnetism and the strength of their message. However, it is not wise to downplay the basic role of critique within leadership. Critique is not only a result of leadership practices but is constitutive of those practices: leadership always has one face turned towards change, and change involves the critical assessment of current situations and an awareness of future possibilities.

In summary, the political-historical model emphasizes the following ideas:

- Leadership is a construct describing relationships between individuals.

- Such relationships involve dimensions of power, in the sense that the desire for power and for empowerment is a fundamental feature of social life.

- Certain types of (transforming) leadership involve the "leader" and the "follower" in a cognitive redefinition of social reality.

- Understanding leadership is best approached through historical study.

The Bureaucratic-Managerial Model

A second and more influential model (at least by the number of pages devoted to it in business texts and journals) is the bureaucratic-managerial one. As the label implies, this model of leadership normally describes the way business and other managers, and scholars of management, talk about the concept of leadership. This model contains a number of prime assumptions. Among them is the assumption that leadership is a function of organizational position; the "leader" is the person of superior rank in an organization. This assumption is almost universally held among management writers and forms the basis for the various models of leadership which have been developed in the last thirty years. A related assumption is that leadership is goal-centered *and* that the goals are driven by organizational needs. Thus the reason for exerting leadership at all is not social change, or meeting followers' needs, but achieving certain organizational goals. The leader is a conduit between organization and labor, and has a clearly defined role of motivating and producing. Indeed the production function is the legitimation of the exercise of leadership.

Each of these assumptions stands out clearly in an analysis of the major models of leadership in this area. If one examines, for example, the popular treatises on leadership, such as "situational leadership" or Fiedler's (1967) contingency model of leadership, the entire thrust is towards developing effective management skills. In these approaches one needs to be concerned with the nature of the task assigned to employees, with their level of ability and maturity, and with the leader's own position in the firm. Leadership essentially becomes getting the employees to do what management wants them to do.

The idea of the "leader" in these presentations depends on the *prior* context of an organization. Leaders can only exercise their powers within an environment bounded by certain task responsibilities, and the leader's role is assumed to be one of determining how these tasks can be accomplished most effectively and efficiently. The strong assumption here is that leadership *only* occurs as a result of position. Top executives control their organizations through the manipulation of power designed to make individuals perform (task) and feel good about performing (consideration) at their level of competency (maturity).

The origins of all this, of course, lie in a brand of Taylorism, with a healthy respect for the volatile possibilities of "human relations" thrown in for good measure. Taylor suggested how we could design the workplace to be error-free, through the development of ever more specific tasks which even the most unorganized amongst us could accomplish. Human relations, the title given the series of research studies undertaken at the Western Electric plants in the late 1920s, cautions us, however, about the reflexivity that social groups tend to display, and that they might, indeed, penetrate the nature of the system and thus prove to be recalcitrant to even the harshest of managerial measures.

These two staples of industrial relations, Taylorism and human relations, form the core of contemporary leadership approaches in management. As appealing as they have been to industrial managers, with their assurance of providing a modicum of control over the production process, it was only a matter of time before they spilled over into all other areas of life, from "domestic management" to "educational management." Not only is the situational leader ensconced in the boardroom, but now he or she "leads" in the school and the bedroom.

If one accepts the assumption of leadership as position, then it is necessary to accept the other assumption that was discussed: leadership is dedicated to organizational goal-achievement. The bureaucratic-managerial model of leadership ties the exercise of leadership closely with performance, and performance is defined by goal-achievement, whether those goals have to do with productivity or other organizational concerns.

At this point the administrator might object to the discussion, claiming that achieving organizational goals, assuring productivity and achieving standards of performance are indeed the stuff of leadership; these are what leaders *do*. Failure to exert some measure of control over the organization and its membership is an assurance of failure, and with failed organizations nobody wins.

This is a telling objection only if we continue to confuse leadership with management (See Rost, 1985). Leadership is not organizational management, and it is of no use to the concept of leadership continually to equate it with position or managerial effectiveness. It is crucial to understand that while leadership may occur in organizational settings, and may be exercised by position holders, there is no necessary or logical link between the two concepts. Yet this conflation of terms persists, and the most obvious culprits are those writing in the administrative/management literature. The lack of distinction between management and leadership has become such a common feature of our language that we are often hard pressed to recognize that leadership can be unorganized, little concerned with production, uncaring of feelings and still be effective if the power of ideas is commanding. The effects of this confusion will be examined next.

The "Translation" of Leadership

In many ways the concept of leadership has been chewed up and swallowed down by the needs of modern managerial theory. The idea of leadership as a transforming practice, as an empowerment of followers, and as a vehicle for social change has been taken, adapted and co-opted by managerial writers so that now leadership appears as a way of improving organizations, not of transforming our world. What essentially has happened is that the language of leadership has been translated into the needs of bureaucracy.

One finds scholars such as Bennis (1984) talking about the leader's transformational role, the need for vision and for the empowerment of employees. The transformational leader is now a popular concept for organizations (Tichy and Devanna, 1986). But the concept has been denuded of its original power; transformational leaders are now those who can lead a company to greater profits, who can satisfy the material cravings of employees, who can achieve better performance through providing the illusion of power to subordinates. Transformational leadership has gone from a concept of power to a how-to manual for aspiring managers.

It would be welcome news if the words above prove to be too harsh an appraisal of the current condition of leadership study. The indications are, however, that they are not. This is not to say that those prescriptions which use the idea of transformational leadership as their base do not offer good advice to managers; assuredly they do, and in doing so may increase the attractiveness of the workplace for many. However, this is not to say that this is leadership in practice. To repeat some of our claims, leadership is and must be socially critical, it does not reside *in* an individual but in the relationship between individuals, and it is oriented toward social vision and change, not simply, or only, organizational goals.

The reasons for and consequences of the translation of the language of leadership into the language of management are aptly if severely described by MacIntyre, a philosopher, and it will be useful to review his claims here.

MacIntyre (1981) has identified three "characters" which are archetypes in twentieth century culture. His three characteristic types *define* in a sense contemporary life: these are the Rich Aesthete, the Therapist and the Manager. These three are "characters" in that they are more than roles people play; rather, they are symbols of a culture, carriers of a history and representatives of current social consciousness. In MacIntyre's words, these characters:

are, so to speak, the moral representatives of their culture and they are so because of the way in which moral and metaphysical ideas and theories assume through them an embodied existence in the social world. *Characters* are the mask worn by moral philosophies. (MacIntyre, 1981, p. 27)

The last two are of immediate relevance to leadership: the Therapist and the Manager are of such common currency in our language that they have come to dominate our way of thinking about certain issues, such as leadership. Each character can be readily seen in many of our social situations: the teacher, for example, acts as a therapist in the one instance and as a manager in the next. The therapist is, of course, interested in *adjustment,* the adjustment of the individual to the current social condition. The manager is interested in *control,* the control of the social environment for personal and organizational gain. Each character seems to be endemic to our modern form of highly routinized and organized life—one to manage it for us and the other to accommodate us to it. The relationship of these two concepts to the task-consideration dichotomy prevalent in leadership studies is quite clear.

This concept of characters is an attempt to delineate the central moral philosophies of the age, as these are carried by everyday actors and agents. The manager and the therapist are not simply social roles but symbols of our major beliefs, presuppositions and ways of acting. Yet these characters are based on a false sense of control over human nature. At best the therapist and the manager can provide only a temporary security: therapy ultimately leads to resignation or acceptance, while management never really knows whether the decisions made have had the effects intended. MacIntyre talks about management as follows:

It is specifically and only managerial and bureaucratic expertise that I am going to put in question. And the conclusion to which I shall finally move is that such expertise does indeed turn out to be one more moral fiction, because the kind of knowledge which would be required to sustain it does not exist. But what would it be like if social control were indeed a masquerade? Consider the following possibility: that what we are opposed by is not power, but impotence; that one key reason why the presidents of large corporations do not, as some radical critics believe, control the United States is that they do not even succeed in controlling their own corporations; that all too often, when imputed organisational skill and power are deployed and the desired effect follows, all that we have witnessed is the same kind of sequence as that to be observed when a clergyman is fortunate enough to pray for rain just before the unpredicted end of a drought; that the levers of power—one of managerial expertise's own key metaphors—produce effects unsystematically and too often only coincidentally related to the effects of which their users boast. (MacIntyre, 1981, p. 73)

Such a conclusion about managerial effectiveness and bureaucratic expertise is not idiosyncratic to MacIntyre, although he does put it so well; rather a whole host of organizational studies carry the same theme. Weick's (1976) concept of loose coupling certainly carries an implicit suggestion that rational and goal-oriented control of organizations is an illusion; in this world events are only loosely coupled to each other and causality (read power) is both multiple and recursive. March and Olsen (1976) address the fundamental ambiguities in the manager's job, observing that rationality tends to take place largely as post hoc rationalization, and that organizations simply do not function in the efficient, Tayloristic view promulgated by a self-labeled "management science." Lincoln (1985) similarly questions the rational, cause-effect view of management, arguing that a new "paradigm" is well under way. Benson (1977) suggests that the goal-seeking, rational model of management and organization is a popular fiction. Various other views of managerial behavior, such as that contained in the "organizational culture" school of thought (Smircich, 1983), and in those schools concerned with the analysis of "sensemaking" in organization (Weick, 1979) further reflect the variability, not to say ineffectiveness, of managerial authority.

If we accept MacIntyre's concerns with managerial power, then what implications are there for leadership? The first is that to let the concept of leadership be captured by management is to emasculate any power the idea of leadership offers to us. To see it as a managerial virtue is to see it as a powerless attempt to control and predict human action. Yet this is probably the main thrust of most authors on leadership: any discussion of leadership seems to dissolve into a discussion of effective management techniques. Burns' work, which, as we noted above, served at first to define the idea of leadership and to show its relevance to the political arena, has now been condensed, changed and otherwise manipulated to justify and in many ways shore up extant power relationships existing in organizations.

If leadership cannot be reduced to management, then it must involve something more than management. We will make the claim here that leadership is fundamentally addressed to social change and human emancipation, that it is basically a display of social critique, and that its ultimate goal is the achievement and refinement of human community.

The Creation of Community

It is an enduring feature of human life to search for community; to attempt to establish patterns of living based on mutual need and affection, development and protection. But this communitarian impulse is never "accomplished"; rather it is an ongoing and creative enterprise in which actors or agents continually re-create social structure, and it is this which allows us to identify "communities." Giddens (1984) has proposed a theory of "structuration" which takes as an essential focus the *duality* of structure: that "the structural properties of social systems are *both medium and outcome* of the practices they recursively organize" (Giddens, 1984, p. 25, emphasis added). Individuals, in other words, engage in social practices which are the foundation for social structure, yet social structure limits and enables the type of practices that can be engaged in. Giddens provides this analysis:

> According to structuration theory, the moment of the production of action is also one of reproduction in the contexts of the day-to-day enactment of social life. This is so even during the most violent upheavals or most radical forms of social change. It is not accurate to see the structural properties of social systems as "social products" because this tends to imply that pre-constituted actors somehow come together to create them. In reproducing structural properties . . . agents also reproduce the conditions that make such action possible. Structure has no existence independent of the knowledge that agents have about what they do in their day-to-day activity. (1984, p. 26)

This property of social structures, and thus of communities, is why leadership can be effective and important. Certain agents can engage in transformative practices which change social structures and forms of community, and it is this that we label leadership. But for leadership to exist in this capacity requires that it be critical of current social arrangements and that this critique be aimed at more emancipatory types of relationships; any other type of "leadership" is basically oriented toward the accumulation of power and, while this is certainly a feature of all relationships within social structures, such accumulation indicates a personal rather than communitarian impulse. Emancipation, it should be stressed, does not mean total freedom; rather, the concept as it is used here means the gradual development of freedoms, from economic problems, racial oppression, ethnic domination, the oppression of women and so on (each of which has its own heroes and heroines: Roosevelt, Churchill, Gandhi, King, Anthony are just some examples).

Emancipatory leadership, however, is not just the property of enlightened individuals. The idea that leadership occurs within a community suggests that ultimately leadership resides in the community itself. To further differentiate leadership from management, we could suggest that leadership is a communal relationship, that is, one that occurs within a community of believers. Leadership, then, is not a function of position but rather represents a conjunction of ideas where leadership is shared and transferred between leaders and followers, each only a temporary designation. Indeed, history will identify an individual as the leader, but in reality the job is one in which various members of the community contribute. Leaders and followers become interchangeable.

Certain Conceptual Demands for Leadership

When leadership is separated from a simple legitimation of a managerial philosophy, it then adopts certain characteristics which particularly define it as a subject of attention. These serve as distinguishing criteria for leadership, whether practiced in business, education, the arts or elsewhere. Leadership, in this sense, is to be quite differentiated from decision-making, from goal-setting, or from authority: in other words, it serves in a different way than the type of authority necessary to run an organization, build cars or accumulate real estate. There are, in this new way of thinking about leadership, at least four criteria for the definition and practice of leadership:

1. Leadership must be critical;
2. Leadership must be transformative;
3. Leadership must be educative;
4. Leadership must be ethical.

Leadership as Critical

Leadership as a critical practice depends largely on one's worldview of human activity: whether one conceives of human activity as essentially "received," passed down from generation to generation without much change, or as "constructed," passed down but reinterpreted and re-created in that passing. If one conceives of human activity in the latter sense, then it becomes clear that a particular aspect of leadership is to examine the previous conditions of social life and subject them to critique; to find, indeed, that there are possibly various conditions of domination which have been resisted.

Seeing human practice as constructed allows us to see humans as agents who can intervene in their affairs. This is an important distinction because it suggests that humans are not just objects of scientific inquiry; that they use social scientific knowledge to change and reorder their particular universes, and that each is his or her own sociologist (see Giddens, 1984).

Theories of leadership are essentially based in the social science disciplines. As must be the case with all such disciplines, the theory itself must be critical. Giddens (1984, p. xxxv) observes that "the formulation of critical theory is not an *option*." This is because all social science knowledge is, first, dependent on the commonsense constructions of those being observed, in the sense that a social scientific statement, such as the fictitious "Birth order will determine success in school," depends for its understanding on commonsense notions of schooling, birth, the timing of children and particular formulas for school success. Even if this principle could be reduced to a formula, such as Bo=S.Su, that formula itself would in turn depend for its interpretation on the preunderstandings of the social scientific community, which in turn depend on lay agents' understandings.

It is because of this first feature that the second feature comes into play. This is, secondly, that social science findings ultimately reflect back upon previous commonsense knowledge in a reflective and critical manner. In this example the critical aspect is suggesting that our previous commonsense knowledge of the relationship of order of birth to school success is faulty to some extent; that recent findings suggest other conclusions, and so on. All social science is critical in some sense, and cannot be anything other than critical; as social science moves into more theoretical and less empirical studies, this becomes even more pronounced.

This feature is a circular one. The findings of social science are circulated among the lay agents (because it is for them that the entire enterprise takes place), and these agents adopt those findings and incorporate them into their new sets of common knowledge, which in turn becomes the foil for social science critique, and in this way a progressive spiral is born.

At the heart of social science is its critical aspect. As Giddens says:

> The point is that reflection on social processes (theories, and observations about them) continually enter into, become disentangled with and re-enter the universe of events they describe. No such phenomenon exists in the world of inanimate nature, which is indifferent to whatever human beings might claim to know about it. (Giddens, 1984, p. xxxiii)

This critical aspect suggests for leadership research in particular that it must always be a critical *practice*. Grob (1984) tells us the following:

In pointing to the critical spirit as the ground of all leadership, my intent has been to argue that without that willingness to examine one's life, alleged leaders in any and all areas of human endeavor must, of necessity, become identified with their purposes, purposes which inevitably congeal into fixed doctrines or dogma. In short, potential leaders *without this ground* find themselves in the service of fixed ideas or causes, and thus agents of the use of power in their behalf. *No longer nourished by a wellspring of critical process at its centre, leadership "dries up" and becomes, finally, the mere wielding of power on behalf of static ideals.* (p. 270, emphasis in original)

Leadership is at its heart a critical practice, one that comments on present and former constructions of reality, that holds up certain ideals for comparison, and that attempts at the enablement of a vision based on an interpretation of the past. In being critical, then, leadership is oriented not just toward the development of more perfect organizational structures, but toward a reconceptualization of life practices where common ideals of freedom and democracy stand important.

Leadership as Transformative

The critical spirit of leadership leads naturally to the notion of transformation. Leadership is and must be oriented toward social change, change which is transformative in degree. That leadership is transformative is easily demonstrated by human history: there have been periods of progress and development which have transformed the course of human events, and these have been called leadership. Burns' view of transformational leadership documents many of these; Gandhi is one example, Martin Luther King another. Transformation of *consciousness* is what took place, and as a result of that, a transformation of social conditions. But this required a community of believers, not just a "leader." Certainly one person helped to serve as a catalyst, but if the full story be known, such transformations occurred because of a community of leaders.

Transformation though is not a special or unique occurrence, one that is found only in certain grand moments of human history. Rather, it happens in everyday events, when "commonplace" leaders exert some effect on their situations. Bhaskar (1975, p. 196) has commented that "it is not necessary that society should continue. But if it is to do so, then men must reproduce (or more or less transform) the structures (languages, forms of economic and political organization, systems of belief, cultural and ethical norms, etc.) that are given to them." Transformation of social relations is a basic feature of all our social living; such transformation may occur as reproduction, wherein social structures may be changed but slightly, or as a true transformation, where structures are changed significantly. It is in the latter case that we claim that leadership has been exerted.

Transformation does involve social change. But this does not necessarily mean *societal* change. Social change can be accomplished without the complete restructuring of any given society; in fact, social change occurs frequently, in small doses, in the actions and activities of various groups and individuals who hope to make some sort of difference. A number of movements, from feminism to racial awareness, can make a claim to transformative leadership and accomplished social change. In some instances this is societal in nature; in others it is much more regionalized. Nevertheless, the balance to the critical aspect of leadership is indeed transformation and change.

Leadership as Educative

If leaders are both critical and transformative agents when engaged in their leadership capacity, so too are they educators. Fay (1987, p. 9) has observed that "humans are not only active beings, but they are also embodied, traditional, historical, and embedded creatures: as a result their reason is limited in its capacity to unravel the mysteries of human identity and to make the difficult choices with which humans are inevitably faced; and their will to change is circumscribed in all sorts of ways." Human agents are, in other words, *located* in a specific history and set of circumstances, one which to some degree controls their behavior, ways of seeing and options for acting. This history is their tradition, a tradition which suggests how one is to live, what one is to value and often how one is to think. We are both victims and beneficiaries of this tradition: on the one hand, it closes down many options for living free and independent lives; on the other hand, it provides meaning and a sense of place for those lives we do live.

But while tradition can provide meaning, it can also be oppressive. This is why education is such an important part of leadership. To the degree that leadership can critique traditions which can be oppressive, and aims for a transformation of such conditions, then it must be educative.

But what does being educative mean for a leader? In this context it means that a leader can present both an analysis and a vision. The analysis means that the leaders enable self-reflection to occur; in an organizational context this means devoting some time to talk about organizational history, organizational purpose and the distribution of organizational power. Such analysis represents the concerted efforts of various members of the organization to deal with the received structures that orient their working lives. This is not to say that such analysis takes place in the context of commitments to massive organizational change; rather the purpose remains simply to reflect upon institutional arrangements, to reveal the "taken-for-granted" features of institutional life, and to allow for commentary on the ways and means that the institution either restrains or promotes human agency.

Vision is another aspect of education. It is not enough to reflect on current social and organizational conditions; in addition, a vision of alternative possibilities must be addressed. Such a vision pertains to how traditions could be altered, if necessary, so that they meet human needs while still providing a sense of meaningfulness. This is perhaps the most crucial and critical role of leadership: to show new social arrangements, while still demonstrating a continuity with the past; to show how new social structures continue, in a sense, the basic mission, goals and objectives of traditional human intercourse, while still maintaining a vision of the future and what it offers.

Vision involves what both MacIntyre (1981) and Fay (1987) have discussed as narratives, stories of human lives, stories that have a sense of meaning and continuity, and which provide to future generations a degree of connectedness to the past. Narratives provide a community with its history, its unique place in the course of human events, its significance in the world order. Each community, and each organization, must have some kind of narrative in order to remain cohesive as a community and organization. But the retelling of narratives is hardly enough; vision describes the telling of possible narratives and the presentation of new narratives. It is here in particular that one can see how leadership is a shared, communitarian role, one in which different narratives are presented by different individuals, each presenting a possibility for a new narrative and interpreting the previous narratives in their own fashion.

This analysis and envisionment obviously results in education; this educative aspect of leadership is intended to have citizens and participants begin to question aspects of their previous narratives, to grow and develop because of this questioning, and to begin to consider alternative ways of ordering their lives. The educative aspect, in other words, attempts to raise followers' consciousness about their own social conditions, and in so doing to allow them, as well as the "leader," to consider the possibility of other ways of ordering their social history.

Leadership as Ethical

A final dimension to leadership is its ethical commitment. This occurs in two ways: the first is the individual ethical commitments of various leaders; the second is the overall ethical commitments to a community of followers.

In regard to the first, we are concerned with the use of leadership to attain various objectives through the use of power. Leadership will involve power relationships, and these can in turn be used in a positive or negative fashion. A negative power relationship involves the use of power to achieve those ends desired by the "leader," what Burns (1978) would label "power wielding." This means that the individual entrusted with some position of power uses that position to achieve objectives that are not of communal benefit, but of benefit to the aspirations of only that individual. Burns would not, and we agree, consider this leadership at all.

This use of power to achieve an individual's ends only often results in treating people as means rather than as ends-in-themselves. Treating people as means is to dehumanize them, yet this is often the result of "leadership" training programs which see the task as the end and the person as the means to accomplish that end. Here, there is an ethical slide: from a type of Kantian idealism found, for example, in Burns' work, to a form of utilitarianism found, for example, in the work of most management-oriented writers on leadership. In utilitarianism the focus is on achievement, and "what works" is "what's right."

But leadership is founded on the fact of moral relationships; it is intended to elevate people to new levels of morality. This is because of what leadership means to a community of followers: it critiques social conditions, and the followers' role in maintaining such conditions; offers new possibilities for social arrangements, and the followers' role in making such arrangements; and in so doing helps to raise the level of followers' moral consciousness regarding their received situation.

However, the ethical aspects of leadership go further than the particular leader's relationship with given followers, and how he or she demonstrates a morality. Rather, leadership in general must maintain an ethical focus which is oriented toward democratic values within a community. This has to do with the meaning of ethics historically—as a search for the good life of a community; an attempt to come to some understanding regarding the various options available for living that life. Ethics here refers to a more comprehensive construct than just individual behavior; rather, it implicates us and how we as a moral community live our communal lives.

Consider for a moment Sullivan's (1982) comments on how a liberal philosophy in modern society contributes to an erosion of community:

> Liberal thinkers rightfully decry the encroachment on individual life of the administrative state, and, though less often, the bureaucratic corporation and mass media. But they see no relationship between willful abnegation of an ethics of mutual concern, announced as freedom, and weakening of social solidarity outside those encroaching structures. Yet, as some thinkers sympathetic to the liberal tradition have come to see, if personal dignity and self-determination are to survive the constraints and potentiality for social control found in modern society, it can only be through the political action of citizens joined in active solidarity. (p. 155)

His argument, also expressed in such places as Bellah et al. (1985), is that such factors as individualism, arising out of the shattering of tradition caused by the Enlightenment and its search for non-mystical and objective knowledge, also parade as freedom in contemporary societies. There is also a tendency toward a shunning of community and a concern with utilitarian self-aggrandizement. Lost is the precious community connection wherein *ways* to live figure prominently; where the search for the good and the right life predominates; and where leadership turns into the development of strategies for success. The result is an atomistic citizenry which acquiesces to even the most irresponsible of governments if only they are left alone.

Sullivan (1982) points out a possible solution: "the achievement of maturity, or moral virtue, consists in a genuine transformation of motives, not simply their combination. And this takes place only through a certain kind of educative social interaction. Civic moral education is, then, natural in that it fulfils humanity's distinctive need to be at once self-reflective and yet interdependent members of a community" (p. 170). This, in particular, is constitutive of the social and generative aspect of leadership, as a moral undertaking. Leadership carries a responsibility not just to be *personally* moral, but to be a *cause* of "civic moral education" which leads to both self-knowledge and community awareness. This is a central, defining aspect of leadership; leadership which is ethically based takes on the task—indeed, a shared task among community members and leaders—of critique and vision: critique in the sense that it remains unsatisfied with social conditions which are either dehumanizing or threatening, and vision in the sense of searching for a kind of life which realizes more closely the Aristotelian ideal.

We have outlined above some aspects of leadership which seem important to the intellectual consideration of the subject. We can summarize some of these ideas and attempt to present them in a way which might have an impact on individuals who hope to be leaders in their own fashion.

1. Leadership and management are not interchangeable concepts. Leadership comes in a number of forms: it has been exerted intellectually, charismatically, modestly, passively, actively. What these forms share in common is a commitment to social change and development, not to control and production. While management might be an essential tool for modern society (and then again it may not be), leadership occurs as a form of communal life concerned with how lives should be lived, not how they should be controlled.

2. Leadership is communal and shared. This has come up a number of times in this reading, yet has never been addressed completely satisfactorily. The issue is that *leaders* are embodied individuals, while *leadership* is a shared and communal concept. This means that while leaders occur in a certain time-space context, it is neither necessary nor sufficient that leadership be identified for all of time and space with these individuals. One of the generative aspects of leadership is that leaders exist only because of the relationship attained with followers, and that this relationship allows followers to assume leadership and leaders, in turn, to become followers. Leaders, in short,

create other leaders, and it is in this fashion that leadership becomes a shared and communal process.

3. Leadership involves self-criticism and self-clarity. While the need for each of these should by now be apparent, it will help to cast them in the terms that Fay (1987) has used. Self-criticism and self-clarity lead to what he calls "genuine narrative." A critical theory, of the self or the society, "will see the lives of its audience as composed of two levels of being: the manifest, in which there is confusion and frustration; and the latent, in which there is an underlying order which is the mainspring of their behavior" (p. 69). The genuine narrative addresses the latent level, the underlying unity of human consciousness and human activity: "This narrative depicts the underlying principle of change at work in the emergence and disappearance of the numerous forms of human life and the countless welter of human activities and relationships": (Fay, 1987, p. 69).

Developing a genuine narrative means for leadership to be both clear and critical regarding the circumstances of its influence and the circumstances of its followers. A genuine narrative is a story of human history and how it is accomplished; a story of the basic drives, wants and needs of a people. In modern life such a narrative becomes clouded and opaque, not the least because a market-centered economy dominates our relationships and a utilitarian philosophy controls our goals

Leadership and leaders can and should be concerned with the discovery of this narrative: Is there, indeed, an underlying, thematic unity to the lives of followers? Are there wants and needs which lie beyond the surface of conscious awareness? Is there a search for a sense of place and a sense of meaning? Finding the genuine narrative in our lives could be the major contribution of leaders to their community. At the same time traditions can be oppressive: a cursory look at racial and gender traditions in various countries certainly reveals this. This is why leaders and leadership need to be critical of those same traditions. Leadership thus turns into a dialectic: it must in turn strive for a sense of community based in tradition, while still based in a search for justice, freedom and equality, those guiding beacons which help to reorient our daily lives to issues of major humanitarian concern.

Conclusion: Implications for Education

Bellah and his colleagues (1985) have written:

The tension between private interest and the public good is never completely resolved in any society. But in a free republic, it is the task of the citizen, whether ruler or ruled, to cultivate civic virtue in order to mitigate the tension and render it manageable.

As the twentieth century has progressed, that understanding, so important through most of our history, has begun to slip from our grasp. . . . The citizen has been swallowed up in "economic man." (pp. 270–271)

This is why leadership has become both so rare and so crucial in different world communities. Indeed, where people gather to conduct commerce, to educate each other, to watch each other's performances, to evaluate each other's artistic abilities, to gather in friendship or debate, there is a need for a leadership conscious of civic responsibility.

We live in an age of instrumentalities, where people themselves become instruments for the achievement of organizational goals; where people are driven by the need to achieve, with achievement defined by economics; and where the individual, rootless and guide-less, strives for a sense of identity and meaning. If we are to climb out of this valley of depression, then we certainly do need leaders, but leaders who are not managers, leaders who can see beyond the immediate needs of the organization, and leaders who can provide a "genuine narrative" for our lives.

How can such leadership exert itself in a community? Think, for example, of a school, but a school as a community of agents, not as an organization of members. Rather than seeing children as individual products being processed through the system, certified according to their achievement test scores, what would it be like to consider the children and the adults as participants in a practicing democracy, where each has the chance to live out a meaningful narrative of their own lives, and where all can exert leadership?

Such a situation seems, perhaps, too idealistic, and to a certain degree it might be. Yet it appeals to all of us in a fundamental way: it suggests that our experiments with democracy might well be lived ones, occurring beyond just the voting booth; it suggests, further, that republican ideals can be reproduced in everyday settings, and this reinforces our belief in a polity where each one can have a say; and finally it suggests that the vital spark which keeps democracy alive, and which prevents a benign government from deciding for us, is that spark which occurs in a specific community of believers. (For a discussion of how participatory democracy can be accomplished in school settings see White, 1983.)

Such experiments in democracy are not unknown, however, and thus not completely idealistic. Certain guidelines do pertain. First, it is leadership that contributes to the development of such a situation. This is to say that the existing administration, if it is concerned with leadership ideas, will adopt a program of self-critique, ethics, transformation and education. Secondly, this attempt at democratization does not mean that every decision is open to full community participation: rather, adjustments have to be made for the type of decision and its importance to the community. In addition, recognition has to be given to the fact that students, and their parents, have to be educated to the responsibilities of participation in a democratic regime; it is the responsibility of participation in a *government* as opposed to participation in an *anarchy*. Thirdly, recognition must be given to the words of those with experience and with wisdom; a community requires its elders, those with a sense of the past and a vision for the future.

Leadership in such a situation is concerned with the meeting of followers' concerns, and with transforming the values of followers so that they too exert leadership. In a school setting it should be recognized that followers come in all sizes, ages and shapes; that each of these, from students to teachers to administrators, can in fact be leaders with respect to their influence over others. Nicoll (1986) has put this well. Asking about the relationship between followers and leaders, he finds that:

Our answer—if we ever are going to find one that is satisfactory—will require leaders to accept and believe that *followers use leaders to make a path.* This is fundamental. Our leaders must allow themselves—and us—to believe that followers are *not* passive, reactive tools of charismatic power figures. They are, instead, the creators of energy. They are the architects of the open moments into which some people must be the first to step. As followers, they are the agents who show their leaders where to walk. They are the ones who validate their leaders stepping out in a direction that has meaning for all of us. (1986. p. 34)

It must be admitted that there are two major issues which make the achievement of a true democracy in education difficult to achieve. The first is the issue of size; the second, that of values.

Size pertains, of course, to the basic structure of schooling in many countries, where the sheer size of the institution makes it difficult if not impossible for administrators to exert the degree of influence over school processes that might be desired. The move toward comprehensive schools, with rigidly departmentalized faculty, curricula and students, argues against the establishment of a community of students, each with the possibility of some input into the way things are organized and reproduced in that setting.

The second issue is concerned with values. In modern society the guiding principles have had to do with the provision of equality and liberty. These are, indeed, *public* values, one that cut across a number of various groups and interests. Yet for a strong public value system to exist, Strike (1982) claims that it is *private* values that must be taught. Private values have to do with a sense of important religious and ethical beliefs, the same beliefs that a fully public system may have trouble addressing because of its diversity and accommodation of various beliefs. Thus a democratic regime depends on the inculcation of various values which are ethical in degree, and which depend often on religious belief. Public schools, however, cannot be overly dependent on the presence of private values in their students; they must to some degree be neutral in their acceptance of various values, treating each as equally worthy.

These two issues pose a basic problem for leadership in education, yet neither is unsolvable. Smaller schools are certainly an option, but so are schools within schools, and schools with differentiated representation patterns so that all students can feel that they can participate in some fashion in the formulation of important policy. The second problem is a harder one. Yet leadership is concerned with the transformation of values, and here school leaders can address basic social end values such as democracy, justice and liberty. These are, indeed, public values in the sense that a society will depend on their formulation for its success as a caring society.

Finally, leadership can surmount such problems by its concern with establishing a true narrative for all participants. This is not something given, but rather something searched for. It suggests that *conscious* attention be paid to the way the organization serves its members, to the stories and even culture that have evolved, to the levels of participation in the formation of new policy, and to the meanings that have evolved in the organizational context.

Leadership, in the final analysis, is the ability of humans to relate deeply to each other in the search for a more perfect union. Leadership is a consensual task, a sharing of ideas and a sharing of responsibilities, where a "leader" is a leader for the moment only, where the leadership exerted must be validated by the consent of followers, and where leadership lies in the struggles of a community to find meaning for itself.

References

Bellah, R. N., Madsen, R., Sullivan, W. M, Swidler, A., and Tipton, S. T. (1985) *Habits of the Heart: Individualism and Commitment in American Life,* Berkeley and Los Angeles, University of California Press.

Bennis, W. (1984) "The 4 competencies of leadership," *Training and Development Journal,* August, pp. 15–19.

Benson, J. K. (1977) "Innovation and crisis in organizational analysis," in J. K. Benson (Ed.), *Organizational Analysis: Critique and Innovation,* Beverly Hills, CA, Sage Press.

Bhaskar, R. (1975) *A Realist Theory of Science,* Leeds, Leeds Books.

Burns, J. M. (1978) *Leadership,* New York, Harper and Row.

Fay, B. (1987) *Critical Social Science,* Cambridge, Polity Press.

Fiedler, R. (1967) *A Theory of Leadership Effectiveness,* New York, McGraw-Hill.

Giddens, A. (1984) *The Constitution of Society,* Berkeley and Los Angeles, University of California Press.

Grob, L. (1984) 'Leadership: The Socratic model,' in B. Kellerman (Ed.), *Leadership: Multidisciplinary Perspectives,* Englewood Cliffs, N.J., Prentice-Hall.

Lincoln, Y. (Ed.) (1985) *Organizational Theory and Inquiry: The Paradigm Revolution,* Beverly Hills, Calif., Sage Press.

MacIntyre, A. (1981) *After Virtue,* Notre Dame, Ind., University of Notre Dame Press.

March, J. G. and Olsen, J. P. (1976) *Ambiguity and Choice in Organizations,* Bergen, Universitetsforlaget.

Nicoll, David (1986) 'Leadership and followership,' in J. D. Adams (Ed.), *Transforming Leadership: From Vision to Results,* Alexandria, Va., Miles River Press.

Rost, J. (1985) 'Distinguishing leadership and management: A new consensus,' Paper presented at California Principals Conference, Anaheim, Calif., November.

Smircich, L. (1983) 'Concepts of culture and organizational analysis,' *Administrative Science Quarterly,* 28, September, pp. 339–358.

Strike, K. A. (1982) *Educational Policy and the Just Society,* Urbana, Ill., University of Illinois Press.

Sullivan, W. M. (1982) *Reconstructing Public Philosophy,* Berkeley and Los Angeles, University of California Press.

Tichy, N., and Devanna, M. A. (1986) *The Transformational Leader,* New York, John Wiley.

Tucker, R. C. (1981) *Politics as Leadership,* Columbia, Mo., University of Missouri Press.

Weick, K. (1976) 'Educational organizations as loosely coupled systems,' *Administrative Science Quarterly,* 21, pp. 1–19.

Weick, K. (1979) *The Social Psychology of Organizing,* 2nd ed., Reading, Mass., Addison-Wesley.

White, P. (1983) *Beyond Domination: An Essay in the Political Philosophy of Education,* London, Routledge and Kegan Paul.

Article Review Form at end of book.

The use of action words to describe roles in organizations is suggested for what reason? What is conveyed with the use of the terms *management* and *leadership*, and which needs more presence in organizations?

The Problem with "Management"

Perhaps it starts with the choice of word

John Mariotti

John Mariotti, a former manufacturing CEO, is president of The Enterprise Group. He lives in Knoxville, Tenn. His e-mail address is JMariotti@UTK.edu.

A while back, I moved my office. It was a short move—from the top floor of my home to the bottom floor—but it prompted a near-cataclysmic cleaning out of old files and reorganizing of those left over.

One of the tasks I decided to catch up on was that of filing copies of book summaries in the binder provided by the subscription service. As I read the titles on the index tabs, I felt pretty good about the balance of topics in the current management literature (or at least the books they chose to summarize). But as I got further into the project, my feelings changed noticeably.

Here's what struck me so strongly: Over a period of two years, the book-summary company had classified 21 titles as management, only one as manufacturing, two as leadership, and none as human relations. As I scrutinized the list of "management" titles, I realized that part of the problem had to do with the labels that were assigned. Fully half of the "management" books in reality dealt with human relations and organizational issues. And there is little doubt that many of those books pertained to manufacturing settings.

My interest then shifted to the apparent dearth of leadership books. I wondered why there was no tab for "leadership." Could it be that it is harder to define than management?

I checked the *American Heritage* dictionary on my laptop computer for a definition of "management." It said: *1. The act, manner, or practice of managing; handling, supervision, or control; 2. The person or persons who control or direct a business or other enterprise; 3. Skill in managing; executive ability.* The definition underscored part of the problem. Too many people still believe the job of management is to "control and direct." And the dictionary backs them up!

When we name things, there is a powerful tendency to live up to the name—or maybe to "live down" to it. That's why buyers usually "buy," instead of selecting and developing strong suppliers; or why customer-service reps usually "service" the customer, instead of satisfying or delighting them.

Graduates with a master's degree in business administration, I fear, may be far too inclined to "administer." And managers certainly will have a greater tendency to "manage" than to lead, inspire, coach, or support their organizations.

Because titles matter a lot; the blocks and lines on organization charts create far more barriers than results. Check out the companies you are familiar with. How far down the organization chart must you go to find a title that uses an action verb to specifically describe the role?

Something is wrong here. What we call jobs creates powerful mental pictures about what the people who hold them are expected to do.

Reprinted with permission from Industry Week, 1997. Copyright Penton Publishing, Inc., Cleveland, Ohio.

A few years ago, I was seriously tempted to change the titles of my direct reports and others in senior roles—from the conventional vice president or manager of this or that function to titles like "leader of customer care," or "leader of making and delivering," or "leader of people and teamwork." I didn't do it, because I was assured by my very traditional-thinking vice president of human resources that not only would I "never get it past corporate," but I might be viewed as too much of a free thinker. I should have done it anyway.

Last year, I spoke with a CEO who had similar inclinations and who also opted not to change the titles in his organization. He felt it would be too "risky." But the risk of sticking with generic names may be even greater. Another company I deal with calls its employees "*partners*," and its floor supervisors "*coaches*." I think it makes a difference in how they feel and behave.

> "Because titles matter a lot, the blocks and lines on organization charts create far more barriers than results."

Management of "things" is important. But leading people is more important. Rearranging charts of accounts or asset allocations is important, too, but not nearly as important as actually making something of value—and doing it well.

The names and words we use paint a more vivid picture than we realize in the minds of everyone who encounters them—customers, suppliers, peers, and outsiders. Big, broad, unemotional terms like "management" may make categorizing and filing easier, but they can make success more elusive. In today's chaotic, fast-moving, technology-intensive environment, people-oriented, action-describing leadership terms and job titles are needed—not bland, one-size-fits-all generalities from the past. More important, we need people who understand that leadership is an important job of "management"—whether there is a file tab for it or not.

Article Review Form at end of book.

What are the implications for principals in understanding teachers' expectations of their role? According to teachers, what are the top five attributes of effective educational leaders?

Teachers' Perceptions of Principals' Attributes

Michael D. Richardson

Kenneth E. Lane

Jackson L. Flanigan

Michael D. Richardson is a professor of educational administration at Georgia Southern University, Statesboro; Kenneth E. Lane is a professor of educational administration at California State University–San Bernardino; and Jackson L. Flanigan is a professor and coordinator of educational administration at Clemson University, Clemson, South Carolina.

During the 1980s, no professional position received more attention, nor was given greater latitude to articulate a new role, than that of the school principal (Bolman and Deal 1992; Thomson 1992; Cunningham and Gresso 1993). A cursory review of the literature reveals that considerable debate about the future of the position continues (Rashford and Coghland 1992; Thomson 1992). The general public, and the educational community in particular, should understand the role of today's principal, however, before any consideration can be given to changing future roles (Richardson and Lane 1993; Prestine 1993). Principals today find themselves in a magnified fish bowl (Fowler 1991; Moorthy 1992); they are bombarded by changing expectations and responsibilities and often find themselves without the knowledge to adequately address such challenges (Lane 1992; Thomson 1992; Richardson and Lane 1993).

Overall, educational researchers have identified the principal as the critical element in a school's success. The traditional concept of the school principal as a passive, reactive manager has grudgingly given way to a perception of the administrator as an active leader and learner (Glasman and Heck 1992; Bauer 1992; Lane 1992; Duke and Iwanicki 1992; Cunningham and Gresso 1993; Strange 1993).

The principal assumes the awesome responsibility for all aspects of school life (Frase and Melton 1992) and often has difficulty rationalizing his or her changing role and the increased demands of the position. In fact, those changes in the nature of the principalship were a prime reason that large numbers of principals left the profession during the past decade (Stein and King 1992). The principal in the 1990s is challenged to facilitate administrative vision, demonstrate concern for students' learning processes, and relate to faculty, staff, and community in a cooperative environment (Silins 1992; Moorthy 1992; Lane 1992). Those new demands require the principal to implement and institutionize new strategies for leading change (Stein and King 1992; Cunningham and Gresso 1993). Educational reform literature abounds with articles that describe the ideal school headed by a strong, visionary leader who promotes an atmosphere of collegiality and participation in a learning environment (Hansen and Liftin 1991).

The Clearing House, v69, n5, pp. 290–292, May/June 1996. Reprinted with permission of the Helen Dwight Reid Educational Foundation. Published by Heldref Publications, 1319 Eighteenth St., N.W., Washington, D.C. 20036-1802. Copyright © 1996.

Numerous studies also have illustrated the dynamic nature of the principalship by producing lists of attributes or skills of good principals (Kimbrough and Burkett 1990; Thomson 1992; Kowalski, Reitzug, McDaniel, and Otto 1992); most of the lists, however, serve only to demonstrate the varied nature of the position (Fowler 1991). Our research effort was based on the assumption that teachers' attitudes toward those litanies of traits and skills should be examined (Estabook 1992). Many studies had looked at the principal's role in change efforts, site-based management, and other reform efforts (Drury 1993; Liontos 1993; Rallis and Goldring 1993; Duden 1993). However, no study had compared principals' attributes with the attributes of effective business managers.

Methodology and Data Analysis

Kouzes and Posner (1987), in their outstanding book, The Leadership Challenge, listed twenty characteristics that business managers thought leaders should possess (see table 1*). Using Kouzes and Posner's instrument, we asked 1,225 teachers, "What are the characteristics of principals that make them leaders?" The responses were obtained from teachers in four states without regard to randomness. The teachers were participants either in our graduate education classes or executive seminars.

Because the characteristics were ranked from most to least popular for both samples, the primary data analysis technique was the Spearman's rank correlation (r ranks) (Glass and Hopkins 1984). The Spearman rank correlation ranges from –1 to 1, with values near zero indicating a lack of correspondence between the two sets of ranks and values near one indicating high levels of correspondence between the two sets of ranks.

Teacher responses were ranked with percentages of respondents indicated. The responses were analyzed to determine whether there was a relationship between the reported values of teachers and those of business managers. According to the study conducted by Kouzes and Posner (1987), the top five descriptions of superior leaders were that the leaders were honest, competent, forward-looking, inspiring, and intelligent (table 1).

Teachers differed very little from the business managers in their perceptions of the ideal attributes of principals, as reported in table 2*. For example, four of the first five responses are identical to those of business managers. The only difference was that teachers chose "caring" as the fifth most important attribute, compared with "intelligent" for business managers. The perception of teaching as a nurturing or compassionate profession could help explain why teachers thought principals should be "caring." For business managers the old adage about being "smarter than the competition" may have influenced the perception of certain business employees that "intelligent" was a highly desirable attribute. Probably the most surprising finding was that teachers and business managers agreed on the fourth most important attribute, "inspiring."

For this data, Spearman's rank order technique was used to correlate the ordinal ranks of both teacher and business leaders with the following result: r ranks = .7774 (t = 5.24, p [less than or equal to] .01). Therefore, that correlation, statistically significant at the .01 level, indicates a positive association between the two sets of ranks. The analysis leads to the conclusion that teachers and managers have a high degree of similarity in their perceptions of the characteristics that business leaders and principals should possess.

It should be noted that regardless of the high level of similarity, there were several exceptions. For example, business managers ascribed more value to broad-mindedness (ordinal rank of 7) than did teachers (ordinal rank of 14). Teachers indicated that a principal should be caring (ordinal rank of 5), yet business managers perceived this characteristic as less important (ordinal rank of 13). In a parallel perception, teachers believed that principals should be supportive (ordinal rank of 6), while business managers sensed this trait was less important (ordinal rank of 11).

Overall, the similarities between business employees' perceptions of managers and teachers' perceptions of principals' characteristics were striking. The implication for principals is clear. The better a principal understands teachers' expectations, the more likely a principal can fulfill the expectations of the role. Valid and reliable data on teacher expectations will assist principals to understand more thoroughly how those expectations can influence teacher behavior, which, ultimately, affects student achievement.

---

* Table 1 does not appear in this publication.

* Table 2 does not appear in this publication.

References

Bauer, S. C. 1992. Myth, consensus, and change. *Executive Educator* 14(7): 26–28.

Bolman, L. G., and T. E. Deal. 1992. Leading and managing: Effects of context, culture, and gender. *Educational Administration Quarterly* 28(3): 313–29.

Cunningham, W. G., and D. W. Gresso. 1993. *Cultural leadership.* Boston: Allyn and Bacon.

Drury, W. R. 1993. The principal's role in site-based management. *Principal* 73(1): 16, 19.

Duden, N. 1993. A move from effective to quality. *School Administrator* 50(6): 18–21.

Duke, D. L. 1992. Concepts of administrative effectiveness and the evaluation of school administrators. *Journal of Personnel Evaluation in Education* 6(2): 103–121.

Duke, D. L., and E. Iwanicki. 1992. Principal assessment and the notion of "fit." *Peabody Journal of Education* 68(1): 25–36.

Estabrook, R. 1992. Constellation building: Leadership for effective schools. *Contemporary Education* 63(2): 91–92.

Fowler, W. J., Jr. 1991. What are the characteristics of principals identified as effective by teachers? (Eric Document Reproduction Service ED 347–695.)

Frase, L. E., and R. G. Melton. 1992. Manager or participatory leader? What does it take? *NASSP Bulletin* 76(540): 17–24.

Glasman, N. S., and R. H. Heck. 1992. The changing leadership role of the principal: Implications for principal assessment. *Peabody Journal of Education* 68(1): 5–24.

Glass, G. V., and K. D. Hopkins. 1984. *Statistical methods in education and psychology.* 2nd ed. Boston: Allyn and Bacon.

Hansen, J. H., and E. Liftin. 1991. *School restructuring: A practitioner's guide.* Swampscott, Mass.: Watersun Publishing.

Kimbrough, R. B., and C. W. Burkett. 1990. *The principalship: Concepts and practices.* Englewood Cliffs, N.J.: Prentice-Hall.

Kouzes, J. M., and B. Z. Posner. 1987. *The leadership challenge.* San Francisco: Jossey-Bass.

Kowalski, T. J., U. C. Reitzug, P. McDaniel, and D. Otto. 1992. Perceptions of desired skills for effective principals. *Journal of School Leadership* 2(3): 299–309.

Lane, B. A. 1992. Cultural leaders in effective schools: The builders and brokers of excellence. *NASSP Bulletin* 76(541): 85–96.

Liontos, L. B. 1993. Transformational leadership: Profile of a high school principal. *OSSC Bulletin* 36(9).

Moorthy, D. 1992. The Canadian principal of the '90s: Manager or instructional leader? or both? *Education Canada* 32(2): 8–11.

Ornstein, A. C. 1993. Leaders and losers. *Executive Educator* 15(8): 28–30.

Prestine, N. A. 1993. Shared decision making in restructuring essential schools: The role of the principal. *Planning and Changing* 22(3): 160–77.

Rashford, N. S., and D. Coghland. 1992. Effective administrator through organizational levels. *Journal of Educational Administration* 30(4): 63–72.

Richardson, M. D., and K. E. Lane. 1993. Principal preparation: From training to learning. *PSSAS Notes* 9(2): 6–7.

Silins, H. C. 1992. Effective leadership for school reform. *Alberta Journal of Educational Research* 38(4): 317–34.

Stein, R., and B. King. 1992. Is restructuring a threat to principal's power? *NASSP Bulletin* 76(540): 26–31.

Strange, J. H. 1993. Defining the principalship: Instructional leader or middle manager. *NASSP Bulletin* 77(553): 1–7.

Thomson, S. D. 1992. National standards for school administrators. *International Journal of Educational Reform* 1(1): 54–58.

Article Review Form at end of book.

How is personal accountability in the workplace defined? What steps can a leader take to improve his or her accountability in the workplace?

How Accountable Are You for Your Success?

The key to career and personal empowerment is taking responsibility for yourself and others.

Cassandra Hayes

An African American female manager is promoted to head a business unit at a large corporation. Over the past three years, she has proven herself to be an excellent candidate, possessing all the technical qualifications necessary for the post. But her employees resent the appointment. They feel that the job should have gone to a white male, long rumored to be next in line for the position.

The employees begin to sabotage her efforts. A small faction of managers in her unit spread rumors that her appointment was a classic case of reverse discrimination. Department productivity and morale take a plunge.

Not surprising, the manager is called in by her superiors and told she has three months to reverse the situation. It doesn't happen. The company vice president then informs her that "things aren't working out" and offers her a lateral move—a position with less prestige and responsibility. Instead of accepting a job she views as a demotion, the manager resigns.

Clearly, this woman was faced with what for some would be insurmountable odds, suffering unfair treatment and discrimination. But could she have prevented her failure? It's easy to place blame elsewhere, but how different would things have been if she had been more accountable for her own success?

Whose Fault Is It, Anyway?

It is no secret that racism and sexism exist in the workplace. Despite the fact that many organizations are now addressing diversity, these company initiatives are not salves for the wounds caused by decades of social inequality in the workplace. But you can't expect your company to do everything. You have to hold yourself accountable for your future.

"Personal accountability is the willingness to claim 100% ownership for the results produced as a consequence of your involvement, both individually and collectively, with others in your workplace," says William A. Guillory, CEO and founder of Innovations International Inc., a management consulting firm in Salt Lake City, Utah. "The lack of empowerment for African Americans is partly discrimination, but the other part is preparing ourselves," he adds. "Ask yourself, "If discrimination disappears tomorrow, am I still prepared?"

Although the manager was capable of handling the position from a technical standpoint, she had limited skills and experience in managing people—the case for most women and minorities moving up the corporate ladder. "Many women don't trust the system or believe the rules will work in their favor," says Tina Scott Lassiter, president of Business of Women's Business, a New York-based personal and professional development firm.

Copyright 1997. Reprinted with permission of **BLACK ENTERPRISE** Magazine, New York, NY. All rights reserved.

Quiz: Measure Your Accountability

Being more accountable involves giving up some behaviors, beliefs, attitudes, etc. rather than concentrating on behaving a different way. One of the most common defense mechanisms used to avoid accountability or responsibility is to become upset. Obviously, if you're upset, you can't handle the matter.

Going "unconscious," is another, says Guillory. "This is done by simply tuning someone out, or by having your own mental conversation while someone is attempting too point out how you could have assumed greater responsibility."

Playing the role of victim is another way to escape accountability, adds Guillory. Expressions common to the victim are "I can't" and "I'm unable." These statements are really, "I am unwilling."

To see how accountable you really are, take the test below:

SA	Strongly Agree
A	Agree
N	Neutral
D	Disagree
SD	Strongly Disagree

1. I am totally responsible for my success at work.
   _____

2. I am exceptionally productive, irrespective of the work environment.
   _____

3. I am accountable for the results I produce, even if a situation is unfair.
   _____

4. I take training to upgrade my skills and competencies on a regular basis, without having to be told.
   _____

5. I am exceptionally skilled at the work I do as demonstrated by my performance.
   _____

6. I trust co-workers (or employees) without interference when I delegate tasks vital to my own success.
   _____

7. I have demonstrated exceptional interpersonal skills where mentorship or coaching is concerned.
   _____

8. I hold co-workers to their commitments, even when it provokes confrontation.
   _____

9. I hold others proactively accountable for their commitments, regardless of how it may affect our personal relationship.
   _____

10. I am willing to work through in-depth personal issues in order to achieve team success.
    _____

SA responses _____ × 4.0 = _____
A responses _____ × 3.0 = _____
N responses _____ × 2.0 = _____
D responses _____ × 1.0 = _____
SD responses _____ × 0.0 = _____
                              Total _____

Multiply the total by 2.5 to obtain your total percentage of personal empowerment based on a scale of 100%.

Total _____ × 2.5 = _____ %

Average score is 77%

91–100 Extremely empowered. Your success is ensured. You accept unfairness as something you have to deal with and ask, "How do I get beyond this?"

81–90 Very empowered and successful most of the time, except if you are put in an extremely unfair situation.

71–80 Somewhat empowered and probably experience success 50% of the time if you are in a fair system.

70 or below Marginally empowered and your success rate is low. These are the people who have long conversations about how racist society is. If it weren't, they'd be successful.

"But they are afraid to be viewed as unable to do a job without support and, as a result, don't ask for help. This can be a detriment."

The company said it would "treat her equally"—and that's where the problem began, Guillory explains. Under the rules of diversity management, people shouldn't be treated alike, but as individuals.

The manager was not equipped to handle her new role without proper skills and support. While the company should have recognized the manager's unique circumstances and put the proper systems in place, she should have asked about the support she would receive during her transition, i.e.: "How will things be set up to ensure the highest probability of my success?"

Her objective should have been to produce the results required even though her subordinates didn't want her to. One way to do this would have been to go to her superiors and inform them of the difficulties she was having with her staff. She should have also developed a support network of people who she could go to for advice and build alliances with superiors.

How to Improve Your Accountability Quotient

- Change your attitude about colleagues and work. Take 100% responsibility for events in your life. Ask yourself, "Am I avoiding responsibility?"

- Learn self-management skills. Managers may be disappearing, but managing is not. Plan, prioritize, execute and focus on your own work.

- Assess your competency level. Your skills should be consistent with the market. Make sure you're not easily replaceable.

- Accept continuous learning as a way of life. Take advantage of the training programs at your organization. Tapes, books, classes, seminars and, most of all, a personal and professional mentor should be mainstays. White males take five times, and white women three times, more training classes than African Americans.

- Knowledge is the only key to security. It's also the ability to integrate information to create new systems. Learn all you can, process it and then apply it.

Resources: "Empowerment for High-Performing Organizations" by William Guillory and Linda Galindo ($12.95) and "Realizations" by William Guillory ($7.95). Both books are published by Innovations International. To order, call 800-487-3354.

If she had done all that and still felt that the level of support offered was not adequate, she could have then chosen not to take a job where she would inevitably fail. If by resigning, she walked away feeling as though she was set up for failure, then she has learned nothing. Her experience was a self-fulfilling prophecy. On the other hand, if she learned to assess her strengths and weaknesses, continuously upgrades her skills and requests the tools needed to work efficiently, then her experience was a success.

Article Review Form at end of book.

Climbing the executive ranks in corporate America depends on what four factors for women and minorities? What qualities have women and minorities projected in order to secure top leadership positions in America?

The New Power Elite

Women, Jews, African Americans, Asian Americans, Latinos, gays and lesbians

Richard L. Zweigenhaft

G. William Domhoff

Richard L. Zweigenhaft is Charles A. Dana Professor of Psychology at Guilford College in Greensboro, N.C.; G. William Domhoff is Research Professor of Psychology at the University of California at Santa Cruz.

A study of the experiences of six groups—women, Jews, blacks, Asians, Latinos, and gay men and lesbians—as they move into the ranks of America's traditionally white, male, heterosexual, and Christian power elite shows that the more things change, the more they stay the same.

Today, more than 20 years since the beginning of affirmative action programs and the social change that led to them, Jews, women, African Americans, Latinos, and Asian Americans sit on the boards of the country's largest corporations; presidential cabinets have become increasingly diverse; and the highest ranks of the military are no longer filled solely by white men.

The rules, however, remain the same as in 1956 when C. Wright Mills' *The Power Elite* described the exclusively white, male, and Christian makeup of the leading members of America's political, military, and business institutions. The broad social movements of the 1960s and '70s sought to diversify this elite—and, in the process, shift its values to reflect greater social equity—but failed to change the most important factors in attaining membership. Indeed, the diversity "forced" upon the power elite has given it buffers, ambassadors, and tokens through the women and minorities who share its prevailing values. Discrimination is still widespread, and the ascension of different groups, albeit uneven, depends on four factors:

Class: For the most part, it takes at least three generations to rise from the bottom to the top. Fully one-third of women in the elite are from the upper class. Most of the Cuban Americans and Chinese Americans come from ruling-class families displaced by political upheaval. The Jews and Japanese Americans are the products of two- and three-generational climbs up the social ladder. And the first African Americans to serve in cabinets and on the boards of large corporations tended to come from the small black middle class that predated the civil rights movement.

Education: The women and minorities who make it into the corporate elite are typically better educated than the white males who are already a part of it, but time and again they emerge from the same institutions: Harvard, Yale, Princeton, and MIT on the East Coast; the University of Chicago in the Midwest; Stanford and the University of California at Berkeley on the West Coast.

Excerpt from the book *Diversity in the Power Elite: Have Women and Minorities Reached the Top?* Developed for publication in *Mother Jones*, vol. 22, no. 2, March/April 1998. Originally from *Blacks in the White Establishment* by Richard L. Zweigenhaft and G. William Domhoff. Copyright 1998 Yale University Press.

Skin color: African Americans and Latinos who do make it into the power elite are lighter-skinned than other prominent members of their racial group. As Colin Powell told Henry Louis Gates Jr. in the New Yorker, explaining his popularity among whites: "Thing is, I ain't that black."

"Identity management": As Terie Miyamoto, an Asian American U.S. West executive, puts it, the challenge is to move into a "comfort zone" with those who decide who is and is not acceptable for inclusion. Cecily Cannan Selby, the first female board member of Avon Products, cites her first dinner with the previously all-male Avon board: The tension in the room, she says, was visibly reduced when she lit up a cigar. Hedging against traditional stereotypes, Jewish and black executives must be properly reserved, Asian American executives properly assertive, gay executives traditionally masculine, and lesbian executives traditionally feminine.

The new members of the corporate elite may differ in appearance from the old guard, but their actions are strikingly similar. When Linda Wachner, one of the few female CEOs of a Fortune 100-level company, the Warnaco Group, concluded in 1996 that Warnaco's Hathaway Shirt Co. was unprofitable, she decided to close down the factory. It didn't matter to her that Hathaway had been making shirts there since 1837, that almost all of the factory's 500 employees were women, or even that the workers had given up a pay raise to hire consultants to teach them how to work more effectively. The company was not making enough money, and she deemed the average worker's $7.50 hourly wage too high. (In 1995, Wachner received $10 million in salary and stock.)

While the new members of the corporate elite mostly have the same background as their white counterparts, the relatively few rags-to-riches stories occur among politicians who come up through the electoral process, usually within the Democratic Party. In general, Congress is more diverse than the corporate world, and elected women and minorities are more likely to be Democrats than Republicans. Meanwhile, the new corporate elite members tend to join the GOP. Thus both Republicans and Democrats can claim they represent women and minorities.

In the 1960s, those who challenged the homogeneity of the country's boardrooms and halls of government had hoped new perspectives would bring greater openness throughout society. But as activists, political leaders, and the courts came to focus more and more on individual rights, the emphasis on social class and "distributive justice" was lost. The age-old American commitment to individualism, reinforced at every turn by corporate leaders, won out over the commitment to a greater equality of income, once a central strand of New Deal liberalism. The power elite now simply has a kinder, gentler, more diverse face.

Women

Hazel R. O'Leary, 60; president of Hazel R. O'Leary Associates; B.A., Fisk University; J.D., Rutgers University

In 1992, the soon-to-be secretary of energy commented on the value of fitting into corporate culture: "Without losing your own personality," said Hazel O'Leary, then an executive vice president at Northern States Power in Minnesota, "it's important to be part of the prevailing corporate culture. At this company, it's golf. I've resisted learning to play golf all my life, but I finally had to admit I was missing something that way." Hazel O'Leary now plays golf.

As women climb the corporate ladder, they adapt their behavior to fit in. White male managers, according to a 1995 Federal Glass Ceiling Commission report, support hiring women and minorities as long as they are not too different. "What's important," said one manager, "is comfort, chemistry, relationships, and collaborations."

Women directors most frequently take the business route to corporate board membership. But while men typically spend 15 years moving up the ranks, eventually joining the board, women are more likely to head small companies or work as consultants and serve as outside directors. Other common paths include academia, volunteer jobs (top positions with charitable and cultural organizations), and legal careers.

Channeled into labor relations and PR, women at the top not only present an image of diversity, but also provide a buffer between the corporation's managers and those who provide its labor force (as well as the public). In this "velvet ghetto," women play an important corporate role, yet few hold positions with responsibility for the bottom line.

Jews

Michael Eisner, 55; CEO and chairman of Walt Disney; B.A., Denison University

On December 14, 1973, the *Wall Street Journal* announced "Boss-to-Be at DuPont Is an Immigrant's Son Who Climbed Hard Way." Irving Shapiro was the first Jew to achieve such a prominent position in a corporation that had not been founded or purchased by Jews.

No such headline greeted the 1984 announcement that the Walt Disney Co., founded by a man who had refused to hire Jews, picked as its CEO Michael Eisner, a Jew from a wealthy New York family. By 1995, while Jews totaled 2.5 percent of the U.S. population, they represented 7.7 percent of those on corporate boards.

Being Jewish has become a progressively less important cause for discrimination, in part due to assimilation. Second- and third-generation Jews among America's economic elite are less involved in Jewish circles and less likely to marry Jews.

In a study of Harvard Business School graduates, Jewish and non-Jewish managers both noted that certain Jews were more likely to be successful than others. "If an individual is perceived as quite Jewish . . . it may have a negative impact," said one Jewish respondent. "Those who have moved faster are the less visible Jews."

An even more pointed comment came from a non-Jew: "I think at the top levels being Jewish will hurt a person's chances. But it depends on how he plays his cards. This one man I know is so polished, such an upper-class person, there's no way to know he's Jewish. I'll admit I'm prejudiced. There are certain aspects of Jewish people I don't like—they're pushy, they're loud, especially those damn New York bastards. My friend is fine, however. He's an upper-class-type person, the kind who could make it to the top."

African Americans

Vernon E. Jordan Jr., 62; senior partner at Akin, Gump, Strauss, Hauer & Feld; B.A., DePauw University; J.D., Howard University School of Law

At the annual General Motors stockholders' meeting in the spring of 1970, a group calling itself Campaign GM attacked the company's minority-hiring policies. At the time, there were no blacks on GM's board of directors and blacks owned only 14 percent of the 13,600 GM dealerships.

Responding to the group's questions, CEO James Roche made an embarrassing slip: "We are a public corporation owned by free, white . . . ," he said, finally adding, "umm . . . and . . . and . . . and black and yellow people all over the world."

Several months later, Roche asked Leon Sullivan, an activist minister in Philadelphia, to join the board. Unlike other blacks on corporate boards, Sullivan came from an impoverished background and had attended a non-elite college. Even today, his appointment is more the exception than the rule.

African Americans remain underrepresented on corporate boards. Although blacks accounted for about 11 percent of the population in 1964 and about 12 percent in 1995, the percentage of seats held by blacks on Fortune-level boards during the same period rose from zero to only about 3.6 percent. Most black board members come from outside corporate ladders—law firms, universities, or black-owned businesses.

Politically, they include both conservatives and liberals—though the traditionalists far outnumber the activists. Even the few activists tend, over time, to become part of the establishment. A 1993 profile in *Current Biography* explains Democrat Vernon Jordan's willingness to join corporate boards: "During his 10 years at the helm, he greatly expanded the influence of the National Urban League by enlisting the cooperation of some of the largest corporations in the United States. As part of that effort, he began serving on the boards of directors of such corporate giants as J.C. Penney, Xerox, and American Express." Jordan was also expanding his own influence. And no doubt his close friendship with Bill Clinton, and reported role in the Monica Lewinsky affair, now qualifies him as the ultimate insider.

Asian Americans

Wendy Lee Gramm, 53; consultant; B.A., Wellesley College; Ph.D., Northwestern University

From 1992 to 1995, the number of Asian Americans on the boards of 750 publicly held companies rose from 15 to 26. Most are Chinese Americans or Japanese Americans; one is Korean American: economist Wendy Lee Gramm, who's married to conservative GOP Sen. Phil Gramm. Born in 1945 in Hawaii (her father was a sugar company executive), she met Gramm in the 1970s, when they both taught economics at Texas A&M. George Bush appointed her to the Commodity Futures Trading Commission in 1988; she served on the board of the Chicago Mercantile Exchange in the '90s and is now a director of Enron.

Given the relatively small number of Asian Americans in the U.S. and the stereotypes they face, Asian Americans' record of corporate involvement is impressive.

26   Educational Leadership

Chinese Americans are more likely to be founders of their own companies, joining boards of other companies by invitation. Unlike Chinese immigrants before 1965, those who have immigrated since then are generally from well-to-do, well-educated families in China, Taiwan, or Hong Kong. Japanese Americans usually climb the corporate ladder or come from legal or academic backgrounds. Significantly, 63 percent of Asian Americans identify themselves as Christian.

Many Asians face difficulties advancing up the corporate ladder due to discriminatory stereotypes that they lack interpersonal, leadership, and English language skills. Thus, despite high education levels and generally wide acceptance by whites, they may not attain positions in the highest ranks of the power elite for at least another decade. Owing to their concentration in small businesses in low-income areas where big corporations such as Safeway, Revco, and Sears fear to tread, Asian Americans have often served as "middlemen."

Latinos

Robert Goizueta, deceased; former CEO of Coca-Cola; B.S., Yale University

On a 1996 Hispanic Business list of the 75 richest Latinos in the U.S., 27 were Cuban Americans and 25 were Mexican Americans (even though Hispanic Americans of Mexican origin outnumber those of Cuban origin 15 to 1). At the top was Roberto Goizueta, then head of Coca-Cola, whose net worth was estimated at $574 million. Goizueta left Cuba in the late 1940s and attended Yale. A member of the wealthy upper class, he returned to Havana after earning an engineering degree and worked for the Coke subsidiary there. He emigrated to the U.S. after Castro came to power and quickly rose through the Coca-Cola ranks, becoming chairman and CEO in 1981. Before his death last year, he also served as an outside director on the boards of Ford, Kodak, Sonat, and SunTrust Banks.

While Goizueta was typical of the Cuban Americans who belong to the power elite, the number of Latinos in the elite is small: Latinos now make up about 10 percent of the population but less than 1 percent of all corporate directors. They are even underrepresented in general management positions at companies that employ a large percentage of Latinos.

Hispanic Business found that most Latino executives worked in telecommunications, commercial banking, or the food industry. Few held top positions in industries, such as retailing, that do very little business with the federal government and therefore don't have to follow federal guidelines for minority hiring to bid for contracts.

The majority of Latinos in the elite come from the upper or at least middle class and went to a prestigious institution at the undergraduate or graduate level.

Gays and Lesbians

Allan Gilmour, 63; retired vice chairman of Ford Motor; B.A., Harvard University; M.B.A., University of Michigan

Allan Gilmour chose to wait until two years after his retirement from his post as vice chairman of the board at Ford to reveal his homosexuality in December 1996. "I perceived the risk of coming out in the business world as fairly substantial," he told the *Advocate*. Gilmour, a graduate of Harvard and a lifelong Republican, remained on the boards of Prudential Insurance, Dow Chemical, Detroit Edison, U.S. West, and Whirlpool. After he went public, none of these boards asked Gilmour to leave. "I was told uniformly that it makes no difference," he says.

Gilmour may serve as an important role model for younger gay men and lesbians in the corporate world. Still, it's unlikely that, in the near future at least, they will be able to rise high in the corporate boardroom if openly gay.

Nevertheless, a gay person working for a Fortune-level company today suffers less discrimination than in the past. The larger culture has undergone dramatic changes in attitudes about sexuality in general and so have some corporations. Now many companies extend health benefits to the domestic partners of their employees, a development that was unthinkable just a decade ago.

In spite of these changes, gays and lesbians continue to encounter the "lavender ceiling." Some very wealthy and influential men in less buttoned-down industries have been able to be openly gay. Media mogul David Geffen acknowledges that being gay influenced his decision to pursue a career as a music producer. "I decided that the entertainment business was a profession in which being gay was not going to be unusual or stand in my way," he told the *Advocate* in 1992. Homosexuality, however, is less acceptable in the higher ranks: No openly gay man or woman holds a senior executive position on a Fortune-level board.

Article Review Form at end of book.

What is cultural competence? What are the abilities necessary for an instructional leader to become skilled as a cultural mediator?

The Instructional Leader as Cultural Mediator

Joseph Khazzaka

Joseph Khazzaka is an associate professor of education at the University of Scranton, Scranton, Pennsylvania.

The research literature that supports American instructional leadership theory and practice has limited transferability in other cultural contexts because of its basic premises. In other words, the way in which an effective leader in an educational institution—an administrator or teacher—functions in Chicago or Los Angeles may not transfer to educational institutions in England, the Congo, India, or Egypt (Donohue-Clyne 1993). Similarly, the student of instructional leadership in Egypt, for example, will find American leadership theory of only limited value in Egyptian schools. We are all embedded in our respective cultures, and our responses to individuals and groups relate to our learning in very specific cultural contexts. Furthermore, it is difficult for a person of one ethnicity to really understand the cultural context of another ethnic group (Schein 1982). The implications of this limitation for leadership are significant.

To understand our culture beyond the experience of our basic personal socialization requires careful study of its realities. Few of us even consider what these realities may be. It is difficult to understand our own behavior and motivation because we take them for granted and accept what we do as normal. It is when we are confronted with the behavior of others, particularly the leadership behavior of a person from another culture, that we become acutely aware of differences that trigger questions about why the person acted in a particular way. It is also true that when we are in another culture, one in which our own habitual behaviors differ from those of the people around us, we become more conscious of our own actions. We begin to ask ourselves questions, to analyze our customs and the values on which they are built (Jacoby 1994). When we are confronted by the assumptions, beliefs, and attitudes of other cultures—their affective domain—we begin to challenge our own world view (Santos 1986).

The process of analyzing our attitudes and behavior in foreign situations is difficult because we lack an awareness of our own culture's structure. One of the first steps, then, is to examine some of the integrating factors in our own culture, those factors that determine how we behave (Mackwood 1992).

Treatises on Cultural Differences

There have been some excellent treatises on this subject by people who may be considered bicultural. One frequently quoted historian and cultural analyst is Alexis de Tocqueville, who, in *Democracy in America* (1835, 1947) portrayed Americans to Americans in terms of the essential supporting premises of our culture. For instance, Tocqueville looked at Americans' ways of creating and structuring organizations. As educators we understand immediately his point that Americans have a fondness for creating organizations, clubs, and associations. We need only look at the vast array of professional education organizations—the Association of Teacher Educators (ATE), the National Education Association (NEA), the American Federation of Teachers (AFT), the National Association of Secondary School Principals

(NASSP), the Association for Supervision and Curriculum Development (ASCD), and so forth. Tocqueville states that Americans make associations to give entertainment, to build inns, to construct churches, to diffuse books, to send missionaries to other countries, and to establish hospitals, prisons, and schools. Americans continue to create and support organizations at an ever-increasing rate and use them as a means of affiliation, of controlling power, and of creating personal social credentials.

Another cultural analyst, Francis Hsu (1981), has provided a sensitive account of the ways in which Americans behave within their own culture by contrasting those cultural patterns to Chinese behavior patterns. The Chinese social system reinforces conformity to group norms and to higher authority from an early age. Individuals are considered in relationship to the groups in which they work. The group is primary. In contrast, Hsu describes individuals in American society as learning to be independent and autonomous, and to expect that society will acknowledge their rights. Thus, American educational programs focus on satisfying the individual learner's needs.

E. H. Schein (1982), in his study of Japanese leadership styles, devised the paradigm of locus of control, which is useful in looking at American leadership patterns. This paradigm has been widely used to describe some of the basic assumptions of American culture. In the United States we operate under the premise that nature should be conquered and that humans are moving forward toward greater perfectibility. We have internalized cultural motifs such as "Where there's a will, there's a way" and "If at first you don't succeed, try, try again." The cultural tone we grow up with is that if a person is willing to put in the time and effort, he or she can "get to college" or "get to be somebody." Educational administrators and classroom teachers believe problem solving is simply a matter of trying, of finding new ways to change what needs to be changed. In one sense, that belief could be viewed as a cultural internal locus of control because it places responsibility for possible change on individuals. Frequently, that cultural theme is at variance with the external locus of control of many subcultural groups in America, who believe that they do not have the power to control their fate. They accept things as they come, as one way of coping with their perceived lack of control over the power structure (Justin 1979).

Teachers and administrators not only mold the environment in which they work but are in turn molded by the cultural climate of the school.

Differences in Instructional Leadership

The way Americans view the world affects their leadership style. The Western world of technology is a world of exploration. This world has become known through confrontations with nature (the "taming" of the frontier and the "conquering" of space), through overcoming problems, through the use of the scientific method to determine fact. The basic assumptions we live by in the West have become the rules for our interactions. In schools, those rules translate into learning from experience, learning by experimentation, learning by debating the facts, and relying on accuracy of measurement to establish what we perceive to be reality. Even ideas that allow for subcultural expression, such as educational pluralism, are closely related to the assumption that truth can be discovered only through open confrontation and that truth can come from anyone. Thus, leadership in classrooms deals with the pluralistic realities of self-expression, individualism, and the expectation that all groups will have a voice (Shaver 1988; Banks 1988).

Another basic assumption we deal with as instructional leaders in the United States is a strongly held rule of interaction relating to consensus formation. It is interesting that in a culture that values the individual, arriving at operational goals is frequently accomplished through collective agreements by the group. However, the group also identifies an individual who will be accountable—who will ensure that the group voice is heard and that the intentions of the group are carried out (Shaver 1988; Banks 1988).

In Japan, as in South America and in other places around the world, the concept of the group is built on different assumptions. A quality of relationship called *ie no tame ni* operates to develop in an individual a family-type loyalty to the group, thereby enhancing cooperation among group members (Rohlen 1974; Rynn 1996). *Ie no tame ni* includes the leader's understanding of the need to create security and in any workplace, to support individuals by avoiding layoffs by enhancing group compliance, and by providing company benefits (in the workplace, the quality relationship is called *kaisha no tame ni*). Community is the central theme in Japan and intensive socialization to enhance community cohesiveness occurs throughout a person's life. The sought-after leader is the person who has a harmonious personality, who supports the group's needs, and who creates security but expects compliance. Transferred to schools, the quality relationship is called *gak ko no tame ni* (Rynn 1996).

In contrast, Americans have a very proactive, individual-oriented value system. We believe in equality of opportunity and in the efficacy of education. The idea of accepting one's fate is simply not part of the underlying American ideology.

Implications

So, what are the implications of such profound differences in basic assumptions and premises for leadership in the educational community? Simply put, educational leadership involves contact with others from subcultures whose basic assumptions may differ radically from ours. Classrooms in which there are young people from other cultures pose a significant challenge for most educators. At best, we may be able to sensitize ourselves to a few basic realities of their experience and to learn to restrain our own ethnocentric responses (Escalante 1993).

Research suggests that effective leadership in the classroom requires people whose basic assumptions and premises are similar to those of their students. Garcia and Otheguy (1985), in reporting on a bilingual education program to help Cuban immigrants make the transition to American culture in Dade County, Florida, attribute the success of the program to the Cuban Americans who ran it, who were themselves bilingual and bicultural and who understood well the needs of the newcomers. Arnau and Boada (1986), discussing research on languages and schools in Catalonia, Spain, concluded that the most important factor in influencing student achievement is having a teacher whose linguistic abilities and background are similar to those of his or her students. Those studies highlight the fact that effective leadership requires subcultural sensitivity coupled with the ability to help minority youth prepare themselves to compete in the dominant culture by using its tools and artifacts (such as computers) and being familiar with its values and ideologies (Escalante 1993).

Bedrosian (1987) and Banks (1988) stressed the need in schools for diversity in unity, student self-identity, and social coherence, and they argued that schools should provide immigrant and minority students with every opportunity to become integrated into the dominant language and culture. In short, the schooling of immigrants and minorities should result in their being able to compute, to read, write, and speak standard English and to express and to act on the nation's democratic ideas and beliefs.

Teachers need to understand the assumptions, values, and artifacts of the major culture. At the same time, they must be sensitive to subcultural values in order to provide educational structures that allow students to develop personally and to make the transition to the dominant culture. The ideal, therefore, in both instructional leaders and in students, may be the bicultural person who can move with ease in both dominant and subcultural milieus (Escalante 1993). Both leaders and students should acquire what Vanikar (1985) called "cultural competence"—the ability to draw on any culture, native or other, with a sense of discernment and purpose.

Instructional Leadership and Educational Policy/Practice

Teachers and administrators not only mold the environment in which they work but are in turn molded by the cultural climate of the school. Ethnic minorities in the schools affect leaders and are affected by them. This reciprocal influence is what John J. Patrick (1986) called "pluralistic integration," a process that seeks to balance ethnic or cultural identity with acculturation. Ethnic or cultural identity cannot be ignored by educational leaders; it is a persistent and pervasive force. Samuel Bell and Mary Soley (1986) maintained that immigrant and minority students must have educational experiences based upon a fundamental respect for them, their respective cultures, and their personal histories. The school should be an environment that is positive and allows for ethnic expression. Leaders who support such environments create classes that lead to heightened participation and empower both teachers and students to share and achieve.

Immigrant and subcultural groups in this country bring their own cultural systems into the schools with them. Those groups must adapt to both the new environment and the dominant culture. They need to learn new cultural values and customs and to master the use of new artifacts if they hope to work and live successfully in the new society. Immigrants who must learn the new language and adjust to the complex cultural systems of their adopted country face a life-long task of adjustment. Seldom do such people aspire to high leadership roles, simply because they lack the socialization that is necessary to deal with native people using appropriate culture values unconsciously. The few immigrants who become truly bicultural are highly prized as leaders because they can help others build cultural bridges (Escalante 1993).

The Bicultural Leader

Teachers and other educational leaders are faced with the task of creating structures and processes that value minority students' previous experiences and help them become bicultural (Chattergy 1992). Bicultural adaptation means having a deep understanding of the adopted culture to the point of sensing its assumptions and premises unconsciously and having a good grasp of the tools that are the creations of the dominant culture, particularly its language and its technological artifacts, so that a person can compete successfully as an individual (Banks 1988).

The cultural pluralism we espouse in education requires leaders of a special kind. Teachers in mono-cultural societies operate using but one set of values. Teachers in multicultural classrooms need to "become" immigrants and minorities—to intellectually transpose themselves into the realities in which their students operate. Teacher education programs must help future teachers to adapt to this situation by exposing them to learning styles from a variety of cultures. In addition, such programs must develop an understanding of the need for multicultural education and a commitment to its implementation. Multicultural teacher education, according to Santos (1986), can succeed only if the affective domain is addressed, if we can understand the beliefs, attitudes, and opinions of other cultures—and the challenges they pose to our own.

References

Arnau, J., and H. Boada. 1986. Language and schools in Catalonia. *Journal of Multilingual and Multicultural Development* 6 (2–3): 107–22.

Banks, J. A. 1988. Education, citizenship, and cultural opinion. *Education and Society* 1 (1): 19–22.

Bedrosian, M. 1987. Commentary: Multi-ethnic literature: Mining the diversity. *Journal of Ethnic Studies* 15 (3): 125–34.

Bell, S. R., and M. E. Soley. 1986. The new immigration and social education. *Social Education* 50 (3): 170–71.

Chattergy, V. 1992. Bridging two worlds: The teacher and the immigrant Filipino student. *Kamehameka Journal of Education* 3 (2): 23–28.

Donohue-Clyne, I. 1993. "Children only go to school to colour in . . ." Overseas educated teachers' perceptions of Australian schools. *Multicultural Teaching to Combat Racism in School and Community* 11:3.

Escalante, J. 1993. Diversity seminar. Adams State College, Alamosa, Colorado (July).

Garcia, O., and R. Otheguy. 1985. The masters of survival send their children to school: Bilingual education in the ethnic schools of Miami. *Bilingual Review* 12: 1–2, 3–19.

Gifford, B. R., and P. Gillet. 1986. Teaching in a great Age of Immigration. *Social Education* 50 (3): 184–88.

Hsu, F. L. K. 1981. *Americans and Chinese, passage to differences*. Honolulu: University of Hawaii Press.

Jacoby, R. 1994. Developing and implementing increasing awareness of cultural diversity in early childhood curriculum through teacher training and participants. Practicum paper. Fort Lauderdale, Fl.: Nova Southern University.

Justin, N. 1971. The relationship of certain sociocultural factors to academic achievement of male Mexican-American high school seniors. Doctoral diss. Tucson: University of Arizona Press.

Mackwood, G. 1992. Postmodernism and the social studies curriculum. *Canadian Social Studies* 26 (3): 100–101.

McKenzie, V. M. 1985. Ethnographic findings on West Indian-American clients. *Journal of Counseling and Development* 65 (1): 40–44.

Patrick, J. J. 1986. Immigration in the curriculum. *Social Education* 50 (3): 172–76.

Rohlen, T. 1974. *For harmony and strength*. Berkeley: University of California Press.

Rynn, M. 1996. Cultural anthropology course lectures. University of Scranton, Scranton, Pennsylvania.

Santos, S. L. 1986. Promoting intercultural understanding through multicultural teacher training. *Action in Teacher Education* 8 (1): 19–25.

Schein, E. H. 1982. Does Japanese management style have a message for American managers? *Sloan Management Review* 23 (1): 55–68.

Shaver, J. 1988. Cultural pluralism and a democratic society. *Education and Society* 1 (1): 11–17.

Stack, S. 1990. Instilling cultural awareness: The Vietnamese experience. *Southern Social Studies Quarterly* 15 (2): 27–34.

Stoddard, E. 1969. The U.S./Mexican border as a research laboratory. *Journal of Interamerican Studies* 11: 447–48.

Swisher, K. 1986. Authentic research: An interview on the way to Ponderosa. *Anthropology Education Quarterly* 17 (3): 1985–88.

Tocqueville, Alexis de. 1835, 1947. *Democracy in America*. New York: Oxford University Press.

Vanikar, R. 1985. Crossing cultural bridges: A model for mapping the extent of bicultural awareness. *Journal of Multilingual and Multicultural Development* 6 (6): 437–447.

Wilson, A. 1986. The immigrant student challenge. *Social Education* 50 (3): 189–193.

Zanger, V. V. 1988. Teachers debate solutions to cross-cultural dilemmas. *Equity and Choice* 4 (3): 13–18.

Article Review Form at end of book.

What is leadership? How do subordinates, peers, and supervisors evaluate leadership effectiveness? Managerial incompetence is associated with what characteristics?

What We Know About Leadership

Effectiveness and personality

Robert Hogan, Gordon J. Curphy, and Joyce Hogan

Robert Hogan and Joyce Hogan, Department of Psychology, University of Tulsa. Gordon J. Curphy, Personnel Decisions, Inc., Minneapolis, MN.

Although psychologists know a great deal about leadership, persons who make decisions about real leaders seem largely to ignore their accumulated wisdom. In an effort to make past research more accessible, interpretable, and relevant to decision makers, this article defines leadership and then answers nine questions that routinely come up when practical decisions are made about leadership (e.g., whom to appoint, how to evaluate them, when to terminate them).

According to the political scientists, the fundamental question in human affairs is "Who shall rule?" As psychologists—who are less infused with the spirit of realpolitik—we believe the question is "Who *should* rule?" The question must be answered during national elections, when CEOs are replaced, and when university presidents retire. The question concerns how to evaluate leadership potential. When it is answered incorrectly, teams lose, armies are defeated, economies dwindle, and nations fail.

In terms of the number of printed pages devoted to the subject, leadership appears to be one of the most important issues in applied psychology. Volumes appear on the topic every year, and a recent review lists over 7,000 books, articles, or presentations (Bass, 1990). However, the rules of psychological research are such that we tend to focus on narrowly defined issues. The result is that our research is primarily read by other psychologists. Although J. P. Campbell (1977) and Mintzberg (1982) recommended that researchers pay more attention to applications, what we know seems to have little impact on the people who actually make decisions about leadership. The gap between what we know and what leadership decision makers want to know may explain the popularity of such books as *In Search of Excellence* (Peters & Waterman, 1982), *The Change Masters* (Kanter, 1983), *Leaders: The Strategies for Taking Charge* (Bennis & Nanus, 1985), and *The New Leaders* (A. M. Morrison, 1992). These books are not intended to be scientific dissertations; rather, they offer practical suggestions about how to identify and evaluate leadership. To reduce the gap between researchers and the lay public, this article answers nine questions that psychologists are often asked by persons who must choose or evaluate leaders.

What Is Leadership?

Various writers have argued that our evolutionary history makes us both selfish (Dawkins, 1976) and yet able to identify with the welfare of our social unit—perhaps because individual survival sometimes depends on group survival (Eibl-Eibesfeld, 1989; J. Hogan, 1978). It is important to distinguish between a person's short-term and long-term self-interest; actions that promote the group also serve an individual's long-term welfare. History mournfully suggests, however,

Copyright © 1994 by the American Psychological Association. Reprinted with permission.

that without an external threat to their group, people largely pursue their short-term interests.

This article provides a context for understanding leadership. In our view, leadership involves persuading other people to set aside for a period of time their individual concerns and to pursue a common goal that is important for the responsibilities and welfare of a group. This definition is morally neutral. A Somali warlord who is trying to bring together a group of clansmen to control food supplies needs the same skills as an inner-city Chicago minister who is trying to bring together a group of parishioners to help the homeless.

Leadership is persuasion, not domination; persons who can require others to do their bidding because of their power are not leaders. Leadership only occurs when others willingly adopt, for a period of time, the goals of a group as their own. Thus, leadership concerns building cohesive and goal-oriented teams; there is a causal and definitional link between leadership and team performance.

What is it that leaders do? Beginning with the Ohio State studies in the 1940s and 1950s, several taxonomies of leadership behaviors have been proposed, including those by Borman and Brush (1993), Davis, Skube, Hellervik, Gebelein, and Sheard (1992), and Yukl, Wall, and Lepsinger (1990). They differ primarily in terms of their specificity. Yukl et al.'s list is the broadest; it identifies 14 categories of leader behavior, including planning and organizing, problem solving, clarifying, informing, monitoring, motivating, consulting, recognizing, supporting, managing conflict and team building, networking, delegating, developing and mentoring, and rewarding. Although these actions are required by persons ranging from first-line supervisors to CEOs, their relative importance differs by organizational level.

These taxonomies tell us what people in leadership positions typically do, and the various commercially available, multirater assessment instruments (e.g., Personnel Decisions, Inc., 1991) tell us about the degree to which a particular leader does these things. However, there is little published research concerning what effective leaders actually do. Effectiveness concerns judgments about a leader's impact on an organization's bottom line (i.e., the profitability of a business unit, the quality of services rendered, market share gained, or the win–loss record of a team). Indices of effectiveness are often hard to specify and frequently affected by factors beyond a leader's control. Nevertheless, effectiveness is the standard by which leaders should be judged; focusing on typical behaviors and ignoring effectiveness is an overarching problem in leadership research.

Does Leadership Matter?

In 1910, the Norwegians and the English engaged in a dramatic and highly publicized race to the South Pole. It was an epic contest, and the contrast between the performance of the Norwegian team led by Roald Amundsen and the English team led by Robert Falcon Scott provided a real-life study in leadership and team performance. Scott's incompetence cost him the race, his life, and the lives of three team members, although, as often happens when high-level leadership fails, the details were covered up for years (cf. Dixon, 1976).

The fact that Lincoln's army was inert until Ulysses S. Grant assumed command and that some coaches can move from team to team transforming losers into winners is, for most people, evidence that leadership matters. Psychologists, as researchers, are (properly) more skeptical; they often explain differences in effectiveness in terms of the factors in the "environment" in which a team operates. Perhaps because effectiveness is influenced by so many factors, there are only a handful of studies evaluating the impact of leadership on an organization's bottom line. Some of the best evidence we have concerns the performance of flight crews (Chidester, Helmreich, Gregorich, & Geis, 1991), military units (Curphy, 1991, 1993), U.S. presidents (House, Spangler, & Woycke, 1991), and Methodist ministers (Smith, Carson, & Alexander, 1984). These studies show that certain leader characteristics are associated with enhanced team performance—when the appropriate indices of effectiveness are studied.

There is a second and less direct way of answering the question "Does leadership matter?" At the historical level one might reflect on the horrific consequences of the leadership of Adolph Hitler in Germany from 1933 to 1945 and Joseph Stalin in Russia from 1927 to 1953. Millions of people suffered and died as a consequence of the megalomaniacal visions of these two flawed geniuses, and the baleful consequences of their rule persist even today.

A third way to decide whether leadership matters is to ask the consumers of leadership (i.e., a manager's direct reports). Several patterns of leadership behavior are associated with subordinates' performance and satisfaction (cf. Bass, 1990; Hughes, Ginnett, & Curphy, 1993; Yukl, 1989). Conversely, reactions to inept leadership include turnover, insubordination, industrial sabotage, and malingering. R. Hogan, Raskin, and Fazzini (1990) noted that organizational climate studies from the mid-1950s to the present routinely show that 60% to 75% of the employees in any organization—no matter when or where the survey was completed and no matter what occupational group was involved—report that the worst or most stressful aspect of their job is their immediate supervisor. Good leaders may put pressure on their people, but abusive and incompetent management create billions of dollars of lost productivity each year. Dixon's (1976) book, *The Psychology of Military Incompetence,* provides a graphic and almost unbearably painful account of the consequences of bad leadership in the military. Reactions to inept leadership can be extreme. In the spring of 1993 articles in several major newspapers (e.g., the *New York Times,* the *Washington Post*) noted that poor first-line supervision was associated with the deaths of numerous postal workers over the past decade.

To stimulate research on the topic of inept management, R. Hogan et al. (1990) proposed that the base rate for managerial incompetence in America is between 60% and 75%. DeVries (1992), in a fascinating brief review, estimated that for the past 10 years the failure rate among senior executives in corporate America has been at least 50%. Shipper and Wilson (1991), using data from 101 departments in a large southwestern hospital, reported that the base rate for incompetent management in that organization was 60%. Millikin-Davies (1992), using data from a large aerospace organization, estimated a 50% base rate. She gathered critical incidents of managerial incompetence, which she rank ordered in terms of frequency. The most common complaints from direct reports concerned (a) managers' unwillingness to exercise authority (e.g., "is reluctant to confront problems and conflict"; "is not as self-confident as others"), which characterized 20% of the sample of 84 managers, and (b) managers tyrannizing their subordinates (e.g., "manages his/her employees too closely, breathes down their necks"; "treats employees as if they were stupid"), which characterized 16% of the sample.

In summary, a growing body of evidence supports the common sense belief that leadership matters. Consequently, psychologists need to better determine when, where, and how leadership affects organization effectiveness and help organizations choose better leaders.

How Are Leaders Chosen?

Psychologists have known for some time that measures of cognitive ability and normal personality, structured interviews, simulations, and assessment centers predict leadership success reasonably well (cf. Bass, 1990; Howard & Bray, 1990; Hughes et al., 1993; Sorcher, 1985; Yukl, 1989). Nonetheless, many organizations seem either unaware or reluctant to take advantage of these psychological selection services. As a result, first-line supervisors are often chosen from the workforce on the basis of their technical talent rather than their leadership skills. Examples include academic department chairs, petty officers in the military, sergeants in the protective services, and shop supervisors in manufacturing organizations. Typically, someone who is good at the activity of the unit is made a supervisor on the basis of his or her proficiency. As a consequence, the organization loses, for example, a good scholar or sailor and acquires a supervisor whose talent for management is unknown.

We believe that middle managers (e.g., academic deans) are often chosen from the ranks of first-line supervisors on the basis of likeability and perceived ability to work with senior management. This, however, is speculation; few data illuminate the topic. Nor is there much data available concerning how CEOs (e.g., university presidents) are chosen. In many cases, an executive search firm puts together a slate of candidates, each of whom seems to fit the corporate culture and seems acceptable to the key decision makers. A search committee—often composed of board members with limited experience in the business of the organization—interviews the candidates and makes a choice (cf. DeVries, 1992).

Why aren't psychologists more involved in the process of executive selection? There are several reasons: (a) Our empirical research is often so narrowly focused that it seems irrelevant; (b) we are so cautious about generalizing beyond our data that we seem to have nothing to say; (c) our services appear expensive to organizations who overlook the costs of making poor selection decisions; (d) we may lack sufficient status in an organization for our views to be considered; and (e) we often do not understand the political realities surrounding the selection.

How Should Leaders Be Evaluated?

We suggested earlier that the appropriate way to measure leadership is in terms of team, group, or organizational effectiveness. This criterion will always be contaminated; unexpected external events can disrupt the best efforts of anyone. Jimmy Carter's presidency was largely undone by an OPEC oil embargo and a riot in Iran, events over which Carter had no control. Nonetheless, we think team performance must always be kept in mind when one evaluates a person's leadership ability.

The literature on leadership effectiveness can be organized in terms of five categories of studies. In the first category, leaders are evaluated in terms of the actual performance of their team or organizational unit. Examples include studies by Chidester et al. (1991), Curphy (1993), House et al. (1991), and Smith et al. (1984).

In the second category, subordinates', peers', or supervisors' ratings are used to evaluate leaders. Examples include studies by Bass and Yammarino (1991), Bray (1982), Harris and Schaubroeck (1988), Hazucha (1991), and Nilsen and Campbell (1993). One implication of this research is that subordinates are often in a unique position to evaluate leadership effectiveness. Sweetland's (1978) review of managerial productivity concluded that effective leadership and increased group output were a function of the interaction between managers and their subordinates. Murphy and Cleveland (1991) noted that the evaluation of a manager's performance depends, in part, on the relationships that the person has established with his or her subordinates. Hegarty (1974) found that university department chairs who received feedback from subordinates improved their performance, both as judged by subordinates and in comparison with control participants who received no subordinate evaluations. Similarly, Bernardin and Klatt (1985) found that managers who were involved in multirater appraisal systems received significantly higher mean effectiveness ratings than those who received no subordinate feedback. McEvoy and Beatty (1989) compared the predictive validity of subordinate evaluations with assessment center ratings and concluded that subordinate ratings were as effective (and less expensive) as assessment center data in forecasting managerial performance seven years later.

Because subordinates are in a unique position to judge leadership effectiveness, what leadership characteristics do they feel are most important? Research by D. P. Campbell (1991), Harris and Hogan (1992), and Lombardo, Ruderman, and McCauley (1988) indicates that a leader's credibility or trustworthiness may be the single most important factor in subordinates' judgments of his or her effectiveness. For example, Harris and Hogan asked subordinates ($N = 301$) to evaluate their managers ($N = 49$) using a 55-item questionnaire that assessed growth versus stagnation, interpersonal competence, managerial values, and technical competence. Subordinates also rated their managers for overall effectiveness. Each manager and his or her boss completed a parallel questionnaire. Subordinates' and bosses' evaluations of a target manager's performance were reasonably consistent ($rs > .50$). In addition, managers' self-ratings were uncorrelated with the ratings provided by the other groups; this is consistent with the meta-analytic results of Harris and Schaubroeck (1988). Perhaps most important, bosses' ratings of a manager's overall effectiveness were largely influenced by judgments of his or her technical competence (e.g., "Supervisor is a flexible and far-sighted problem solver"), whereas subordinates' ratings of a manager's overall effectiveness were largely influenced by judgments of integrity (e.g., "My supervisor has earned my trust"). Thus, although subordinates and bosses tend to agree in their evaluation of a manager's overall effectiveness, they also evaluate rather different aspects of that performance. Although subordinates' ratings will be to some degree contaminated by rating errors, research shows that these ratings also reflect some knowledge of a person's actual performance in a leadership role. For example, Shipper and Wilson (1991), using data provided by managers and their subordinates from 68 subunits of a large southwestern hospital, showed that subordinates' ratings of managerial effectiveness were correlated (rs between .22 and .46) with engineered standards of productivity. These findings provide strong support for the use of subordinates' evaluations of managerial effectiveness.

A third category of studies evaluates the leadership potential of strangers on the basis of their performance in interviews, simulations, assessment centers, or leaderless group discussions. Examples include studies by Albright, Kenny, and Malloy (1988), Howard and Bray (1990), and Lord, De Vader, and Allinger (1986). The leaderless group research provides virtually no information about effectiveness; rather, it tells us about what a person must do in order to be perceived, in the short term, as leaderlike. On the other hand, assessment center research often uses organizational advancement as a criterion, and it tells us about the characteristics related to getting ahead in large, complex organizations. In the AT&T Managerial Assessment Project, for example, subsequent management level was best predicted by assessment center ratings for need for advancement, general mental ability, written communication skills, overall communications skills, flexibility, creativity, and organizing and planning (Howard & Bray, 1990).

Fourth, self-ratings of leadership have also been used as evaluative criteria (Farh & Dobbins, 1989). The evidence is clear, however, that self-ratings tell us little about leader effectiveness. But there is a kind of manager who routinely over evaluates his or her performance, and that tendency is associated with poor leadership (Atwater & Yammarino, 1992; Nilsen & Campbell, 1993; Van Velsor, Taylor, & Leslie, 1992).

In the fifth category of research, effectiveness is defined by the low end of the continuum—by persons whose careers are in jeopardy or who have derailed. The fact that a person has been passed over for promotion or fired reflects an evaluation of his or her performance in a negative direction. Early research on derailment includes articles by Lombardo et al. (1988) and McCall and Lombardo (1983). Hellervik, Hazucha, and Schneider (1992), Peterson (1993), and Peterson and Hicks (1993) studied managers whose careers were in trouble, using a wide variety of assessment techniques, such as multirater assessment instruments and psychological tests, to identify different jeopardy and derailment factors. This research reveals managerial incompetence to be associated with untrustworthiness, over control, exploitation, micromanagement, irritability, unwillingness to use discipline, and an inability to make good staffing or business decisions (or both).

We can summarize this section as follows: The answer to the question "How should leaders be evaluated?" is "In terms of the performance of their teams." Realistically, the data needed to make this evaluation are often difficult to obtain or badly contaminated by external factors. Perhaps the best alternative is to ask subordinates, peers, and superiors to evaluate a leader. The empirical literature suggests that these sources of information are correlated; that the respondents tend to key on different aspects of a leader's performance; and that, taken together, these evaluations are moderately but significantly related to team performance (D. P. Campbell, 1991; Harris & Hogan, 1992). Finally, because subordinates', peers', or bosses' ratings involve judgments about the frequency of certain behaviors, researchers typically find stronger links between personality and these ratings than between personality and indices of effectiveness.

Why Do We Choose So Many Flawed Leaders?

The 1992 U.S. presidential election is an example of how important leaders are often chosen. A group of candidates make public statements; the voters, aided by promptings from journalists, evaluated the leadership potential of the candidates and then chose one. The process involves estimating the leadership qualities of strangers. DeVries (1992) noted that, of all the methods available to chose senior executives, organizations overwhelmingly rely on search firm nominations, background checks, and interviews. The standardized and well-validated methods developed by psychologists are used in only a tiny fraction of cases. We believe the less valid methods continue to be used (in spite of what we know) because of the reasons cited earlier and because candidates for executive positions often refuse to submit to psychological assessment. The 50% failure rate among senior executives may well be the result of these widely used but invalid selection procedures. Again, the hiring problem typically involves evaluating the leadership potential of strangers.

There has been considerable research concerning the characteristics of persons who, in the absence of performance data, nonetheless seem leaderlike. This research fits nicely into two categories. These include (a) studies of the relation between personality and indices of emergent leadership, and (b) research on implicit leadership theory.

Emergent Leadership

Research on emergent leadership identifies the factors associated with someone being perceived as leaderlike when there is only limited information about that person's actual performance; this research typically involves leaderless discussion groups. Stogdill (1948) reviewed research on personality and emergent leadership in a variety of unstructured groups. He concluded that measures of dominance, extraversion, sociability, ambition or achievement, responsibility, integrity, self-confidence, mood and emotional control, diplomacy, and cooperativeness were positively related to emergent leadership.

The personality descriptors identified in Stogdill's (1974) review easily map onto the big-five model of personality structure endorsed by many modern personality psychologists (cf. Digman, 1990; Goldberg, 1993; R. Hogan & Hogan, 1992; McCrae & Costa, 1987; Passini & Norman, 1966). This model holds that personality, from the view of an observer, can be described in terms of five broad dimensions—surgency, agreeableness, conscientiousness, emotional stability, and intellect —and it provides a common vocabulary for interpreting the results of personality research. In the past, this research was often hard to interpret because different studies used different terminology. For example, the conscientiousness dimension has been called conformity (Fiske, 1949), prudence (R. Hogan & Hogan, 1992), constraint (Tellegen, 1982), will to achieve (Digman, 1990), and work

Peabody & Goldberg, 1989). These different terms refer to the same broad construct; similar trends for the other four personality dimensions can be found in the Appendix.*

Returning to Stogdill's (1948) review, dominance, extraversion, and sociability reflect surgency; responsibility, achievement, and integrity fall into the conscientiousness dimension; self-confidence, mood, and emotional control are part of emotional stability; and diplomacy and cooperativeness resemble agreeableness. Mann (1959) reviewed 28 studies concerning the relation between personality and observer ratings of emergent leadership in small groups and essentially replicated Stogdill's (1948) findings.

More recent studies of personality and leadership emergence reached similar conclusions (Gough, 1990; J. Hogan, 1978; Kenny & Zaccaro, 1983; Lord et al., 1986; Rueb & Foti, 1990; Stogdill, 1974; Zaccaro, Foti, & Kenny, 1991). Gough (1984, 1990), for example, reported that the Dominance, Capacity for Status, Sociability, Social Presence (i.e., surgency), Self-Acceptance, Achievement via Independence (i.e., emotional stability), and Empathy (i.e., agreeableness) scales of the California Psychological Inventory (Gough, 1987) are significantly correlated with peer and staff ratings for emergent leadership in leaderless discussion groups. Lord et al. (1986) used meta-analysis to estimate the correlations between various personality traits and leadership emergence in the studies reviewed by Mann (1959) and 13 other studies. They reported that the "true" correlations between masculinity–femininity, dominance, extraversion–introversion,

*Does not appear in this publication.

adjustment, conservatism (which correspond to surgency, emotional stability, and conscientiousness), and leadership emergence in small groups are $r = .34, .13, .26, .24$, and $.22$, respectively. Although the correlations tend to be low, many studies in this meta-analysis examined leadership emergence in a single situation, and these single situation ratings are necessarily less reliable than ratings from a variety of situations.

Looking across a number of leaderless discussion groups, Kenny and Zaccaro (1983) found that between 48% and 82% of the variance in leadership emergence rankings was due to personality. Ellis (1988), Rueb and Foti (1990), and Zaccaro et al. (1991) have shown that the ability to control one's expressive behaviors (i.e., self-monitoring) is positively related to leadership emergence. Snyder's (1974) self-monitoring scale consists of three dimensions —concern for social appropriateness, sensitivity to social cues, and the ability to control one's behavior according to social cues (cf. Briggs, Cheek, & Buss, 1980)—and these dimensions correspond to the big-five dimensions of surgency, agreeableness, and emotional stability. In summary, this research reveals a fairly consistent association between high scores on the dimensions of surgency, agreeableness, and emotional stability and being perceived as leaderlike in a group with no appointed leader.

Assessment centers and employment interviews are often used to evaluate the leadership potential of strangers; data are sometimes gathered to determine the validity of these evaluations. Bray (1982), for example, reported that assessment center data were reasonably valid predictors of a person's promotion record at AT&T. The performance dimensions identified in the AT&T Managerial Assessment Project—need for advancement, behavior flexibility, creativity, organizing and planning, and so on—correspond to the dimensions of surgency, conscientiousness, emotional stability, and intellect.

These results suggest that the big-five model provides a convenient way to summarize both leaderless group discussion and assessment center research. The results also suggest that measures of surgency, agreeableness, conscientiousness, and emotional stability can be used to predict the leadership potential of strangers. Implicit leadership theory research also supports the utility of the big-five taxonomy.

Implicit Leadership Theory

The second line of research concerning how we evaluate the leadership potential of strangers is called *implicit leadership theory*. Starting with Hollander and Julian (1969), implicit leadership theory argues that people are seen as leaderlike to the degree that their characteristics (i.e., intelligence, personality, or values) match other peoples' preconceived notions of what leaders should be like. Eden and Leviathan (1975), Lord, Foti, and De Vader (1984), Rush, Thomas, and Lord (1977), and Weiss and Adler (1981) have shown that people do in fact have generalized ideas about leadership, and they use them to evaluate the leadership potential of strangers. Specifically, most people seem to regard intelligence, honesty, sociability, understanding, aggressiveness, verbal skills, determination, and industriousness as important aspects of leadership, regardless of the team task or situation. Note that these attributes can be organized using the big-five model.

To return, finally, to the question of this section, "Why do we choose so many flawed leaders?," the answer may be that search committees choose candidates not on the basis of established principles of personnel selection but on the basis of the principles that guide leadership emergence—namely, those candidates who seem most leaderlike are most likely to be anointed. The problem is that persons who seem leaderlike may not have the skills required to build and guide an effective team. The result is a leadership failure rate in the range of 50% to 60%.

How to Forecast Leadership?

In our judgment, the best way to forecast leadership is to use a combination of cognitive ability, personality, simulation, role play, and multirater assessment instruments and techniques. Although personality assessment is part of this, there is some disagreement as to whether personality measures on their own can predict leadership potential. We believe that terminological confusions have obscured the usefulness of personality measures for assessing leadership potential and that the big-five model substantially enhances our ability to integrate this research.

Personality and Rated Leader Effectiveness

Several lines of evidence show that certain personality dimensions are consistently related to rated leadership effectiveness. The first evidence comes from Stogdill's (1974) review. Stogdill found that surgency (i.e., dominance, assertiveness, energy or activity level, speech fluency, sociability, and social participation), emotional stability (i.e., adjustment, emotional balance, independence, and self-confidence), conscientiousness (i.e., responsibility, achievement, initiative, personal integrity, and ethical conduct), and agreeableness (i.e., friendliness, social nearness, and support) were positively related to rated effectiveness. Stogdill (1974) did not organize his findings as we describe them; nonetheless, his findings support the idea that there is a relationship between personality and leadership.

Bentz (1985, 1987, 1990) reported similar findings from his research on executive selection at Sears. Using the Guilford-Martin Personality Inventory, Bentz (1985, 1990) noted that executives promoted to the highest levels at Sears were articulate and active (i.e., surgency), independent, self-confident, and emotionally balanced (i.e., emotional stability), and hard working and responsible (i.e., conscientiousness). The median multiple correlations between these dimensions and subordinates' ratings of operating efficiency, personal relations, satisfaction, financial rewards, and job conditions were about $R = .50$ (Bentz, 1985). Bentz (1985) reported comparable multiple correlations between these personality factors and leaders' compensation, immediate and second-level superiors' ratings and rankings, and peer groups' ratings of effectiveness over a 21-year period.

Bray and Howard (1983) and associates reported similar findings with AT&T executives. Those personality traits that best predicted managerial advancement—and we assume that most of those who advanced were also effective—were the desire for advancement, energy-activity level, and the readiness to make decisions (i.e., surgency); resistance to stress and tolerance for uncertainty (i.e., emotional stability); inner work standards (i.e., conscientiousness); and range of interests (i.e., intellect; Bray, Campbell, & Grant, 1974; Bray & Howard, 1983; Howard & Bray, 1990).

Personality and Effective Team Performance

Two sets of studies illustrate the link between personality and team performance. The first concerns charismatic leadership. House (1977) used biographical materials to identify three themes in the careers of charismatic leaders. First, they have a vision that others find compelling; second, they are able to recruit a group of people who share that vision, and these people resemble a team; and third, by virtue of the relationships they develop with the team members, such leaders are able to persuade them to work for and to support the vision.

Charismatic leaders can be quite effective; relative to non-charismatic leaders, they have substantially higher (a) promotion recommendations or performance appraisal ratings from superiors; (b) satisfaction, morale, or approval ratings from subordinates; (c) historians' ratings of greatness; or (d) levels of team performance (Avolio, Waldman, & Einstein, 1988; Bass, 1985; Bass, Avolio, & Goodheim, 1987; Bass & Yammarino, 1991; Conger & Kanungo, 1988; Curphy, 1991, 1993; House et al., 1991; Howell & Frost, 1988).

House et al. (1991) reported that charismatic U.S. presidents have strong needs for power and high energy levels and they are socially assertive (these themes resemble surgency) and achievement oriented (i.e., conscientiousness). Using self-ratings from the Adjective Checklist (Gough & Heilbrun, 1983) and subordinates' ratings for charisma, Ross and Offermann (1991) reported that charisma ratings are positively correlated with self-confidence and personal adjustment (i.e., emotional stability), feminine attributes and nurturance (i.e., agreeableness), and the need for change (i.e., intellect).

Foushee, Chidester, Helmreich, and their associates studied the personality measures that influence team performance—in this case, the performance of commercial airline flight crews (cf. Chidester et al., 1991; Foushee & Helmreich, 1988). This research is important because breakdowns in team performance are the primary cause of air transport accidents (Cooper, White, & Lauber, 1979). Chidester et al. showed that flight crew performance—defined in terms of the number and severity of the errors made by the crew—is significantly correlated with the personality of the captain. Crews with captains who were warm, friendly, self-confident, and able to stand up to pressure (i.e., agreeableness and emotional stability) made the fewest errors. Conversely, crews with captains who were arrogant, hostile, boastful, egotistical, passive aggressive, or dictatorial made the most errors. Despite these results, Chidester et al. pointed out that personality is not taken into account in the process of airline pilot selection.

Why Do Leaders Fail?

Leaders fail for a variety of reasons—product lines no longer interest customers, services are no longer required, and companies reorganize and downsize. Nevertheless, a number of leaders fail for personal rather than structural or economic reasons. They may be skilled in a particular area, such as accounting, engineering, or sales. They fail because they can no longer rely solely on their own skills and effort; that is, they have been promoted into positions that require them to work through others to be successful. Because they are unable to build a team, their management careers come to a halt. Derailment is curiously understudied given the frequency with which it occurs.

Bentz (1985) essentially founded modern derailment research while analyzing the correlates of executive performance at Sears. He reported that among the persons with the appropriate positive characteristics (i.e., intelligence, confidence, ambition), a subset failed. Bentz catalogued the themes associated with failure (e.g., playing politics, moodiness, dishonesty) and concluded that the failed executives had an overriding personality defect or character flaw that alienated their subordinates and prevented them from building a team.

Research on managerial incompetence at the Center for Creative Leadership and Personnel Decisions, Inc., has come to similar conclusions; many managers who are bright, hard-working, ambitious, and technically competent fail (or are in danger of failing) because they are perceived as arrogant, vindictive, untrustworthy, selfish, emotional, compulsive, overcontrolling, insensitive, abrasive, aloof, too ambitious, or unable to delegate or make decisions (Hazucha, 1991, Kaplan, Drath, & Kofodimos, 1991; Lombardo et al., 1988; McCall & Lombardo, 1983; Peterson & Hicks, 1993).

The big-five model reflects the "bright side" of personality. Effectiveness requires both the presence of these positive characteristics and the absence of what we call "dark side" characteristics —irritating tendencies that alienate subordinates and interfere with a person's ability to form a team. Research shows that these dark side characteristics are negatively related to ratings of team performance and that subordinates are almost always aware of them (Harris & Hogan, 1992). Nonetheless, they are hard to detect using interviews, assessment centers, or inventories of normal personality because they coexist with high levels of self-esteem and good social skills (Harris & Hogan, 1992). Because managers with dark side tendencies often do well in procedures that evaluate the leadership potential of strangers, their counterproductive tendencies will be apparent only after they have been on the job for some time.

Can dark side characteristics be changed? The best evidence here comes from an evaluation of the Individual Coaching for Effectiveness program at Personnel Decisions, Inc.—an intensive intervention that may last for a year. The program is designed for managers whose careers are in jeopardy. Reviewing the results for 370 candidates over a five-year period, Peterson (1993) and Peterson and Hicks (1993) reported that the majority of managers were able to change a number of targeted behaviors, and these behavioral changes were still in place six months after the training had ended. Many of these candidates had previously attended three- to five-day standardized leadership training programs, but these programs produced little behavioral change (Peterson, personal communication, November 18, 1993). These findings imply that many managers who are performing poorly can make the changes necessary to maintain their careers, but they need more intensive training than that found in most leadership development programs.

How Do Leaders Build Teams?

The key to a leader's effectiveness is his or her ability to build a team. Hallam and Campbell (1992) identified eight problems for leadership that affect team performance; six problems are task related and two involve team maintenance. On the task side, successful leaders communicate a clear mission or sense of purpose, identify available resources and talent, develop the talent, plan and organize, coordinate work activities, and acquire needed resources. On the maintenance side, they minimize and resolve conflicts among group members and they ensure that team members understand the team's goals, constraints, resources, and problems. These team-building tasks obviously overlap with the taxonomy of leader behaviors developed by Yukl et al. (1990).

We believe that a leader's personality has predictable effects on team performance. For example, leaders with higher surgency scores communicate more with their teams, which increases the possibility that the team understands its goal and the performance standards required to achieve it. Moreover, these leaders are better able to build alliances with people outside of the team, which allows them to secure necessary equipment and resources. Conscientiousness is related to being perceived as trustworthy, planful, and organized. Agreeableness is related to communication, trust, and morale. Emotional stability is associated with seeming steady under pressure, able to resolve conflicts, and to handle negative feedback, all of which promote team effectiveness. Thus, four of the five big-five personality dimensions are related to Hallam and Campbell's (1992) team building tasks and to Yukl's (1989) taxonomy of leader behaviors.

The discussion so far concerns the relationship between personality and leadership in general. But practitioners also know that leadership is relative to the group in question. Although there are few data available on this point, we suspect that two considerations are important. The first is the group's developmental history; the second concerns the major tasks the group performs.

One can speculate that the qualities needed to form a group may be different from those required to maintain it. Persons leading organizations in the start-up phase may be more effective if they have a credible and strategic vision of what the group can do. Such people will also need to withstand the discouragement associated with the inevitable failures in the start-up phase. On the other hand, successful leaders of established organizations will probably need to be more orderly, more ceremonial, more concerned about details, and less visionary. Thus, leaders with higher surgency, intellect, and emotional stability scores may be more successful in organizations developing new products or services, whereas leaders with higher conscientiousness scores may be more effective in organizations having established products, services, and procedures.

Leadership is also relative to the task of the group, but how should that relationship be conceptualized? Holland's (1985) theory of occupational types provides a clue. Holland proposed that people's interests, talents, abilities, values, and motives cluster in six broad types. Realistic types (e.g., engineers) are procedural, action oriented, and concrete. Investigative types (e.g., scientists) are abstract, original, and independent. Artistic types (e.g., painters, writers, philosophers) are unconventional, nonconforming, and imaginative. Social types (e.g., teachers, clergy, personnel managers) are friendly, idealistic, and altruistic. Enterprising types (e.g., lawyers, politicians) are outgoing, assertive, and manipulative. Finally, conventional types (e.g., accountants, computer programmers) are conforming, practical, and conservative. Schneider (1987) proposed that the culture of an organization depends on the Holland types of the senior management, that people will join organizations whose activities and values are consistent with their own preferences, and that they leave organizations whose culture is inconsistent with their preferences.

Moving to the level of the work group, R. Hogan and his associates (Driskell, Hogan, & Salas, 1987; R. Hogan, Raza, & Driskell, 1988) showed that teams can be classified in terms of their primary tasks using the Holland model. Realistic and conventional groups (e.g., athletic teams, police departments) respond to task-oriented and authoritative leadership and resent participatory management, which they see as weak. Enterprising and social groups (e.g., management teams, school faculties) respond to process, interaction, and participation and resent task-oriented leadership, which they see as authoritarian. In our view, the familiar Fleishman and Harris (1962) leadership typology of initiating structure versus consideration only applies to realistic, conventional, enterprising, and social groups; we know little about the leadership style that is best suited for artistic and investigative groups (e.g., theater companies, research teams)—meaning, we know little about the process of managing creativity.

What About Leadership in Workforce 2000?

Historically, the typical American worker has been a White man with a high school education employed in a manufacturing (i.e., realistic and conventional) job. Our models of leadership largely focus on how to lead that kind of person in those kinds of jobs in those kinds of organizations. All of the projections suggest, however, that the economy will shift from manufacturing to service (i.e., more social and artistic) jobs and that the workforce will become older, less well trained, more diverse, and more female (Hamilton, 1988; Johnston & Packer, 1987; Offermann & Gowing, 1990). For example,

"Only 15 percent of the new entrants to the labor force over the next 13 years will be native white males, compared to 47 percent in that category today" (Johnston & Packer, 1987, p. xiii). The labor market for skilled workers will tighten, and there will be increased competition for talented personnel: "The fastest-growing jobs will be in professional, technical, and sales fields requiring the highest education and skill levels" (Johnston & Packer, 1987, p. xxi). As organizations shrink, fewer middle managers will be needed, and the responsibilities of first-line managers will expand.

We see these trends as having five implications for leaders, organizations, and psychologists. First, because competition for talented employees will increase and because managerial responsibilities will expand, the overall quality of management will need to improve. Corporate failures are increasing—there were 57,000 failures in 1986 (Ropp, 1987)—and this may reflect the combination of incompetent management and changes in labor and market forces. If current estimates of the base rates of bad management are realistic, then organizations in which 60% of the managers are incompetent will likely be at a serious competitive disadvantage. Psychologists can help organizations by verifying estimates of the base rate of incompetent management, exploring the relationships between these estimates and organizational effectiveness, and by doing a better job informing organizations about our managerial selection, coaching, and promotion expertise.

Second, with an increased emphasis on productivity, we suspect that the performance of senior managers will be more closely scrutinized. Derailed managers are typically good at selling themselves upward in their organizations, but they are less successful when dealing with peers and subordinates; thus these groups have access to unique information. Consequently, if effectiveness becomes a criterion for managerial evaluation, then multiple perspective appraisals (e.g., those that include bosses', peers', and subordinates' ratings) may become more widespread. Psychologists have played a key role in the development and refinement of multirater assessment instruments, and they should play an equally important role in the adoption of these instruments in the future.

Third, management practices will have to change as we move toward a service economy and the workforce becomes more diverse—what is the best way to manage female and minority employees in social and artistic (service) organizations? Moreover, we will likely have the same percentages of women and minorities in management as are currently in the workforce. Are there significant gender or cultural differences in leadership style, and will these styles be more or less effective for building teams in tomorrow's organizations? These are questions that psychologists are uniquely qualified to answer.

Fourth, although psychologists know more about leadership than the public apparently recognizes or, indeed, than we are often willing to admit (cf. Meindl & Ehrlich, 1987), there is one aspect of leadership about which we know very little: how to manage creative talent. There is good reason to believe that successful organizations will increasingly rely on innovation and the development of new products and services—meaning, on the performance of their investigative and artistic teams. We understand something about the characteristics of individual creativity (Barron, 1965; Cronbach, 1984), but we know little about how to manage teams whose primary tasks are problem solving and the development of new knowledge, methods, and products (cf. J. D. Morrison, 1993). How to manage creativity is one of the most important problems of the future, and it is a problem to whose solution psychology can make an important contribution.

Fifth, given that personality measures can predict leadership effectiveness, how can psychologists best use this information? We recommend selecting personality predictors on the basis of job analysis results because measures chosen in this way have significantly higher correlations with performance (Tett, Jackson, & Rothstein 1991). Next, we recommend matching measures and criteria in terms of their specificity (Pulakos, Borman, & Hough, 1988). Although the big-five dimensions are useful for summarizing results, they are the wrong band width for many prediction problems; narrower measures of personality often yield higher validity coefficients (Cronbach, 1984; Hough, 1992; Shannon & Weaver, 1949). We also recommend screening candidates for dark side tendencies using measures of the *Diagnostic and Statistical Manual of Mental Disorders*, 3rd edition (*DSM-III*, Axis 2; American Psychiatric Association, 1980) personality disorders or using structured interviews with their direct reports.

Finally, because bad managers often have exaggerated views of their talents, psychologists may want to use observers' ratings as predictors of leadership potential. Our first two recommendations often lead to correlations in the .20 to .40 range; observers' ratings lead to correlations in the .30 to .60 range (Curphy & Osten, 1993; Nilsen, 1992). Although these results are promising, considerably more research is needed here.

Finally, as a profession we need to recognize that we can improve the lives of the incumbents in many organizations (as well as productivity and organizational climate) by improving leadership selection. Nevertheless, organizations will not ask for our help if we continue to argue that there is no such thing as leadership; that leadership has little impact on group, team, and organizational effectiveness; or that personality and leadership are unrelated. Practitioners do not believe these behaviorist-inspired arguments, and we must get beyond them if we want to make an impact on important selection decisions.

References

Albright, L., Kenny, D. A., & Malloy, T. E. (1988). Consensus in personality judgments at zero-acquaintance. *Journal of Personality and Social Psychology, 55*, 387–395.

American Psychiatric Association. (1980). *Diagnostic and statistical manual of mental disorders* (3rd ed.), Washington, DC: Author.

Atwater, L. E., & Yammarino, F. J. (1992). Does self–other agreement on leadership perceptions moderate the validity of leadership and performance predictions? *Personnel Psychology, 45*, 141–164.

Avolio, B. J., Waldman, D. A., & Einstein, W. O. (1988). Transformational leadership in a management game simulation. *Group and Organizational Studies, 13*, 59–80.

Barron, F. (1965). The psychology of creativity. In *New directions in psychology II* (pp. 1–134). New York: Holt, Rinehart & Winston.

Bass, B. M. (1985). *Leadership and performance beyond expectations*. New York: Free Press.

Bass, B. M. (1990). *Bass and Stogdill's handbook of leadership* (3rd ed.). New York: Free Press.

Bass, B. M., Avolio, B. J., & Goodheim, L. (1987). Biography and the assessment of transformational leadership at the world class level. *Journal of Management, 13,* 7–20.

Bass, B. M., & Yammarino, F. J. (1991). Congruence of self and others' leadership ratings of naval officers for understanding successful performance. *Applied Psychology: An International Review, 40,* 437–454.

Bennis, W. G., & Nanus, B. (1985). *Leaders: The strategies for taking charge*. New York: Harper & Row.

Bentz, V. J. (1985, August). *A view from the top: A thirty year perspective of research devoted to discovery, description, and prediction of executive behavior*. Paper presented at the 93rd Annual Convention of the American Psychological Association. Los Angeles.

Bentz, V. J. (1987, August). *Contextual richness as a criterion consideration in personality research with executives*. Paper presented at the 95th Annual Convention of the American Psychological Association, New York.

Bentz, V. J. (1990). Contextual issues in predicting high-level leadership performance. Contextual richness as a criterion consideration in personality research with executives. In K. E. Clark & M. B. Clark (Eds.). *Measures of leadership* (pp. 131–143). West Orange, NJ: Leadership Library of America.

Bernardin, H. J., & Klatt, L. A. (1985). Managerial appraisal systems: Has practice caught up to the state of the art? *Personnel Administrator, 30,* 79–86.

Borgatta, E. F. (1964). The structure of personality characteristics. *Behavioral Science, 12,* 8–17.

Borman, W. C., & Brush, D. H. (1993). More progress toward a taxonomy of managerial performance requirements. *Human Performance, 6,* 1–21.

Bray, D. W. (1982). The assessment center and the study of lives. *American Psychologist, 37,* 180–189.

Bray, D. W., Campbell, R. J., & Grant, D. L. (1974). *Formative years in business: A long-term AT&T study of managerial lives*. New York: Wiley-Interscience.

Bray, D. W., & Howard, A. (1983). The AT&T longitudinal studies of managers. In K. W. Schaie (Ed.), *Longitudinal studies of adult psychological development* (pp. 112–146). New York: Guilford.

Briggs, S. R., Cheek, J. M., & Buss, A. H. (1980). An analysis of the self-monitoring scale. *Journal of Personality and Social Psychology, 38,* 679–686.

Campbell, D. P. (1991). *Manual for the Campbell Leadership Index*. Minneapolis, MN: National Computer Systems.

Campbell, J. P. (1977). The cutting edge of leadership: An overview. In J. G. Hunt & L. L. Larson (Eds.), *Leadership: The cutting edge* (pp. 221–246). Carbondale: Southern Illinois University Press.

Chidester, T. R., Helmreich, R. L., Gregorich, S. E., & Geis, C. E. (1991). Pilot personality and crew coordination. *International Journal of Aviation Psychology, 1,* 25–44.

Conger, J. A., & Kanungo, R. N. (1988). *Charismatic leadership: The elusive factor in organizational effectiveness*. San Francisco: Jossey-Bass.

Cooper, G. E., White, M. D., & Lauber, J. K. (Eds.). (1979). *Resource management on the flight deck* (NASA Conference Publication No. 2120; NTIS No. N80–22083). Moffett Field, CA: NASA—Ames Research Center.

Cronbach, L. J. (1984). *Essentials of psychological testing* (4th ed.). San Francisco: Harper & Row.

Curphy, G. J. (1991). *An empirical investigation of Bass' (1985) theory of transformational and transactional leadership*. Unpublished doctoral dissertation, University of Minnesota, Minneapolis.

Curphy, G. J. (1993). An empirical investigation of the effects of transformational and transactional leadership on organizational climate, attrition, and performance. In K. E. Clark, M. B. Clark, & D. P. Campbell (Eds.), *Impact of leadership* (pp. 177–188). Greensboro, NC: Center for Creative Leadership.

Curphy, G. J., & Osten, K. D. (1993). *Technical manual for the Leadership Development Survey* (Tech. Rep. No. 93–14). Colorado Springs, CO: U.S. Air Force Academy.

David, B. L. Skube, C. J., Hellervik, L. W., Gebelein, S. H., & Sheard, J. L. (1992). *Successful manager's handbook: Development suggestions for today's managers*. Minneapolis, MN: Personnel Decisions.

Dawkins, R. (1976). *The selfish gene*. New York: Oxford University Press.

DeVries, D. L. (1992). Executive selection: Advances but no progress. *Issues & Observations, 12,* 1–5.

Digman, J. M. (1988). *Classical theories of trait organization and the Big Five factors of personality*. Paper presented at the 96th Annual Convention of the American Psychological Association. Atlanta, GA.

Digman, J. M. (1990). Personality structure: Emergence of the five-factor model. In *Annual review of psychology* (Vol. 41, pp. 417–440). Palo Alto, CA: Annual Reviews.

Dixon, N. F. (1976). *On the psychology of military incompetence*. London: Futura.

Driskell, J. E., Hogan, R., & Salas, E. (1987). Personality and group performance. In C. Hendrick (Ed.), *Personality and social psychology review* (pp. 91–112). Beverly Hills, CA: Sage.

Eden, D., & Leviathan, U. (1975). Implicit leadership theory as a determinant of the factor structure underlying supervisory behavior scales. *Journal of Applied Psychology, 60,* 736–741.

Eibl-Eibesfeld, I. (1989). *Human ethnology*. Chicago: Aldine.

Ellis, R. J. (1988). Self-monitoring and leadership emergence in groups. *Personality and Social Psychology Bulletin, 14,* 681–693.

Eysenck, H. J. (1970). *The structure of human personality* (3rd ed.). London: Methuen.

Farh, J. L., & Dobbins, G. H. (1989). Effects of self-esteem on leniency bias in self-reports of performance: A structural equation model. *Personnel Psychology, 42,* 835–850.

Fiske, D. W. (1949). Consistency of the factorial structures of personality ratings from different sources. *Journal of Abnormal and Social Psychology, 44,* 329–344.

Fleishman, E. A., & Harris, E. F. (1962). Patterns of leadership behavior related to employee grievances and turnover. *Personnel Psychology, 15,* 43–56.

Foushee, H. C., & Helmreich, R. L. (1988). Group interaction and flight crew performance. In E. L. Weiner

& D. C. Nagel (Eds.), *Human factors in aviation* (pp. 189–227). San Diego, CA: Academic Press.

Goldberg, L. R. (1993). The structure of phenotypic personality traits. *American Psychologist, 48*, 26–34.

Gough, H. G. (1984). A managerial potential scale for the California Psychological Inventory. *Journal of Applied Psychology, 69*, 233–240.

Gough, H. G. (1987). *California Psychological Inventory administrator's guide.* Palo Alto, CA: Consulting Psychologists Press.

Gough, H. G. (1990). Testing for leadership with the California Psychological Inventory. In K. E. Clark & M. B. Clark (Eds.), *Measures of leadership* (pp. 355–379). West Orange, NJ: Leadership Library of America.

Gough, H. G., & Heilbrun, A. B., Jr. (1983). *The Adjective Checklist manual: 1983 edition.* Palo Alto, CA: Consulting Psychologists Press.

Guilford, J. P. (1975). Factors and factors of personality. *Psychological Bulletin, 82*, 802–814.

Hallam, G. L., & Campbell, D. P. (1992, May). *Selecting team members? Start with a theory of team effectiveness.* Paper presented at the 7th Annual Meeting of the Society of Industrial and Organizational Psychology, Montreal, Quebec, Canada.

Hamilton, M. H. (1988, July 10). Employing new tools to recruit workers. *Washington Post,* pp. H1, H3.

Harris, G., & Hogan, J. (1992, April). *Perceptions and personality correlates of managerial effectiveness.* Paper presented at the 13th Annual Psychology in the Department of Defense Symposium. Colorado Springs, CO.

Harris, M. M., & Schaubroeck, J. (1988). A meta-analysis of self-supervisor, self-peer, and peer-supervisor ratings. *Personnel Psychology, 41*, 43–62.

Hazucha, J. F. (1991). *Success, jeopardy, and performance. Contrasting managerial outcomes and their predictors.* Unpublished doctoral dissertation, University of Minnesota, Minneapolis.

Hegarty, W. H. (1974). Using subordinate ratings to elicit behavioral changes in supervisors. *Journal of Applied Psychology, 59*, 764–766.

Hellervik, L. W., Hazucha, J. F., & Schneider, R. J. (1992). Behavior change: Models, methods, and a review of the evidence. In M. D. Dunnette & L. M. Hough (Eds.), *Handbook of industrial and organizational psychology* (2nd ed., Vol. 3). Palo Alto, CA: Consulting Psychologists Press.

Hogan, J. (1978). Personological dynamics of leadership. *Journal of Research in Personality, 12*, 390–395.

Hogan, R., & Hogan, J. (1992). *Hogan Personality Inventory manual.* Tulsa, OK: Hogan Assessment Systems.

Hogan, R., Raskin, R., & Fazzini, D. (1990). The dark side of charisma. In K. E. Clark & M. B. Clark (Eds.), *Measures of leadership* (pp. 343–354). West Orange, NJ: Leadership Library of America.

Hogan, R., Raza, S., & Driskell, J. E. (1988). Personality, team performance, and organizational context. In P. Whitney & R. B. Ochsman (Eds.), *Psychology and productivity* (pp. 93–103). New York: Plenum.

Holland, J. L. (1985). *Making vocational choices: A theory of careers.* Englewood Cliffs, NJ: Prentice-Hall.

Hollander, E. P., & Julian, J. W. (1969). Contemporary trends in the analysis of leadership processes. *Psychological Bulletin, 71*, 387–91.

Hough, L. M. (1992). The "Big Five" personality variables–construct confusion: Description versus prediction. *Human Performance, 5*, 139–155.

House, R. J. (1977). A 1976 theory of charismatic leadership. In J. G. Hunt & L. L. Larson (Eds.), *Leadership: The cutting edge* (pp. 189–207). Carbondale: Southern Illinois University Press.

House, R. J., Spangler, W. D., & Woycke, J. (1991). Personality and charisma in the U.S. presidency: A psychological theory of leadership effectiveness. *Administrative Science Quarterly, 36*, 364–396.

Howard, A., & Bray, D. W. (1990). Predictions of managerial success over long periods of time: Lessons for the Management Progress Study. In K. E. Clark & M. B. Clark (Eds.), *Measures of leadership* (pp. 113–130). West Orange, NJ: Leadership Library of America.

Howell, J. M., & Frost, P. (1988). A laboratory study of charismatic leadership. *Organizational Behavior and Human Decision Processes, 43*, 243–269.

Hughes, R. L., Ginnett, R. A., & Curphy, G. J. (1993). *Leadership: Enhancing the lessons of experience.* Homewood, IL: Irwin.

Johnston, W. B., & Packer, A. H. (1987). *Workforce 2000.* Indianapolis, IN: Hudson Institute.

Kanter, R. M. (1983). *The change masters.* New York: Simon & Schuster.

Kaplan, R. E., Drath, W. H., & Kofodimos, J. R. (1991). *Beyond ambition: How driven managers can lead better and live better.* San Francisco: Jossey-Bass.

Kenny, D. A., & Zaccaro, S. J. (1983). An estimate of variance due to traits in leadership. *Journal of Applied Psychology, 68*, 678–685.

Lombardo, M. M., Ruderman, M. N., & McCauley, C. D. (1988). Explanations of success and derailment in upper-level management positions. *Journal of Business and Psychology, 2*, 199–216.

Lord, R. G., De Vader, C. L., & Allinger, G. M. (1986). A meta-analysis of the relationship between personality traits and leadership perceptions: An application of validity generalization procedures. *Journal of Applied Psychology, 71*, 402–410.

Lord, R. G., Foti, R. J., & De Vader, C. L. (1984). A test of leadership categorization theory: Internal structure, information processing, and leadership perceptions. *Organizational Behavior and Human Performance, 34*, 343–378.

Mann, R. D. (1959) A review of the relationships between personality and performance in small groups. *Psychological Bulletin, 56*, 241–270.

McCall, M. W., & Lombardo, M. M. (1983). Off the track: *Why and how successful executives get derailed* (Tech. Rep. No. 21). Greensboro, NC: Center for Creative Leadership.

McClelland, D. C. (1975). *Power: The inner experience.* New York: Irvington.

McClelland, D. C., & Burnham, D. (1976). Power is the great motivator. *Harvard Business Review, 25*, 159–166.

McCrae, R. R., & Costa, P. T., Jr. (1987). Validation of the five-factor model of personality across instruments and observers. *Journal of Personality and Social Psychology, 52*, 81–90.

McEvoy, G. M., & Beatty, R. W. (1989). Assessment centers and subordinate appraisals of managers: A seven-year examination of predictive validity. *Personnel Psychology, 42*, 37–52.

Meindl, J. R., & Ehrlich, S. B. (1987). The romance of leadership and the evaluation of organizational performance. *Academy of Management Journal, 30*, 91–109.

Millikin-Davies, M. (1992). *An exploration of flawed first-line supervision.* Unpublished doctoral dissertation. University of Tulsa, Tulsa, OK.

Mintzberg, H. (1982). If you're not serving Bill or Barbara, then you're not serving leadership. In J. G. Hunt, U. Sekaran, & C. A. Schriesheim (Eds.), *Leadership beyond establishment views* (pp. 239–259). Carbondale: Southern Illinois University Press.

Morrison, A. M. (1992). *The new leaders: Guidelines on leadership diversity in America.* San Francisco: Jossey-Bass.

Morrison, J. D. (1993). *Group composition and creative performance.* Unpublished doctoral dissertation, University of Tulsa, OK.

Murphy, K. R., & Cleveland, J. N. (1991). *Performance appraisal.* Boston: Allyn & Bacon.

Nilsen, D. (1992). Using observers' judgments for selection. In R. T. Hogan (Chair). *The future of leadership selection.* Symposium conducted at the 13th Biennial Psychology in the DoD Conference, U. S. Air Force Academy, Colorado Springs, CO.

Nilsen, D., & Campbell, D. P. (1993). Self-observer rating discrepancies: Once an overrater, always an overrater? *Human Resource Management, 32,* 265–281.

Norman, W. T. (1963). Toward an adequate taxonomy of personality attributes: Replicated factor structures in peer nomination personality ratings. *Journal of Abnormal and Social Psychology, 66,* 574–583.

Offermann, L. R., & Gowing, M. K. (1990). Organizations of the future. *American Psychologist, 45,* 95–108.

Passini, F. T., & Norman, W. T. (1966). A universal conception of personality structure? *Journal of Personality and Social Psychology, 1,* 44–49.

Peabody, D., & Goldberg, L. R. (1989). Some determinants of factor structures from personality-trait descriptors. *Journal of Personality and Social Psychology, 57,* 552–567.

Personnel Decisions, Inc. (1991). *The PROFILOR.* Minneapolis, MN: Author.

Peters, T. J., & Waterman, R. H. (1982). *In search of excellence.* New York: Harper & Row.

Peterson, D. B. (1993). Measuring change: A psychometric approach to evaluating individual training outcomes. In V. Arnold (Chair), *Innovations in training evaluation: New measures, new designs.* Symposium conducted at the Eighth Annual Conference of the Society for Industrial and Organizational Psychology, San Francisco.

Peterson, D. B., & Hicks, M. D. (1993, May). *How to get people to change.* Workshop presented at the Eighth Annual Conference of the Society for Industrial and Organizational Psychology, San Francisco.

Pulakos, E. D., Borman, W. C., & Hough, L. M. (1988). Test validation for scientific understanding: Two demonstrations of an approach for studying predictor-criterion linkages. *Personnel Psychology, 41,* 703–716.

Ross, S. M., & Offermann, L. R. (1991, April). *Transformational leaders: Measurement of personality attributes and work group performance.* Paper presented at the Sixth Annual Conference of the Society for Industrial and Organizational Psychology, St. Louis, MO.

Ropp, K. (1987, February). Restructuring: Survival of the fittest. *Personnel Administrator,* pp. 45–47.

Rueb, J. D., & Foti, R. J. (1990, April). *Traits, self-monitoring, and leadership emergence.* Paper presented at the Fifth Annual Conference of the Society for Industrial and Organizational Psychology, Miami, FL.

Rush, M. C., Thomas, J. C., & Lord, R. G. (1977). Implicit leadership theory: A potential threat to the internal validity of leader behavior questionnaires. *Organizational Behavior and Human Performance, 20,* 93–110.

Schneider, B. (1987). The people make the place. *Personnel Psychology, 40,* 437–453.

Shannon, C., & Weaver, W. (1949). *The mathematical theory of communication.* Urbana: University of Illinois Press.

Shipper, F., & Wilson, C. L. (1991, July). *The impact of managerial behaviors on group performance, stress, and commitment.* Paper presented at the Impact of Leadership Conference, Center for Creative Leadership, Colorado Springs, CO.

Smith, J. E., Carson, K. P., & Alexander, R. A. (1984). Leadership: It can make a difference. *Academy of Management Journal, 27,* 765–776.

Sorcher, M. (1985). *Predicting executive success: What it takes to make it in senior management.* New York: Wiley.

Snyder, M. (1974). The self-monitoring of expressive behavior. *Journal of Personality and Social Psychology, 30,* 526–537.

Stogdill, R. M. (1948). Personal factors associated with leadership: A survey of the literature. *Journal of Personality, 25,* 35–71.

Stogdill, R. M. (1974). *Handbook of leadership.* New York: Free Press.

Sweetland, J. (1978). *Work in America Institute studies in productivity: Highlights of the literature: Managerial productivity.* Scarsdale, NY: Work in America Institute.

Tellegen, A. (1982). *Brief manual for the Multidimensional Personality Questionnaire* (mimeograph). (Available from A. Tellegen, Department of Psychology, University of Minnesota, Minneapolis, MN 55455)

Tellegen, A. (1985). Structures of mood and personality and their relevance to assessing anxiety, with an emphasis on self-report. In A. H. Truman & J. D. Maser (Eds.), *Anxiety and anxiety disorders* (pp. 681–706). New York: Erlbaum.

Tett, R. P., Jackson, D. N., & Rothstein, M. (1991). Personality measures as predictors of job performance: A meta-analytic review. *Personnel Psychology, 44,* 703–742.

Tupes, E. C., & Christal, R. E. (1961). *Recurrent personality factors based on trait ratings* (ASD-TR-61-96). Lackland Air Force Base, TX: Aeronautical Systems Division, Personnel Laboratory.

Van Velsor, E., Taylor, S., & Leslie, J. B. (1992, August). *Self/rater agreement, self-awareness and leadership effectiveness.* Paper presented at the 100th Annual Convention of the American Psychological Association, Washington, DC.

Weiss, H. M., & Adler, S. (1981). Cognitive complexity and the structure of implicit leadership theories. *Journal of Applied Psychology, 66,* 69–78.

Yukl, G. A. (1989). *Leadership in organizations* (2nd ed.). Englewood Cliffs, NJ: Prentice-Hall.

Yukl, G. A., Wall, S., & Lepsinger, R. (1990). Preliminary report on the validation of the management practices survey. In K. E. Clark & M. B. Clark (Eds.), *Measures of leadership* (pp. 223–238). West Orange, NJ: Leadership Library of America.

Zaccaro, S. J., Foti, R. J., & Kenny, D. A. (1991). Self-monitoring and trait-based variance in leadership: An investigation of leader flexibility across multiple group situations. *Journal of Applied Psychology, 76,* 308–315.

Article Review Form at end of book.

What are the three sets of skills for leading innovation-stimulating environments? What are the characteristics of a good vision?

Before Looking for the Gas Pedal

A call for entrepreneurial leadership in American schools

Kyle L. Peck, Ph.D.
The Pennsylvania State University
University Park, Pennsylvania 16802

Most of today's schools are "run" by "administrators" who "manage" existing educational systems. What is needed today is not management, but leadership. And, the leadership that's needed is not the traditional leader/follower relationship, but a newer, more democratic type in which individuals are motivated and empowered. Rather than promoting their own ideas, successful leaders of educational reform efforts will help teams of educators create powerful, shared visions and will provide the encouragement and support necessary to streamline the progress. A democratic "player/coach," the entrepreneurial leader will bring out the best in each member of the team, helping them see the need for dramatic change, design exciting alternatives to traditional practices, and identify and remove significant obstacles.

A popular metaphor describes today's schools as vehicles for which "everyone has a brake pedal, but nobody has a gas pedal." But the gas pedal is not the only feature missing, nor should it be the first missing part to be restored. America's schools need a vital form of leadership that gives each school its own gas pedal—but only after first giving it a steering mechanism, and perhaps even wings.

As a symptom of how deeply rooted certain outdated notions are in American education, consider the words we use to describe the jobs and responsibilities held by our professionals. "Teacher" implies a person who has information and labors to move that information into the heads of students. Although teaching is certainly one way to establish a knowledge base, there is considerable and increasing sentiment that the role played by the professional in the classroom must change to include the identification, coordination, and management of educational experiences in which student activity, rather than teacher activity, is emphasized. This new role will involve the creation and maintenance of important personal relationships with students and parents, the development of creativity, research and problem-solving skill, and verbal, numerical, and technological literacy. Teaching, the delivery of information to groups of students, will become a much less prominent responsibility. The word "classroom" also implies a single function we may find occupying considerably less time in the near future, as educators develop and implement logical responses to the problem of educating tomorrow's citizens.

The teacher's boss in an "administrator," a term that implies running or "administering" an effective operation or process.

"Before Looking for the Gas Pedal: A Call for Entrepreneurial Leadership in American Schools" by Kyle L. Peck. Copyright 1991 Project Innovation. Reprinted with permission.

46 Educational Leadership

Likewise, "management" and "supervision" are verbs that make sense only when the process is working and all are happy with the status quo. This is not the case with education today. We need leadership, not administration or management. The "principal," a term that implies primary importance, may prove to be an appropriate term in many schools, but the jury is still out.

According to statistics cited by Keith Geiger, President of the NEA, there have been over 20,000 reports written by credible authors calling for significant reform since the publication of "A Nation at Risk" in 1983. There seems to be agreement that nothing short of a paradigm shift—dramatic changes in the very nature of what we do in the name of education—will be sufficient. Any process or technology has its limits. "Tinkering" with today's system may bring small gains in effectiveness, but efforts aimed at improving the present system, no matter how diligent the small-step reformers may be, can only increase the speed at which we "hit the wall" (O. Botlik, personal communication, September 12, 1990). For example, as long as travel was constrained by contact with the ground, speeds were relatively low. By leaving the ground, a new range of speeds many times the original range became possible. It's time education left the ground. It's time education addressed the important question asked by John Naisbitt and Patricia Aburdene (1985, p. 120) in Reinventing the Corporation: "What would education look like if we were to invent it right now?"

An interesting debate concerns who will design the dramatically different educational systems called for by a dynamic future. Will it be the teachers and administrators who spent 15,000 hours as successful students, then spent another four to seven years in collegiate and graduate preparation before gaining several years of experience doing for others what had been done for them? Or, is it more logical to expect that "outsiders" with a less thorough grounding in today's methods will create radical, yet effective alternatives, despite minimal understanding of "what kids and learning are about?" Current opinion seems to indicate that change must be driven by educators, but with significant input from outsiders. The perspectives that both groups bring to the drawing board will be critical during the "reinvention" of education.

Instead of (or perhaps, during the early stages, in addition to) "management" or "administration," what is needed is entrepreneurial educational leadership (no acronyms or logos, please). Kanter's (1983) description of entrepreneurs and their organizations sounds like just what education needs:

> Entrepreneurs—and entrepreneurial organizations—always operate at the edge of their competence, focusing more of their resources and attention on what they do not yet know (e.g., investment in R & D) than on controlling what they already know. They measure themselves not by the standards of the past (how far they have come), but by visions of the future (how far they have yet to go). And they do not allow the past to serve as a restraint on the future, the mere fact that something has not worked in the past does not mean that it cannot be made to work in the future. And the mere fact that something has worked in the past does not mean that it should remain. (p. 27–28)

Many of the people in power in today's educational organizations were appointed to administer, not chosen to lead (Boles Davenport 1975). They were not selected based on a rich set of ideas, nor based on their abilities to inspire creative thinking, to help groups define and implement a shared vision, or to identify and eliminate obstacles to innovation. Yet that is precisely what is needed. According to H. Ross Perot, while inventories can be managed, people must be led.

In education, "leadership" is another term that may be approaching the end of its useful life. While leadership has been subdivided into many styles and types including "democratic," it implies the presence of "followers." Rather than an image of a single leader providing direction to a body of followers, better images might look more like what Smyth (1986, p. 7) called "a form of leadership that stimulates dialog and mutual learning." This type of leader serves as a catalyst, causing important processes to happen, rather than as the primary source of innovation and direction. According to Taylor and Rosenbach (1989), the leader's real challenge is to gain commitment to achieve common goals. An effective entrepreneurial leader will strive to create "a team of leaders," encompassing all of the team's members. That is, in tomorrow's entrepreneurial educational organizations, all team members will be providing both innovation and support to promote a shared vision developed and "owned" by the team.

How does one gain an unwavering commitment to achieve common goals—a commitment so strong that it will endure the inevitable snags and pitfalls? In success stories from industry and education alike, the answer seems to be "vision," a word found in nearly every contemporary definition of leadership (Taylor & Rosenbach, 1989). Successful teams have a powerful, shared vision. "Goals" are not enough. A vision is an image of the ideal state that team members carry around in their heads as a constant reminder of the prize the struggle will ultimately bring. Pursuit of this vision becomes a passion, not a pastime.

What are the characteristics of a good vision, and how can educational leaders help their teams develop this critical component for progress? First, the vision must describe a "transcendent purpose" for the organization that "infuses their work with meaning, meaning beyond just making a living" (Taylor & Rosenbach, 1989, p. 10). "Improving test scores" does not qualify, nor does "a computer in every classroom." Second, a vision must be "so clear that every person in the organization can express it, from the CEO to the janitor" (Sashkin, 1989). And third, as the word "vision" implies, it must be rich in imagery, composed of pictures of what the desired end product will be. Joiner (1987) summarizes the characteristics of a good vision particularly well:

> This vision is no more than a mental picture of where the organization is headed and what it can become. It is a picture that taps key human emotions and wraps the dreams of individuals into a goal that they could never achieve on their own. It is an ideal and worthwhile dream for employees to pursue as part of a social organization. It is a clear picture of an exciting and possible future that is attainable only through participation in cooperative action. (p. 166)

I believe it is safe to say that few schools have such a powerful vision. Having a vision does not make life easy (Sheive & Schoenheit, 1987). A compelling picture of a clearly superior alternative breeds dissatisfaction with traditional practices. The more compelling the vision, the less willing employees are to tolerate obstacles. They want to see progress! These people no longer look for "management," nor do they need to be "led" in the conventional sense. Their leader's role is more "catalyst" than "administrator." When a catalyst is added to a mixture, things happen!

What process is recommended for entrepreneurial educational leaders? In *The Leadership Challenge*, Kouzes and Posner (1987) found that successful leaders:

1. Challenge the existing process
2. Inspire a shared vision
3. Enable others to act
4. Model the way
5. Encourage the heart.

Rather than promoting their own ideas, these successful leaders helped their teams establish powerful, shared visions and provided the encouragement and support necessary to enable progress. A democratic "player/coach," the entrepreneurial leader brings out the best in each member of the team, melding the group into a body more powerful than the sum of its parts and eventually creating a team so strong and cooperative that tasks once the domain of the leader are shared as leadership is dispersed throughout the group. The leader generally begins as the most eloquent "storyteller" (Taylor & Rosenbach, 1989), best able to captivate outsiders with the team's vision. Ultimately, however, the successful leader makes a single point of leadership unnecessary.

How will the process begin? Who will the initial leader be? Will it be the principal? Perhaps. Principals often are in their positions because of exemplary performance in the classroom, driven by a sincere desire to do their best for students. That sincere desire is critical, but not sufficient. Kanter (1983, pp. 35–36) proposes three sets of skills required to lead in innovation-stimulating environments: 1) power skills—persuading others to invest information, support, and resources; 2) the ability to manage the problems associated with the greater use of teams and employee participation; and 3) knowledge of how change is designed and constructed. Additional attributes generally listed for successful innovative leaders include integrity, confidence, passion, strong belief in people, pursuit of excellence, and a bias for action (Joiner, 1987). Each of these attributes exist to varying degrees, in all of us. Some attributes will need to be developed, not just in the leader, but in all team members.

Perhaps the most important attribute of tomorrow's leaders is rarely listed. Tomorrow's leaders will not necessarily be the most visible members of the team. Because they will be so convinced of the merit of the reforms they seek and correspondingly reinforced by progress toward their vision, they will not need the glory and status historically awarded to successful leaders. They will, instead, divert attention to it's appropriate target—the vision itself. If outsiders insist on calling attention to the people who created, nurtured, implemented, nursed, revised, and evaluated the vision, this attention will be appropriately focussed on the team, since the vision was grander than what any subset of the team could have brought to being. If examples in industry serve as models for education, once the vision approaches completion entrepreneurial team members will turn it over to managers and administrators, moving on to a new challenge or to replicate their vision in a more demanding environment, for vision and the pursuit of it are addictive and the need for passionate educational leaders is great.

As Campbell (1989, p. x) puts it:

Leadership is where the action is. It is bright orange, there's nothing gray about it (except of course the early interminable mindless ploughing of the furrows). To be in charge means to be alive, to unleash your own personal potential, to be able to watch your ideas blossom, to escape Thoreau's life of "quiet desperation." To lead is to be.

But leadership need not be the domain of one individual per school. In fact, it cannot be. Each professional in education has an obligation to lead. There's an old saying, "If you're not part of the solution, then you're part of the problem." Work with the other professionals in your school to "reinvent" education. Value the contributions of outsiders. And remember, don't do it for the inevitable excitement and attention, do it for the students.

References

Boles, H. W. & Davenport, J. A. (1975). *Introduction to Educational Leadership.* New York: Harper Row.

Campbell, D. (1989) In R. L. Taylor & W. E. Rosenbach (Eds.). *Leadership: Challenges for Today's Manager.* (pp. ix–x). New York: McGraw-Hill.

Joiner, C. W. (1987). *Leadership for Change.* Cambridge: Ballinger.

Kanter, R. M. (1983). *The Change Masters: Innovation and Entrepreneurship in the American Corporation.* New York: Simon & Schuster.

Kouzes, J. M. & Posner, B. Z. (1987). *The Leadership Challenge: How to Get Extraordinary Things Done in Organizations.* San Francisco: Jossey-Bass.

Naisbitt, J. & Aburdene, P. (1985). *Reinventing the Corporation.* New York: Warner Books.

Sashkin, M. (1989). The visionary leader. In R. L. Taylor & W. E. Rosenbach (Eds.), *Leadership: Challenges for Today's Manager.* (pp. 45–52). New York: McGraw-Hill.

Sheive, L. T. & Schoenheit, M. B. (1987). Vision and the work life of educational leaders. In L. T. Sheive & M. B. Schoenheit (Eds.), *Leadership: Examining the Elusive.* (pp. 93–104). Alexandria: Association for Supervision and Curriculum Development.

Smyth, W. J. (1986). *Leadership and Pedago.* Victoria: Deakin University Press.

Taylor, R. L., Rosenbach, W. E. (Eds.). (1989). *Leadership: Challenges for Today's Manager.* New York: McGraw-Hill.

Article Review Form at end of book.

WiseGuide Wrap-Up

- Leadership is a consensual process, a sharing of ideas and responsibilities toward a common vision and goal.

- Leadership differs from management in many significant applications, including intent, interaction, persistence, and effectiveness.

- Leadership style is strongly affected by one's deep-seated values and beliefs about how people learn.

- Important leadership qualities include honesty, competence, caring, vision, human relations skills, and knowledge of change.

- Visionary and entrepreneurial leaders inspire a shared vision, model the way, and encourage the heart.

R.E.A.L. Sites

This list provides a print preview of typical **Coursewise** R.E.A.L. sites. There are over 100 such sites at the **Courselinks**™ site. The danger in printing URLs is that web sites can change overnight. As we went to press, these sites were functional using the URLs provided. If you come across one that isn't, please let us know via email to: webmaster@coursewise.com. Use your Passport to access the most current list of R.E.A.L. sites at the **Courselinks**™ site.

Site name: Mistakes Educational Leaders Make
URL: http://eric.uoregon.edu/publications/digests/digest122.html
Why is it R.E.A.L.? Understanding the kinds of leadership behaviors that create problems for principals can guide new and continuing leaders. This ERIC Digest investigates three types of flawed leadership and summarizes six suggestions for improving leadership effectiveness.
Key topics: accountability, attributes, behaviors, collaboration, communication, cooperation, ethics, human relations, team, trust
Try this: After reviewing this web site, detail the common mistakes made by leaders and the actions they can take to avoid committing them.

Site name: American Association of School Administrators
URL: http://www.aasa.org/
Why is it R.E.A.L.? This web site, hosted by the largest school administrators' association in the nation, contains a variety of resources. Sections include online publications on major issues and topics of interest, legislative alerts, leadership news, job bulletins, etc. Links to membership information, state organizations, and other administrator web sites complete this well-organized and comprehensive site.
Key topics: communication, community, education, empowerment, goals, human relations, instructional leadership, leadership, management, politics, reform
Try this: Select "AASA Publications," the "School Administrator magazine." Review the articles in October 1998 addressing administrator evaluation. What are the criteria used in principal evaluation, and how is the process contributing to the professional development of each leader?

section 2

Ethical Dimensions of Leadership

Learning Objectives

- Identify the organizational traits that lead to increased employee job satisfaction. Describe how leaders develop these traits.

- Discuss how values, virtue, and character relate to effective leadership in today's organizations. Describe the elements and importance of each.

- Define intellectual capital and explain its association to the development of leadership.

- Compare and contrast authentic leadership and value-based leadership. Explain how each promotes effectiveness within an organization.

- Summarize the characteristics of change within an organization and discuss how change elements affect employees and leaders.

WiseGuide Intro

Ethics and *leadership:* These terms are not mutually exclusive. Any discussion of leadership must include an investigation into this important dynamic. Leadership ethics involves two aspects. One aspect we see as evidence of the success and outcome of a leader. This includes ethical "artifacts" from an administrator's daily role within and outside the organization. These involve developing a vision, making decisions, building teams, empowering, and collaborating, to name only a few. The second aspect of leadership ethics defines who the leader is, and it is from this source that the "artifacts" of leadership emerge.

Why do some organizations excel, while others struggle and fail? The authors in this section would attribute success to leadership ethics. Webster's dictionary provides one useful definition of ethics: "philosophy dealing with values relating to human conduct, with respect to the rightness and wrongness of certain actions and to the goodness and badness of the motives and ends of such actions."

Ethical leadership provides schools with vision, inspiration, value, and purpose. Employee job satisfaction increases and productivity improves in organizations led by ethical leaders. It becomes difficult to ignore this very powerful yet personal leadership factor. Business and educational literature is now filled with research on various dimensions of ethical leadership, including value-centered leadership, intellectual capital, and authentic leadership.

As E. Thomas Behr, one of the authors in this section, states, "Every day should serve as a living example of your values." This section provides insight into ethical leadership, its value in schools today, and its importance to educational change and reform efforts.

In Lieber's article, "Why Employees Love These Companies (100 Best Companies to Work For in America)," three important organizational traits are identified. Ethical dimensions figure prominently in Lieber's analysis of best-loved organizations.

Yates takes us from ethics to goodness in "Good Leaders Must First Be Good People." He makes the connection between leadership and values that sustain a democratic society—"a good society."

Focusing on value-centered leadership, Behr discusses organizational success in a climate of change in his article "Acting from the Center." He explains why facing current leadership challenges must be grounded in personal values.

Vision, character, and intellectual capital highlight Loeb's "Where Leaders Come From." His analysis of leadership character is particularly powerful for today's administrators.

This inner, personal process of leadership is continued in "Leadership: A Journey That Begins Within" by Pigford. She shares her own world-perspective of this inner journey, learned from her varied experiences.

Finally, Carrow-Moffett's article "Change Agent Skills: Creating Leadership for School Renewal" wraps up this section by discussing the ethical leadership dimensions needed for change in organizations.

Questions

Reading 9. What are the three organizational traits which positively impact employee job satisfaction? Why should leaders focus attention on organizational facilities?

Reading 10. A leader's virtue is dependent on what values? What is virtue, and how does it relate to leadership?

Reading 11. What is value-centered leadership? What are two simple lessons of value-centered leadership?

Reading 12. What is the "tripod of forces" that constitutes a leader's character? What is intellectual capital, and how does an effective leader use it within his or her organization?

Reading 13. What is authentic leadership? What is meant by the phrase "leadership shared is leadership multiplied"?

Reading 14. What are the six steps to becoming a successful change agent? What are personal and environmental barriers and enhancers to change?

What are the three organizational traits which positively impact employee job satisfaction? Why should leaders force attention on organizational facilities?

Why Employees Love These Companies

(100 best companies to work for in America)

Ronald B. Lieber

It isn't complicated: We found that most of the raves workers give their employers are based on just three corporate traits. For many companies they're within reach.

By now, most of us have been schooled to believe we'll spend the rest of our careers jumping from job to job, working ever harder to prove our mettle to cranky bosses, and getting promoted much less often than our predecessors. We've been told over and over that this Darwinian odyssey is the new workplace reality, bleak though it may be. Yet the cheerful employees of our 100 Best companies face a far different, far more benign daily work life. These workers sing their employers' praises and—though it's very un-'90s—even declare pride in their corporate affiliation.

Why? What makes employees not just like but love these companies? We looked hard and found three recurring traits that seem to explain a lot. The great majority of our 100 Best have at least one, and many have all three. The good news is, they're within the reach of just about any employer.

First, many of our 100 Best are run by a powerful, visionary leader. Superstar CEOs like Bill Gates of Microsoft (No. 8), Andy Grove of Intel (No. 32), and Larry Bossidy of AlliedSignal (No. 96) are among the most demanding bosses in business, yet workers seem to feel inspired rather than oppressed by them; non-celebrities running many lesser-known companies have the same effect. Second, many of these companies offer a physical work environment that employees adore. Third, these companies often frame their work as part of a deep, rewarding purpose that employees find fulfilling. Here's a closer look at how a few companies on our list wow their workers.

Inspiring Leadership

Exhibit A is Herb Kelleher, the Southwest Airlines CEO perched at the pinnacle of our 100 Best list. He spends his business life making sure his employees believe in him and in the operation he has muscled into the top tier of a savagely competitive industry. He smokes, he arm-wrestles, he drinks large quantities of Wild Turkey, he raps in music videos—and it is only slight hyperbole to say nearly all his employees worship the ground he walks on. But even he can't match the act of devotion displayed for Dave Duffield, the founder and CEO of PeopleSoft (No. 20), the software maker in Pleasanton, Calif. A few years ago employees formed a garage band and decided to call it The Raving Daves.

Remarkably, the well-worn story of Mary Kay Ash also retains its power to inspire. Those who know her well—and almost all who work for Mary Kay Inc. (No. 82) seem to think they do—

Reprinted from the January 12, 1998 issue of FORTUNE by special permission; copyright 1998, Time Inc.

describe her as a sort of corporate Everywoman: Pushed aside by her male superiors as a saleswoman in the 1950s, she quit her job and built a sales organization intended to empower other women.

Mary Kay's saga of how she grew her business and made a fortune is the chief inspiration for many of the 475,000 women who sell her products. "I was a secretary. I was not voted most likely to succeed in high school," says Lisa Madson, 37, who started selling for the company 11 years ago. "But she reaches so many people by talking about the potential that everyone has inside. And she's the living example."

Though Mary Kay herself is a millionaire many times over, the people who work for her marvel at her ability to remain accessible. Before she suffered a stroke in 1996, she used to invite employees to her home for tea several times a year. "I've sat on her bed and had cookies at her table," says Gloria Mayfield Banks, 41, an executive senior sales director based in Baltimore. "It takes away the mystery when someone totally opens herself up to you like that."

The effective leader inspires employees not just to work hard and succeed but also to become miniversions of the leader. That seems to be happening at Mary Kay. "People understand that for Mary Kay, it was all about fulfilling a mission that was bigger than just her," says Janice Bird, 42, who works at corporate headquarters in Dallas. "They've increased their own self-esteem by being around her, and they want to pass that on to others the same way she did."

Knockout Facilities

These may be the most persuasive ways to tell employees they're valued. Top management at USAA (No. 39), the San Antonio-based insurance and financial services company, demonstrates the value of wooing employees with an impressive corporate compound. "Anywhere you go in town, if you tell someone you work for USAA, they're impressed," says Jeannette Leal, a service adviser in the life/annuity service and claims department. "You become a part of this place, and it becomes everything that you're about."

The amenities begin with an on-site child care center. The facility can handle 300 kids, and there's car-seat storage for families where the mom drops off and the dad picks up. In Tampa, where the company also has a large presence, they've even thought to add industrial-strength fencing around the kiddie playground in case marauding alligators show up in search of snacks. "My wife and I visited ten or 12 day-care facilities all over town," says Raul Nevarez, 30, a USAA security officer. "There was no competition at all."

If you don't want to drive to work, the company sponsors a van pool. If you ruin your hose, you can pick up a pair at the on-site store. There's a dry-cleaning service, a bank, and several ATMs. Even the cafeteria food is tasty enough that, several years ago, employees began demanding dinner to go. At Thanksgiving they purchased 5,620 pies and 188 turkeys to take home to their families.

Then there are the athletic facilities. The three gyms are indistinguishable from those at many upscale health clubs, and one is open all night long. Outside, employees compete in intramural leagues on basketball and tennis courts and softball and soccer fields. If you want to work on your backswing at lunch, there's a driving range too.

USAA employees clearly enjoy these breaks from their desks during the workweek, but they often return to the campus on the weekend with their families. "I enjoy bringing my kids here," says Donna Castillo, 34, a sales manager in consumer finance and auto service. "There are playgrounds where they can run around, and it's nice to take pictures of them here when the bluebonnets come out in the spring."

Amenities like these cost a company a lot, but they buy a lot too. "The facilities say that the company cares about us, that we're a valued asset," says security guard Nevarez. "People are dying to get in here. I have to go direct traffic when the parking lot at the employment center overflows. It makes me feel really good that I work for a company that is sought out like that, but it also means that I have to produce in order to earn the right to stay."

A Sense of Purpose

What sort of mission turns employees on? Well, it's not shareholder value, that's for sure. "I always try to make this very clear to analysts who cover our company," says Bill George, 55, CEO of Medtronic (No. 47), a medical-products company in Minneapolis. "Shareholder value is a hollow notion as the sole source of employee motivation. If you do business that way, you end up like ITT."

Most of those analysts love Medtronic anyway, largely because its employees turn out so many great new gizmos that a full 50% of revenues come from products introduced in the past 12 months. Shareholder value? The company's total return to shareholders has averaged about 34% annually over the past decade. But that isn't what gets workers out of bed and into a lab coat in the morning. Rather it's the notion of helping sick people get well. Instead of concentrating on shareholders or doctors, workers at Medtronic concentrate on the people who will have the company's products implanted inside them.

This is hardly a new approach for companies in the health and medical industries. Employees at Merck (No. 9), a perennial all-star in surveys of worker satisfaction, have long since memorized the mantra that the medicine is for patients, not profits. Medtronic finds novel ways to teach similar lessons, embodied in the company motto, "Restoring patients to full life." Its symbol is an image of a supine human rising toward upright wellness.

The resurrection imagery comes to life each December at the company's holiday party, where patients, their families, and their doctors are flown in to tell their survival stories. It sounds like the stuff of a made-for-TV tearjerker, but this is not PR gimmickry; journalists are generally not invited. Instead, it's the employees who are moved to tears year after year. "I remember going to my first holiday party, and someone asked me if I had brought my Kleenex," recalls Medtronic President Art Collins, 50, a strapping guy with a firm handshake who is generally not prone to crying fits. "I assumed I'd be fine, but then these parents got up with their daughter who was alive because of our product. Even the surgeons who see this stuff all the time were crying."

Improving human health, though in a much different way, was the deep purpose motivating John Mackey, 44, when he helped start Whole Foods Market (No. 34), a chain of natural-foods grocery stores. That clearly stated mission has helped him draw motivated employees who are more educated than the average grocery worker. Take Lisa Shaw, 30, a Wellesley College graduate who works in Brighton, Mass., for one of the company's Bread & Circus stores. "I remember going to a wedding after I graduated and seeing the looks on people's faces when I told them what I was doing," she recalls. "I just hang on to the fact that my job is good in some larger sense. If people buy the sprouts, they're eating healthier foods, the farmer is doing well, and it's good for the planet because they're grown organically."

Such high-minded talk makes it tempting to dismiss Whole Foods employees as a bunch of hippies running an overgrown cooperative. But Whole Foods is a public company whose margins are roughly 50% higher than the average grocery chain's; its total return to shareholders over the past five years has averaged about 23% annually. And the people who work there make explicit connections between the company's financial success and its larger goals. "We're going to pass a billion dollars in sales this year," says Linda Fontaine, 38, the national tax coordinator at corporate headquarters. "All that means is that we've just made that much more of a difference in the world."

Blissed-out employees working in the best of economic times are fairly easy to please, of course. A better test of worker resolve comes when a company slams up against a serious crunch.

TDIndustries (No. 5), a specialty construction and service-repair business in Dallas, fell on hard times when building in that area practically stopped at the end of the 1980s. The company's bank had failed, and private investors wouldn't touch the place. So in 1989 CEO Jack Lowe took the problem to employees, who decided to terminate their overfunded pension plan. They could have put the $4 million thus liberated directly into their IRAs, but instead many of them elected to bet their retirement money on Lowe's bailout plan. All told, TDI employees put about $1.25 million back in the company in return for shares in an ESOP account.

A risky investment? Absolutely—but the value of those shares has more than doubled since then. Besides, it wasn't the money that people were worried about anyway. "Sure, we were fixing to lose a lot of our retirement funds if the company failed," says senior project manager Laura Price. "But the real fear was of having to go work for someone else."

"Everyone, from the highest executive to the maintenance staff, lives the corporate philosophy."
—Anjanette Schmelter, marketing manager, Medtronic

"People are dying to work here, and I like being at a company that is sought out like that." —Raul Nevarez, security officer, USAA

"I'm absolutely tied to my benefits here, and I also feel that what I'm doing is good in some larger sense."
—Lisa Shaw, body-care buyer, Whole Foods Market

"This is a company that understands that positive emotions can be good for the soul." —Gloria Mayfield Banks, senior sales director, Mary Kay

Article Review Form at end of book.

A leader's virtue is dependent on what values? What is virtue, and how does it relate to leadership?

Good Leaders Must First Be Good People

Dr. Albert C. Yates

President; Colorado State University and Chancellor of Colorado State University System

I pursued a career in education because I have faith in the future, and because I believe in the ability of great leaders to emerge from each generation—leaders who can restore our faith, return us to our foundations and help us to took toward the future with optimism and spirit. One of the greatest challenges facing education today is to help our students understand the vital link between leadership and those values that sustain a democratic society—and, most important, a good society.

We expect our leaders to have a glimpse of the future, of a time and place better than now. We expect them to coalesce and focus our concerns and dreams and inspire us to action in pursuit of this collective vision. But more, we want to trust our leaders; we want our passion to be their passion. We want to have faith in them, to be assured of their virtue and know they will make the right choices.

But what is virtue? I've come, over time, to think of "virtue" as the embodiment of what is good and right in human life, as the understanding, embrace and employment of values that teach us how to be better people. Virtue is possible through the consideration of values such as truth, integrity, competence, commitment and, above all, compassion.

- **Truth.** I include truth because without it achieving intellectual and psychological equilibrium seems virtually impossible. Rationalizing to avoid the truth is one of the easiest things we do. "I have no time to get involved." "One person can't make a difference." "It's really none of my business." How often do we lie to ourselves to bring comfort in our isolation, selfishness, and cynicism?

- **Integrity,** surely, is our most precious commodity. It is the quality that allows us to remain steadfast in our convictions, to resist the temptations of power, status and money. It is the voice of conscience, the inner compass that allows us to steer a steady and true course.

  A world of options opens up to us when we are not saddled with integrity. Opportunity abounds when we abandon what we know is right. The newspapers are filled with examples of the wealth and notoriety of those unburdened by integrity. They also are filled with the pathetic words, actions and attitudes of those so unburdened. If you accept the challenge to make the world a little bit better, then there is no better guide than integrity.

- **Competence.** Through competence we assure our usefulness—to ourselves and others. Competence is an acknowledgment that one of our most important duties as human beings is first to determine and then to cultivate our abilities.

  Not everyone plays power forward well—there are few Michael Jordans. Not everyone can design scientific experiments—there are few George Washington Carvers. Not everyone can teach well. Or cook well. Or play the guitar well. But all of us can try our best to do our best. I believe all of us incur a special debt to the world from the simple act of being: We owe our best efforts to humanity simply because we are a part of it.

Reprinted by permission of Black Issues in Higher Education.

- **Commitment** is not just duty or obligation or responsibility. It instills a reason to be, a passion for life. To live life without commitment, without passion, seems hardly a life worth living.
- **Compassion.** Perhaps our most uniquely human quality is compassion. Moving toward a better world seems to require at least two critical ingredients: an acceptance of those things about ourselves and others that we—or they—cannot change, and a recognition that "reverence for life" is not merely a noble phrase, but a necessity for survival.

Virtue derives from the interplay of all these values—how they function in concert, one to another.

On their own, they don't amount to much. Lacking integrity and truth, committed and competent criminals are a dime a dozen. Lacking compassion, subjective truth becomes the rationale for much evil—the basis of slavery and the Holocaust. Commitment on its own may lead to fanaticism. Compassion alone can lead to helplessness and despair. Even integrity, without these other values, can be reduced to rigidity and narrow-mindedness. But taken together, they can lead one toward virtue—each depends on another and only together are they complete.

Of course, we can have leadership without virtue—and we often do. Virtue is not something you earn along with your high school or college diploma. Highly intelligent people will not automatically choose "good over evil." Indeed, our society seems to be making a long steady slide into the void of selfishness and cynicism under the leadership of "very intelligent people."

But virtue enhances the probability that leadership will be successful and good. Virtue allows one to take the high ground, to transcend the petty, the routine and the mundane, to fight the urge to succumb to temptations of power or status or money, and to pursue a true course for collective good.

What seems true is this: Good leaders must first be good people.

Article Review Form at end of book.

What is value-centered leadership? What are two simple lessons of value-centered leadership?

Acting from the Center

Your response to today's leadership challenges must be grounded in personal values

E. Thomas Behr

E. Thomas Behr is president of Horizons Unlimited Inc., a consulting firm based in Millington, N.J. He is the author of The Tao of Sales: The Easy Way to Sell in Tough Times *(Element Book 1997).*

To succeed in a fast-moving, unpredictable economy, companies across America have been "breaking up the machine" for the next decade. They have focused on dismantling the bureaucratic "silos" that fragmented energy upward in the organization instead of outward to customers, replacing top-down directives with "boundaryless" communications networks and transforming command-and-control cultures into self-directed work groups guided by ownership and accountability.

In the process, managers are discovering that it's much easier to tear down a dysfunctional system than to construct a new organization that operates efficiently and competitively. In particular, the shift of power from the top of a company to lower levels has created a new set of problems for today's leaders.

"In 'flattening' the company, we also wound up flattening the few managers that survived," says one hard-pressed veteran of downsizing. "My span of 'non-control' is so wide now I spend most of my day just keeping up with what's going on. Forget getting anything done. We flattened the company by driving over it with a steam roller; most days I feel like a road-killed chipmunk."

For this manager and many others, the traditional power that derives from one's position in a hierarchy has been lost. But in its place, a very different kind of leadership power has begun to emerge. This new power is rooted in a leader's personal values and convictions and his or her willingness to act on them in the face of uncertainty. Those who practice "value-centered leadership" create the organizational integrity needed to compete in an ever-changing world.

Leading through Change

What's driving the need for such leadership? Consider a conversation I had some years ago with the new CEO of a Fortune 500 company. His mandate was to remake the company's culture so that it was more responsive to customers, more entrepreneurial in nature, more personally accountable for decisions and more open to constant, unpredictable change.

His comment summed up the burden felt by many managers these days: "Does anybody out there really have answers, or are we all making this up as we go?"

Reprinted from *Management Review*, March 1998 © 1998. American Management Association International. Reprinted by permission of American Management Association International, New York, NY. All rights reserved. http://www.amanet.org.

This new leader faced some familiar obstacles in changing the company's culture: a management team so comfortable with the "old way" of doing things that achieving any substantive change would be like pulling teeth; an existing culture in which people had learned, often painfully, to "ask for permission" rather than take initiative; a preference for power and blame over accountability; and a competitive, even arrogant, attitude toward the marketplace in which customers were seen as "the enemy" and valued for their revenue, not their loyalty.

"I took this job to change things," said the CEO, "and I'm ready to lead the troops into battle. But how do I know that when I step out in front enough people will follow me?"

"Change means fear," he continued. "Not just employees' alarm for their jobs, although that's real enough, but the fear that the people at the top don't have a clue and are trying just another experiment—another 'change agenda.' And in a way they're right. This is an experiment that's never been done before."

In short, the change sweeping through corporate America has produced a common result: Not only is it difficult for executives to be certain the course they've chosen will produce promised results, but it's also terribly hard for them to acknowledge their own uncertainties. This CEO's name has been withheld for that very reason. His arrival at the troubled company prompted a desperately needed upsurge in its stock price. The last thing Wall Street would want to hear is that he doesn't have "the answer."

Similar discussions with leaders at all levels of today's companies reveal that the loss of conventional power is a widespread problem. This loss seems to be the inevitable result of the de-layering of companies, the empowering of managers and employees and the inversion of the organizational pyramid so that leadership exists at the bottom.

However, an upside-down pyramid will stay balanced—if it's centered. The same principle applies to leadership. It comes down to knowing what you really believe, trusting in those beliefs and acting on them accordingly. Every day should serve as a living example of your values.

A leader has power when that example touches the lives of others in the organization. He or she must be able to influence "upward" within an inverted pyramid, and that means letting go of traditional notions of command, control and coercion as sources of power. Today's leaders must rely on core values to keep the organization centered and balanced. This kind of power can exist only when all stakeholders—employees, suppliers and customers—voluntarily choose to support the same principles the company's leadership has made a commitment to live by.

That makes it tough for a leader who needs to initiate broad-scale change. After all, it's impossible to achieve different results without altering the habitual actions and deeply ingrained processes that create those results—that is, the organization's entire culture. But this is just where value-centered leadership may pay its greatest dividends. It offers leaders at all levels the opportunity to affect the basic culture positively, powerfully and quickly.

Stand by Your Values

Value-based leadership requires a pivotal change in perspective. The leader can no longer view the company as a machine that needs to be controlled. Instead, he or she must see it as a living community centered on the shared goals, values and commitments that provide a sense of organizational integrity. The leadership serves as the source and model of that integrity.

For example, John Gillespie, former CEO and vice president of operations at Innovation Luggage, Secaucus, NJ., helped spearhead an organizational transformation at the firm that began with his willingness to take a personal stand on the values he believed were essential to the company's growth. He committed himself to achieving specific results and living by his values, even in the face of skepticism from the CEO and initial resistance to change from key managers and employees.

"Forget all the fluff about mission statements," Gillespie says. "Most of that language is 'consultant talk,' anyway. The real questions are: What do you believe in? What are you committed to accomplish? I found that if I wanted people to follow me, I had to be the first person to take risks and work without a safety net under me."

Gillespie acknowledges that he also had to address his own fears. "You can feel like 'The Emperor's New Clothes,' exposed and naked," he adds. The act of becoming accountable is scary at first, but the fear is a gift because it tells you you're completely involved. And the feeling of acting out of choice and commitment is exhilarating."

Two years after the transformation began, Innovation Luggage had funded an aggressive expansion from 21 to 39 stores out of operating cash flow, while reducing expenses by almost 4 percent, doubling its market share in New York City and increasing its operating earnings 68 percent.

Earning Influence

Once leaders have made a personal commitment to certain core principles, they must grapple with another challenge: How can they help others in the organization evolve so that they, too, reflect and embody those values?

Don Makie, vice president of quality assurance at Lear Corp., Southfield, Mich., is one executive who has faced this challenge. He was a key change agent within Masland Industries in the late 1980s and has continued to serve in that role since Masland was purchased by Lear in 1996.

Over an eight-year period he and other senior leaders transformed Masland from a traditional manufacturer struggling to meet increasing competition and control escalating costs, into the world's highest-quality, lowest-cost producer of automobile interiors.

"I'd like to say we began initiating change in 1987 just because it was common sense to do so," Makie reflects. "But given the truly global level of competition in the auto industry, we really didn't have a choice. The alternative to common sense was extinction."

At Masland, the "common sense" need for change took two forms: developing a shared awareness of new values on which the company's future success would depend and a shared sense of purpose in choosing to live and work by those values.

Looking back over nearly a decade of successful change, Makie observes, "We had to get everyone in the company—and I mean everybody from top management to hourly unionized workers—to make some critical transitions. They had to shift from a narrow focus on the numbers to being process-oriented systems thinkers. Instead of hiding from problems or passing the buck, they had to welcome problems as treasures. If you don't know what the problem is, you can't do anything about it; thus, the flawed system continues to generate flawed results."

Makie and the other senior executives challenged plant managers to create an environment they would choose to work in themselves. If they weren't willing to do the toughest, most "menial" job on the plant floor with enthusiasm and commitment, why think anybody else would want to do the job?

"We were looking for managers who wanted to get on the shop floor, communicate with people and learn," Makie says. "You can't manage change from a distance. So we did away with all the executive perks and changed the whole meaning of the manager's job. Their one purpose was the same as senior management's: to create a work environment that strongly supported the values we wanted to create throughout the company."

In this case, the vehicle for change was Masland's "Compass Program," adapted from Toyota's kaizen philosophy of continuous improvement, organizational integrity and workforce accountability. Makie singles out two core values—trust and nonjudgmental behavior—as principles that needed to be lived at every level of the organization.

"Trust is a two-way street," he says. "Our employees, especially the unionized hourly workers, had to be able to trust that we were serious in our commitment to change, and that this wasn't just another 'flavor of the month.' That kind of trust is like customer loyalty. You have to earn it every day. And we had to trust that if we turned planning and operational control over to the workforce that they'd accept that challenge."

To develop a companywide commitment to nonjudgmental behavior, the leaders had to create a culture that did away with recrimination, personal criticism and finger-pointing. At the same time, victimization, helplessness and lack of accountability were no longer acceptable. "When things go wrong," says Makie, "95 percent of the time it's a flawed process, not a flawed person. So if you want better results, fix the process, not the person. And the best people to fix a flawed process are the people who actually perform it every day."

Masland's approach to value-centered leadership has produced impressive results. Under the Compass Program, the company has made improvements in measures such as lead time, rework and average daily production.

Values As a Defense

A commitment to value-based leadership also provides a stabilizing force when the going gets tough. At PR Newswire, a business communications company based in New York, CEO Ian Capps and other top executives focused on values such as "mutual respect" and "ongoing learning" to transform the company from a price-sensitive, commodity—style business into an industry-leading service provider.

As described in my book, *The Tao of Sales: The Easy Way to Sell in Tough Times,* these leaders recognized that their daily treatment of each other set the standard or the company's treatment of customers. No respect for each other, no respect for and from customers. And as a company that relied on technology for its competitive advantage, PR Newswire had to become what Peter Senge has called "a learning organization."

According to Capps, the company initially tried to manage the changes brought by fast growth and changing technologies. But no sooner would it initiate a top-down directive to "control" one part of the service process and "fix" a problem than another part would start to malfunction. Then the company got lucky. Its major competitor launched a price war, offering customers discounts of up to 50 percent for "comparable" service.

The only way PR Newswire could fight back was to fully trust its values and make them the centerpiece of its response. In essence, it turned the price war into a choice between cost and quality service. Capps says the company examined its assets—including the quality of its people, a commitment to value-added service and technological investments that allowed it to customize offerings—and decided to meet the challenge with those strengths.

Instead of yielding to price pressure, the company held the line on the importance of client relationships and the cost benefits of value-added service. Instead of reducing its own prices, it invested in new technological resources and additional training companywide that would allow it to deliver even better service to clients in a cost-effective manner.

In the process, PR Newswire changed the dialogue with clients. A superficial, myopic focus on the bottom-line gave way to a more collaborative commitment to service as a shared investment. A year after the initial competitive attack, the company had not only preserved its customer base but was actually taking clients away from the competition. In the ensuing four years, revenues tripled.

Getting Centered

As the companies discussed here illustrate, value-centered leadership rests on some surprisingly simple lessons. Here are two points to keep in mind as you adopt this leadership approach:

- Let your actions do the talking. A leader's day-to-day interactions with managers and employees set the pattern for employees' treatment of each other, customers and suppliers. Ultimately, those daily behaviors determine the actions that create the company's performance and results. People are what they do. And the more consistent everyone's behavior, especially when things get tough, the more focused the response and the more powerful the results.

    Managers who don't "walk the talk" will not fool employees. Say what you will about the company's values, but employees will still reflect the behavior and attitudes they see exhibited by management.

- Focus on work processes. According to Makie, one of the toughest challenges for Masland was to shift people's attention from results to processes. "Results are what you did last month or last year," he says. "It's like driving down the highway at 90 mph with your eyes fixed on the disappearing white line in your rearview mirror." Rather than dwell on bygone results, the company should focus on how work gets done. "If your processes keep improving, so will your numbers," Makie adds.

With a commitment to value-centered leadership, success becomes easy to measure because people's attention shifts from after-the-fact results to daily relationships and personal commitments. "If you want people to tell you the truth because you think that's a critical business value," Gillespie says. "be truthful with them and expect truth in return. You'll know where you are as soon as they open their mouth."

Lear Corp.'s success stems from the same sense of organizational integrity grounded in core behaviors. There is no apparent clutter, confusion or waste—on the plant floor, in people's actions or, implicitly, in their minds—in a facility that has embraced the values of the Compass Program.

Ethical Dimensions of Leadership **61**

By its very nature, value-centered leadership is neither a panacea nor an easy answer to today's challenges. It can, however, be a powerful choice for leaders who must compete in a global marketplace characterized by constant, unpredictable change.

The clear, daily focus on values and core behaviors can create both immediate profits and long-term resilience. More important, leaders who trust their own values enough to offer them to others, to choose or reject, benefit from one thing that is often lacking in more traditional command-and-control companies—honest feedback.

Article Review Form at end of book.

What is the "tripod of forces" that constitutes a leader's character? What is intellectual capital, and how does an effective leader use it within his or her organization?

Where Leaders Come From

Marshall Loeb

Half a dozen CEOs of major global corporations—men from the worlds of autos, banking, oil, railroads, electronics—met privately in Chicago not long ago to assess the future of world business. What worried them most was not production or profits or competition but this: Where have all the leaders gone? The chairman of this powerhouse group, Henry Kissinger, leaned into his cold beef fillet and lamented that in previous times of crisis, great leaders always appeared on the scene just in time to pull the world through. But now, try to name only one larger-than-life leader, one who could fill the role of F.D.R. or Ike or De Gaulle or Churchill. And in business, look at how the icons have fallen at IBM, GM, Kodak, countless others.

Wherever you go in business as in government these days, you hear people ask, plaintively, Where are the leaders? Perhaps we demand too much. Perhaps memory has inflated the images of yesterday's business heroes— Sloan, the Watsons, David Rockefeller, Sam Walton. Perhaps a brilliant new generation of boomer CEOs—their eyes on the horizon as much as the bottom line—is about to burst upon us. But don't hold your breath.

Instead, seek answers. And fresh blood. How do we find leaders? How do we create leaders? What makes a good leader today? If all happy families are alike, what characteristics are common to all successful leaders?

Ask the man who knows more about the subject than anyone else, Warren Bennis. Psychologist, sociologist, economist, USC professor, former university president, author of two dozen books on the subject, Bennis, 69, has spent years intensely studying 150 leaders— mostly corporate chiefs. When this silver-haired, perpetually tanned man shows up at a business conference, he's the Pied Piper; expectant executives crowd the hall to hear him tell (for up to $20K) what qualities are needed for a mere manager to grow into a real leader.

The indispensable first quality, Bennis says, is a guiding vision, a clear idea of what he wants to do. "All the leaders I know have a strongly defined sense of purpose. And when you have an organization where the people are aligned behind a clearly defined vision or purpose, you get a powerful organization." Thomas Carlyle had it right: All history is biography—so great companies are indeed the direct reflection of their leaders.

The most exemplary leaders are also pragmatic dreamers. Banker Walter Wriston once told Bennis that he regarded his long-term plan for Citicorp as a dream with a deadline.

The best leaders have a potent point of view. Bennis quotes Mike Eisner, Disney's lion king, as saying: "You know, we don't have a vision statement, but we have a strong point of view. What amazes me is that it's always the person with the strong POV who influences the group, who wins the day. Around here, a powerful POV is worth at least 80 IQ points."

Another quality the leader needs is constancy. "One of the things you hear about the least effective leaders," says Bennis, "is that they do whatever the last person they spoke to recommended." Or that they plunge forward with the latest good idea that pops into their head. To trust the leader, followers have to know what to expect. So sometimes the leader has to put off a

Reprinted from the September 19, 1994 issue of FORTUNE by special permission; copyright 1994, Time Inc.

grand idea or a glorious opportunity until he has had a chance to convince his own allies of it. A main problem for imaginative, impetuous Bill Clinton as leader is that he plunges ahead with the idea of the hour without first checking it out and selling it to his stakeholders. In business as in politics, the effectiveness of a decision is the quality of the decision multiplied by the acceptance of it.

And the leader—or the leader in training—needs candor. That's tough because Bennis's studies show that seven of ten people in organizations don't speak up if they think their point of view will vary with the conventional wisdom or their boss's POV—even if they believe their boss is going to make an error. What the leader needs to cultivate are firm-minded subordinates with the wisdom and courage to say no.

The effective leader, Bennis believes, limits himself to several key objectives. "GE's Jack Welch says, 'Look, I have only three things to do. I have to choose the right people, allocate the right number of dollars and transmit ideas from one division to another with the speed of light. So I'm really in the business of being the gatekeeper and the transmitter of ideas. And we'll plagiarize from anybody.'"

For example, Welch was among the first to send his executives to Bentonville, Arkansas, to study Wal-Mart's selling methods. Bennis paraphrases Welch: "No more of this not-invented-here stuff. We'll take ideas from anywhere and deploy them and use them as quickly as we can." Or as Picasso is said to have remarked, "Good artists copy; great artists steal." Bennis will tell you that seven characteristics define a leader.

- **Business literacy:** Does he know the business? Does he know the real feel of it?
- **People skills:** Does he have the capacity to motivate, to bring out the best in people?
- **Conceptual skills:** Does he have the capacity to think systematically, creatively, and inventively?
- **Track record:** Has he done it before and done it well?
- **Taste:** Does he have the ability to pick the right people—not clones of himself but people who can make up for his deficiencies?
- **Judgment:** Does he have the ability to make quick decisions with imperfect data?
- **Character:** The core competency of leadership is character, but character and judgment are the qualities that we know least about when trying to teach them to others.

The leader's character is made up of a tripod of forces: ambition and drive; competence and expertise; integrity and moral fabric. All three are needed, and all three have to be in balance, or the tripod topples. Get a leader with only drive but not competence and integrity, and you get a demagogue. Get someone with competence but absent integrity and drive, and you get a technocrat. Get seduced by someone who has ambition and competence but lacks integrity, and you get a destructive achiever.

The key to competitive advantage in the Nineties and beyond, says Bennis, "will be the capacity of top leadership to create the social architecture capable of generating intellectual capital. I mean an organizational environment that will be not only fast, focused, flexible, and friendly but also fun. By intellectual capital, I mean know-how, expertise, brainpower, innovation, ideas. All the good CEOs tell me that their major challenge is, 'How do I release the brainpower of the people in my company?'"

You do that only by leading, not simply managing. "Leaders are people who do the right things. Managers are people who do things right. There's a profound difference. When you think about doing the right things, your mind immediately goes toward thinking about the future, thinking about dreams, missions, visions, strategic intent, purpose. But when you think about doing things right, you think about control mechanisms. You think about how-to. Leaders ask the what and why question, not the how question. Leaders think about empowerment, not control. And the best definition of empowerment is that you don't steal responsibility from people."

In their bad old days, IBM, GM, and Sears were overmanaged and underled. Success had made them content. (Much the same fate befell the Mafia, but that's another story.) Says Bennis: "Those whom the gods want to fail, give them 20 or 25 years of success. Just when you start thinking you're really terrific, you start dictating to the market instead of listening to the customers."

He likes to quote from the late Grace Hopper, a management expert who was the first woman admiral in the U.S. Navy. Said she: "You manage things, but you lead people." And we lost our leadership, she added, "largely because of this tremendous push to financial management. The business schools taught it. The whole thing was business management, not leadership."

What employees want most from their leaders, says Bennis, "is direction and meaning, trust and hope. Every good leader I have spoken with had a willful determination to achieve a set of goals, a set of convictions about what he or she wanted his or her organization to achieve. Everyone had a purpose." And here Bennis quotes his hockey hero, Wayne Gretzky: "It's not where the puck is that counts. It's where the puck will be."

Are leaders born or made? Bennis gets off the droll crack about the martinet CEO's dull son who comes home with a report card loaded with D's and F's. "Well, Dad," asks the kid, "is it nature or nurture, genes or the environment?"

Leaders are made, concludes Bennis, usually self-made. But it's very helpful to have had a strong, determined set of parents. His studies of leaders show they usually had someone in the family who said, "Go for it, you can do it." It's wise also to have as wide a set of experiences as possible. One of the flaws of American business is that we have too much vertical mobility. Managers inch up the same smokestack, learning more and more about less and less. But really smart companies—like Glaxo and Arco, to name a couple—move promising people around horizontally, having them serve time in most of the major divisions to give them a kaleidoscopic view of the organization and the mentoring of a variety of bosses.

"I used to think that running an organization was equivalent to conducting a symphony orchestra. But I don't think that's quite it. Now it's more like jazz. There is more improvisation, the sound of surprise."

How do you go about becoming a good leader? Professor Bennis's short course. "Be yourself. Figure out what you're good at. Hire only good people who care. Treat them just the way you want to be treated. Switch from macho to maestro. Identify your one or two key objectives or directions. Ask your co-workers how to get there. Listen hard. Get out of their way. Cheer them. Count the gains. Start right now."

Article Review Form at end of book.

What is authentic leadership? What is meant by the phrase "leadership shared is leadership multiplied"?

Leadership

A journey that begins within

Aretha B. Pigford

Aretha B. Pigford is professor of educational administration at the University of South Carolina, Columbia.

In 1991, the Kellogg Foundation gave me an incredible gift—the opportunity to be a Kellogg Fellow and participate in its three-year leadership development program. Among a host of learning opportunities, this gift would allow me to experience cultures throughout the world and to explore leadership firsthand.

My explorations would take me to a quaint, intimate Amish community in Pennsylvania Dutch country; to a dirt-poor sugar cane plantation in Guatemala; to a cramped, crowded township in South Africa; to a garbage-strewn community in the Philippines; to a condemned public housing project in Houston; to an opulent presidential palace in Central America.

During my three-year journey, I would observe the leadership styles of the rich and powerful as well as the poor and victimized. I would meet with an internationally acclaimed Nobel Peace Prize recipient, with powerful heads of governments, with impoverished Chiapa women weavers, with frustrated South African students, and with grief-stricken Guatemalan mothers.

So What?

As I traveled the world examining leadership, I realized that the most powerful travels were not to faraway lands, but rather the journey taken within. Whether in the barren hills of Guatemala or the violent township of Umlazi, my personal journey always brought me back to the poignant question the Kellogg Foundation posed to the Fellows at our first meeting, "So what?"

What did an experience mean to each of us at a personal level? At a professional level? How did our visiting a given community make a difference for the residents there? For us? Were we merely another group of tourists who, after photographing our hosts and expressing dismay about the situations in which many of them lived, retreated to our more-than-comfortable lifestyles in America? In other words, so what?

It has been almost two years since my fellowship and the "so what" question continues to challenge me personally and professionally. On a professional level, my approach to both thinking about leadership and to preparing leaders has changed. As a professor of educational administration who has both participated in and supervised several leadership development programs, I have begun to see leadership through new eyes.

Instead of focusing on preparing students who can demonstrate a knowledge of and ability to apply selected theories, my emphasis has shifted to helping my students approach leadership as a personal journey, a journey that focuses primarily on discovering *who one is*—not on what one does. Authentic leadership, leadership based solely on the will of the followers, is really about "being" (i.e., one's values and beliefs) and not about doing. My commitment now is to preparing authentic leaders.

If there is sufficient time for interacting with persons who hold leadership positions, it is relatively easy to identify those who are authentic leaders. It is never so much what they do or the titles they hold as who they are. Authentic leaders are people who

---

"Leadership: A Journey That Begins Within," by Aretha B. Pigford. *NASSP Bulletin*, January 1996. Reprinted with permission. For more information concerning NASSP services and/or programs, please call (703) 860-0200.

have well-defined belief systems, people who know the values that guide them and the principles they hold inviolate, people whose actions are consistently congruent with the values they espouse.

While my experiences in the varied cultures I visited taught me a lot about leadership, I returned home still unable to identify the defining qualities of leadership. I did, however, reach some conclusions about this elusive phenomenon.

1. Leadership Is a Sacred Trust—Not a Bestowed Right

Although many persons I met during my travels occupied positions of leadership, some were not authentic leaders. Their followers responded to them out of fear, not trust. Remove the fear and there would likely have been no followers. Authentic leadership is based on mutual trust, a trust the leader respects and honors. Since the only prerequisite to leadership is the willingness of someone to follow, the leader who abuses the trust of his or her followers is doomed to fail.

2. Leadership Is About Hearing All the Voices

Authentic leaders hear all the voices, including those that may be silent, and feel a responsibility to respond not only to the squeaky wheel but to the missing wheel as well. They understand the objective of the squeaky wheel, to communicate loudly the position of those who stand to benefit in a given situation. The important and often unasked question, though, is who stands to lose? Authentic leaders ask this unpopular question and make decisions only after careful consideration of the perspectives of both the squeaky and the missing wheels.

3. Leadership Is About Creating a "Surplus of Vision"

Authentic leaders grow and nurture other leaders. Because they do not regard power as finite and realize that leadership shared is leadership multiplied, authentic leaders enthusiastically empower those around them. By doing so, they create a "surplus of vision." While authentic leaders are likely to amass considerable power, the acquisition of power is never a goal; instead, it is a by-product of leadership and merely a means to realizing a vision.

4. Leadership Is About Being Uncomfortable

Authentic leaders are comfortable with being uncomfortable. They understand that while comfort is likely to promote complacency and stagnation, discomfort stretches them and thereby facilitates their growth and development. The authentic leaders I observed expressed a gnawing sense of discomfort, an intolerable frustration with the status quo, and a strong commitment to bringing about change. It was this sense of discomfort that seemed to propel them into action. Whether their efforts proved successful or not, what mattered most was that they were in fact "doing something."

The Journey

The journey to authentic leadership begins with introspection. Given the flaws one is likely to uncover, such a journey can indeed be intimidating. Those who dare to undertake the journey, however, are likely to make discoveries that will provide them with the commitment and courage to ask the unpopular questions, to speak out when it's easier to remain silent; to hear all the voices; to be comfortable with discomfort: to continue to ask "so what?" Only persons who have taken such a journey can hope to be truly authentic leaders.

Article Review Form at end of book.

What Teens Are Saying

A survey of high achieving teens reveals a strong relationship between close family activity, such as eating dinner together, and students' sense of personal responsibility and emotional well-being. According to the *Who's Who Among American High School Students' Special Report on Teens and Their Families*:

- Eight in 10 students have a great deal of confidence in their parents.
- More than two-thirds would raise their children as they were raised.
- More than a quarter choose to confide in one of their parents.
- The "decline of the family" is a greater crisis facing our nation than AIDS, the national debt, racial tensions, and inadequate health care.
- Students who say their life at home is unhappy most of the time are almost three times as likely to engage in sexual intercourse than those who say their life at home is happy.

The survey was conducted among 3,351 high-achieving 16 to 18-year-old students, all of whom have an A or B average, and 98 percent of whom plan to attend college after high school graduation.

What are the six steps to becoming a successful change agent? What are personal and environmental barriers and enhancers to change?

Change Agent Skills

Creating leadership for school renewal

To be an effective change agent one must be willing to commit to a lifelong process of self-examination. The six-step process outlined here is designed to help.

Patricia A. Carrow-Moffett

Patricia A. Carrow-Moffett is a consultant to public and private organizations in the area of leadership development, and an adjunct faculty member in the Department of Educational Services at the University of North Florida.

In the 21st century, the one constant we can rely on is change. One need only consider the revolutionary changes—demographic, sociological, and technological—that have already affected us. Such dramatic change introduces added stressors and anxiety into our personal and work lives on a daily basis.

Both the private and public sectors are feeling the need to respond to these global changes. American corporations are responding to the challenges of the 21st century by adopting more participatory management styles, learning how to manage a more culturally diverse workforce, and addressing the needs of families as well as the corporation (Morgan, 1989). In the public arena, educators are challenged to reform our system of education. There is movement toward greater teacher participation in decision making, accountability for producing skilled workers for the future, year-round schooling, etc., (Laguna, 1989; McConnell, 1989; Wilson and Burbach, 1989). It's difficult to keep up, much less welcome and embrace the barrage of change that is upon us. Many of us don't like it one bit!

It is increasingly clear that to meet the challenges ahead, we must develop leaders throughout every level of the system. We will need leaders who are change agents, who have vision and purpose, and who understand the big picture (Faidly and Musser, 1989). We will need leaders who are able to set directions and facilitate those involved in working cooperatively to meet the challenges of a diverse world.

Developing Leaders

The ideas and procedures outlined on these pages evolved from consultation with public and private sector organizations who were faced with system-wide changes and the implications of managing those changes for employees. The essence of the approach is to plan as fully for the impact of change on the people involved as we do for the impact on resources. School leaders can guide themselves and those they lead through a specific change process. It is much easier to focus on the paper plan since it deals in a step-by-step manner with tangibles such as material resources, funding, FTE's, time factors, etc.

What is often taken for granted is the impact that even minor changes have on the people who are tasked with implementation. The old adage, "the best laid plans of mice and men,"

"Change Agent Skills: Creating Leadership for School Renewal," by Patricia A. Carrow-Moffett. *NASSP Bulletin,* April 1993. Reprinted with permission. For more information concerning NASSP services and/or programs, please call (703) 860–0200.

reminds us of what often happens when we transfer a paper plan to the real world. Leaders must consider not only the rational plan—i.e., the logical, sequential way it should work—but also the "arational" or human system factors. This "arational" system, with its human emotions and values, affects the rational plan. Often overlooked, it is the source of much frustration and anger when things don't go as planned. However, to become effective change agents, we must first challenge ourselves to explore and develop our awareness of the barriers and enhancers that we bring to the change process. This process is the prerequisite for effectively leading others through change.

Analyzing the Impact of Change

Would-be change agents are encouraged to begin by examining the meaning they give to change, both in their personal and external environments. It may help to identify a specific change in which you are currently engaged, or one that you anticipate will occur within the year. The change may be personal or work related. Identify the change as either "self-selected" or "other-imposed." This distinction is important. We are more likely to have the greatest degree of resistance to change when it is experienced as other-imposed.

With the advent of any change we are required not only to learn something new; we must also "unlearn" something. Part of the process of change is the integration of new perceptions, attitudes, and behaviors into one's sense of self. If we can see how a change or even a part of the change can fit with our personal vision, the integration process is enabled. However, it is the unlearning process that is at the root of most resistance (Schein, 1987). Therefore, effective change agents recognize the need to deal with issues of loss, even when the losses appear minor—old habits and procedures—or major—as when one's identity or sense of values is perceived to be threatened.

Six steps have proved helpful for a number of leaders and managers tasked with becoming change agents. They are identifying and speaking vision: yours, mine, and ours; empowerment of self and others; knowing your values; personal barriers and enhancers to change; environmental barriers and enhancers to change; and resisting the change-back phenomenon.

1. Identifying and Speaking Vision: Yours, Mine, and Ours

One of the hallmarks of change agents is their sense of a personal vision that becomes their "frame for action" (Morgan, 1989). It is this well-defined vision that provides stability and guidance in the same sense as one's personal identity, philosophy, or core values do. In a phrase, it is "what we're about in life." This first step is critical; it determines the clarity with which our vision is heard by others. If a leader lacks clarity of vision—e.g., purpose and direction—this becomes a barrier to effectively leading others through change.

Leaders and change agents are cautioned not to "impose" their visions on those they would lead. Rather, they should encourage others to discuss their individual visions. It is finding the "overlap," the place where individual visions become shared, that provides the leverage needed to enroll people for change (Senge, 1990). If you speak your vision broadly enough, others will find a place within it to actualize their visions as well as yours. In fact, the very process of talking to your people about your sense of vision will help them to articulate theirs.

We do not always know exactly how others perceive us, and may assume they are as clear about our vision as we may think we are.

Videotape yourself speaking your vision. Describe the changes you are currently challenged by, and then talk about your vision. Ask a colleague or friend to view your videotape and give you feedback on the clarity of your vision statement. Do you come across as rigidly imposing your vision as the only right and true one? Or, is it broad and flexible enough that others feel invited to contribute a part of their vision as well?

Though this exercise may feel awkward, it is a powerful tool to increase your awareness of how others perceive you This process can provide you with new skills to articulate your vision more effectively.

2. Empowerment of Self and Others

Empowerment means to give power to or authorize; to enable or permit. When change agents are committed to the process of self-examination, the result is increased awareness of self and others. Their deeper understanding of the psychological impact of change on people's sense of security enables them to not take resistance personally. Putting their own and others' feelings into perspective, they can acknowledge those feelings as "normal" under the circumstances, and not make them wrong or bad.

They often reframe the change(s) and their view of the people involved; where there was once only resistance, they are enabled to see possibilities for fulfilling their visions. In short, they are empowered to take action. Such a leader/change agent can effectively enhance others' sense of self-efficacy and confidence and challenge them to determine their own course of action, thus empowering them. Bass and Avolio (1990) refer to these leaders as transformational rather than transactional.

3. Knowing Your Values

Values—our judgments of right/wrong, good/bad, true/false, that we received from our families and subculture—contribute substantially to our world view. Our world view, in turn, determines our daily interactions with others and our view of change. Massey (1979) introduced the concept of four basic, differing value systems based on the particular time period in which our values were developed. Most values programming occurs before the age of 10, and it will not change unless we experience what Massey calls "a significant emotional event." Few of us take the time to carefully examine and question our values. They are such a part of us we are often unaware of their influence on our attitudes.

Differing values within a work group can present a formidable barrier to change if each person holds his or her value system, or world view, as the "right, good, and true" one. Effective change agents are not without values, but they are more keenly aware of them than most of us. They also listen for, recognize, and validate the values of others. By doing so, they create a truly safe, collaborative environment where people feel less threatened by the changes around them.

Our value systems are often ignored when we are faced with change. As a change agent, you can ill afford to ignore or discount the influence of values, your own or others. You can begin this exploration of your own values by listing all your "shoulds" about an emotional topic.

For example, your school is considering moving to year-round classes. Write the change at the top of a piece of paper. Then, as quickly as you can, complete the stems, "Schools should. . . . parents should. . . . students should. . . . teachers should. . . . I should . . . ", etc. Your value system will come forth! If you want a more in-depth look at your values and how they shape your interactions with others, consider taking a formal instrument such as, Massey's Values Analysis Profile (1985).

4. Personal Barriers and Enhancers to Change

Openness and willingness for self-examination, and a lifelong commitment toward personal mastery is critical for anyone who takes up the challenge of being a change agent. For in truth, we cannot change others, but only ourselves (Corey, 1989; Senge, 1990).

Throughout the planning and implementation process, effective change agents are committed to ongoing self-examination. They are open to and integrate information about their own and others' value systems, request feedback from those they lead, and own their strengths and weaknesses. They look for the patterns of how they typically react to change, what their thresholds are, types of changes that are perceived as most threatening to them, etc. This process helps them to understand their own thoughts, feelings, and behaviors triggered by change.

5. Environmental Barriers and Enhancers to Change

A process similar to the one above can be used to scan the outside environment for resistance and support for a particular change. What are the "shoulds," or values of the people/system involved? Have you listened for and heard their visions? What are the strengths and skills they bring to this task?

These are questions you cannot answer alone. As you move through and practice steps one through three, you will begin nurturing an environment when true team synergy can flourish. You may want to consider some team-building exercises with an external facilitator/consultant who works with team building around a shared vision. You will need a team environment in which people can openly explore and identify the barriers and the possibilities that exist in today's world to tackle the next component.

The additional component to be considered is the tangibles, such as lack of material resources, funding, etc. Essentially, the change agent asks, "What or who can get in the way of this change? What or who can contribute to this change?"

It is equally, if not more important to recognize your sources of strength and support as it is to anticipate potential problems. Again, focus is on the thoughts, feelings, and behaviors of self and others affected by the change. What often appears to be the "reality" of shrinking resources and insurmountable barriers begins to alter as you open yourself to the synergy of a committed team with a shared vision.

6. Resisting the "Change-Back" Phenomenon

One of the most overlooked factors in the change process is the human factor. Change agents are themselves quite human, and like those they would lead through change, are members of this arational system. They are subject to similar thoughts, feelings, and behaviors. They may approach their work or home environment filled with ideas for "improving" a situation.

How often have we met with apathy or resistance from those we believe will benefit most from these changes? Discouragement, disillusionment, frustration, and anger at those who do not welcome our wonderful new changes are very human feelings. Unprepared to deal with this resistance, we may eventually give up, give in, and "change back" to more familiar ways of doing things.

Effective leaders and change agents are aware of the early warning signs of the change-back phenomenon. They recognize the feelings and emotions that signal it. They are patient with themselves and others, and keep their focus on the shared vision, They continue to be open to inquiry about how their "team" can work more effectively to realize their vision. Change agents recognize conflict as a necessary and valuable ally, designed to bring into the open unforeseen barriers and possibilities.

Conclusion

Dealing with change in our personal and work lives is a daily occurrence. We don't always like it, and many of us resist it. To keep up in a changing world, we will need leaders who are change agents at every level of the system; leaders who are willing to embrace change and direct it. This requires that we understand the process of change as it applies to human systems.

References

Bass, B. M., and Avolio, B. J. *Transformational Leadership Development.* Palo Alto, Calif.: Consulting Psychologists Press, Inc., 1990.

Corey, S. *The 7 Habits of Highly Effective People.* New York: Simon & Schuster, 1989.

Faidly, R., and Musser, S. "Vision of School Leaders Must Focus on Excellence, Dispel Popular Myths." *NASSP Bulletin*, February 1989.

Laguna, J. "Managing Change and School Improvement Effectively." *NAASP Bulletin*, September 1989.

Massey, M. *The People Puzzle.* Reston, Va.: Reston Publishing Co., 1979.

———. *The Values Analysis Profile System.* Indianapolis, Ind.: Performax Systems International, Inc., 1985.

McConnell, D. "Teacher Empowerment and the Waves of Reform." *NAASP Bulletin*, December 1989.

Morgan, G. *Riding the Waves of Change.* San Francisco: Jossey-Bass, 1989.

Schein, E. *Process Consultation Volumes I and II.* Reading, Mass.: Addison-Wesley, 1987.

Senge, Peter. The Fifth Discipline. New York: Doubleday, 1990.

Wilson, B., and Burbach, H. "The Renewal Factor—Important for Success in School and Business." *NAASP Bulletin*, November 1989.

Article Review Form at end of book.

WiseGuide Wrap-Up

- Key organizational traits, including vision, excellent facilities, and sense of purpose, lead to higher levels of employee job satisfaction.

- Values and ethics are important parts of an effective leader—these include truth, integrity, competence, and compassion.

- A leader's character is also an important part of effectiveness. Character includes expertise, integrity, ambition, and moral fabric.

- Emotional intelligence and authentic leadership impact leadership effectiveness.

- Becoming a successful change agent requires specific ethics-related skills, including vision, values, empowerment, and persistence.

R.E.A.L. Sites

This list provides a print preview of typical **Coursewise** R.E.A.L. sites. There are over 100 such sites at the **Courselinks**™ site. The danger in printing URLs is that web sites can change overnight. As we went to press, these sites were functional using the URLs provided. If you come across one that isn't, please let us know via email to: webmaster@coursewise.com. Use your Passport to access the most current list of R.E.A.L. sites at the **Courselinks**™ site.

Site name: Ethical Leadership
URL: http://eric.uoregon.edu/publications/digests/digest107.html
Why is it R.E.A.L.? Real leaders concentrate on doing the right thing, not on doing things right. To be an ethical school leader, then, is not a matter of following a few simple rules. This ERIC Digest focuses on the leader's responsibility as complex, multidimensional, and rooted less in technical expertise than in simple human integrity.
Key topics: behavior, beliefs, communication, community, empowerment, ethics, honesty, motivation, trust, values, vision
Try this: Review the article and discuss ways leaders can resolve ethical dilemmas.

Site name: The Centrality of Character Education
URL: http://www.aasa.org/sa/may9801.htm
Why is it R.E.A.L.? From the journal *The School Administrator*, this article discusses the importance of character education. This web site discusses the "sacred duty" of school leaders in building a better world and future.
Key topics: beliefs, change, communication, community, culture, ethics, honesty, reform, trust, values
Try this: According to this article, what are the imperatives for character education in schools?

Site name: Test Your Ethics Quotient
URL: http://www.aasa.org/sa/oct02.htm
Why is it R.E.A.L.? This web site provides an opportunity to take a brief quiz on ethics for school leaders. Each of the realistic scenarios poses an ethical dilemma for school district administrators. This was part of a study on superintendent ethics.
Key topics: ethics, behavior, beliefs, honesty, responsibility, values
Try this: Take this test and compare your answers with those proposed by the American Association of School Administrators (AASA) Code of Ethics.

section 3

Connecting: To People and Community

WiseGuide Intro

Leaders lead. This is the very nature of the leader's role, but leadership is not conducted in a vacuum. It is not a solitary process. Leading can take place only with others. A leader, together with others, addresses interests and goals common to both. This coming together of individuals for a common purpose creates a social entity, or grouping. As a social entity, organizations are our vehicles for addressing goals and common objectives. Businesses, government agencies, community associations, clubs, and schools are all organizations that bring people together to address shared interests.

Successful leadership, therefore, requires extraordinary people skills. People *are* the organization. Enhancing one's skills in working with people is critical to aspiring and current leaders. Ancient philosophers, such as Aristotle, struggled to address key concepts of human nature, such as motivation, satisfaction, and meaningfulness. We can gain insight from these famous thinkers, as well as from other, more current researchers. Their guidance provides answers for leaders attempting to understand and work productively with others.

A knowledge of human nature includes an understanding of motivation, spirit, communication, and trust. The effects of environment, respect, and belongingness also influence individuals. A leader's understanding and intimate knowledge of these and other aspects of human nature are critical to working with individuals and leading effectively. However, working with individuals is just one aspect of the people skills required by today's leader.

All of our organizations, including schools, operate in a larger context. We are more than just individual-to-individual relationships. Our organizations include teams, divisions, departments, neighborhoods, and communities. The process of community building is also an important responsibility of leaders. From team building to networking with community agencies, leaders are continually involved in demonstrating effective human relations skills.

"Relationships rule the world," claims author Jennifer Laabs. This is true of our organizations as well. The interdependence of individuals and agencies, particularly in education, continues to grow, so the building and strengthening of relationships become even more important for today's and tomorrow's leaders. Author Martie Lubetkin shared her experience in a neighborhood collaborative and concluded, "Our experience clearly demonstrates how much caring educators, a willing community, and empowered families can achieve when they work together."

Working well with people involves understanding individual human nature and team/community building. It also involves a knowledge of the complexities of group and interagency collaborations. Pursuing the highest levels of excellence for the individual, organization, and community should be the goal of every leader.

Learning Objectives

- Identify and discuss successful human relations practices related to motivation, trust, and meaningfulness at work. Summarize various perspectives from ancient and current educational thinkers.

- Discuss the importance of trust in the development of leadership. Identify trust-builders and the warning signs of lack of trust.

- Analyze the purposes of delegation and subservient management to leadership. Describe the advantages of both for leaders and for employee development.

- Summarize the challenges and implementation strategies for community development collaborations. Cite advantages and partnering practices for successful educational improvement.

- Detail the practice, structure, and advantage of community forums for discussing important issues among citizens at the local level. List the partners who should be included in this dialogue.

- Describe the "new role" schools will play in an "ecosystem" perspective of education in the larger community. Detail the issues educators will need to consider in this type of community development.

> **Questions**
>
> **Reading 15.** What are the four points of Aristotle's insights? What is meant by Plato's statement "It's not until philosophers become kings or kings become philosophers that we're going to have a good society"?
>
> **Reading 16.** What is the difference between human and social capital? What are the "four Cs" essential for a leader to develop trust?
>
> **Reading 17.** What are some of the signs of low trust in an organization? What are the ten "trust builders"?
>
> **Reading 18.** What is subservient management? Why are some managers uncomfortable with subservient management?
>
> **Reading 19.** What was the purpose of the Hattiesburg Area Education Foundation? What did participants in the town forum indicate were benefits of the process?
>
> **Reading 20.** What is the purpose of educational community forums? What four recommendations enhance the success of educational community forums?
>
> **Reading 21.** What changes in governance will be necessary for community development? In community development, what issues will educators need to consider?
>
> **Reading 22.** Neighborhood teamwork can achieve differences for students when which partners are included? What challenges did this community partnership face and overcome?

This section focuses on developing this broad range of skills for leaders in a collection of articles ranging from the philosophical to the practical to the clinical:

In "Aristotle's Advice for Business Success," Laabs interviews business philosopher Tom Morris, who encourages the engagement of workers' hearts and souls. Morris describes Plato's perspective on leadership and human nature and recommends how today's leaders can learn from those teachings. In addition, he shares Aristotle's four insights about people and applies them to today's organizations.

Trust is one of Aristotle's four insights, and it is the focus of Kerfoot's article "Creating Trust." She describes the difference between human and social capital in an organization and the reasons that both are important. She also shares the four Cs leaders can use to develop trust.

Glaser continues the dialogue in his article "Paving the Road to TRUST." He claims that trust is the "cement that binds together all relationships." He then details the warning signs for lack of trust and the costs to leaders and organizations. His ten trust-builders support leaders' efforts to develop strong, purposeful relationships.

Broadening our perspective on people skills for leaders is the article by Davis. In "The Art of Subservient Management," Davis directs responsibility to leaders for employee needs. He describes the six attributes of subservient management and holds leaders accountable for the well-being of their employees.

Highlighting the process of collaboration is van Slyke's article "Building Community for Public Schools: Challenges and Strategies." Van Slyke describes the development and implementation of the Hattiesburg Area Education Foundation. She highlights the challenges faced by and strategies used in this collaboration between school and community. Her recommendations provide leaders with keys to successful collaborations of their own.

Continuing the discussion of community building is Jennings' article "An Experiment in Democracy." Jennings describes the use of community forums for discussing important issues among citizens at the local level.

In the article by Timpane and Reich, our perspective of school is reframed as part of a larger ecosystem. In "Revitalizing the Ecosystem for Youth: A New Perspective for School Reform," community development is discussed in the larger context of schools as a member of the ecosystem, not necessarily the leading organization.

This section concludes with Lubetkin's article "How Teamwork Transformed a Neighborhood." This case study perspective provides readers with applications found throughout this section. It describes the positive differences teamwork can make when all partners are included.

What are the four points of Aristotle's insights? What is meant by Plato's statement "It's not until philosophers become kings or kings become philosophers that we're going to have a good society"?

Aristotle's Advice for Business Success

(Interview with business philosopher Tom Morris)

Engaging workers' hearts and souls, not just their minds, will be the next catalyst for success in business.

Jennifer J. Laabs

Jennifer J. Laabs is the associate managing editor at WORKFORCE. E-mail laabsj@workforcemag.com to comment.

Tom Morris is a modern-day business philosopher. A former professor of philosophy at Notre Dame for 15 years, Morris is now Chairman of the Morris Institute for Human Values in Wilmington, North Carolina, and author of *If Aristotle Ran General Motors: The New Soul of Business*, which was just published by Henry Holt and Company, New York, last month. Here, in an exclusive interview, Morris discusses such time-tested ideas as truth, beauty, goodness and unity, and why HR professionals, and the workforces they serve, can benefit by tapping the wisdom of the ages.

Q: Although the ideas in your book also come from the teachings of other ancient philosophers from Greece, Rome and China, why do you focus on Aristotle?

A: Well, I started off surveying all the ancient thinkers and all the great philosophers throughout the centuries looking for the most powerful wisdom I could find to apply to modern-day business. Over and over again, I kept coming back to Aristotle, the person who had the most powerful perspective on any given issue. For example, what really motivates human beings? Many of the great thinkers had a lot of insightful things to say, but it was always Aristotle who seemed to really hit the nail on the head. Then, when I was thinking about what really holds an organization together and how people in an organization should view what they're doing together, it was Aristotle, again, who had the key that unlocked the door to all kinds of powerful insights. Aristotle gives us the way to make the next step forward in our understanding of organizations, of motivation, and those kinds of things.

"Aristotle's Advice for Business Success" by Jennifer J. Laabs, copyright October 1997. Used with permission of ACC Communications Inc./*Workforce*, Costa Mesa, CA. All rights reserved.

Q: What was the practical advice Aristotle proposed in his day that applies to us now in business?

A: Aristotle helps us to understand human motivation: that human beings are searching for happiness in everything they do—in their private lives, in their family lives and in their work lives. Aristotle helps us understand, at a deeper level, what that's all about. If business managers can understand what motivates people, they can understand the leverage points in their workers' personalities for helping them attain the highest levels of excellence along with the greatest levels of satisfaction. Too often in modern work, those two things come apart. People are being driven to higher levels of excellence, but it's being attained at the expense of their satisfaction. They feel nothing but stress and pressure. They're disgruntled. Aristotle helps us, as business people, understand human nature so we can see how to build higher levels of excellence on a foundation of happiness and satisfaction, so people feel good about what they're doing in the long run and, thereby, can sustain the kind of excellence businesses hope to achieve.

Q: In your book, your first point is truth. How does truth fit into the business picture?

A: We're hearing a lot nowadays about businesses being "information societies" and "learning organizations." People appreciate the importance of ideas. But so many organizations are almost desert landscapes when it comes to people telling each other the truth, the whole truth, and nothing but the truth. Because of organizational politics, people fear open candor about the problems they're facing and what really needs to be done. But human beings need truth just like they need air, water and food. It's that important. I give lots of examples in the book about how truthfulness, truth-telling in the right way, always strengthens an organization. I show places where it has worked beautifully and try to show how to avoid misusing truth-telling because sometimes it can be a harmful exercise if people are uttering brutal truths in an uncaring and unfeeling way. So I help people understand the importance of truth in organizations and how they can inject more truth into the workplace.

Q: Do you think modern businesses have been withholding truth?

A: Yes, I do. And it's based on a misunderstanding of a famous insight from philosopher Francis Bacon centuries ago. Bacon said, "Knowledge is power." And a lot of people in modern business concluded from that, "If you want power, hoard knowledge." They think that if you give away knowledge, you give away power. They don't understand there are some things in human life (like love and knowledge) that when they're shared, they're actually multiplied: To share truth in the right way multiplies truth and strengthens the organization as a result. In the book, I show how that works.

Q: How does Aristotle's second point, beauty, fit into the business arena?

A: Beauty is seen in the workplace on many different levels: cleaning up a factory, repainting a facility, beautifying a place where people work. Hospitals discovered a long time ago that if you hang beautiful paintings in recovery rooms and if you paint the walls a nicer color, people physically recover from surgery faster. The same thing holds true in the workplace. If people have more pleasant surroundings to work in they're going to feel better about their workplace; they're going to enjoy being there, and they'll work at higher levels. So I talk about that sort of beauty at work. But I also talk about other levels of beauty: performance beauty, for example, delighting a customer, delighting an associate, empowering people to create beautiful solutions to business problems. Nobody wants to feel like a robot. People essentially are creative beings. HR professionals need to turn people loose to be artists, to be creators. There will always be constraints, but if they can help people feel that kind of beauty in their work, they will be helping employees achieve greater satisfaction.

Q: How does the third point, goodness, fit in?

A: Thoreau once said goodness is the only investment that never fails. Goodness is the power behind business ethics, and I'm talking about the deepest perspective on ethics there is. Ethics isn't about staying out of trouble. Ethics is about creating strength. A nice side effect typically is staying out of trouble. But goodness is about something positive. That was the perspective of the ancient Greek and Roman philosophers. They believed goodness is a foundation for long-term excellence. So if you have an organization in which people feel they're treated fairly with kindness and respect, that's going to be a stronger organiza-

76 Educational Leadership

tion. We hear so much about how loyalty has been lost in the business world in the last few decades. Goodness brings loyalty back into the equation. Goodness makes a huge difference in both little and big issues.

Q: What about the fourth point, unity? How does unity help workers?

A: Unity is the target of what I call the spiritual dimension of human experience. Everybody wants to feel part of something greater than themselves. They want to feel like they belong, that they're making their contribution in the world along with other people. So I talk about the different spiritual needs everyone has that have been too neglected in the workplace in the last few decades. And I'm not talking about institutionally religious things. I'm just talking about deep, psychological and spiritual needs that all people have: to feel special, to feel important, to feel like they belong, to feel they're useful, to feel like the deepest parts of themselves are being called into play in their work. People don't just show up at work to make money. They want to make a difference. So the fourth part of the book is all about unity and connectiveness.

This fourth foundation of human excellence helps make the workplace a place of meaningfulness for people. As business managers explore the spiritual dimension of human experience, they're exploring an important and powerful leverage point for excellence in any organization that's been unduly neglected. For such a long time, business leaders have just talked about quantifiable stuff, as if these other issues are the soft issues. But what company managers are working with here are soft beings, human beings. These issues end up being the most important issues for a company's sustainable success, I think.

Q: How can human resources professionals begin to influence work processes and people in the workforce with these four points?

A: First of all, they've got to expose people to these four points. Then train people on them. These really are the simplest ideas in the world, but they're also the most powerful ideas in the world. But sometimes people miss the simplest things. William of Ockham, a medieval philosopher, always said, "Simplify, simplify. Find the essential core of any situation. Learn to concentrate on that, and all the complications will fall into place." Too often human resources managers try to institute all these different kinds of training programs that focus on how to do this and that. A philosopher is concerned with the whys. If you don't understand the whys, you won't ever get the hows right. For example, if Hewlett-Packard or Toyota do certain things, many managers at other companies think they should do likewise. But, the ancient philosophers always said, "Know thyself." Companies should make alterations that fit their organizations. So first of all, everybody should be exposed to the deep roots of excellence in human nature, the universal human nature that we all share. What are those leverage points in human nature for making sure people do their best and feel their best about what they're doing? That's what the great philosophers bring to us. So, HR people could start injecting some of these big-picture perspectives into their training and then talk about how these ideas mesh into people's lives. HR people need to realize that new gimmicks come down the pike every month, but what they've got to do is get their bearings with some of the most fundamental ideas that have never changed.

Q: How can American businesses regain the lost hearts and souls of their workers through either Aristotle's plan or your plan?

A: Business executives have thought about numbers more than they've thought about people. Of course, they've got to have sustainable, profitable businesses. But they've also got to remember that with all the emphasis on product quality and on process efficiency, if they lose sight of the spirit of the people who do the work, they lose everything. It's the spirit of the people who do the work that's the core of any sustainable enterprise. By losing sight of that, modern American business has drifted so much so that people are instituting all these policy changes, such as process changes, reengineering and downsizing. Yet, managers are saying, "Why isn't it working the way it was supposed to?" So much of modern business thinking is process-oriented rather than people-oriented. But ultimately, it's the people who are the key to success. Relationships rule the world. And if [managers] ignore relationships for the sake of abstract, quantitatively measured process improvement, they're barking up the wrong tree. The science of business has to do with the philosophy of human nature, ultimately. In his famous book *The Republic,* Plato once said, "It's not until philosophers become kings or kings become philosophers that we're going to have a good society." He believed the people in charge better understand human nature. Yet, that's not what business schools train future leaders in.

Per Morris' words, maybe it's time to return to the ABCs of human nature so companies can lead from a humanistic vantage point. Fortunately, Aristotle and Morris give professionals a good place to start.

Article Review Form at end of book.

READING 16

What is the difference between human and social capital? What are the "four Cs" essential for a leader to develop trust?

Creating Trust

Karlene Kerfoot

Karlene Kerfoot, PhD, RN, CNAA, FAAN, is Internal Consultant, Memorial Hermann Healthcare System, Houston, TX.

One important criterion for success in your organization is the level of trust you create as a leader. Trust leads to social/professional collaboration, which is the key to producing excellent clinical outcomes in an organization. The level of trust is the foundation upon which financial and quality success can be built. Some leaders can create trust in an organization and others cannot. We know that people are happier working in collegial organizations than in competitive and individualistic ones. Organizations and units that can create trust among their members can create a high-performing, synergistic environment that will produce exceptional patient care outcomes.

To get the work of the organization done, we depend on human capital and also social capital. Traditionally, we have thought of capital as the tools, equipment, and buildings required to do the work. However, we are now recognizing that the human side of the enterprise is much more important in determining the outcome of the unit and/or organization. In health care, human capital has always been extremely important, but managing the human side of the organization has not always been done in the most humane way. Human capital is a term used to define the level of knowledge and expertise of the workforce. Social capital by contrast involves the staff's ability to associate with each other and to work together. This ability is totally dependent on the prevalence of trust in the unit/organization. According to Fukuyama (1995), the concept of trust can be defined as "the expectation that arises within a community of regular, honest, and cooperative behavior, based on commonly shared norms, on the part of other members of that community (p. 27)." Fukuyama also makes the point that hierarchies are necessary because not everyone can be relied on at all times to live by ethical rules alone.

How then does the leader create trust? The authors of *Learning to Lead* (1994) note that trust is the essential quality that creates a following. It is the secret of leaders who are able to inspire movements that create great social change and successful organizations that achieve their vision. According to Bennis and Townsend (1995), the "four Cs" are essential characteristics of the leader who will develop trust in the organization. The leader must be congruent, consistent, caring, and competent. When these four states are in place, the interaction between the leader and the led is the ". . . sweeping back and forth of energy" (p. 62) that creates a team. Bennis and Goldsmith (1994) also note four characteristics of leaders who can establish trust: vision, empathy, consistency, and integrity. These authors also write that leaders generate and sustain trust by acting in ways that produce constancy, congruity, reliability, and integrity. Social capital is created out of the interplay of these factors and creates organizations with a high level of positive interactions and relationships. This produces high performance and morale.

These concepts are all very important and deserve a great deal of consideration by themselves. But how do you make all this happen? What kind of leader

---

Kerfoot, K. (1998). Creating Trust. *Nursing Economic$*, 16(1), 48–49. Reprinted with permission of the publisher, Jannetti Publications, Inc., East Holly Avenue, Box 56, Pitman, NJ 08071–0056; Phone (609) 589-7463. (For a sample issue of the journal, contact the publisher.)

behaviors are needed to demonstrate to others that you abide by these concepts? Unfortunately, leaders can demonstrate the characteristics listed above. But unless people can experience you practicing these behaviors, they won't know you as a trustworthy leader.

Availability and Accessibility

The first leader behavior to consider is your availability and accessibility. You can religiously abide by the characteristics just mentioned, but if people can't experience you in action living out these concepts, they won't know what kind of person you are. You must manage your schedule to be accessible, so people will have the opportunity to test you and learn that you are a person who can engender trust.

To be perceived as accessible, people must see and talk with you. That can take the form of regular rounds where you personally communicate with people. And it can also be accomplished by structured time with staff such as regularly scheduled brown-bag lunches and coffees where people work or in your office. If you manage a 24-hour unit, your visibility on the off-shifts must be there also. How can you manage something with which you do not have first-hand experience? Being available also means that you are reachable in the off hours when people are in need. And yes, this means giving out your home number and saying that you are available if the need arises.

Just being around people who report to you is not sufficient. People should feel comfortable and at ease when talking with you. Listening and hearing what people are saying to you is a science and an art. After one has been in a management/leadership position for awhile, it becomes easy to anticipate what people are going to say and to immediately jump in and start to provide solutions. This doesn't work. Instead, one should approach listening as an opportunity to learn appreciation for a totally different perspective and a cultural perspective of the organization that is different than yours as a manager/leader.

When you are the leader of a larger organization or have a large span of control, it is imperative that a communication plan is devised so that people feel they are in touch even though you might be geographically separated or unable to personally touch people often. A newsletter with personal notes from you, e-mail, and voice mail are all ways of personally being in touch. For example, one executive invited people to e-mail him with suggestions. He read these messages every night and sent back a reply. Although many people do not have e-mail access at work, many do with their home computers and they can connect with their leader from their home.

Communicate with Candor

The second behavior to consider is your ability to communicate with candor. This involves talking about ourselves with frankness. At times our actions may appear to lack integrity. However, discussing the event with openness and disclosing your motives and rationale will be much more helpful than avoiding the issue, and/or appearing defensive. You build confidence and trust when you disclose the thinking process that went into your decision versus an approach that dogmatically just states you did it with no rationale. Candor does not require full disclosure. But it does demand that you provide the rationale for why you cannot discuss the particular issue. For example, employment issues or information about mergers could be off limits to open discussion. But people need to be reminded and told why that is the case rather than to just be brushed aside with an autocratic statement about it being none of their business. Storytelling is a great vehicle to disclose your thoughts and actions and a superb way to build relationships. Candor involves the willingness to share as much information as possible and the willingness to volunteer information. Leaders who are not open do not generate trust. And leaders who cannot dialogue in an open manner do not win the trust and approval of their people.

Willingness to Invest

Bower (1997) points out that respect and trust are only the price of admission for a leader. In his view, the leader must demonstrate a real willingness to invest in the development of junior people and to show a genuine concern for junior people as human beings. Leaders and managers who are viewed as always putting themselves and the company first over the needs of their followers will not be viewed as trustworthy although they meet all the previously mentioned criteria such as honesty and predictability. When the frontline people are treated like paper towels, to be used up and thrown away, the leader will suffer from a lack of followers because this leader will be perceived as not willing to invest in people who get the work done. This is a common complaint among nurses in the last few years; they are seen as disposable widgets rather than contributing people who are hungry for development and growth. Leaders who create trust have the ability to reach out with empathy, to listen, but in a manner that says they are truly interested in their staff.

Summary

We can list the characteristics of trustworthiness in leaders much as we have just done. But unless leaders know how to communicate and demonstrate how they actualize these traits in daily life, they will fail. Trustworthy people can be perceived as not to be trusted by failing to address their availability and accessibility, ability to operate with candor, and by not demonstrating a real willingness to invest in the development of junior staff.

References

Bennis, W., & Goldsmith, J. (1994). *Learning to lead.* Reading, MA: Addison Wesley.

Bennis, W., & Townsend, R. (1995). *Reinventing leadership.* New York: William Morrow & Co.

Bower, M. (1997). *The will to lead.* Boston: Harvard Business School Press.

Fukuyama, F. (1995). *Trust.* New York: Free Press Paperbacks.

Article Review Form at end of book.

What are some of the signs of low trust in an organization? What are the ten "trust builders"?

Paving the Road to TRUST

Robert Glaser

Robert Glaser, an associate with Blanchard Training and Development, San Diego, is responsible for the design of training programs.

Trust and leadership. In successful organizations, the two go hand in hand. Too often, however, managers and leaders toss around the idea of trust without having a clear understanding of its meaning, its importance in relationships and its impact on the long-term success of an organization.

From Abstract to Concrete

Trust is not merely an abstract concept. It is the cement that binds together all relationships and provides the foundation from which society operates, leadership flourishes and changes occur.

Trust is vital within an organization because leadership cannot exist without some level of trust. In order to influence one another or be influenced, there must be a belief by both parties that the other is trustworthy and credible.

The Waning of Trust

Mergers and downsizing—whether they are ongoing, rumored or anticipated—continue to erode the trust of employees at all levels within an organization. Low levels of trust adversely affect relationships, stifle innovation and risk taking, and hamper the decision-making process. Employees in organizations marked by a decrease in trust usually operate under higher levels of stress, constantly looking over their shoulders, justifying their decisions and searching for scapegoats when things go awry. This prevents them from focusing on the fundamental problems of the organization that need to be addressed if the organization is to remain competitive.

The slide into low levels of trust does not happen overnight. Here are some of the warning signs:

- High turnover, especially the loss of talented personnel;
- Active rumor mill;
- Low productivity; and
- Increased absenteeism.

Companies must heed these warnings and ensure that management does more than simply talk about trust—it must put trust at the core of every relationship, communication and decision.

Trust Builders

While enhanced levels of trust may not always be needed for routine work, it is essential when leaders are trying to achieve significant goals.

Here are 10 ways leaders can earn the trust of their followers.

1. Narrow the gap between your intentions and your behavior. The road to trusting relationships is filled with good intentions, but if the behavior does not match, good intentions mean little. Practice what you preach, and set the example.

2. Declare your intentions to others and invite feedback from them regarding your progress or performance. We all have distorted perceptions about how others see us and judge our actions. Feedback is critical if we are to learn to behave in more consistent and trusting ways.

Reprinted from HRFOCUS, January 1997. Copyright © 1997 American Management Association International. Reprinted by permission of American Management Association International, New York, NY. All rights reserved. http://www.amanet.org.

3. When things go wrong and problems arise, look for solutions—not people to blame. It is very tempting to point the fingers at others. Instead, look inward to determine if you could have contributed to the problem. See problems as learning opportunities.

4. Keep confidential information confidential. If an employee learns that you have revealed a personal matter to someone else, trust will be lost forever.

5. Let others know what you stand for, what you value and what you wish for. This allows others to know you and creates an environment of openness.

6. Make it safe for others to be with you and share with you. Listen carefully, be nonjudgmental and offer feedback only when it is wanted and requested.

7. Demonstrate competence and commitment in your professional position. Be seen as the person who has something of value to contribute and has a successful track record of performance as a leader and team player.

8. Maintain a high level of integrity. Be honest and keep your personal and professional commitments to others. Build a reputation of "doing the right thing" regardless of the political consequences.

9. Know yourself! Be clear about what you value, your biases and how your personality type may be perceived by others.

10. Build credibility with others by being consistent, delivering on your promises and building a track record of reliability.

Like a plant, trust must be nurtured before it can be harvested. While trust is established through many small interactions over time, it can also be destroyed in an instant and lost forever.

Article Review Form at end of book.

What is subservient management? Why are some managers uncomfortable with subservient management?

The Art of Subservient Management

Thom Davis

Thom Davis is proprietor of Thomas P. Davis & Associates, a quality-assurance and regulatory compliance consulting firm. He is an AMA individual member and can be reached via e-mail at tpdavis@community.net. Visit his Web page at www.community.net/~tpdavis.

Once upon a time, a miller used a wheel-shaped grindstone to turn grain into flour on a flat millstone. A beast pulled the grindstone, traveling in a circle around the mill. The miller noticed that when grain was thrown onto the mill, some of it scattered on the path of the beast, which would end up eating it. Looking to improve his profitability, the miller decided to bind the beast's mouth. At first, he had to beat the beast more often to make it produce. But the beast eventually went slower despite this treatment. Finally, the beast died and the miller was forced to tie himself to the grindstone.

Most often, this story is synopsized as "do not bind the mouths of the kind that tread the grain." The meaning is clear: Don't kill the source of your livelihood.

There is, however, a deeper meaning to this story that is applicable to management in the 21st century. When you are in a position to benefit from another's labor, you have a responsibility to meet that person's needs. In other words, you must assume the role of a "subservient manager."

Many managers are uncomfortable with the concept of subservient management. With this approach, one of a manager's key responsibilities is to provide the best rewards available to employees, ensuring that their pay, vacation, perks, training and so on are commensurate with performance. In discussing these concepts over the years with "dictatorial managers" (nonsubservient managers), the arguments against this management style appear to be derived from attitudes.

Dictatorial managers say, "I don't work for them; they work for me." These managers can get the identical results as subservient managers in any given management situation. In many cases, the immediate success or failure of either type of manager is more a matter of dealing with specific circumstances and operational problems. As in the case of the miller, however, more threats and firings eventually decrease production.

Which Type of Manager Are You?

When an employee asks for guidance, do you give him or her your complete attention (that is, does the employee's need for guidance or your work come first)? Is your attitude during performance reviews one that aims to provide the best possible compensation for your employees, including any necessary training, given acceptable performance? Are the reviews timely? Are you willing to fight your boss for improvements in your employees' compensation packages? Do you ask for help from your staff rather than give orders?

If all of your employees were asked to anonymously assess whether you have the following

---

Reprinted from *Management Review*, May 1998 © 1998. American Management Association International. Reprinted by permission of American Management Association International, New York, NY. All rights reserved. http://www.amanet.org.

attributes, would they respond "yes"? Approachability, good communication skills, integrity, honesty, fairness and compassion. Unless you yourself can answer an emphatic "yes" to all the questions posed above, you have dictatorial manager tendencies.

The good news is, you can change. The difference between dictatorial managers and subservient managers is a matter of attitude, and people can change their attitudes by changing their behaviors. To achieve that goal, make a conscious effort to exhibit the behaviors identified in the questions above. Depending on how frequently you exhibit these behaviors, you will soon become a worldclass manager of the 21st century.

Article Review Form at end of book.

What was the purpose of the Hattiesburg Area Education Foundation? What did participants in the town forum indicate were benefits of the process?

Building Community for Public Schools

Challenges and strategies

Ms. van Slyke describes the reasons for and the outcomes of Hattiesburg's participation in the national demonstration project "Public Conversations About the Public's Schools."

Sue van Slyke

Sue van Slyke is executive director of the Hattiesburg (Miss.) Area Education Foundation.

Positioned in the heart of south Mississippi's rolling piney woods, Hattiesburg provides a unique blend of affordability and a high standard of living for nearly 50,000 residents. Hattiesburg is the educational, retail, and medical center for more than a quarter of a million people who live throughout southeastern Mississippi and is home to the University of Southern Mississippi, William Carey College, and Camp Shelby, the largest National Guard training facility in the U.S. Known as the "Hub City," Hattiesburg is located within 100 miles of the state capital, Jackson; the Gulf Coast; New Orleans; and Mobile. The growing micropolitan area that includes Hattiesburg, Forrest County, and neighboring Lamar County was designated a Metropolitan Statistical Area in 1994, with a combined population of more than 100,000 residents. During recent years, Hattiesburg has been honored nationally in a number of different ways:

- ranked number one in health care and desirability by G. Scott Thomas, author of the Rating Guide to Life in America's Small Cities (1990);

- received "1992 City Livability Award" for cities with populations under 100,000, awarded by the National Conference of Mayors;

- cited for two years as one of the 10 most popular destinations for Americans relocating to small cities, according to the Ryder Relocation Report (1994–95); and

- named as Mississippi's first certified retirement community (1995).

Continued economic expansion during the past few years has made Hattiesburg one of the most dynamic and fastest growing areas in the southeast. From its economic beginnings in the timber industry of the late 1800s to the prosperous growth of the 1990s, Hattiesburg stands ready to move into the 21st century as a progressive, economically healthy community that nurtures a quality of life second to none.

With all its successes, Hattiesburg is divided by the fault lines that plague many cities of similar size, especially in the South—but here, these divisions

"Building Community for Public Schools: Challenges and Strategies" by Sue van Slyke. Copyright © 1997. Reprinted with permission from Phi Delta Kappan and the author.

are often obscured by the area's attractiveness. Differences of race, class, and politics tend to go unresolved and become barriers to addressing important issues and solving community problems. In addition to the divisions typically found in other cities, the greater Hattiesburg area is served by five school districts, each characterized not only by distinct demographics but also by different priorities and leadership.

Two of these districts have recently engaged in strategic planning, involving significant numbers of constituents from distinct geographic segments of the community. Opportunities for constituents from all five districts to come together to discuss issues important to education in the entire community have been rare, and they have been related only to specific projects or activities. There has been little discussion about a communitywide vision for public education that can be understood and supported by all stakeholders.

The Hattiesburg Area Educational Foundation (HAEF), a local education fund that has attempted to serve the educational interests of the community since 1988,[1] recently undertook an evaluation that looked not only at its own organizational effectiveness but also at contextual issues that are part of the educational, social, and demographic climates in which it works.[2] Through interviews with community leaders and focus group discussions with parents, teachers, and employers, the evaluation identified the following issues as barriers to HAEF's work:

- **A multidistrict environment.** HAEF attempts to meet the needs of disparate school districts. There is no apparent forum through which parents, students, educators, or employers can come together across district lines to discuss issues important to education for all children in the community. Indeed, for many participants, the discussions among parents, educators, and employers that were initiated during the evaluation were their first experience at talking to their counterparts from other districts.

- **Business ambivalence about public education.** The Hattiesburg area has been remarkably successful in attracting economic enterprise at a time when competition for it is fierce. Yet significant business leaders do not appear to see public education as crucial to near-term economic development or to enhanced quality of life. Frustrated by a perceived failure of the local schools to prepare students adequately for the work force, coupled with their own inability to engage in meaningful dialogue about these issues with local educators, members of the organized business community have focused on other means of economic development.

- **White flight.** As in many southern communities, a result of years of litigation and resistance to desegregation in Hattiesburg was substantial white flight from the city's public schools. Within a few years after the final desegregation of the city's schools, the Hattiesburg School District had lost approximately 25% of its white student population. As whites deserted the city for surrounding areas, they left behind a population that was not only increasingly black but also significantly less well-off. An outgrowth of this situation is that there does not seem to be a place where whites and blacks come together to discuss and deal with important community issues.

- **An apparent lack of commitment to the public schools by a significant number of affluent whites.** Communitywide, there seems to be no sense of urgency about public education's important role in community development and economic growth or its centrality to a democratic and civil society. Concerned more about their own children's day-to-day educational experiences and achievement levels than about these philosophical issues and finding no forum for addressing their concerns, many white parents have opted to leave the system. The apathy about public education may be due, at least in part, to the fact that the schools, in spite of contentious social and demographic conditions, are doing so well. Things just haven't been "bad enough" to stimulate change. Local school districts, surpassing others statewide, consistently boast high numbers of National Merit semifinalists, millions of dollars in scholarships, and national recognition for many of their programs. Indeed, of the five teachers in the state certified by the National Board for Professional Teaching Standards, three come from the Hattiesburg district.

Like many other local education foundations in the South, HAEF was begun in the late 1980s amid the dislocation that followed efforts to desegregate the public schools.

Leaders in the business community—fearing disinvestment in public schools by a significant population, continued abandonment of the city by whites, and eventually a depressed economy—created HAEF with the hope of encouraging people to remain supportive of the schools. With pledges of support and genuine concern about the quality of public education, but with no real consensus about specific goals or strategies for realizing them, business leaders connected to the Chamber of Commerce initially made up the board of directors of HAEF and provided the bulk of financial support for its operations.

In its early years, HAEF focused on such traditional projects for local foundations as making grants to teachers to support innovative classroom instruction (awarding approximately $200,000 to 160 teachers since 1988), coordinating activities of the Adopt-a-School Advisory Committee, developing and implementing teacher workshops on grant writing and student assessment, and developing a collaborative writing improvement project for area teachers and students. Although the organization was successful in achieving the goals and objectives established for these projects, questions remain about their connection to needed systemic change in public education and their contribution to any real educational improvement.

In recent years, motivated by the need to raise additional funds and by pressure from its constituencies to spur systemic change, HAEF has become involved in education reform issues.

A grant from the BellSouth Foundation in 1994 enabled HAEF to conduct a community-planning initiative to develop a long-range plan to improve school readiness among area children. This initiative led to the establishment of a Family Resource Center, located in a major shopping mall in the heart of the city, which has received additional funding from the BellSouth and Mississippi Power Foundations and has engaged significant numbers of people in programs to support early childhood development.

In 1995 HAEF brought together school board members from the five school districts to discuss the feasibility of participating in a national demonstration project, "Public Conversations About the Public's Schools." The purpose of the project, co-sponsored by the Institute for Educational Leadership (IEL) and Public Agenda, was to demonstrate, through a series of town meetings in diverse communities throughout the U.S., effective communication processes to engage the public in dialogue about issues important to public education.

The discussion that began with those school board members was itself a significant step in the direction of effective dialogue across school district lines and, according to IEL's Jacqueline Danzberger, one of the reasons for Hattiesburg's selection as one of eight cities in the U.S. to host the town meetings. In fact, Hattiesburg was the only site chosen with multiple school districts.

The town meeting, held on 21 November 1996, brought together 120 stakeholders of public education—parents, teachers, students, school board members, district administrators, and employers—from all segments of the population and from each of the five school districts to discuss "the purpose of public schools" and "teaching methods." In a questionnaire completed at the end of the meeting, attendees listed "openness of the dialogue" and "hearing different viewpoints and opinions" as what they liked most about the town meeting. When asked what other issues needed to be dealt with in Hattiesburg, participants listed "parent involvement" and "discipline" as their top choices. Asked how the town meeting compared to other experiences in terms of improving their understanding of an educational issue, 62 participants rated it as "better" than other experiences, including school board and other community meetings. Eighty-four participants asked to receive the results of the questionnaire, and 67 indicated a desire to help plan follow-up activities.

With the knowledge gained from its evaluation and from the town meeting, HAEF is poised to bring together representatives from all segments of the community to discuss what changes in the education system and in the community's understanding and attitudes will be necessary to truly support educational excellence. Currently engaged in the development of a strategic plan that will guide the organization's programs and activities for the next three to five years, HAEF is focusing on a theme of readiness—readiness to learn, readiness to work, and readiness of the community at large to support educational excellence.

Facilitating dialogue between parents and teachers about what is important to learn and about ways to support and equitably measure student learning and achievement are central to the plan. Just as significant will be the dialogue between educators and employers about the nurturing and development of skills and attitudes that local graduates must have to succeed in today's work force. Only after such issues are addressed by both groups through meaningful dialogue will the community support and resources needed to ensure success be forthcoming.

Supporting the development of HAEF's strategic plan, which has a target date of August 1997, are the Phil Hardin Foundation (Meridian, Mississippi), the Mary Reynolds Babcock Foundation (Winston-Salem, North Carolina), the Hattiesburg Area Development Partnership, and local school entities in the greater Hattiesburg area.

In a recent issue of Kappan, Gary Henry discussed "community accountability" and the importance of using accurate and understandable information to inform those with a stake in public education not only about the performance of schools and school systems, but also about the community characteristics that affect the difficulty of the educational task. A necessary ingredient for community accountability, according to Henry, is "widespread reporting of performance information that can stimulate enlightened action both inside and outside the education system."[3]

HAEF and other local education funds are well-positioned to stimulate community accountability by collecting and disseminating information about school and community performance, best practices for improving education, and ways citizens can become involved in educational improvement. HAEF recognizes the need to develop a systematic approach for addressing these issues. Currently engaged in strategic planning, it has demonstrated the will and sensibility to connect important educational issues to the perceived needs of the community in order to promote widespread citizen involvement in education reform.

1. HAEF is a member of the Public Education Network (PEN), a national nonprofit association of 47 local education funds in 26 states and the District of Columbia. PEN's mission is to enhance education for all children, especially those who are disadvantaged.
2. HAEF's evaluation report, funded by the Ford Foundation in a grant administered by the Public Education Network, was written by Robert A. Kronley, consultant.
3. Gary T. Henry, "Community Accountability: A Theory of Information, Accountability, and School Improvement," *Phi Delta Kappan*, September 1996.

Article Review Form at end of book.

What is the purpose of educational community forums? What four recommendations enhance the success of educational community forums?

An Experiment in Democracy

Distrust is a very strong element in our society and is influencing our debates on national issues, such as the effectiveness of public education, Mr. Jennings points out. But distrust of and disappointment with the schools are just problems, not immutable conditions, and therefore they can be changed.

John F. Jennings

John F. (Jack) Jennings is director of the Center on Education Policy, Washington, D.C.

Every generation coming of age since the 1950s has been less trusting than the previous one. Furthermore, the most distrustful members of society today are the youngest—those 18 to 23 years of age. These are the sobering results of 31 years of polling data, analyzed by Harvard University, the Henry J. Kaiser Foundation, and the *Washington Post* and published on 28 January 1996. These data help to explain why our public debates are so harsh. To a large degree, we do not believe that others can be trusted to do the right thing.

We can posit many reasons for this situation—from the growing influence of television to the waning feeling of national solidarity after the successful conclusion of the Second World War. Regardless of reason, the important factor is that distrust is a very strong element in our society and is influencing our debates on national issues, such as the effectiveness of public education.

In this special section of the *Kappan*, David Matthews of the Kettering Foundation writes about how the public is "halfway out of the schoolhouse door" in its support for public schools. Deborah Wadsworth explains Public Agenda's assertion that support for the institution of public education is "fragile and porous." In last September's *Kappan* I laid out my own impressions—based on my travels—about the reasons that the public doubts the effectiveness of the public schools.

Great mistrust in society, which leads to inaccurate assumptions, and the perceived shakiness of support for public education were two major—and interrelated—reasons why the Center on Education Policy (CEP) produced two booklets, *Do We Still Need the Public Schools?* and *The Good—and the Not-So-Good News About American Schools*. Phi Delta Kappa printed these publications and distributed them widely last year and is continuing to do so. Our purpose is to remind people of why the U.S. developed public schools and to lay out the facts on the successes and failures of those schools.

The appearance of these booklets led Phi Delta Kappa to suggest a series of local forums on public education to explore the issues as framed in the publications. Lowell Rose, executive director emeritus of Phi Delta Kappa, was put in charge of the forums by the board of directors and by Ron Joekel, executive director. During the course of preparations, the National PTA expressed interest in co-sponsoring the forums, an offer that Phi Delta Kappa eagerly accepted. Lowell Rose's article in this *Kappan* special section explains the organizational aspects of the forums, and Shirley Igo of the PTA articulates in her article the reasons for the PTA's involvement.

"An Experiment in Democracy" by John F. Jennings. © 1997 Phi Delta Kappan. Reprinted with permission.

The basic assumption of the forums is that important issues must be discussed among citizens at the local level. If our democracy is to function, we must dispel distrust among ourselves by talking to one another face to face. National public service advertisements, television programs on important topics, and demonstrations in state capitals are useful, but there is something especially meaningful about people sitting down and talking one-on-one or in small groups about such fundamental issues as why the country developed the public schools, how effective or ineffective they are, and what can be done to make them more effective.

A central requirement of these discussions is that people representing all major points of view in the community must be invited to participate. Homeschoolers, conservative religious critics of the public schools, and private school advocates must be included, along with businesspeople and representatives of community organizations and of ethnic and racial minorities. Teachers, principals, superintendents, and school board members must also be invited, but—if at all possible—people directly involved in the public schools should not make up the majority of participants.

Getting members of society who are not associated with the public schools to attend these local forums has been one of the hardest aims to achieve. The local organizers have frequently spent hours and hours trying to entice and cajole these people to come to the meetings, often with modest success. However, the most successful forums have been the ones in which all points of view were represented and educators were not in the majority.

I would speculate that a major reason why individuals not directly connected with the public schools were hard to attract was the pervasive mistrust that I mentioned above. Some people may have thought that any meeting about public schools sponsored by an educators' group—Phi Delta Kappa—and by the National PTA would be an attempt to persuade them of the need for the public schools and not an honest effort to have a full and open discussion of the issues. I also detected a reciprocal wariness on the part of educators toward those not connected with the schools. They seemed to fear that those people would be too critical of the schools and would not understand enough about the problems educators face. If my speculations are correct, these mutual misunderstandings reinforce the need to have such meetings, in which all points of view are represented. If we truly want a more trusting society, we must meet face to face and talk through our problems.

The National PTA, Phi Delta Kappa, and the Center on Education Policy are all advocates for the public schools, but we all recognize that those schools must be better than they currently are. The first step toward improvement is to agree on why public schools were created and on the facts about their successes and failures. Only then can we try to achieve agreement on how to bring about a better education for children in those schools. Support for public education must be rebuilt community by community, just as public education must be improved school by school while working at the same time to improve the overall system. That is difficult work, but the fruit of this labor is that you achieve lasting change.

I was the moderator at five of the 30 forums and have discussed the other forums with many others who participated. These are the recommendations I would make for future forums, based on those experiences.

First, most people enjoyed the exchange of views and the effort to reach agreement on these issues. It seems that there are very few opportunities today for people with varying points of view to sit down on relatively neutral turf to discuss important issues. Therefore, I conclude that the general idea is on target.

Second, the basic format of roughly three hours of discussion on three questions (an hour apiece) with people sitting at tables of eight to 10 per table is a very good way to structure the meetings. There are many ways to stimulate the conversations, such as using a participant poll and comparing the results to a national poll or using a film explaining why public schools were created. These devices are optional and worked better in some situations than in others. The important point is that the general structure of face-to-face conversations for roughly three hours seems to work. It is best to have few or no presentations by speakers because that allows time for people to talk to one another.

Third, much effort must go into persuading people with varying points of view to attend. Co-sponsorship with the local chamber of commerce, the local alliance of churches, or the local senior center might be a useful way to bring in those with differing views. When educators dominated the forums, less was accomplished than when community leaders, religious figures, businesspeople, and others were in the majority.

Fourth, at the end of the meeting, it is vitally important to discuss and reach agreement on where to go next. Although the organizers of the forums tended to be very tired at the conclusion of the meetings and thus preferred to postpone any discussion of next steps, the people who participated wanted to know where all this activity was leading. Some closure was needed to give a sense of accomplishment. Possibilities for follow-up activities include inviting the school board to respond to the recommendations of the participants, holding additional forums on particular topics, or conducting similar general forums in churches, senior centers, or other locations.

These are the four main recommendations that I would offer. There are some additional points that might help to make future meetings more effective. For instance, some work needs to be done on improving the data presented on the effectiveness of the schools—nationally, at the state level, and locally. Another area for further consideration is the best timing of the events. I found Saturday mornings least effective and after-work and early evening events with boxed meals most effective. The geographical area of focus is also important. I found it easier to get people engaged if the meeting looked at one school district rather than at all school districts in a state because of the variance in conditions statewide.

The most important factor to keep in mind is that holding one of these forums is just the beginning of a long-term process to rebuild support for public education and school improvement. Mounting them is very time-consuming, especially for teachers or parents who do not have ready access to copying machines and free mailing. The honesty involved in facing legitimate criticism of public schools and the courage needed to rebut unfair accusations are also demanding and tiring.

We face great distrust in our society, and many of our fellow citizens are thinking of deserting the basic institution of public education. To address these problems will take time, energy, and nerve. But the distrust of and disappointment with the schools are just problems—they are not immutable conditions—and therefore they can be changed. As citizens we can do no finer thing than use the means of our democracy to rebuild support for our public schools and to make them better for children.

Article Review Form at end of book.

What changes in governance will be necessary for community development? In community development what issues will educators need to consider?

Revitalizing the Ecosystem for Youth

A new perspective for school reform

Community development changes the core identity of schools from isolated, independent agencies to institutions enmeshed with other community agencies in an interconnected landscape of support for the well-being of students and learners, Messrs. Timpane and Reich maintain.

Michael Timpane and Rob Reich

Michael Timpane is vice president and senior scholar at the Carnegie Foundation for the Advancement of Teaching, Princeton, N.J. Rob Reich is a doctoral candidate in philosophy of education at Stanford University, Stanford, Calif., and a research associate for the Pugh Network for Standards-Based Reform. They wish to thank Howard Fuller, Milbrey McLaughlin, Sharon Lynn Kagan, and Terry Peterson for reading an earlier version of this article, prepared for the Aspen Institute Program in Education for a Changing Society, August 1995.

Over the past decade, most people involved in the reform of education have come to espouse a systemic perspective. Some hold out great hopes for improving the schools; others conclude that significant change is improbable at best. But all believe that "everything is related to everything else." Concerns about outcomes beget goals and high standards for all students, which beget curriculum frameworks and assessments, as well as requirements for teacher preparation and performance. Concerns about the limitations of teachers' classroom performance beget new pedagogies and school restructuring strategies, which beget a rethinking of approaches to professional development, as well as calls for autonomy. Concerns about the difficulty of producing sustained and widespread improvements beget critiques of administrators, school boards, and unions, as well as calls for additional research and experimentation.

Finally, Herculean effort has brought into being what have come to be called "alignment strategies," which presume, among other things, a capacity to bring about considerable changes in attitudes and institutional performance through incentives and requirements embedded in new policies. For some, this grand synthesis is the capstone of reform; for others, it is the ultimate indication that the endeavor is doomed and that the system must simply be replaced.

"Revitalizing the Ecosystem for Youth: A New Perspective for School Reform" by Michael Timpane and Rob Reich. © 1997 Phi Delta Kappan. Reprinted with permission.

No one who has been involved in these reform efforts has emerged without changed perspectives and understandings. Indeed, a policy revolution has occurred; systemic reform and choice are the two principal alternatives for today's policy addicts.

There are, of course, other possible perspectives. One of the most powerful is that of teachers, who have proclaimed throughout the reform era that the entire process has lacked their participation and has yet to affect what goes on in their classrooms. Another is the perspective of those who entered the lists with good will and high hopes but have since come to believe that the architecture of the reforms grossly overestimates the strengths of the political and educational materials at hand to build them.

We believe that there is yet another perspective, systemic in a different sense, that must be considered if the impulse to improve education is to sustain its momentum into the next century. We must consider the perspective of the young person, the learner.

To the learner, the "system" is the procession of adults and institutions encountered each day: the family, the neighborhood, private associations, churches, peers, youth programs, social service agencies, health workers, mass communications, the criminal justice system, and, of course, teachers and schools. All of these entities shape the young person. "A child's education," as Harold Howe II said in the fall 1995 issue of Daedalus, "is made up of many activities, most of them occurring outside the schools." It can be significant when one or another of these forces in a young person's life is not working smoothly or efficiently, but it can be disastrous for his or her progress to adulthood if some are absent entirely or are working at cross-purposes to the others.

What is more, each of the entities trying to help young people depends heavily on the effective functioning of the others. Just as no young person can succeed alone, neither can any of the institutions involved. Indeed, all share the tasks of fostering each young person's learning and development. And yet, by tradition and often by law, we view each young person through the lens of one narrow problem at a time—according to whether he or she is in a stable family, healthy or not, pregnant, abusing drugs, homeless, doing poorly in school, in trouble with the law, and so on. In today's policy environment, none of these "special purpose" youth programs is flourishing, and equally tragically, we have no program devoted to seeing that young people "flourish" overall.

Borrowing language from the natural sciences, we believe that the arrangements we need are best thought of as an ecosystem—a total environment supporting the healthy growth and development of America's youth. Today, that environment is perilously frayed and damaged. Like an arid and undernourished field whose topsoil is eroding, where water is in short supply, and in which volunteer firefighters stamp out increasingly frequent brush fires, the environment for youth is beset by the erosion of the family over the past 30 years, by a long dry season of funding for youth programs, and by a landscape of deficit-driven services designed mostly to respond to emergencies, put out fires, and "fix" young people.

Like plants and animals, our young people depend on the existence of a surrounding environment that is conducive to growth. When the ecosystem for youth deteriorates, growth is stunted, warped, or simply impossible. For young people to develop into successful, educated, and healthy adults, we need to revitalize the underlying ecosystem that supports them—and all of us.

The experiences of youth service workers testify to the discord and fragmentation of the environment in which children grow.

- No overarching, systemic vision coordinates the diverse services that seek to help youth. Youth services and supports are delivered in a haphazard and idiosyncratic fashion, unconnected to an overall "strategy for youth."

- Youth workers are underpaid (relative to educators), often lack good initial training, and receive little continuing professional development. Furthermore, while those who teach school are members of a credentialed profession with union bargaining power, youth workers come from extremely varied backgrounds and are unorganized. While one need not envisage a full-fledged credentialing system, youth programs should not have to rely exclusively on the good will, compassion, and caring devotion of adults.

- Youth programs typically survive on hand-to-mouth funding and are dangerously dependent on project-based "soft money" from foundations or philanthropists. This dependence prevents the evolution of long-term strategies for youth and reinforces the categorical nature of youth services. When programs must engage in a constant drive to justify their existence and raise money, there is scant possibility of knitting together the diverse organizations that share the goal of improving the lives of young people.

- Finally, there is no inclination or incentive for coordination or collaboration. Instead, like a parched, untended garden where plants compete for water and soil, youth programs compete with one another for increasingly scarce government and foundation funds. In this way, the current funding mechanisms for youth services indirectly discourage collaboration.

The Default Agency

In this bleak landscape, the school is the single non-needs-based institution that touches the life of every child. As the only universal service provider for young people, the school has become the default agency for addressing the much broader problems of the depleted environment. To be sure, other social services carry important responsibilities for serving young people. But simply because schools are everywhere and have an obvious stake in the well-being of their students, citizens and policy makers often look to them to address and solve a vast array of nonacademic problems. Schools are not at fault for the damaged environment for youth, but rather they have assumed by default the role of providing crucial social support for young people.

Some schools—blessed with leadership, collaborative spirit, and strategic support—have been able to carry out these responsibilities remarkably well. But most lack the conviction or capacity to do so and end up weakening both themselves and the agencies whose services they are supposed to replace. Then all parties are blamed—usually by one another—for the ensuing lack of progress.

In the final analysis, no one institution is responsible for the collapse of the ecosystem for youth. And two corollaries come with this realization: 1) the reform or revitalization of any one institution cannot itself repair the ecosystem, and 2) no single institution can itself be reformed or revitalized without the concomitant strengthening of the other constituent parts of the system.

Thus school reform cannot succeed without community development. School reformers have often been blind to this fact and have sometimes made matters worse by not supporting community reformers, by subordinating community interests to those of the schools, and by turning education inward and focusing on narrowly defined educational goals and outcomes. Schools rarely involve families and communities in educational planning and decision making in any systematic, planned ways. By making schools the sole focal point of change, reformers have ignored the place where reform may do the most good to develop and revitalize the entire environment for children—the community.

Defining Community and Community Development

The notions of "community" and "community development" must be appropriately framed. The community we speak of consists of a web of relationships connecting individuals and institutions whose focus is ensuring that every child has a substantial opportunity to grow up successfully. In this sense community includes families, neighbors, friends, private associations, churches, media, youth organizations, and public institutions—all of which are directly involved in the series of critical transactions that constitute an upbringing. Moreover, a successful community of this sort is characterized by robust, informal, and continuous relationships among its component institutions and the individuals in them. Such interplay lightens the often oppressive character of formal relationships, enables the development of mutual regard and trust, and provides a strong voice for those who wish to speak with those who govern their lives. This is the civil society for which we all yearn.

Proceeding from this view of community, we see community development primarily as the building and strengthening of relationships. Some of this development occurs naturally. But some can be more formally supported through such arrangements as community development councils, compacts, commissions, and collaboratives, on the one hand, and continuously active community organizers and advocacy groups, on the other. Just as there is no single model of school reform that guarantees success in all contexts, so there is no single framework for community development. Each community must create arrangements that build on its strengths and respond to its particular needs.

Government recognition and support for such enterprises, including dollars, will also be needed. Just as ecosystems are delicately balanced and intertwined, with the whole dependent on the vitality of its constituent parts, so every community institution, including the school, must understand its proper role in community development.

Other issues that define a community must also be addressed. What are its geographical boundaries? To what extent should demographics or prior institutional or governmental divisions be taken into consideration? After all, we already have counties, municipalities, school districts, library districts, police precincts, postal zones, religious congregations, and more. But reflecting on this complex list only drives us back to our basic proposition: a locality can create a stable, synergistic, youth-serving ecosystem only within a dense web of relationships; merely redrawing organizational lines and boxes will not do the job.

Community Development and School Reform

A robust community development program is a boon for school reformers, not an additional burden on schools. In our vision of community development, schools cease to be the default agency for youth services and can concentrate on teaching and learning. The new integrated, collaborative model of services will certainly require new structures of power sharing and control that will be difficult for schools to accept. But in the long run, the new vision of coordinated services will lift a large burden from schools and leave them with more freedom to pursue their core academic goals.

However, school reformers should not be misled into believing that community development exists solely in order to help schools. The various components of a community—schools, youth organizations, families, churches, businesses, and so on—depend on the others in order to carry out their missions and reach their goals. The relationship between community development and school reform is reciprocal. Simply put, schools rely on the well-being of families, community organizations, and the economy, and they, in turn, rely on the schools. A community development plan may be beneficial to schools, but it is intended, above all else, to serve children and their families. As a consequence, it requires fundamental redefinitions of the relationship that schools have with other community institutions and organizations.

At its heart, community development constitutes a philosophical change in the way schooling is conceived. Community development changes the core identity of schools from isolated, independent agencies to institutions enmeshed with other community agencies in an interconnected landscape of support for the well-being of students and learners. On the one hand, it beckons schools to consider and respond to learning needs throughout the community, not just to those of children within the school building. On the other hand, it assumes that the community is determined to make its children's welfare a top priority.

Community Development and Teaching and Learning

Within the framework of clear academic standards and high expectations, each school must refine its curriculum so that it recognizes and takes account of the good and bad experiences that students bring from their communities. As John Dewey emphasized long ago, school curricula ought not to ignore students' home lives but should instead incorporate and build on them.

Local educators must find appropriate ways to address the issues that undergird the experiences of young people in their communities—issues of race and social class, of the locus of power in the community, and of the meaning of democratic citizenship in the community setting.

A community-oriented pedagogy must become part of every school's repertoire. It should be based on models of learning that capitalize on young people's relationships with adults in multiple settings, so that students will connect what they learn to what they see and to what they want to be.

Project-based, cross-disciplinary assignments and service-learning initiatives are particularly good examples of curricular and institutional patterns that support academic goals, are conducive to community involvement, encourage the use of extra-scholastic experience, and contribute to multigenerational learning. Yo! Radio in San Francisco, for example, is a student-run radio station that teaches youths solid academic skills and also reaches out into the entire community. Likewise, New York City students, through New Youth Connections, publish a youth newspaper that is read by thousands of young people in the city and provides an outlet for expression on topics and issues seldom covered by traditional school newspapers.

At present, many community-based organizations consider schools to be downright detrimental to the healthy development of young people because of the schools' overemphasis on highly formal and often alienating relationships between teachers and students. Community development would place more emphasis on the "quality of care" in education—not as an alternative to academic instruction, but as a needed complement to it.[1]

Professional development for teachers and administrators would alter dramatically if schools were viewed as central parts of a community development vision. The necessary changes would reverberate throughout teachers' careers, from the very beginning of preservice training. As thinking in terms of community development begins to relocate schools within an integrated, collaborative model of service, support, and accountability, even the basic foundation courses of teacher education must change. To work in successful partnership with community organizations and parents, educators must redefine themselves as professionals. From day one, they need to understand that schools are not islands of education but fundamental components of a larger community whose learning needs they serve.

But it is important to recognize that the necessary changes in training must extend beyond just the professional development of educators. There is currently too little effort to combine the training of the various professionals who share the common goal of serving youth. In a community development model, the preservice and in-service training of teachers, youth workers, healthcare workers, and social service providers should be coordinated and, to a considerable extent, combined.

Community Development and School-to-Work Reforms

A focus on community development gives a strong boost to current school-to-work initiatives that attempt to integrate academic and vocational preparation, strengthen the transition from schooling to the workplace, and build opportunities for lifelong learning into the workplace itself. Preparing for work is central to the identity and development of young people. When we expand our notion of learning beyond the walls of the school building, the workplace becomes an obvious source of potent learning opportunities for all students. Finally, were community development to accomplish all its goals for the healthy development of youth, its success would be for naught if young people were unable to find work in adulthood. Any community development must be linked to economic development.

School-to-work and community development strategies place a premium on building healthy communities, on preparing children for adulthood, on learning in context, on active participation in the learning process, and on providing a broad spectrum of learning opportunities to the entire community. The workplace comes to be seen as a center of learning and is redefined to include community organizations, church groups, and volunteer efforts.

Furthermore, school-to-work strategies open up the schools to the outside community and thereby broaden the conception of a classroom. When the hallmark elements of school-to-work reform efforts—service projects, job internships, apprenticeships, and job shadowing—become part of K–12 school curricula, schools naturally begin to collaborate and involve businesses and community organizations with the mission of education. Local businesses become more fully involved as employers, partners in learning, and beneficiaries of community and school improvement. The workplace becomes an arena in which students can engage in serious learning. Work experience, job training, and apprenticeships are viewed as learning opportunities; school moves out of the school building. Academic outcomes, developmental outcomes, and employment outcomes are sought and accomplished together.

Governance Changes

Because community development holds schools to be only one part of the broad ecosystem for youth development, reforms stemming from a community development perspective will fundamentally change the governance structures of schools at every level. When schools are no longer isolated and autonomous, there are new stakeholders whose voices will figure prominently in the governance of schools. There are also important and challenging implications for other reform policies, including assessment and funding.

School Level

New school governance structures that are cooperative enterprises that rely on and cultivate grassroots community voices will play a crucial role in a model of schools within a community development vision. In these new structures, all stakeholders in the community will have a place, and schools will welcome community input for the curriculum and program within the context of state and local requirements and standards. At the same time, schools will join other service providers in collaborative efforts that take place outside the school building. Educators will identify the new stakeholders, determine with them the new structures, and finally agree on levels of control and how control will be exercised. In developing collaboration, educators should not sacrifice their professional judgment but should seek to extend it through increased mutual understanding and access to local "street wisdom."

The school restructuring agenda will similarly need to involve community stakeholders in setting goals, establishing accountability, ensuring collaboration, and coordinating support. In the new community vision, community-based organizations will play prominent roles in school redevelopment, perhaps even taking charge of the restructuring strategy for some schools. A critical problem in this respect will be to dovetail community strategies with other initiatives to enhance the autonomy and capacity of principals and teachers —and of community and social service providers as well. However, school personnel and social service providers must retain the capacity for day-to-day decision making in their respective workplaces, without endless consultation and paralysis by collaboration.

An important test of these new joint ventures will be sharing control over the use of school facilities. When communities become partners with schools, schools come to be seen as "community" or "public" buildings, especially during nonschool hours. Over time, ownership and management of the facilities may pass from school to community—to the ultimate relief of educators.

District Level

In the past 20 years, school reformers have pursued two dominant strategies—school-by-school reform (e.g., the work of Theodore Sizer, James Comer, Robert Slavin, and Henry Levin) and systemic reforms that stress federal and state frameworks, assessments, and incentives. Both have either overlooked or minimized the influence of the district. But the new governance structures required by community development visions refocus the reform agenda on the basic, accountable, democratic institutions in education: the school district and the school board.

School boards exist—in theory though not always in practice —to represent community interests in education. Districts and boards are thus theoretically in an optimal position to foster community redevelopment and, together with community leaders, to revitalize the ecosystem for youth. In reality, however, school boards sometimes do not work in the best interests of the community and instead become captives of local politics or divided by corrosive political infighting. For this and other reasons, district and administrative leadership is increasingly beset by instability.

Moreover, boards and districts must deal with municipal governments and agencies that are just as overburdened as they are. Yet school districts and local government agencies have indispensable roles to play in fostering community development. They must provide political and financial support; ensure equitable treatment for all youth services; contribute necessary resources, expertise, facilities, and qualified personnel to community services; and organize new structures of collaboration, including joint projects and interprofessional networks.

The creation of such new, broadly inclusive governing structures, for each school will accelerate the current trends away from complete autonomy for educational authorities. The days when school, district, and state education leaders wielded sole authority over schools and educational decision making appear to be ending. One need only note the recent calls for the merger of the federal departments of education and labor, Minnesota's decision to combine its departments of education and social services, the push by New York and Chicago mayors to exert increased influence over school boards and educational affairs, and the growing number of children's councils or child and family services boards in many cities.

Many school districts, particularly in our largest cities, have already taken promising first steps toward implementing a collaborative, integrated community development model. New York and Chicago provide good examples.

- New York's New Visions initiative permits community-based organizations to create their own schools in response to the needs of local communities. High schools for Public Service and the El Puente Academy for Peace and Justice are by now well established and successful. Better known are the Beacons schools, in which local community organizations form partnerships with their neighborhood schools. Educators and youth program leaders share the school buildings, which typically remain open seven days a week, 16 hours a day.

- In Chicago, the Chicago Community Trust created a $30 million Children, Youth, and Families Initiative to stimulate community development reforms. As a result of this initiative and Chicago's almost total devolution of school control to individual school sites, many schools have been reformed or reborn to respond specifically to community needs and desires.

State and Federal Levels

State and federal educational agencies do not possess the necessary local knowledge or clout to direct the transformation of communities, but they can help individual communities to construct visions of change. On a concrete level, they can empower community development by creating new funding mechanisms that:

- permit the combination of funds across different institutional categories into "core" streams;
- delegate more authority to community agencies to use existing funds in new ways;
- establish fiscal incentives for schools to adopt community-centered models of reform; and
- encourage contributions from the private sector and form foundations to expand the capacity and resources of communities.

The likelihood that federal funds will increasingly be distributed to states in the form of block grants creates (along with the dangers of inadequate funding for essential services) an opportunity for states to choose how to spend federal dollars and how to restructure their own finance strategies. States should be careful to ensure that block grants lead to coherent and equitable funding patterns across various services rather than to continued fragmentation among various agencies and programs.

In addition, in an integrated, collaborative model of community services, state and federal agencies must still ensure that legal and constitutional requirements for nondiscrimination and equal opportunity are met. In doing so, perhaps state and federal agencies will learn how to work together themselves!

Most of all, state and federal agencies must develop goals and standards for children that embody the values and outcomes of the broader community and indicate a shared responsibility for the overall well-being of youth. Such goals and standards must explicitly acknowledge the interconnection and interdependence of schools and their communities.

For example, each of the eight goals spelled out in Goals 2000 depends, in part, on community support for learning, and three goals—those concerning readiness to learn, safe and drug-free schools, and parent participation—have community development among their most prominent concerns. Current efforts to devise curricular standards and new assessments and to stimulate state and local demonstrations should not overlook these vital connections.

Societal Commitment to Change

The feasibility and ultimate success of any community development vision depends in the end on a broad societal commitment to change. Such commitment must be shared by a clear majority of citizens who recognize the pressing need to accept responsibility for the well-being of all children. Local and state politicians and community leaders will figure prominently in any broad community agenda, but no less important to change are those who make up the most numerous segment of society and who are often recalcitrant when it comes to youth issues: people without children. Any community redevelopment requires a shared vocabulary, shared values, and common goals concerning children. Community development must be considered a social movement.

In order to build the necessary mandate for change, school authorities should engage in an ongoing public dialogue with all people, inside and outside of education, to foster understanding of the need for change. While educators cannot assume sole responsibility for creating and promulgating such a movement, they can promote the creation of alliances and broad coalitions. Unions, business leaders, parent and family organizations, juvenile justice institutions, civic and fraternal associations, churches, philanthropies, and young people themselves must all be involved. And educators can and must reach out to all in partnership for learning.

The cardinal principle here will be the renunciation of low expectations so that all parties will be held responsible for more than any one of them is doing today. A system that distributes accountability for the healthy development of youth throughout community programs and institutions will bring a quick end to the game of "blame shifting" currently played today. When all stakeholders accept responsibility for youth, praise or blame redounds to the community as a whole.

New Questions and Dilemmas

The evident promise of community development to revitalize the ecosystem for youth masks a host of new questions and dilemmas. The challenges and difficulties in implementing a community-based plan of redevelopment are matched only by the importance of the task. We highlight here four major issues raised by a community development agenda.

1. Redefinition, Not Rearrangement

The stance reformers adopt toward community development plan is of the utmost importance. We must recognize that reform does not involve the rearrangement of different agencies and institutions. There is no jigsaw puzzle waiting to be pieced together by some ingenious authority, thereby "solving" the problem. Instead, community development requires the redefinition of different agencies and institutions. No component of a community will stand alone, independent and isolated from others. Each will assume more interdependent, collaborative roles within a landscape of services and supports.

For those who have been part of largely independent agencies and institutions, such as school systems, this redefinition will be a painful process. For the redefinition of schools will not be left solely to educators; it will be an accomplishment of the community. The precise contours of the redefined roles of various agencies can be dictated neither by state or federal powers nor by individuals within localities; they must be generated by the community, acting in concert. Redefined relationships must be the product of sustained, respectful dialogues.

Educators need to consider the following issues.

- When "learning" is conceived of as an activity that occurs in many settings, not just in schools, teachers must be willing to share responsibility for the learning process with other interdependent actors and agencies in the community.

- Similarly, teachers must be willing to invite into the classroom and school building different community actors and agents to become partners in the learning process. In turn, teachers need to get out of their own classrooms and into the community more often.

- When the school is construed as a public, community-owned facility, educators must be ready to share control and authority over their classrooms and buildings. What will happen when community needs for the school building conflict with teachers' needs? What is a "classroom" when learning is reconceived as occurring in varied settings and at various times?

2. No Guarantee of Consensus

The incorporation of different community stakeholders into the governance structures of schools raises the question of whether consensus among different groups is possible. When businesses, schools, and diverse community representatives meet, there are likely to be real conflicts that go beyond the problem of finding a common vocabulary. Do the business leaders share the same goals as the educators? Businesses may stress vocational skills more than preparation for civic responsibilities and citizenship. Do community groups want the same things in education as teachers? Ethnic groups sometimes see schools as forcing their children to become part of a dominant and alien culture. And, of course, even if people reach consensus on goals, there is no guarantee that people will agree on the means to reach those goals.

The attainment of diverse representation in new governance structures is no guarantee of consensus. The potential is great for the norms and interests of various groups to conflict. What will governing boards do when they cannot agree? We need strategies for, as John Gardner would say, "embracing diversity." We need to emphasize and learn more about ways to build a civil society that places a premium on dialogue and consensus rather than on demagoguery and criticism.

3. School Readiness/ Community Readiness

Serious consideration must be given to school readiness and community readiness before collaboration begins. If a school or district struggles to achieve its core academic goals, it will be unlikely that collaboration will immediately improve matters; it is more probable that the situation will become worse. Likewise, if a community agency or service is unsuccessful or unfocused, a link with schools will only produce confusion and further frustration.

The goal of integration and collaboration is not merely the realization of a process but also a substantive change. Both schools and community programs must be secure and confident about what each does so that coordination involves the combining of strengths rather than a pooling of weaknesses or the thoughtless domination of fragile community programs by large, highly structured school systems.

4. Reexamining School Choice Strategies

Clearly, the perspective of community development implies devolution of power and dissolving of bureaucratic obstacles. At the same time, it places great importance on the need for individuals and families to choose the services they need. Indeed, many of the most stable community-based education programs have been created in the context of school choice. To the extent that choice policies have so far assumed discrete educational or social services to be the unit of choice, unrelated to other needs or to community context, they may need to be redesigned or refined. Each district's solution—no doubt arrived at by vigorous experimentation with choice plans, charter schools, and other institutional patterns of learning—will be different.

Communitarianism, John Dewey, and Jane Addams

The recent interest in community-based models of development in the policy world mirrors current academic work in many fields, especially in political science and political philosophy, which in the past decade have seen a resurgence of interest in exploring the importance of communities. A growing "communitarian" movement views local communities as the preferred locus of meaningful social renewal and deep, lasting change.

Educators, policy makers, and academics who promote community development all lay claim, in some way, to the legacy of John Dewey and Jane Addams. More than 80 years ago, in thought and in practice, they both passionately defended the crucial importance of communities to the social fabric of the nation. They sought to create communities that established norms and assumed responsibility for the well-being of their citizens. At the same time, they argued that communities should allow for ongoing democratic debate about the particularity of those norms and about the ways the well-being of their citizens could be improved.

Those with a feel for history and its ironies will appreciate the fact that the ideas of Dewey and Addams are once more coming into vogue. Like them, we must seize this opportunity and be bold enough to experiment with new structures for schools and social services that respond to community needs and, in the process, take a giant step toward revitalizing the ecosystem for youth.

1. Much recent academic work supports the vital need for schools to become more caring at both the institutional and individual levels. Milbrey McLaughlin (of Stanford University) has researched the importance of caring relationships for young people in community organizations. Eric Schaps' Developmental Studies Project in Oakland has made caring a classroom and school concern, and Nel Noddings (also of Stanford) has done philosophical work on relational ethics. All highlight the centrality of care in teacher/student and school/student relationships for the healthy development of young people.

Article Review Form at end of book.

Neighborhood teamwork can achieve differences for students when which partners are included? What challenges did this community partnership face and overcome?

How Teamwork Transformed a Neighborhood

This is a story of how one elementary school overcame the challenges of neighborhood poverty and crime to build a community coalition.

Martie Thleen Lubetkin

Martie Thleen Lubetkin is a Speech/Language Specialist at Pio Pico Elementary School in Santa Ana and Associate Professor at Saddleback Community College in Mission Viejo.

Pio Pico Elementary is an almost five-year-old school located in a barrio in the center of Santa Ana, California. Nearly every family lives below the poverty level. Most of the adults have had fewer than four years of schooling, and most families double up in overcrowded apartments. More than a third of the children have never seen the ocean, which is fewer than 10 miles away. In most households, both parents work, usually for less than minimum wage. Spanish is the primary language of 98 percent of the residents, as this is a port-of-entry neighborhood populated primarily by families from Mexico and El Salvador.

The students who attend Pio Pico come from one of the poorest, most densely populated neighborhoods in one of the richest counties in California. The one square mile surrounding the school is home to some 26,000 children under the age of 18.

The School Context

The large number of students in the area justified building a new school in close proximity to three other elementary sites. Overcrowding was so severe, in fact, that it became necessary to open the school before the intended site could even be cleared. In August 1991, 330 students began attending classes in a collection of bungalows on the playground of a school a few blocks away from the permanent location.

Because Spanish was the primary language for most of its students, Pio Pico was designated as a Spanish Language Arts Demonstration School. In collaboration with the University of California at Irvine, teachers would help students maintain their primary language skills as well as develop their fluency in English. This approach was very different from the sink-or-swim version of language instruction that many of the parents had experienced. The teachers were eager to share their plans for this program at a Family Night held before the school opened.

It became clear at the meeting, however, that the overriding concern of the parents was the safety of their children. Highland Avenue, where the new school would be located, was a street ruled by gangs. It was a place where drug sales occurred 24 hours a day. Discussions about the curriculum had to be put on hold until the safety issue could be resolved.

That evening, a group of parents developed a plan to escort the children to school and back each day. A short time later, this same group of parents

---

Lubetkin, Martie Thleen (1996). "How Teamwork Transformed a Neighborhood," *Educational Leadership*, v52, n 7, pp. 10–12. Reprinted with permission of the Association of Supervision and Curriculum Development. Copyright © 1996, by ASCD. All rights reserved.

formed the Pio Pico Safety Committee, a group that would continue to grow and evolve. This was the first time residents had joined forces to improve conditions in their neighborhood.

In August 1992, the school moved to new temporary quarters. The campus was now a makeshift group of bungalows on the very street about which the parents had expressed strong concerns the year before. During the first few weeks of classes at this site, staff members sat in the teachers' lounge and watched drug deals occur. Parents continued to escort their children to and from school, and they began to stay and visit after classes had started, talking out their concerns at the lunch tables.

The Catalyst

Initially, the school's principal and teachers had reached out to the families. Now the families were ready to join the school staff and reach out to the community. The Pio Pico Safety Committee enlisted the help of the Santa Ana Police Department, which had a federal grant to redevelop the downtown area and purge it of drug and gang activity. Although Highland Avenue was just outside the prescribed area, the Department agreed to assign a team of officers to do stakeouts and surveillance in the area for two weeks. During that short period, 34 drug busts were made in front of the school. By the end of the two weeks, the drug dealers had gotten the message that the area was no longer safe for them, and they moved on.

With the principal as facilitator, the Safety Committee expanded into a Neighborhood Association made up of three representatives from each building in the area: the apartment owner, the apartment manager, and a member of a family with children at Pio Pico. This group mobilized to assess community needs, and to match school and community resources to meet those needs. The fact that most of the volunteers lived in the neighborhood and shared a linguistic and cultural background with the other residents made them much more effective ambassadors than the teachers or the principal might have been. And, the inclusion of property owners gave added weight to the requests of the group at the city level.

With the drug problem under control, the Neighborhood Association, the school staff, and the groups that had formed partnerships with the school decided to hold their first Operacion Limpieza (Operation Clean-Up). Their goal was to improve physical conditions on Highland Avenue. A week before the event was to take place, parents were asked, via newsletter, to help and to donate ingredients for a luncheon. A group of dads volunteered to grill the carne asada brought by the families, and the teachers chipped in for tortillas, salsa, and other condiments. A local McDonald's agreed to provide punch and cups, and the Boys' and Girls' Club across the street from the new school site opened its kitchen to host the luncheon.

On the day of the clean-up, teachers, other staff members, and students (with their parents, brothers, and sisters) were joined by representatives from the Police Department, Fire Department, Police Explorer Scouts, Home Base of Santa Ana, and the Santa Ana Neighborhood Improvement Program. The work crew also included two city council members, several district assistant superintendents, and two school board members. Even neighbors who had no children attending the school got involved; they were caught up in the feeling of pride and accomplishment.

By lunch time, they had swept the sidewalks, picked up and bagged trash, painted over graffiti, and planted flowers along the sidewalks. Home Base provided the paint, brushes, gloves, trash bags, and plants. The Fire Department used its pump trucks to water the new plants and to clean the fences and walls before they were painted. This was the first time all the groups had come together for such a positive purpose.

The goal was to show the community that the Pio Pico students and their families cared about improving the deplorable conditions in which they lived, and to demonstrate that they could do so. They succeeded: Operacion Limpieza has become an annual event in the Pio Pico neighborhood. The area has remained clean and well cared for, and the people living there take the responsibility to keep it so.

And that's not all. In the last four years, crime in the community has dropped by approximately 35 percent. There have been no homicides, robbery is down 25 percent, and aggravated assault is down 19 percent. Small children can now play safely in their yards.

The Effort Continues

The clean-up was just the first step in reaching out to the families and the community, and in enlisting the help of local businesses. The school's extended family has grown, and the community has become more involved with the school. Partnerships with community organizations such as the Boys' and Girls' Club and the Santa Ana Police Department have led to even more connections with the community, and to other partnerships.

For example, when a group of Korean-American entrepreneurs began building a strip mall near the school, a Korean-American police officer who had participated in the partnership program introduced us to several of the merchants. They visited the school, and in December 1994, they partnered with a class for the annual holiday gift exchange. In June 1995, they joined the Neighborhood Association in a multicultural celebration of independence for the community, with dancers and food and a program that commemorated the struggles for independence of the United States, Mexico, and Korea.

Recently, the merchants invited some of our bilingual 5th graders to administer the oral final examination for their adult Spanish class. The "professors" were invited to attend the dinner held in honor of the "graduates" they had tested. The children honored the adults by singing an impromptu version of "Ari Rang," a Korean anthem.

Four Years of Achievement

These past few years, Pio Pico Elementary School has grown from 10 classrooms located on the grounds of another school to more than 860 students in a brand-new building. The parents have become advocates for their children's education. They are interested and involved in what happens at school, and they are determined to help their children achieve.

The school continues to boast 85 percent parent attendance at PTA meetings and 99 percent attendance at parent-teacher conferences. Adult ESL classes consistently run at full capacity. In addition, 195 parents have graduated from the Parent Institute for Quality Education, a program that teaches parenting skills and encourages parents to be active participants in their children's education. One hundred eighty-five more are enrolled in the program in progress now.

When interviewed, one graduate—a mother of two Pio Pico students—said she now believes that her children can go to the university, and she now knows what she can do to help them get there.

The Pio Pico vision of "lifelong learners, eager and well prepared to make positive contributions to a diverse global society" will take years to evolve, but the physical changes in the neighborhood where its students are spending their childhood already are obvious. Our experience clearly demonstrates how much caring educators, a willing community, and empowered families can achieve when they work together.

Author's note: The principal of Pio Pico Elementary, Judith Magsaysay, was one of three community leaders in the state to win California's 1995 Peace Prize, awarded by the nonprofit California Wellness Foundation. The foundation cited Magsaysay's efforts to increase parents' involvement in education and foster intercultural understanding.

Article Review Form at end of book.

WiseGuide Wrap-Up

- Achieving high levels of excellence by individuals requires addressing the key issues of human nature, including the need for trust, purpose, empathy, consistency, and caring.

- Leadership and trust are key partners for success. Trust-builders include credibility, accessibility, investment in others, integrity, and trustworthy behaviors.

- Successful leaders practice effective delegation for their own and others' growth. They also practice the art of subservient management.

- Community forums can serve as effective communication vehicles for school reform and improvement.

- An "ecosystems" perspective for serving students can promote effective services from a variety of agencies, including schools. Systematic changes will require schools to become part of a larger community partnership.

R.E.A.L. Sites

This list provides a print preview of typical **Coursewise** R.E.A.L. sites. There are over 100 such sites at the **Courselinks**™ site. The danger in printing URLs is that web sites can change overnight. As we went to press, these sites were functional using the URLs provided. If you come across one that isn't, please let us know via email to: webmaster@coursewise.com. Use your Passport to access the most current list of R.E.A.L. sites at the **Courselinks**™ site.

Site name: A Compact for Learning: An Action Handbook for Family-School-Community Partnerships

URL: http://www.ed.gov/pubs/Compact/

Why is it R.E.A.L.? This sixty-page online booklet is sponsored by the U.S. Department of Education. It provides detailed directions for implementing successful family-school-community partnerships by developing commitments and responsibilities for key players.

Key topics: behavior, change, collaboration, community, communication, empowerment, human relations, motivation, reform, responsibility, shared leadership, success, team, vision

Try this: Use this site to implement a partnership in your school. Review the five examples of school compacts. Develop a compact for your school, including evaluating and strengthening your partnership.

Site name: Schools as Communities—ERIC Digest

URL: http://eric.uoregon.edu/publications/digests/digest111.html

Why is it R.E.A.L.? ERIC Digests, sponsored by the U.S. Department of Education, present concise information summarizing the latest research. This digest presents evidence demonstrating that a strong sense of community in schools has benefits for both staff members and students. In addition, community building provides a necessary foundation for school improvement.

Key topics: attitudes, behavior, change, collaboration, community, culture, human relations, job satisfaction, motivation, reform, shared leadership, team

Try this: Review the web site for the characteristics of community in schools. How does this sense of community affect staff and students? List the factors that affect community in schools.

section 4

Collaborating: Building Teams and Leadership Capacity

Learning Objectives

- Identify and discuss leadership as an individual and a collective process. Describe the characteristics and skills necessary for leaders in today's and tomorrow's schools.

- Describe the advantages for individuals and organizations of building collaborative teams in schools. Explain the difficulties in accomplishing true collaboration at the school-site level.

- Explain the administrator's role in guiding the collaboration/team-building process. Describe the steps that lead to successful collaborative change.

- Identify the characteristics of effective work groups and explain how highly effective work groups have improved change efforts in schools.

- Analyze the cycle of change and describe the impact/purpose of collaboration in achieving change in school reform.

- Discuss the importance of leadership capacity and constructivist leadership to the future of educational reform initiatives.

WiseGuide Intro

Collaboration can best be referred to as the emerging skill for the new millennium. The process of collaboration is one of the most productive and fundamental forces in human nature. Collaboration, as a problem-solving and creative tool, serves the participants who share a vision for collective benefit. The U.S. Department of Education, the National Governors' Association, the National Association of State Boards of Education, and the National Council of Chief State School Officers have specifically called for education to invest its time, energy, and resources in collaborative efforts and have clearly emphasized the importance for school administrators to collaborate to improve services to students. In addition to federal, state, and other formal mandates for collaboration, pressure for collaboration has also come from the local level. The growing emphasis on school-based leadership, school-community partnerships, and joint decision making requires that school administrators possess and demonstrate skills in collaboration.

Some educational leaders are using collaboration to address the current challenges in delivering services to students. These collaborative activities include both interagency collaboration, (multiple organizations, including education, as stakeholders) and collaboration, between staff, students, administration, and parents/community on individual school sites. As education professionals attempt to practice the art of collaboration, how can they best be prepared with the skills and experience necessary to build confidence for effective collaborative endeavors?

Although growing in importance and emphasis at the federal, state, and local levels, collaboration will have little impact in education unless school administrators understand its definition and have an opportunity to practice it. I believe that applying the principles of collaboration to current challenges facing education is an effective method of meeting those challenges.

This section begins with a close look at collaborative efforts in Donaldson's article "Working Smarter Together." He discusses team efforts in relation to creativity, resources, hazards, productivity, and operating principles.

There is more to collaboration than simply working well as a team. Moravec, Johannessen, and Hjelmas introduce the concept of a self-directed team process in their paper "The Well-Managed SMT." They look closely at organizations that have successfully implemented this concept and its advantages for the organization, employee empowerment, and increased individual initiative.

Short draws our focus into the educational arena of employee-directed collaboration in her article "School Empowerment Through Self-Managing Teams: Leader Behavior in Developing Self-Managing

Work Groups in Schools." She highlights the advantages for teachers, an effective process for administrators to follow, and defines the term *unleader*.

The actual collaboration process in one school is detailed by Benjamin and Gard in "Creating a Climate for Change: Students, Teachers, Administrators Working Together." This hands-on view outlines specific strategies and human interest stories to inspire others.

Lambert contributes an excellent conclusion to this section with her article "How to Build Leadership Capacity." In her discussion of constructivist leadership, she examines the contribution each educator can make to promote learning and school reform in a culture of supportive collaboration.

Questions

Reading 23. What steps can a leader take to contribute and guide successful collaborative change? What are the components of the five-stage model of the cycle of change while working together?

Reading 24. How can team members practice self-management and develop qualities of a leader? What are the benefits of self-managed teams?

Reading 25. What are the characteristics of self-managing work groups? What are the three themes of the principal's role in facilitating self-managing teams?

Reading 26. Describe the programs initiated at Highland Park High School that encouraged collaboration and shared leadership. What are the four types of communication identified in this article?

Reading 27. Define constructivist leadership and explain how this perspective is supporting collaborative school improvement. What is leadership capacity?

What steps can a leader take to contribute and guide successful collaborative change? What are the components of the five-stage model of the cycle of change while working together?

Working Smarter Together

Leading collaborative change in schools means helping staffs become more productive without substantially depleting their resources.

Gordon A. Donaldson, Jr.

In *What's Worth Fighting For?* Michael Fullan and Andrew Hargreaves compellingly argue that working collectively in schools is the best way to improve them (1991). Yet throughout the book they weave cautions about the hazards of collective action. Faculties can develop group think. They can balkanize. They can stop at "contrived collegiality" and never arrive at true collaboration. Threatened principals can undermine efforts at working together.

The transition from traditional patterns of faculty problem solving and decision making to more collaborative ones is fraught with difficulties. As Fullan and Hargreaves note, "Building collaborative cultures involves a long developmental journey; there are no shortcuts." For the principal bent on supporting this type of restructuring, the challenge is to lead a faculty that may not wholly support, understand, or have the energy and time to navigate this fundamental change. Teachers and principals commonly compare their restructuring efforts to "rebuilding a 747 while it's in the air."

Principals, teachers, and other staff have responded to the criticisms of their schools by working longer and harder. They have added new programs and spent hours planning change. These efforts are well intentioned, but we are beginning to realize how little they are changing what teachers do daily, and thus what students learn (Toch 1991, Sizer 1992).

Working Smarter, Not Longer

Simply working longer and harder will not significantly change our performance; we must learn to work smarter. Peter Vaill persuasively argues that "working smarter" requires shifting our habits of work "collectively, reflectively, and spiritually" (1989). What does working smarter collectively look like in schools?

At first glance, it's easier to see what working smarter collectively should not be. It should not involve every teacher in more meetings that identify problems without showing promise of resolving some. It should not add more responsibilities onto teachers' already heavy workloads. It should not expect educators to instantly function as a team without the group skills to do so.

Working smarter means monitoring the efficiency of faculty work from two standpoints: (1) how productive it was in reaching desired student outcomes, and (2) how much it depleted important resources, including the human ones. The goal of working smarter is to be more productive without substantially depleting resources. That means devoting time and energy, both individually and together, to activities that demonstrate true benefit to children and that do not threaten, over the short or long haul, to exhaust teachers, principals, children, parents, or physical resources.

Donaldson, Gordon A. Jr. (1993). "Working Smarter Together," *Educational Leadership*, v51, n2, pp. 12–16. Reprinted with permission of the Association of Supervision and Curriculum Development. Copyright © 1993, by ASCD. All rights reserved.

Instrumental to "working smarter" is developing the ability to monitor what we do. We can only know if our efforts are wisely directed if we can step back and see what they produce and what they deplete. Every school staff must learn to reflect on its daily work in the light of student outcomes and its bank of resources. What came from that three-day unit on tropical rain forests? What time, energy, talents, and materials went into it? Was it worth it? What came from those workshops on cooperative learning? What went into them? Were they worth it?

Where We Are? Where We Are Going?

To help school staffs judge their new efforts and whether they are paying off, Figure 1 provides a five-stage model of the cycle of progress. Each stage is characterized by both "possibility" and "danger." The possibility is for potential growth and positive outcomes: the danger describes what can happen to the faculty if its new efforts come close to depleting its store of resources. Schools attempting to improve pass through these stages. Whether they emerge with gainful change depends on the staff's collective success at maximizing the possibilities while minimizing the dangers.

If some staff members are excluded, the school flirts with the danger of disenchantment. The collective "resource meter" begins reading "not worth the effort." Staff members dwell on the problems they or their colleagues experience, lose sight of the goals of the new practice, and grow impatient with the costs, disorder, and slow pace of change. Conversations in corridors and parking lots grow cynical, and staff members mutter about "what new idea we'll be forced to try next."

A staff that works smarter together can use this five-stage model to ask, "Where are we in this cycle now? Are we realizing the possibilities? Or are the dangers taking over?" The group needs to share evidence of positive developments to create the affirmative spirit needed to sustain progress. On the other hand, if the human resources are being depleted more rapidly than the possibilities promise to bring

---

Stage 1: Criticism. Externally or internally expressed dissatisfaction with the school's performance launches a period of criticism. From every substantial criticism, the school staff can learn what may not be functioning well. The "possibility" is for staff to use the criticism to identify ways to improve performance. The "danger" is that the faculty will feel overwhelmed and unappreciated. For staff whose resources are nearly depleted, defensiveness can spread rapidly; blaming others both externally and internally seals off the criticism, the facts underlying it, and often the critics as well.

Stage 2: Self-examination. If criticism is faced and defensiveness held to a minimum, staff can objectively examine the student outcomes in question and how its own practices affect them. Teachers can collect and use evidence to pinpoint what is working and what is not.

The danger in this stage is discord. The source of the problem could be identified as "the math department" or "the cross-age grouping team," and other staff members may disassociate themselves from those sources. This is particularly dangerous for a staff whose resources are "running on empty" already and who is consequently wary of sharing responsibility for all students.

Stage 3: Goal Setting. Once a staff succeeds at objectively appraising outcomes and practices without feeling overcome by discord, collective goal setting can occur. The data from Stage 2 can help identify specific goals, and the absence of discord, enables everyone to support the proposed goals. Stage 2 data will also reveal staff successes that can be celebrated.

That goals will be too grandiose or numerous to be achieved is this stage's danger. In this case, defeatism among the staff is practically inevitable. Working smarter in this stage means choosing goals that can be attained in a reasonable time frame with the resources available.

Stage 4: New Efforts. The school staff that emerges from Stage 3 with achievable goals will enter into planning and implementing new efforts without wondering, "oh, what's the use?" or feeling "here we go again!" To realize the possibilities of the new practice, however, requires that collective energies be focused on specifying that practice, the people responsible for it, the training they need, and the time required to plan and assess implementation. Most important, the entire staff needs to commit itself to helping it work, as any new practice will draw down resources and energy from the whole system's "bank."

The danger in this effort is that staff commitment will wane, leaving only a small group to effect the change; the collective effort will disintegrate. The effects of disintegration can be devastating as the staff divides itself between "true believers" and "foot draggers." Staff members take sides, and innovations become the target of arguments over resources.

Stage 5: Consolidation. New efforts backed by an "integrated" faculty and based on careful goal setting and honest assessment are most likely to succeed. With effective monitoring, the success or failure of the new practice becomes plain to all. Adjustments can be made, and its consolidation into the school's patterns realized. The entire staff needs to be privy to this monitoring, celebrating the successes and solving the difficulties that will accompany consolidation.

Figure 1

benefits, the staff will wisely heed the danger signals.

A school faculty that continuously monitors its own progress through collective reflection becomes self-aware, permitting course corrections before the five dangers or "Killer Ds" take over. Even if that course correction means abandoning a major effort, the faculty can make that decision with full recognition of the imbalance that exists between the potential for gain and the depletion of resources. This awareness keeps a school staff from feeling it's spinning its wheels or falling into the "we-tried-that-once-and-it-didn't-work" syndrome. In contrast, a staff beset by the "Killer Ds" is stuck in a cycle of hopelessness and routine work. Theirs is not a cycle of progress but an endless revolving around halfhearted attempts at change.

Staffs that are working smarter can adjust their plans, activities, and even their ambitions to see that progress occurs. As they live through the cycles of renewed effort, each cycle builds on the previous one, and a spiral of collective progress is born.

Redefining Staff and Leadership

Principals and teacher leaders play important roles in the development of faculties that work smarter together. They act very different, however, from the "strong leaders" of the Effective Schools era. A strong leader who is in control, who must direct traffic at all the crossroads of decisions, has no place in a school where all adults share responsibility in these areas (National Leadership Network 1991).

School staffs that seek creative solutions, that feel stewardship for the institution, and that shoulder a share of the toughest decisions facing the school will constantly chafe under the limits of leaders who must control, direct, and ultimately decide. Such leaders, however well intentioned, will soon be driven beyond their own human limits by their desire to support and monitor their staffs. Eventually they will sanction only those activities that will not deplete their personal and professional resources (Donaldson 1991).

This pattern is all too familiar in our schools. At first, such leaders work longer and harder to keep up with all the initiatives spawned by eager attempts at improvement. As they discover the incredible size and variety of activities and people, they learn to work "together"—denying their own personal needs and sometimes those of their colleagues as they drive for excellence, asking more and more from themselves and from others. Such leaders—and there are many that seem caught between paradigms—are finding that they eventually deplete their own resources and come dangerously close to depleting those of the faculty. Many retreat behind governing councils, behind office doors, to the central office, or unfortunately, out of the profession altogether. When the dangers outweigh the possibilities for the leader, the staff has little chance of working smarter collectively.

The cycle of progress requires that a school staff redefines itself as a community responsible for setting and reaching its own goals and capable of managing its own resources. Such redefinition means nothing less than establishing new working relationships among all players. As the formal leader of this group, the principal must not control, monitor, and direct, but must treat this group as a responsible community of adults. Staffs and principals who have historically divided responsibility for decisions unequally, reserved "final say" for the principal, and expected the principal to ride herd on "quality control" cannot overnight share responsibility as a community. They must start by setting in place together the groundwork on which future collective action can occur.

The principal's and teacher leaders' first task is to shift the group's compact. Three operating principles form the foundation of a new compact to work smarter collectively:

1. Responsibility and authority go hand in hand;

2. Children and adults learn best in trusting communities in which every person is both a learner and a resource for learning; and

3. All adult members of the school staff care for the institution and community as a whole as well as for their primary roles in it.

These principles make good intuitive sense, and decades of experience in schools and other group settings support them (Rost 1991, Sergiovanni 1992). As a staff considers taking responsibility for all five phases of its own progress, leaders must first help it assess each member's understanding of and commitment to these principles. Are we willing to be responsible for the actions and decisions we will have the authority to make? Are we willing to confront our own blind spots and see our colleagues, students, and their parents as important resources for our learning? Are we willing to set aside what might be best for me or for "my" students to build something better for the entire school?

Leaders Who Work Smarter

If principals and teacher leaders are to help staff make these significant shifts, they, too, face personal and professional challenges. They must ask: Am I willing to cede both authority and responsibility to others? Am I willing to reveal my blind spots, to appear unknowledgeable and vulnerable? Am I able to trust the group to accept responsibility and to exercise power? Am I capable of sharing information about the many aspects of the school that the staff needs to know in order to understand and make effective decisions?

Until these questions are answered in the affirmative and acted upon by the leaders, working smarter together cannot succeed. Not only must leaders facilitate public commitment to these principles initially, but they must also find ways to revisit them as the group moves along. Commitment to the ideal of working together requires constant attention and discussion. How the principal and teacher leaders respond to each phase of the cycle of progress can spell the difference between success and failure for the whole staff.

Figure 2* describes some strategies for leading a "smarter working" staff and contrasts them with commonly observed "harder and tougher" work strategies. Each is keyed to a phase of the cycle of progress and

*Does not appear in this publication.

can be used by principals and others as a device for monitoring how they are functioning. Each of the "working smarter" strategies directs the leader back to the three operating principles. To work smarter, a leader:

- Faces criticism: The leader listens and asks for evidence in the face of criticism, placing responsibility on the critic for specifying problems and helping to resolve them. Defensiveness and blaming are avoided, and trust grows.

- Welcomes self-examination: The leader involves the responsible players in examining teacher practices and student outcomes. Stewardship for the institution grows, and discord is minimized.

- Sets achievable goals: The leader helps the staff to meet the challenges of self-improvement by celebrating strengths and setting achievable goals. Assuring a proper balance between seeking improvement and depleting available resources fends off defeatism.

- Nurtures new efforts: The leader involves the entire staff in implementing a change or monitoring its progress, building collective stewardship, and minimizing disintegration at this crucial point when new efforts require changes in everyone's work patterns and resource distribution.

- Monitors and celebrates: The leader celebrates staff and student successes and acknowledges the many adjustments necessary in school improvement. The leader enables the staff as a group to acknowledge what works and what needs to be tackled next. The disenchantment with change that schools often experience is offset by a sense of collective efficacy.

Leaders play essential roles in developing collaborative cultures that "lie within the control of those who participate in them, [where] teachers and members together make their own schools" (Nias, quoted in Fullan and Hargreaves 1991). In a culture where all staff members work smarter together, each leader—including the principal—must ask: What is the balance between my productivity and the depletion of my own resources?

In the mid-1990s, the dangers of depleted resources will not diminish for school staffs and leaders. Physical and human resources will continue in short supply; good will and optimism, worn down by a decade of diverse reforms, may be hard to come by. If school staffs are to build on the progress they have begun, working smarter together will be more important than ever. They will need to know where their efforts are paying off and whether their resources will permit them to sustain those efforts. Most school staffs have the capacity for such collective reflection and action. Leaders in both administrative and teacher ranks must redefine their purposes and relationships to tap and build on this capacity.

References

Donaldson, G. (1991). *Learning to Lead; The Dynamics of the High School Principalship.* Westport, Conn.: Greenwood.

Fullan, M., and A. Hargreaves. (1991). *What's Worth Fighting For? Working Together for Your School.* Andover, Mass.: Regional Laboratory of the Northeast and Islands.

National Leadership Network. (1991). *Developing Leaders for Restructuring Schools: New Habits of Mind and Heart.* Washington D.C.: OERI, U.S. Department of Education.

Rost, Joseph. (1991). *Leadership for the 21st Century.* New York: Praeger.

Sergiovanni, Thomas. (1992). *Moral Leadership: Getting to the Heart of School Improvement.* San Francisco: Jossey-Bass.

Sizer, Theodore. (1992). *Horace's School: Redesigning the American High School.* Boston: Houghton Mifflin.

Toch, Thomas. (1991). *In the Name of Excellence: The Struggle to Reform the Nation's Schools, Why It's Failing, and What Should Be Done.* New York: Oxford University Press.

Vaill, Peter. (1989). *Managing As a Performing Art: New Ideas for a World of Chaotic Change.* San Francisco: Jossey-Bass.

Article Review Form at end of book.

How can team members practice self-management and develop qualities of a leader? What are the benefits of self-managed teams?

The Well-Managed SMT

Milan Moravec, Odd Jan Johannessen, Thor A. Hjelmas

Milan Moravec of Moravec and Associates, Walnut Creek, Calif., consults on creating high-performance organizations (e-mail: Moravec@Pacbell.net). Odd Jan Johannessen is the principal of Feedback Fundamentals Scandinavia, and Thor A. Hjelmas is production manager at BP Norge. Both are from Stavanger, Norway.

With proper guidance, self-managed teams can learn to assume responsibility for their actions and results.

How can you stimulate a sense of individual initiative in your company? And how can you renew the spark and energy that earned your success in the first place? As organizations around the world have discovered, it's impossible to achieve those goals when relationships are defined by hierarchical control. Many of these companies have opted for a new form of control called self-managed teams (SMTs).

Robert Haas, CEO of Levi Strauss, says, "I see us moving into a team-oriented, multi-skilled environment in which the self-managed team takes on work that only they as a work unit can accomplish.... These teams are a most powerful and proven empowerment strategy that accelerates productivity and quality and enhances human competencies and commitment."

Companies such as Asea Brown Boveri, a Swedish-Swiss firm, 3M in the United States and BP Norge in Norway have found that self-managed (or self-directed) teams create a work environment that stimulates people to become self-motivated. Besides speeding up decision making and innovation, SMTs inspire employees to connect with the company's vision in a very personal way: They experience the company as the means by which they can affect key issues and develop their leadership skills.

Before they get to that point, however, they have to let go of a host of old assumptions, fears and habits. Managers often fear that their jobs will disappear if work teams become self-directed. Specialists and support employees, such as engineers and HR professionals, may have similar reactions if they will have to share their special knowledge with SMTs, relinquishing a traditional source of self-esteem and status.

For this reason, the implementation of SMTs must be carefully planned. Good intentions are not enough, as plenty of companies have learned. A business needs a disciplined execution methodology if people are to make the transition from work groups to teams.

But old behaviors and attitudes are amazingly resilient. As Asea Brown Boveri's CEO, Percy Barnevik, put it when talking about the opportunities and frustrations he encountered during the introduction of SMTs, "I found myself trying to implement third-generation strategies through second-generation organizations run by first-generation managers." In any company that has introduced SMTs, people move back and forth between resistance and exploration, testing new behaviors and expectations, as they make the journey from the familiar to the unfamiliar. This is perfectly normal and requires only that the company assist teams in understanding situations, their causes and the appropriate SMT behaviors.

Reprinted from *Management Review*, June 1998 © 1998. American Management Association International. Reprinted by permission of American Management Association International, New York, NY. All rights reserved. http://www.amanet.org.

Defining 'Self-Managed'

Employees and managers alike may have trouble grasping the essence of "self-managed." Employees may hear the term and think, "Great! Now I don't need a manager." They act on their new "rights" without understanding their new accountabilities.

Similarly, managers may become confused about what they should and shouldn't do. One manager found herself being held hostage to the notion that "We are empowered and don't need your input." When she finally used her regular style to influence a decision, she was told, "You're not acting in a self-managed way."

Varying interpretations of "self-managed" or "self-directed" can lead to confusion and missteps. Essentially, the concept means that team members share or rotate leadership and hold themselves mutually responsible for a set of performance goals, an approach to their work and deliverables that reflect the company's mission, vision and business plan.

Some teams are slow to assume that responsibility. John Vemmestad, a senior manager at BP Norge (the Norwegian arm of British Petroleum), tells the story of two SMTs—an instrument group and an electrical group—that had adjacent workshops. At one point, they asked the project leader if they could remove the wall between them. The leader told them to do what they thought was right.

"Sometime later," Vemmestad says, "they came back and said, 'We've noticed that both our groups have the same lathe; can we locate them next to one another?' The project leader said, 'I'm not sure why you're asking me that.'"

Two weeks later, the representatives reported to the project leader, "We decided that two lathes were too many, so we only have one now." These teams had assumed self-accountability, but it took some time and a bit of nudging.

No group has ever become an SMT until it could hold itself accountable as a team. This is a heavy responsibility, especially since SMT members determine how they will organize themselves to get their work done and are responsible not only for their own output, but for that of others as well.

And what becomes of the former manager? In many well-functioning SMTs, that person begins as a team leader, keeping projects on track and ensuring that everyone is working with the same information, understands the business vision and has set appropriate goals. Management helps teams get started by broadly framing the company's performance requirements, while the leader explains the jobs to be accomplished, assists the team as it is performing those tasks and reviews the end products.

Gradually, he or she relinquishes certain decision-making and conflict-resolution responsibilities as the team members gain skill and competence. The leader serves more as a coach and an adviser as the team matures, but he or she always remains a member of the team, participating in decisions and supplying expertise, knowledge and resources.

Therefore, "self-managed" does not mean "without management." Rather, it implies self-responsibility and self-accountability. Initially, the manager/team leader needs to reinforce this accountability. An astonishing number of managers are neither aware of nor comfortable with the need to hold team members accountable for their new responsibilities and actions.

Managers and team leaders must strike a careful balance between too much involvement and not enough. If they step too far back from the team process, letting them struggle and make mistakes, they may have to jump back in.

If they don't hand off responsibilities in a timely fashion, however, people will assume that SMTs are a nice concept but do not produce real transformation. In our research on the false-starts of SMTs, a typical comment was, "Things haven't changed much. The supervisor still makes most of the decisions."

General Electric Co.'s CEO, Jack Welch, has no fear of letting his SMTs struggle for a while—but he demands performance and accountability from them. Laughing, he says, "Give them a chance to struggle together and even flounder and fight. Lock them into a room if necessary until they come out with a distinctive, agreed set of outputs and measures for the team as a work unit. Then get out of the way."

As managers loosen the reins of day-to-day control, they must ensure that SMTs have clear sets of behavioral competencies and performance standards, such as financial targets. SMTs require a compelling performance context. These expectations, more measurable than the vision statement yet more broadly framed than a line item in the annual budget, determine the height of the bar and define the conditions for self-accountability (autonomy). In an apparent paradox, such parameters actually give teams more freedom to take risks.

3M, which has leveraged 100 core technologies into 60,000 products, has maintained its market nimbleness by creating self-directed teams that thrive on risk-taking and creativity. The basic business requirement, communicated to all teams, is that 30 percent of 3M sales must come from products introduced within the previous four years. It's a strong demand for new products, and the SMTs have delivered.

Andy Grove, chairman of Intel, says that "building a collective identity does not mean losing a sense of individual responsibility." Teams, he maintains, must ensure that collectivity does not degenerate into undisciplined "group think," time-wasting bureaucracy and individual free riding.

The identity of Intel's SMTs supports exceptional human activity, similar to the passion and collaboration exhibited by emergency workers. With his leadership and his motto of "Only the-paranoid survive," Grove has made sure everyone understands that the business requires them to anticipate charge, shift and innovate more rapidly than the competition and pull together to meet extraordinary challenges.

The Challenges

SMTs resemble more of a process than a structure. As such, they evolve, change course, make adjustments and grow. Successful ones build in adjustment mechanisms from the start.

For example, the team leader might place a list of responsibilities on the wall and negotiate the degree of latitude team members will have for each one: Recommend, act and report immediately, act and report routinely or just act. Periodically, the team examines the chart with an eye to revision. Members provide examples of what they mean by each item so that everyone is clear about specific actions, accountabilities and measures. As teams and individuals become more able and more credible, accountabilities and responsibilities are pushed further down or away from the team leader.

Team members also need to assume responsibility for the process itself. They must measure their progress against the agreed-upon goals and approach, as well as assess their skills and competencies to determine where they require development, on-the-job training or coaching. Then it's up to them to obtain what they need through the team leader. They also may need training in communication skills, performance management or conflict resolution.

Like the team itself, the individual members need to practice self-management. Each must develop the qualities of a leader to complement his or her technical expertise. These qualities include taking risks, being receptive to new ideas and pathways and going beyond the "next logical step." The former manager can be an excellent resource for this learning process, but leadership is best developed in practice.

When they are introduced skillfully and guided along the way, SMTs can empower employees and managers. The discipline of a rigorous process diminishes the fear and resistance associated with SMTs and helps people integrate self-management into their business processes. Time is not the only element required for SMTs to take hold and succeed. It's what you do during that time that counts.

Briefcase

Employees and managers alike must shake off old behaviors and attitudes to make self-managed teams work. Those that succeed can become truly accountable for their results.

How to Let Them Manage

Managers can remove themselves as barriers to the self-management process, while retaining the role of adviser and resource person, by asking these questions of team members:

- What is the cause of the problem?
- What are you doing to fix it?
- How will you know when it is accomplished?
- How can I help?

This process sounds deceptively easy, and managers may have to be coached a bit until the behavior becomes a natural habit.

Article Review Form at end of book.

What are the characteristics of self-managing work groups? What are the three themes of the principal's role in facilitating self-managing teams?

School Empowerment Through Self-Managing Teams

Leader behavior in developing self-managing work groups in schools

Paula M. Short

*The Pennsylvania State University
University Park, Pennsylvania 16802*

The reform literature has advocated the empowerment of school staff (Frymier, 1987; Lightfoot, 1985; Maeroff, 1988; Massachusetts Department of Education, 1988). The assumption in the literature is that a positive work environment, brought about by school participants who are able to initiate and carry out new ideas, results in enhanced learning opportunities for students. In particular Maeroff (1988) cites key empowerment components for teachers to be increased status, highly developed knowledge base, and autonomy in decision making. In searching for avenues for creating a collaborative school environment where teachers have the autonomy and competence to act to affect the outcomes of schooling and students become independent learners and problem-solvers, there is increasing interest in "self-managing work groups." It is possible for schools to function with groupings that function as self-managing work teams. This study identified empowered schools where participant groupings are functioning as self-managing work teams and studied the role of the principal in the growth and development of such groups.

Introduction

The reform literature has advocated the empowerment of school staff (Frymier, 1987; Lightfoot, 1985; Maeroff, 1988; Massachusetts Department of Education, 1988). The assumption in the literature is that a positive work environment, brought about by school participants who are able to initiate and carry out new ideas, results in enhanced learning opportunities for students. In particular Maeroff (1989) cities key empowerment components for teachers to be increased status, highly developed knowledge base, and autonomy in decision making.

For the purposes of this study, empowerment is defined as a process whereby school participants develop the competence to take charge of their own growth and resolve their own problems. Empowered individuals believe they have the skills and knowledge to act on a situation and improve it. Empowered schools are organizations that create opportunities for competence to be developed and displayed.

"School Empowerment Through Self-Managing Teams" by Paula M. Short. Copyright 1994 Project Innovation. Reprinted with permission.

In searching for avenues for creating a collaborative school environment where teachers have the autonomy and competence to act to affect the outcomes of schooling and students become independent learners and problem-solvers, there is increasing interest in "self-managing work groups." Hackman (1986) characterized self-managing work groups as collections of people who take personal responsibility for the outcomes of their work, monitor their own performance, manage their own performance and seek ways to improve it, seek needed resources from the organization, and take the initiative to help others improve (Hackman, 1986). Tom Peters (1987, p. 282) states, ". . . there is no limit to what the average person can accomplish if thoroughly involved . . . this can most effectively be tapped when people are gathered in human-scale groupings—that is, teams, or more precisely, self-managing teams."

It is possible for schools to function with groupings that function as self-managing work teams. In a recent study, interdisciplinary teaching teams in a newly-opened middle school in the Midwest were well on their way to functioning as self-managing work teams (Kasten, Short, & Jarmin, 1988). Other configurations such as departmental teams in secondary schools, cross-grade level teaching teams in elementary schools, small school faculties, and certain highly function school-based committees could be examples of self-managing work groups. By definition, self-managing work groups function with empowered team members (Hackman, 1986). Therefore, the concept has merit for efforts in schools to empower all school participants.

Objectives of the Study

Objectives of this study were to identify empowered schools where participant groupings are functioning as self-managing teams or are well on the way to functioning at that level and to study the role of the principal in the growth and development of such groups. The primary research question guiding the study focused on identifying the attitudes, roles, and knowledge utilized by the principals in each empowered school that facilitate self-managing work groups to become self-evaluative, self-monitoring, and self-reinforcing?

Conceptual Framework

Frymier (1987, p. 9) states that "In any attempt to improve education, teachers are central." Rosenholtz (in press) suggests that ". . . the culture of a school changes significantly when experienced teachers top functioning in isolation and start solving problems related to students' learning collectively." In any attempt to improve schools, attention must be given to roles in decision making and increased opportunities for meaningful, collective participation in the critical areas of activity in the organization which focus on organizational goals.

Empowerment

Rappaport and his colleagues have described empowerment as a construct that ties personal competencies and abilities to environments that provide opportunities for choice and autonomy in demonstrating their competencies (Zimmerman & Rappaport, 1988). Although the construct can be applied to organizations, persons, and social policies, it appears to be a procedure whereby persons gain mastery or control over their own lives and democratic participation in the life of their community (Katz, 1984; Rappaport 1987; Zimmerman & Rappaport, 1988).

Dunst (1991) has suggested that empowerment consists of two issues: (1) enabling experiences, provided within an organization that fosters autonomy, choice, control, and responsibility, which 2) allow the individual to display existing competencies as well as learn new competencies that support and strengthen functioning.

School restructuring has, as one of its components, the empowerment of teachers, administrators, and students (Murphy and Evertson, 1990; Short et al., 1991). In fact the restructuring paradigm of Murphy and Evertson includes empowerment as a integral part of reform. Lortie (1975) depicts teachers as working in isolation from other teachers. Little collegial contact is ever realized as teachers perform their craft in separate rooms. In addition to working in isolation, teachers are expected to complete reports and maintain orderly classrooms. These "around the clock" tasks tend to absorb available time for collegial interaction and contribute to the isolation of teachers.

Research by Gruber and Trickett (1987) conducted in an alternative school identified the importance of control over decision making in empowering participants in school organizations. Rinehart and Short (1991), in a study of empowerment of teacher leaders in the national program calling Reading Recovery, found that teacher leaders saw opportunities for decision making, control over their daily schedule, high levels of teaching competency, and opportunities for growth and development, as empowering aspects of their work. In addition, their work (Short & Rinehart, 1992) identified six empirically-derived dimensions of teacher empowerment: involvement in decision making, teacher impact, teacher status, autonomy, opportunities for professional development, and teacher self-efficacy.

Self-Managing Teams

In recent years, the concept of self-managing work groups has been utilized in business and industry to further the cause of employee empowerment (Manz & Sims, 1987). In self-managing teams, employees take personal responsibility for the outcomes of their work, manage and monitor their own performance, seek needed resources, and take the initiative to help others improve (Hackman, 1986).

Hackman (1986) defined self-managing work groups by placing them on a continuum extending from management-led groups at one end to self-governing groups at another. Minimal criteria for self-managing groups were identified by Hackman and Oldham (1980):

(1) that the group be intact and identifiable—if sometimes small or temporary—social system, (2) that the group be charged with generating an identifiable product whose acceptability is potentially measurable, and (3) that the group have the authority to determine how members will go about working together to accomplish their task (p. 184).

While self-managing teams are generally portrayed as a way to increase worker autonomy and responsibility, organizational context is an important variable. Manz and Angle (1987) studied the introduction of self-managing work groups into an organization that had traditionally relied on individual self-management. In the context of an independent property and casualty insurance firm, self-management work groups were found to threaten the personal control and autonomy of employees and to result in reduced services to customers. Self-managed work groups were introduced in this firm without worker participation or approval and were used as a means of increasing management control. Manz and Angle concluded that additional research is needed on the effects of introducing self-managing work groups in service occupations, particularly when employees have a history of individual autonomy.

Researchers have also been interested in the functions of leaders in organizations with self-managing teams. Most writers on the subject have concluded that leadership is at least as important in organizations with self-managing work groups as it is in traditionally structured organizations (Cummings, 1978; Hackman, 1986; Lawler, 1986; Manz & Sims, 1987). Leadership is however, different. Manz and Sims (1984) describe the leader in an organization with self-managing work groups as an "unleader," "one who leads others to lead themselves" (p. 411). Hackman (1986) noted that "leadership is both more important and a more demanding undertaking in self-managing units than in traditional organizations" (p. 119). Leaders must monitor the work of the groups by diagnosing and forecasting from available data and leaders must take action to create or maintain favorable conditions for the group. In Manz and Sims' study of a small parts manufacturing plant that operated with self-managing work groups, the most important leader behaviors were "encourage self-reinforcement" and "encourage self-observation/evaluation" (p. 124).

Organizations that utilize self-managing work groups operate with a bottom-up perspective and "the leader's job is to teach and encourage subordinates to lead themselves effectively" (Manz & Sims, 1987, p. 121). In the organization that Manz and Sims studied, top management called themselves "the support group." Skills that leaders working with self-managing groups must develop were listed by Cummings (1978), Hackman (1986), and Lawler (1986). While their particular lists differ, human relations skills are emphasized over technical skills, including the abilities to build trust, understand group dynamics, develop group members' capacities for autonomy, and empower others.

Middle School Interdisciplinary Teaching Teams

Kasten, Short, & Jarmin (1989) found that interdisciplinary teaching teams in a midwestern middle school exhibited characteristics of a self-managing work group: an intact and discrete social system, responsibility for an identifiable part of the work, and authority to determine how members would work together to accomplish the task (see Hackman & Oldham, 1980).

Interdisciplinary teams are utilized in the middle grades in response to the unique needs of the early adolescent learner (Gatewood & Dilg, 1975; Merenbloom, 1986). Interdisciplinary teams involve a group of teachers who plan together and provide instruction to a particular group of students (Grooms, 1967). As an example, a team of four teachers representing mathematics, science, social studies, and language arts may plan together for the same cadre of students (George, 1973). They may meet one or more times a week to discuss strategies for addressing needs of certain students. They may also plan interdisciplinary teaching units to be taught cooperatively by the four teachers. The interdisciplinary team approach to planning curriculum allows for the integration of content areas and provides a means for teaching basic skills throughout all discipline areas (Merenbloom, 1986). The interdisciplinary team structure may facilitate the formation of collegial relationships to a greater extent than the traditional structure of the self-contained classroom (Alexander & George, 1981). Teachers on interdisciplinary teams generally have the discretion to select content, correlate units of instruction, and manage instruction to meet the needs of a particular group of students (Whitford & Kyle, 1984). This flexibility enhances the teachers' sense of control. In addition, interdisciplinary teams usually operate within a large block of instructional time (Merenbloom, 1986). Because each team is responsible for a particular group of students during this block of time, teachers may make decisions relative to the use of that time and have the flexibility to determine both content and the organization of instruction. Teachers on interdisciplinary teams make decisions that greatly affect the nature of their work. These decisions can involve the scheduling of classes, integration of curriculum, grouping of students, and organization of instruction, all decisions not generally within the purview of the teacher. (Alexander & George, 1981).

Teachers on teams have the power to make decisions about those things that directly affect the classroom and teaching. At the same time, it must be noted that work in teams cuts against many of the occupational norms of teaching, including norms of individuality, privacy, and isolation.

The investigation of the interdisciplinary teams as self-managing teams in middle school study (Kasten et al., 1988) suggests that the role of the principal must be further investigated in school settings where attempts at school empowerment, using the concept of self-managing work groups, is evident. Is it a unique role as suggested in the research literature on self-managing work groups in business and industry (Cummings, 1978; Lawler, 1086; Manz & Sims, 1987)? Is it a role that indeed empowers others in the organization? Does the principal role vary relative to the type of self-managing work group (cross grade level teams vs. departmental teams in high schools, for example)? Is that role affected by school contextual variables (size SES, teacher level of education and experience, for example).

Method

The study employed qualitative research methods (observations, interviews, document analysis) to answer the primary research question. The qualitative approach, an interpretive, naturalistic model, analyzes phenomena based on assumptions which accommodate a small number of subjects. The conceptions, value orientations, and understandings of those being studied are discovered through personal observation and shared communication. Information is acquired from individuals at separate times to establish patterns of behavior, attitudes, and motivations. Qualitative inquiry operates in real situations and contexts, utilizing researcher-subject interaction to uncover information not otherwise accessible. This "intersubjectivity" is best achieved when the number of participants is small (Merriam, 1986). Researchers utilize several sources of data including historical and current documents, structured interviews, and field notes from observations.

Types of Data Collected at Each Site

The four sites for the study were selected based on researcher knowledge that forms of self-managing work groups currently exist in the schools in the form of interdisciplinary teaching teams. University professors, public school personnel from regional service units, and school administrators identified schools using interdisciplinary middle school teams. The researcher visited a sample of ten sites and selected four that approximated self-managing work groups based on (1) autonomous functioning and (2) self-direction exhibited by the teams within the school. The researcher spent two days in each of the four schools conducting observations and interviews in order to select the four schools for the study.

To collect the data required, it was necessary to observe self-managing team interactions. Observations were conducted over a six month period with three days per month spent at each of the four sites. Observations of full school operations established the context in which the teams function. Observations of principals focused on those behaviors, actions, and roles that foster, within the teams, those attitudes and activities that establish the teams as autonomous and self-directing. Intensive interviews were conducted every other month at each site with the principal and teachers on teams. On three visits over the six months, focus-group interviews were held with a sample of students from the teams. Two interviews were conducted with the counselors and other special teachers over the six months.

Data Analysis

Data analysis included the coding of role behaviors, attitudes, and knowledge of principals, specifically in developing the self managing team, obtained from field notes from observations, interview transcripts, and school documents such as principal memos, team documents, and other principal/team-related materials. Content analysis was used to organize responses to interview questions. Procedures followed those prescribed by Holsti (1968). Content analysis is a technique for objectively and systematically identifying those characteristics of messages which bear relevance to some theoretical construct. This technique analyzes communication content by consistently applying selected criteria to verbal messages and categorizing responses according to those criteria.

The process used for theory building is known as analytic deduction, in which data are collected and categorized through two interconnected processes—enumerative deduction and eliminative deduction (Miles & Huberman, 1984). The former process collects and records data by number and type of response. The later probes for alternative or rival explanations which might affect the emerging construct. This second process eliminates the threat of an analysis in which only information supporting the researcher's original notions is examined (Holsti, 1968; Merriam, 1986). The two processes systematically elicit both similar and dissimilar patterns which point out relationships and help specify appropriate organization of variables.

After preliminary coding and display, all data were reviewed for parallel and dissenting responses and for pattern recognition. Frequently occurring variables and those variables which showed interactions were identified. Variables were assembled in clusters which illuminated patterns of response. Observational data were coded and analyzed for trends, themes, categories and relationships relative to the research questions. To triangulate the data collection, document analysis, observations, and structured interviews were used. Documents reviewed were principal communiques, materials sent home to parents, newspaper articles, minutes of any team meetings, communique among faculty both within and among teams, school goal-statements, any additional material related to self-managing teams and the principal. These multiple sources of information—observation, document analysis, and intensive interviews—were used because "no single source of information can be trusted to provide a comprehensive perspective . . ." on a program (Patton, 1990, p. 157). By using this combination of sources, the various data facilitated validation and cross-checking of the findings. To provide additional triangulation, multiple researchers collected and cross-checked the emerging themes from the data during data reduction.

Participant Schools

All of the schools in the study are located in the eastern and central part of a middle Atlantic state. The schools are from four districts, two suburban and two urban. All schools are organized on the traditional middle school model with interdisciplinary teaching teams. Most have been functioning well as innovative middle schools for some time. The principals in each site have been in their positions for 8 to 10 years.

School A is located in a suburban area with 650 students in grades 6 and 7. The female principal has been providing leadership in the school for 7 years. Teachers indicate that they need to make some improvement in their approach to interdisciplinary teaching. Each team holds formal meetings together two times per week, one meeting to set the agenda for the other meeting. The second meeting is used to discuss specific students who may need additional attention or help. Specialists often are brought in to provide additional insight and expertise. Special teachers such as foreign language, art, and vocational education are not members of the teams. Teachers on each team have a common office space which includes a phone, large desks for each teacher on the team, and conference tables and computers. All teachers in the school are connected to Internet.

School B is located in an urban setting. Approximately 900 students populate grades 7–9 in this popular middle school. The school is characterized as being very innovative with exciting projects and activities motivating the students. Units are taught around broad themes for the entire grade level. In other words, "Hawaii" may be the 6th grade theme for eight weeks with each team using "Hawaii" to teach the core areas.

School C can be found in a largely suburban area and enjoys a student population of 850 in grades 6–8. The busy faculty spend a great deal of time trying new ideas within the teams. Teachers have access to all equipment and materials in the school. The principal has developed some innovative ways to give release time to special teachers who have become members of a interdisciplinary team. There are no bells in this school to indicate the movement of students. The students move from station to station with ease and little noise. The principal holds regular "conversations" with the teams to find ways to assist their efforts.

School D is found in an urban setting with approximately 950 students in grades 6–8. Grades 6 and 7 enjoy an interdisciplinary teaching approach while grade 8 is organized within the teams in the more traditional subjects with little interdisciplinary work.

Findings and Conclusions

Principals in each of the four schools were energetic, enthusiastic about the middle school concept, expressed delight in working with students and great confidence in the teachers in their respective schools. One principal said, "They can make better decisions than I can on things that affect learning." Principals were very knowledgeable about what was happening in the various teams both in terms of what was being taught as well as ongoing issues that the teams were dealing with at various times. One team interviewed said, "He is a conversation person, always talking with us as a colleague-as if he is keenly interested in what we are doing." Another teacher from a seventh grade team felt that the principal ". . . facilitates our problem solving. When we get stuck or complacent, she always asks us questions that make us rethink." One principal attended many of the team meetings at various times but said very little. However, the teachers seemed to believe that his presence ". . . indicated interest and commitment to our work, not surveillance."

Central Themes

Themes have evolved that provide insight regarding the role of the principal in facilitating self-managing teams in the four middle schools in the study.

Facilitates Reflection

A key behavior of the principals in each of the four schools was helping the teams to engage in reflection. It was as if the team learned a process for thinking about events, the ramifications of action taken, and the implications for change. One principal said when talking with a member of a team, "When that happened yesterday, when did the light bulb go off for the members? What principle do you think the team used in making that decision?" Examples of this reflective behavior by principals included refusal to solve the problem experienced by a team but encouraging the team to experiment with alternative solutions with the principal providing any support needed. In one case, a team was experiencing conflict in work style. Instead of reassigning members and instigating a tight supervision of the team, the principal offered several resources, including a psychologist trained in team effectiveness, but let the team decide what resources were needed and how to solve the dilemma.

Facilitates the Focusing of the Team on Goals

The interdisciplinary teams that enjoyed the most success in becoming self-managing appeared to also be the teams most able to establish clear goals and an understanding of what they were about and how to move forward. The concept of the "unleader" (Manz & Sims, 1987) was the most apparent among the three principals where teams operated the most self-managed. These principals refused to impose ideas on the teams but used "conversations" as a means for encouraging team goal-setting. One principal kept the teams focused on kids by attending some of the team meetings and, in a very unintrusive manner, would occasionally say, "How is Johnny doing?" That one statement would cause the team to talk about "Johnny". In interviewing the principal, he stated, "I do that with certain children that I believe are falling through the cracks. I see them on the basketball court at lunch, before school, and in other settings that teachers might miss. I have a big picture of the student that may be helpful to the teaching team. By asking about Johnny in a curious but nonthreatening way, I help the team focus on a specific child."

Facilitates the Self-Criticism of the Team

The principals encouraged the team members to be critical of their performance, especially if progress (with students and with teams) was not up to par. Principals appeared to do this best by modeling self-criticism. One principal would often describe something that she had tried to accomplish, in front of the teams, and then critique her success. This was done in a positive light, always in a supportive environment. These schools modeled risk-taking environments. One teacher said, "I know I can try any new idea here and expect a supportive and helpful critique if something does not go well. I won't get in trouble, instead I have help." In another school, a teacher characterized the role of the principal as ". . . clearly facilitating our own efforts to be superior teachers by asking us to consider how something could be done differently." She went on to say that the principal's questions were not seen as criticism but as an intense interest on new ideas.

Facilitates Team Self-Reinforcement

Another activity of the four principals was to help the teams acknowledge their own successes rather than wait for someone else to provide reinforcement and praise. One principal regularly held "bragging sessions" or a kind of "celebrating that we do not do in schools." Another principal frequently asked teachers, "Are you pleased with what happened? How did the team itself celebrate this achievement?" Teams in these schools were looking within the teams for a sense of accomplishment and, in two of the schools, had begun to develop rituals for acknowledging and celebrating the attainment of certain team goals. All principals in the study engaged in status-building strategies for the teams. For example, principals alerted professional organizations and other groups about the expertise among the team members and encouraged them to invite the teachers in their schools to participate in regional and national conferences. In essence, they nominated their teachers for opportunities to perform as professionals in the public forum. In one school, when a team expressed interest in a new idea or technique, the principal would send a representative of the team to visit the site where the idea was in practice so the teacher could return and try the new ideas in the team.

These four themes dominated the roles and behaviors assumed by the principals in these schools. The roles that facilitated the effective development of the self-managing teaching teams centered around helping teams reflect, therefore, becoming better problem solvers and building expertise (Short & Rinehart, 1993). These principals also engaged in behaviors that fostered self-critique among team members. This attribute of teams is essential for self-management. Principals modeled through the critique of their own actions and decisions when interacting with the teams.

A pervasive behavior of these principals was the facilitation of team goal setting. By using informal "conversation" and constant interaction with the teams, these principals communicated the key expectations for team focus on kids and learning. Most asked teams to talk about where they were and where they wanted to go throughout the year. Observations of team interaction indicated that the teams used terms like "our goal . . . benchmarks . . . short-term planning . . . total quality . . .", indicating a knowledge base around planning and goal setting.

Principals in these schools worked hard to help teams learn to gain reinforcement from within the team itself. In one of the schools, teams had begun to experiment with alternative assessment with students without any prodding by the principal or district office. When the teachers wanted to videotape students to indicate student responsibility in group work to go into student portfolios, the principal quietly bought the video equipment and made it available to all the teams. He never indicated that a team must use it. In an interview, the principal stated, "I am listening when they do not think that I am. I heard them talk about videotaping so I made sure the resources were available for them. I figured that if getting the equipment was a barrier, then trying innovative ideas would become punishing and frustrating to them. This way, successfully implementing an innovation would be very reinforcing and encourage trying new ideas."

The behavioral themes gleaned from the principals in the schools in this study should be informative to those interested in understanding the kind of leadership that fosters self-managing teams. Further study of principal facilitative behaviors that encourage self-managing work groups to become self-evaluative, self-monitoring, and self-reinforcing would greatly assist reform efforts to create schools where participants feel greatly empowered.

References

Alexander, W., & George, P. (1981). *The exemplary middle school.* New York: Holt Rinehart, & Winston.

Cummings, T. (1978). Self-regulating work groups. A socio-technical synthesis. *Academy of Management Review,* 3, 625–634.

Dunst, R. (1991). Issues in empowerment. Presentation before the annual meeting of Childrens' Mental Health and Service Policy Convention, February, 1991, Tampa, Florida.

Flymier, J. (1987). Bureaucracy and the neutering of teachers. *Phi Delta Kappan* 69, 9–14.

Gatewood, T. E., & Dilg, C. A. (1975). *The middle-school we need.* Report from the ASCD Working Group on the Emerging Adolescent. Washington, DC: Association for Supervision and Curriculum Development.

George, P.S. (1973). The middle school in Florida: Where are we now? *Educational Leadership,* 31, 217–220.

Gruber, J., & Trickett, E.J. (1987). Can we empower others? The paradox of empowerment in a alternative public high school. *American Journal of Community Psychology,* 15, 353–372.

Hackman, J.R. (1986). The psychology of self-management in organizations. In M.S. Pollack & R. O. Perloff (Eds.), *Psychology and work: Productivity change and employment,* (pp. 85–136). Washington, DC: American Psychological Association.

Hackman, J.R., & Oldham, G.R. (1980). *Work redesign.* Reading, MA: Addison-Wesley.

Holsti, D,R. (1968), Content analysis. In B. Lindzey & E. Aronson (Eds.), *Handbook of social psychology: Vol. 2. Research methods* (pp. 596–692). Reading, MA: Addison-Wesley.

Kasten, K.L., Short, P.M., & Jarmin, H. (1989). Using organizational structure and shared leadership to enrich the professional lives of teachers: A case study in self-managing teams. *The Urban Review,* 21(2), 63–80.

Katz, R.F. (1984). Empowerment and synergy: Expanding the community's healing resources. *Prevention in Human Services,* 3, 201–226.

Lawler, E.E., Ill. (1986). *High involvement management: Participative strategies for improving organizational performance.* San Francisco, CA: Jossey-Bass.

Lightfoot, S.L. (1985). On goodness in schools: Themes in empowerment. Paper presentation at Macyie K. Southall Distinguished Lecture on Public Education and the Futures of Children, Vanderbilt University, Nashville, Tennessee.

Manz, C.C., & Angle, H. (1987). Can group self-management mean a loss of personal control: Triangulating a paradox. *Group and Organizational Studies,* 11 309–334.

Manz, C.C., & Sims, H.P., Jr. (1987). Leading workers to lead themselves: The external leadership of self-managing work teams. *Administrative Science Quarterly,* 32, 106–128.

Manz, C.C., & Sims, H.P., Jr. (1984) Searching for the "unleader": Organizational member views on leading self-managing groups. *Human Relations,* 37, 409–424.

Maton K.I., & Rappaport, J. (1984). Empowerment in a religious setting: A multivariate investigation. *Prevention in Human Services,* 3, 37–72.

Merenbloom, E.Y. (1986). *The team process in the middle school: A handbook for teachers.* Columbus, OH: National Middle School Association.

Merriam, S. (1986, October). Qualitative research in adult education. Paper presented at the meeting of the American Association of Adult and Continuing Education, Hollywood, FL.

Miles, M.B., & Huberman, A.M. (1984). *Qualitative data analysis.* Beverly Hills, CA: Sage.

Murphy J., & Evertson, C. (1990). Restructuring schools: Capturing the phenomena. Paper presentation at the annual meeting of the American Educational Research Association, Boston.

Patton, M.W. (1990). *Qualitative evaluative methods.* Beverly Hills, CA: Sage.

Peters, T. (1987). *Thriving on chaos: Handbook for a management revolution.* New York: Alfred A. Knopf.

Rappaport, J. (1987). Terms of empowerment/exemplars of prevention: Toward a theory for community psychology. *American Journal of Community Psychology,* 15, 121–148.

Rinehart, J.S., & Short, P.M., (1992). Reading recover as an empowerment phenomenon. *The Journal of School Leadership,* 1(4), 379–399.

Short, P., & Greer, J.T. (1989). *The empowered school district project.* Grant funded by the Danforth Foundation.

Short, P.M., & Greet, J.T. (1989). Increasing teacher autonomy through shared governance: Effects on policy making and student outcomes. Paper presented at the annual meeting of the American Educational Research Association, San Francisco.

Short, P.M., Greer, J.T., & Michael, R. (1991). Restructuring schools through empowerment: Facilitating the process. *Journal of School Leadership,* 1(2), 525.

Short, P. & Rinehart, J. (1992). School Participant Empowerment Scale: Assessment of the level of participant empowerment in the school. *Educational and Psychological Measurement,* 54(2), 951–960.

Short, P.M. & Rinehart, J.S. (1993). Using reflection to development expertise. *Education Administration Quarterly,* 29(4), 501–521.

Whitford, B.L., & Kyle, D.W. (1984). Interdisciplinary teaming: Initiating change in the middle school. Paper presented at the annual meeting of the American Educational Research Association, New Orleans, April 1984.

Zimmerman, M.A., & Rappaport, J. (1988). Citizen participation, perceived control, and psychological empowerment. *American Journal of Community Psychology,* 16(5), 725–750.

Article Review Form at end of book.

Describe the programs initiated at Highland Park High School that encouraged collaboration and shared leadership. What are the four types of communication identified in this article?

Creating a Climate for Change

Students, teachers, administrators working together

Here's a look at how one school changed its organizational structure to allow for collaboration and shared leadership.

Susan Benjamin and Jane Gard

Susan Benjamin is English department chair and Jane Gard is principal, both at Highland Park (Ill.) High School.

While having adequate resources can be helpful in initiating change, the starting point for school improvement can be simply a matter of attitude or point of view. For change to occur, school leaders must first believe that change is possible and necessary through simple and pragmatic means.

Recently at Highland Park (Ill.) High School, we adopted the point of view that we needed to challenge all previously held assumptions about the way we did things. That attitude alone was responsible for helping to set the tone that would provide the context in which meaningful change could—and would—occur.

Knowing the Culture

The first assumption we considered was that the operation of our school rested on the view of school as bureaucracy. As we looked closely at the way things work, both when they work effectively and when they do not, we discovered that such concepts as a hierarchy of roles, a pyramidal structure with power at the narrow top, a chain of command, and tightly structured procedures do not typify the way our school functions.

Instead, what we found was that we preferred to view organization as a culture, and to acknowledge that what worked best in our culture operated on the premises of collaboration and shared leadership, investment in the decision-making process by those affected by the decisions, and a flat rather than pyramidal organizational structure. One of the first items of discussion for our administrative team was styles and types of communication, since communication embodies our values, our attitudes, our ideas, and our practices.

We identified four important elements of the kind of communication we believed matched our approach: conflict resolution or win/win—addressing tough issues with positive outcomes for all involved; empathic communication, implying good listening skills to support and nurture; professional communication, which identified ways in which we could, as a school, effectively and efficiently communicate needs, decisions, and plans; and communication for mutual support, which entailed ways in which we could talk honestly and directly to one another. We also approached ways in which we could redirect inappropriate criticism into positive channels. Once we had agreed on and practiced these communication patterns with our administrative group, we were ready to act as role models for the communication we believed appropriate for our school.

"Creating a Climate for Change: Students, Teachers, Administrators Working Together," by Susan Benjamin and Jane Gard. *NASSP Bulletin*, April 1993. Reprinted with permission. For more information concerning NASSP services and/or programs, please call (703) 860-0200.

With our focus on effective communication as a base, the members of our administrative council (principal, assistant principals, department chairs, and program directors) discussed concrete ways in which we could set a tone to reflect important premises such as mutual caring, trust, and respect among the entire school community. Our discussion about setting a tone for the school community moved into a practical realm when all department leaders were given an all-school task in addition to their department leadership functions. As a group, we decided that we would enjoy and probably work more productively in pairs or small committees, as opposed to the previous model of each department chair's taking on an individual task.

Working collaboratively, we volunteered for tasks in which we were particularly interested. An important aspect of this process was that the decision about how to lead and what projects we would lead was at least partly in the hands of the individual leaders themselves. That decision-making ability is important in our culture; we, along with our teachers, see ourselves as leaders, as initiators of movement, action, and change. Such collaborative decision making reflects our school's culture.

Values into Practice

The next assumption we challenged was that values could not easily be converted to practice. After defining some of our values, we worked to make them real in practice. We say, for example, that we value empowerment and collaboration; we also say that we value risk-taking toward positive ends. Most of all, we value our students and want to provide a truly positive environment in which they can grow and learn.

As we looked to the new school year, we wanted to find a vehicle to orient and welcome students who were new to the school. Two members of the administrative team were asked to create a freshman orientation program. After determining the precise purpose of the program—a combination of information, entertainment, and tone-setting—we decided to focus on breaking down student anxiety, making freshmen feel truly welcome and important, and perhaps providing a chuckle or two. Because we value student participation, we involved student leaders in organizing and presenting the freshman orientation program.

When students and faculty members work in a true collaboration, the process can be mutually educational and the product can be inspired. As the collaboration progressed, the students and faculty members created a process that involved individuals of both generations in an assembly. The assembly included representatives of many groups, such as our marching band and our pom pon squad. Faculty volunteers performed an original welcoming song (an idea suggested by a student), and upperclassmen welcomed freshmen in the form of "The Freshman Shuffle," an original skit.

The process of creating freshman orientation was important: faculty members and students, working together, created the process and the product. After the assembly, freshmen indicated that they felt Highland Park High School was a comfortable place to be. The collaborative efforts of faculty leaders and students brought about the desired result of making students feel at home in their school.

Sharing the Culture

Another assumption we challenged was that the school culture would automatically become apparent to new faculty members. We created a program to present aspects of the culture before school officially began. Similar to the way the new student orientation program was planned and developed, two department chairpersons developed a program to orient teachers new to the school. After some discussion, they decided that, although much of their charge involved information giving and procedures, providing opportunity for enjoyment and even fun was also important. Therefore, they planned an ice-breaker—a scavenger hunt—to begin the program. Instead of dry, didactic instruction, role-playing of varied situations helped to bring procedures to life.

In order to understand fully the culture of the school, one must have an understanding and appreciation of the culture of the community. At the teacher orientation program, the new teachers were oriented to our community through a bus tour that included lunch at a neighborhood nature center. The community tour included "important" sites of our city, such as where to get a fast food dinner, where well-known athletes live, and locations of feeder schools. Providing visual images of neighborhoods and student gathering spots helped new teachers to understand an important aspect of students' lives. Seeing different neighborhoods, residences, religious institutions, parks, and "hangouts" helped provide new teachers with a context of their school community.

Shared Leadership

Finally, we challenged the assumption that leadership is centralized at the top of a pyramid. Our faculty is composed of strong, diverse, committed leaders. In setting the tone for the school year, we wanted to recognize faculty contributions. Therefore, the opening faculty meeting was divided into segments that emphasized changing directions for the school. Each person who was in charge of a particular area was called on to speak about that initiative. Although the principal led the meeting, the principal did not own the meeting.

Additionally, those who made presentations at the meeting were not just the formally appointed leaders of the school; they were the informal leaders, such as the teacher who was the captain of the faculty baseball team.

All the major initiatives that had preceded the opening faculty meeting were shared with the faculty at large. At this meeting and at subsequent gatherings, whether the faculty has communicated in large or smaller groups, a massive effort toward good communication has taken place. We have set a tone in which we are avoiding "triangulation"; everyone must hear the same thing. Except in instances where confidentiality must be maintained, we avoid secrets. Open communication inspires confidence and empowers our staff to do their best work.

Present Initiatives, Future Promise

We believe that leadership emerges from competence, and competence emerges from successful leadership. Once the tone is set and the model is in place, good things emerge. With our collaborative model of students and teachers working together, we have experienced a number of successes.

For example, we have a new model for student cheerleaders. In our culture, girls feel that they are equal performers, and they do not always enjoy cheering for the boys. A group of boys asked if they could become the cheerleaders and we allowed them to do so. Our cheerleaders are humorous, and they truly lead the cheers for the entire school. This year also featured "Student Stunts," an original musical play, written, performed, and directed by students. The play was a huge success, due to a sparkling script and equally sparkling performances.

Additionally, our entire school was actively involved in a canned food drive for the needy. Mountains of cans, donated by varied constituents of our school community, were stocked in our counseling office. Finally, in our halls, our students and staff exude a spirit of camaraderie and a high sense of energy and purpose.

Despite gloomy reports about American education today and for the future, and despite problems that we face, we look to the coming years with optimism and confidence. We feel that by concentrating on our human resources and by establishing a truly collaborative atmosphere, we can direct change and improve education for our students.

Article Review Form at end of book.

The Benefits of Community Education

Community education—coordinating education, recreation, and social service in the community—benefits the community and the students. According to *Community Education: Building Learning Communities*, published by the National Community Education Association, benefits of community education include:

- Schools and other community agencies are more responsive to parents and other community members
- The learning climate improves, as does student achievement
- The community members work together to solve their problems.

"Community education is a simple idea, bringing to mind the days when the little red schoolhouse functioned, not just as a place to teach children, but as a center for community activities," Larry E. Decker and Associates write in the book's introduction.

Define constructivist leadership and explain how this perspective is supporting collaborative school improvement. What is leadership capacity?

How to Build Leadership Capacity

How can we promote learning and engagement for both adults and students? How can districts support collaborative school improvement efforts?

Linda Lambert

Linda Lambert is Director of the Center for Educational Leadership, California State University-Hayward, Hayward, CA 94542-3080 (e-mail: Llambert@CSUHayward.edu).

Several years ago, I had a conversation with a man considered to be an outstanding principal. I asked, "What happened at the school where you were last principal? Are the reforms still in place?"

"That has been a real disappointment for me," he lamented. "You see, conditions and programs at the school soon returned to the way they were before I got there."

Over the intervening years, I've held several similar conversations. "Returning to normal" is the usual story. It is not surprising that schools do not maintain their improvements. New principals and superintendents often come to a school or district with their own agendas. Or they respond to a charge from the superintendent or board to "turn this school around," "get us back on an even keel," "undo what the incumbent did," or "move us into the future." Such sweeping mandates ignore the history, passions, and qualities of an incumbent staff, choosing instead to import reforms that are both generic and popular.

Less often do new administrators hear, "This is a good school that is getting better. Structures are in place to continue the work. Teacher and parent leadership is strong. We need a principal who can co-lead this school in the direction it is already going."

Most schools cannot yet be described in these glowing terms—they have yet to reach the capacity to sustain improvements on their own. Whether the school is advanced or a beginning in reform, what it does not need is to start over. Each time a school is forced to start over, its staff and community lose some of their personal energy and commitment.

If we are to sustain our improvements and build on the strength and commitment of educators, we need to address the capacity of schools to lead themselves. We need to rethink both leadership and capacity building.

Rethinking Leadership

When we think about leadership, we are accustomed to picturing people in roles with formal authority, such as principals, vice-principals, directors, or superintendents. But we can view *leaderships* as a verb, rather than a noun, by considering the processes, activities, and relationships in which people engage, rather than as the individual in a specific role.

Let's define *leadership* as the reciprocal learning processes that enable participants in a community to construct meaning toward a shared purpose.

Lambert, Linda (1998). "How to Build Leadership Capacity," *Educational Leadership*, v55, n7, pp. 17–19. Reprinted with permission of the Association for Supervision and Curriculum Development. Copyright © 1998 by ASCD. All rights reserved.

This definition is known as "constructivist leadership" (Lambert et al. 1995). Leadership in this context means learning among adults in a community that shares goals and visions. Leadership as learning involves these assumptions:

- *Leadership is not a trait; leadership and leader are not the same.* A leader is anyone who engages in the work of leadership.
- *Leadership is about learning that leads to constructive change.*
- *Everyone has the potential and right to work as a leader.*
- *Leading is a shared endeavor,* the foundation for the democratization of schools.
- *Leadership requires the redistribution of power and authority.* To encourage shared learning, superintendents and principals need to explicitly release authority, and staff need to learn how to enhance personal and collective power and informal authority (Lambert in press).

If leadership is everyone's work, it does not require extraordinary charismatic qualities and uses of authority. If teachers perceive the work as a natural outgrowth of their roles as professional educators, they are less likely to opt out, insisting, "I'm not a leader." Teachers have long attended to the learning of students and themselves; leadership asks that they attend to the learning of their colleagues as well. The skills and dispositions of effective leaders include convening and facilitating dialogue, posing inquiry questions, coaching one another, mentoring a new teacher, and inviting others to become engaged with a new idea. This kind of leadership is naturally engaging and leads to broad-based participation.

Framing Leadership

Building capacity in schools includes developing a new understanding of *leadership capacity*—broad-based, skillful participation in the work of leadership. Leadership capacity can be seen as a complex, interactive framework, with four types of schools and school communities. A caveat is needed here. Frameworks, matrixes, or scales somewhat artificially categorize human behavior. Individuals—and schools—have unique characteristics.

Leadership is the reciprocal learning process that enables participants in a community to construct meaning toward a shared purpose.

- *School 1: Low Participation, Low Skillfulness.* Here, the principal often exercises autocratic leadership. Parents and community members tend to have limited participation. Information flows from the principal to the staff (often originating with the district office), yet is rarely a two-way process. This information often includes rules that govern behavior and practices. Staff often attribute problems to children, family, and the community rather than instructional practices. Collegial work is rare. Staff members—and parents and students—often express resistance by being absent from meetings or school. Teachers rarely initiate new practices, although they may comply with mandates temporarily. Although students may initially show some improvement in achievement when staff members implement mandates, they rarely sustain these gains.

- *School 2: High Participation, Low Skillfulness.* The principal's style is often unpredictable or predictably disengaged. He or she may make unilateral or surprising decisions, often depending on who is asking the question or requesting the action. Information tends to be sparse. Faculty meetings are often composed of "sit and git" sound bites without dialogue. No schoolwide focus on teaching and learning is evident; thus, both excellent and poor classrooms may exist. Many staff work with individual grants, projects, or partnerships that are disconnected from each other. Staff members may not concern themselves with nonachieving classrooms; referrals, attendance, and achievement differ across the school. Roles and responsibilities are unclear. Overall student achievement is often static, with higher achievement for students in particular socioeconomic and gender groups. The range of achievement from high to low is as broad as the range of quality.

- *School 3: High Skillfulness, Low Participation.* This school tends to make concentrated efforts to provide for skillful leadership work for a few teachers and the principal, perhaps as a leadership team. These people may have had opportunities for training through a reform-oriented center, network, or

128 Educational Leadership

coalition. There may be growing polarization among the staff, who may strengthen their resistance as they see favored colleagues leading a change effort. Teams have learned to accumulate and use data to make school decisions, although the data may raise objections or denials from other staff members. Staff caught in the middle (neither thoroughly involved nor disengaged) are often thoughtful allies but relatively unskilled in resolving conflicts. These teachers are unclear what role to play as tension increases between the "haves" and "have nots." Pockets of strong innovation and excellent classrooms tend to exist, but focus on student learning is not schoolwide. Student achievement may show only slight gains.

- *School 4: High Skillfulness, High Participation.* This school tends to have high leadership capacity and broad-based participation. The principal and other leaders make concentrated efforts to include all staff in leadership development and decision making. Staff members have gathered evidence from existing sources or through action research and tend to base decisions on these data. The school has a clear purpose, focusing on student and adult learning. Information loops keep staff, parents, and students informed, with opportunities to discuss, clarify, and refine ideas as they are being formed—long before a final decision is made. Roles and responsibilities are shared and blended, but clear. The school community tends to assume collective responsibility for the work of leadership and learning. Staff members consider themselves to be part of a professional community in which innovation is the norm. Student achievement is high across the student population and within each subgroup as well.

A School on Its Way

New Century High School (a pseudonym) is moving up on the scale of leadership capacity. The school joined a reform network and developed an effective leadership team. The team led in many improvements, including the use of student data to inform decisions. Yet the harder they worked, the more they seemed to alienate some teachers.

"There are some missing pieces here," reflected one team member. "We may have to slow down to speed up." The team then focused on involving more staff, students, and parents in the leadership process. Team members began to converse with staff—to really listen and to engage everyone in schoolwide inquiry.

Six months later, New Century's professional culture is changing. Faculty meetings are devoted to dialogue about teaching and learning. The majority of the staff are involved in the reform effort. People feel that their voices are heard. There are fewer student referrals and failing grades. Schoolwide improvement now seems possible.

Everyone has the potential and right to work as a leader.

Encouraging Leadership

Schools and districts need to create the following conditions if they are to build leadership capacity:

1. Hire personnel with the proven capacity to do leadership work, and develop veteran staff to become skillful leaders.

2. Get to know one another, build trusting relationships.

3. Assess staff and school capacity for leadership. Do you have a shared purpose? Do you work collaboratively? Is there a schoolwide focus on student achievement and adult learning?[1]

4. Develop a culture of inquiry that includes a continuous cycle of reflecting, questioning, gathering evidence, and planning for improvement.

5. Organize for leadership work by establishing inclusive governance structures and collaborative inquiry processes.

6. Implement plans for building leadership capacity—and anticipate role changes and professional development needs.

7. Develop district policies and practices that support leadership capacity building. These practices include district-school relationships built on high engagement but few rules and regulations, as well as shared decision making and site-based school management. Districts should model the processes of a learning organization.

[1] For surveys and rubrics on leadership capacity, as well as extended case studies, see *Building Leadership Capacity in Schools* (Lambert in press).

Collaborating: Building Teams and Leadership Capacity **129**

Sustaining the momentum of our work in schools is essential if we are going to stay the course with program improvements long enough to know whether they succeed. We must institutionalize the processes of collaboration and collective responsibility. Building leadership capacity is not the next innovation, but the foundation for sustaining school and district improvements.

References

Lambert, L., D. Walker, D. Zimmerman, J. Cooper, M. Lambert, M. Gardner, and P.J. Ford-Slack. (1995). *The Constructivist Leader.* New York: Teachers College Press, Columbia University.

Lambert, L. (in press). *Building Leadership Capacity in Schools.* Alexandria, Va.: ASCD.

Article Review Form at end of book.

WiseGuide Wrap-Up

- Effective teams serve organizations and individuals by creating innovation, increasing the performance and self-esteem of employees, and focusing employee efforts.

- The cycle of change in school reform can be successfully directed and enhanced while working in collaborative teams.

- Self-managed work teams take responsibility for outcomes in their work, monitor their own performance, secure resources, and help others improve. They also increase productivity, improve quality, and enhance employees' competencies and commitment.

- Creating a truly collaborative atmosphere requires administrator support and employee initiative, trust, and commitment.

- By building leadership capacity, organizations create broad-based, skilled participation in the work of leadership by others in the organization.

R.E.A.L. Sites

This list provides a print preview of typical **Coursewise** R.E.A.L. sites. There are over 100 such sites at the **Courselinks**™ site. The danger in printing URLs is that web sites can change overnight. As we went to press, these sites were functional using the URLs provided. If you come across one that isn't, please let us know via email to: webmaster@coursewise.com. Use your Passport to access the most current list of R.E.A.L. sites at the **Courselinks**™ site.

Site name: Critical Issue: Building a Committed Team
URL: http://www.ncrel.org/sdrs/areas/issues/educatrs/leadrshp/le200.htm
Why is it R.E.A.L.? This comprehensive report of teams and team building by the North Central Regional Education Laboratory (NCREL) provides specific information for leaders with interconnected links to other resources.
Key topics: collaboration, communication, reform, shared leadership, team
Try this: Review the web site and detail the barriers to building effective teams; how can these barriers be avoided in your school?

Site name: Work Teams in Schools
URL: http://www.ed.gov/databases/ERIC_Digests/ed391226.html
Why is it R.E.A.L.? This well-written digest serves as an executive summary about work teams in schools. It addresses the questions of why use work teams, what are the important team characteristics, what factors are needed for a quality team, and what are the common problems of teamwork and the solutions.
Key topics: change, collaboration, communication, power, reform, shared leadership, team
Try this: Review the digest and identify problems your school has experienced in attempts at teamwork.

Site name: School-Based Reform: A Guide for School Reform Teams
URL: http://www.ed.gov/pubs/Reform/index.html
Why is it R.E.A.L.? A U.S. Department of Education publication, this guide is a resource for school administrators interested in undertaking school-based reforms. It includes examples of promising reform strategies.
Key topics: change, collaboration, communication, power, reform, shared leadership, team
Try this: Describe the suggestions cited in this research-based report for building a school culture that nurtures staff collaboration and participation.

section 5

Instruction: Learning and Leadership

To live a single day and hear a good teaching is better than to live a hundred years without knowing such teaching.

—Buddha

WiseGuide Intro

The concept of instructional leadership is relatively new. Emerging in the early 1980s, this new role changed the responsibilities of school administrators. Expectations of school administrators as managers of school operations shifted to one with a specifically academic mission. Research maintains that high-achieving schools have administrators that lead the academic program, set goals, analyze the curriculum, evaluate faculty, and assess achievement.

The teaching and learning process is at the core of every educational endeavor. Enhancing and increasing the effectiveness of that process must be the goal of every educational leader. However, the road to successful administrator-as-instructional-leader is paved with difficulties, detours, and dead ends. This section highlights the important nature of this work, a successful path to follow, and recommendations for administrators.

In "Instructional Leadership and Principal Visibility," Whitaker details four areas of strategic leadership interaction for higher levels of student achievement. Based on three themes from research on effective instructional leaders, she provides practical avenues for today's educational administrator.

Ovard's article, "Leadership: Maintaining Vision in a Complex Arena," recommends that administrators maintain a vision developed from reliance on values and develop a knowledge that comes from building quality educational programs for all youth, so that each student progresses and finds self-fulfillment in a free society.

Expanding the concept of instructional leadership is "Collegiality: A New Way to Define Instructional Leadership" by Hoerr. He suggests administrators share the responsibility for instructional leadership with teachers, and he outlines steps for building collegiality for teachers in this new role.

Jo and Joseph Blase provide an excellent guide for faculty development in their paper "In the Teachers' Own Words: Six Powerful Elements of Effective Staff Development." Their clear and research-based discussion of powerful elements for staff development provides administrators with a rich resource for teachers.

In his article, "Schools for All Seasons," Goodlad recommends that instructional leaders create "circumstances of richly textured educational environments guided by caring, competent, and professional teachers."

Ediger wraps up the section by discussing teacher motivation, staff development, innovation, and quality instruction through the lens of change. His article "Change and the School Administrator" reviews change from an instructional perspective.

Learning Objectives

- Describe the importance of instructional leadership and its impact on students, faculty, and the community.

- Analyze the patterns of instructional leadership and its impact on major educational reform initiatives.

- Identify the obstacles to instructional leadership and describe their negative impact. Recommend strategies for increasing instructional leadership potential.

- Summarize efforts in shared leadership and the development of leadership teams.

- Explain leadership efforts and the importance of building a culture of lifelong learning through inquiry and collaboration.

- Describe teacher motivation and highlight important criteria to consider in developing effective staff development for teachers.

Questions

Reading 28. Why is instructional leadership such an important part of effective administration? School administrators increase their instructional effectiveness by high levels of performance in what four areas?

Reading 29. Why is education of all youth important? What are the important educational principles for leadership?

Reading 30. How are school leaders joining with teachers in sharing power and developing leadership teams? What are the obstacles to instructional leadership?

Reading 31 How can an instructional leader build a culture of lifelong learning through inquiry and collaboration? What are the six elements of effective staff development that are important for instructional leaders to implement?

Reading 32. How do we create and sustain school programs that cultivate a wide range of human potential? What is the best guarantee for a broadly encompassing intelligence?

Reading 33. What motivates teachers in teaching? What are the important criteria to consider in developing effective staff development for teachers?

Why is instructional leadership such an important part of effective administration? School administrators increase their instructional effectiveness by high levels of performance in what four areas?

Instructional Leadership and Principal Visibility

Beth Whitaker

Beth Whitaker, a former principal, is currently a research assistant and instructor at Indiana State University, Terre Haute, Indiana.

Effective-schools researchers hold that a key element of an effective school is an effective principal. The "principal has to be the person the instructional personnel look to for the instructional leadership in the system. If they do not, the implications for the school are considerably negative" (Edmonds 1981, 26). Weber (1971) listed "strong leadership from the principal" as a characteristic of "successful" schools. Lezotte, Edmonds, and Ratner also identified the principal-as-instructional-leader as one "characteristic of an effective school" (1975, cited in Russell et al. 1985, 3). Andrews and Soder (1987) identified the effective instructional leader as a principal performing at high levels in four areas: resource provider, instructional resource, communicator, and visible presence in the school.

Instructional Leadership

The principal's role in the instructional development of schools has been a focus of educational research for twenty years. The research has demonstrated the great need for strong instructional leadership in schools and has identified several common characteristics of effective leaders. One of those characteristics, extremely important in the life of a school and often neglected, is that of being a visible principal. Many principals get caught up in day-to-day office operations, discipline, paperwork, and telephone conversations. They fail to realize that school business of major importance is found not in the office, but in the classrooms, hallways, playgrounds, and cafeterias. They will never have a sense of the school unless they immerse themselves in the atmosphere beyond the office door. Granted, all principals do their necessary observations, perhaps hand out paychecks, and at times deliver messages of importance to students and staff. But being a part of and knowing the workings of the school extend far beyond these few limited events.

Niece (1983) found three major themes in his qualitative research on effective instructional leaders. First, effective instructional leaders "are people oriented and interactional" (16). These principals did not let themselves become secluded and isolated from the day-to-day operations of the school. They interacted regularly with all people in the school and remained visible and accessible.

Second, effective instructional leaders "function within a network of other principals" (16). The principals made sure they kept in close contact with their peers, on both a formal and informal level. These networks were on local, state, and national levels.

Third, effective instructional leaders were found to have had administrative practitioners who had acted as mentors to them.

Smith and Andrews (1989) identified four areas of strategic

The Clearing House, v70, n3, pp. 155–156, Jan/Feb 1997. Reprinted with permission of the Helen Dwight Reid Educational Foundation. Published by Heldref Publications, 1319 Eighteenth St., N.W., Washington, D.C. 20036-1802. Copyright © 1997.

interaction conducted by instructional leaders that lead to higher levels of student achievement:

- **Being a resource provider.** The teachers in the schools are its greatest resource, and they must be acknowledged for exemplary teaching and encouraged to share with others. The principal must know the strengths and weaknesses of the teachers and show genuine concern for their health, welfare, and professional growth. This caring approach creates a faculty willing to take risks and approach change positively.

- **Being an instructional resource.** The principal identifies good teaching and provides feedback that promotes professional growth.

- **Being a communicator.** The principal must communicate to the staff essential beliefs that (1) all children can learn and experience success; (2) success builds upon success; (3) schools can enhance student success; and (4) learner outcomes must be clearly defined to guide instructional programs and decisions.

- **Being a visible presence.** To create a visible presence in day-to-day activities, principals must model behaviors consistent with the school's vision; live and breathe their beliefs in education; organize resources to accomplish building and district goals; informally drop in on classrooms; make staff development activities a priority; and, most of all, help people do the right things and reinforce those activities. (Andrews, Basom, and Basom 1991, 100)

Modeling Beliefs

Just as teachers need to model appropriate responses and behaviors for their students, the principal must model such actions to teachers, parents, and other staff members, as well as to students. Principals cannot effectively do this without becoming an integral part of the daily operations of their schools. The principal should greet students and staff in the morning. This could mean standing outside the front door with his or her morning coffee or it could mean strolling through the halls to greet teachers by their classrooms and students at their lockers. Sharing welcoming statements allows everyone to start the day in a positive fashion. It also allows principals the opportunity to model appropriate interpersonal interactions for the entire school community.

Effective principals may have students deliver the morning announcements, but they should not neglect the power of their own participation. The principal could share an uplifting thought each day or announce the names of students who have made worthy contributions to the school climate.

Effective instructional leaders must make it a point to visit classrooms daily. These visits should be structured to show that they have meaning and purpose. They validate the idea that the classrooms are where the truly important activities in a school occur and that instructional leadership is the most critical responsibility of the school principal.

Allan Glatthorn (1984) described these visits as administrative monitoring or "drop-in supervision." Their purpose should be to see teachers at work under normal conditions; they should be learning-centered, with emphasis on the teacher's purpose, the learning experience, and the atmosphere of the classroom. The visits are very informal in nature compared with the formal evaluation approach. They can last anywhere from five to fifteen minutes and require no systematic approach by the principal. Afterwards, the administrator must provide feedback to the teacher and use the observational data as part of an ongoing assessment of the instructional program and climate of the school (Glatthorn 1984).

Interaction and Feedback

While the principal is in the classroom, he or she should not only take note of the workings of the classroom, but participate and interact with students if the situation permits. Helping children work on assignments or getting involved in class discussions promotes the principal's belief in the importance of learning. Those interactions could also provide the principal with a better picture of individual students' abilities. That knowledge will help the principal engage in richer and more meaningful conversations with students, parents, and teachers.

After a principal has been in a classroom, he or she needs to take the time to write the teacher a note about the informal observation. The note should be placed in the teacher's mailbox that day and could even be written in the classroom during the observation. The note should contain words of encouragement and praise about specific teaching strategies or management. The principal's drop-in observation could be a catalyst for an informal conversation in the hallway or the teacher's workroom later in the day. The principal could also make note of successful classroom activities in the weekly bulletin. The bulletin can praise good teachers, inform the rest of the staff of classroom activities, and allow the principal to reinforce the effective teaching standards he or she has set forth for the staff.

These practices are supported by Foriska (1994) when he discusses instructional leadership as "critical to the development and maintenance of an effective school" (33). Instructional leaders must influence others to couple appropriate instructional practices with their best knowledge of the subject matter. The focus must always be on student learning, and principals must supply teachers with resources and incentives to keep their focus on students. Principals must keep teachers informed about educational tools and developments in the field of effective teaching. They must also be available to teachers to help critique these tools and teaching practices and to determine their applicability to the classroom.

The visible principal has the opportunity to model his or her beliefs and to promote a positive instructional climate—major leadership behaviors of effective principals (Krug 1992). Principals who create an exciting and reinforcing learning environment will find that students and teachers will want to do what needs to be done.

References

Andrews, R. L., and R. Soder. 1987. Principal leadership and student behavior. *Educational Leadership* 6: 9–11.

Andrews, R. L., M. R. Basom, and M. Basom. 1991. Instructional leadership: Supervision that makes a difference. *Theory into Practice* 30(2): 97–101.

Edmonds, R. 1981. *Improving the effectiveness of New York City public schools*. (ERIC Document Reproduction Service No. ED 243 980).

Foriska, T. J. 1994. The principal as instructional leader: Teaming with teachers for student success. *Schools in the Middle* 3(3): 31–34.

Glatthorn, A. 1984. *Differential supervision*. Alexandria, Va.: Association for Supervision and Curriculum Development.

Krug, S. 1992. Instructional leadership: A constructivist perspective. *Educational Administration Quarterly* 28(3): 430–43.

Niece, R. 1993. The principal as instructional leader: Past influences and current resources. *NASSP Bulletin* 77(553): 12–18.

Russell, J., J. Mazzarella, T. White, and S. Maurer. 1985. *Linking the behaviors and activities of secondary school principals to school effectiveness: A focus on effective and ineffective behaviors*. Eugene, Ore.: University of Oregon, Center for Educational Policy and Management. (ERIC Document Reproduction Service No. ED 258 322).

Smith, W., and R. Andrews. 1989. *Instructional leadership: How principals make a difference*. Alexandria, Va.: Association for Supervision and Curriculum Development (ASCD) Press.

Article Review Form at end of book.

Why is education of all youth important? What are the important educational principles for leadership?

Leadership

Maintaining vision in a complex arena

How does one maintain the vision to provide leadership in the complex world of today's schools? This writer suggests that a reliance on values and principles is still a fundamental.

Glen F. Ovard

Glen F. Ovard is a professor, Department of Educational Leadership, Brigham Young University, Provo, Utah

Never in the history of education has so much been expected from the principal. As a manager, the principal is expected to do things right, and as a leader, to do all the right things. Clear vision is required, but the playing field is muddy.

The principal is expected to have imagination and creativity and build a program of excellence while policy-making bodies mandate a curriculum with less and less opportunity for creativity and choice, two fundamental ingredients for excellence in a society.

A principal is sued for not providing a delinquent student with all his legal rights and proper due process, while elsewhere citizens applaud a principal for carrying a baseball bat while patrolling the halls.

Principals have found, through endless hours of parent conferences, that parents want every student disciplined but their own. Principals have also found, in an age of single parents, that it isn't enough to know the parents of 2,500 students. They must also know who the legal guardian is, and who has custody of the student. Records must be kept on each student and be open to the parents; however, the of-age student can prohibit a parent from seeing them. And the list goes on.

How simple were the administrative problems of yesterday compared with those of today. How does one maintain vision in this complex arena? Perhaps a principal must develop some of the characteristics of the fire walker.

The Fire Walker

A few years ago in Fiji, I witnessed a fire walking exhibition. It was a clear day. A fire was built in a pit approximately 15 feet long and kept burning for hours until there was a bed of red-hot coals. Around the pit were people from many parts of the world, all waiting for the fire walker. Emotions ranged from passive indifference to high expectation, from doubt to belief, from speculation to those who thought they could do better without ever trying to walk the bed of coals.

A hush came over the crowd. A Holy Man and his disciples approached from a nearby sanctuary where they had been meditating and preparing themselves. The Holy Man took off his loose robe, and except for a loin cloth, stood naked before the crowd. He stepped forward and stopped with his bare feet poised at the edge of the pit.

He looked over the heads of the onlookers and doubters, and with deep concentration he slowly walked across the bed of coals, and reentered his sanctuary.

"Leadership: Maintaining Vision in a Complex Arena," by Glen F. Ovard. *NASSP Bulletin,* February 1990. Reprinted with permission. For more information concerning NASSP services and/or programs, please call (703) 860-0200.

While everyone was applauding and praising the remarkable feat, I couldn't help wondering about his concentration, his control of his body's sensory mechanisms. Was his mind focused on the past, the present, or the future?

How does one walk across the red-hot coals of the present and still maintain the vision of the future? How can a principal maintain clear vision for the future of education in a society where values are shifting, where laws become relative, and where serious crimes are resolved through plea bargaining?

Perhaps the stability of vision for the future comes through meditating and holding fast to some long-standing values and guidelines.

Some Principles and Guidelines

Value and Importance of Education

As principals, we must never lose sight of the value and importance of education in our society. Thomas Jefferson said it well: "If a nation expects to be free and ignorant in a state of civilization, it expects what never was and never will be."

We must constantly try to improve the educational program without sacrificing the quality. In the words of Henry Steele Commager, the great educator and historian, "Our schools have kept us free."

In our struggle for efficiency, we must remember the value and importance of education for our society and for each individual. To accept a lesser quality of education is to settle for a form of slavery.

Education for All American Youth

There was a time when the national educational policy was "Education for All American Youth." The achievement of this goal has been a constant force in the developmental pattern of American education. We moved from an education of the elite and education only for those who had leisure time to education for "free" people, education for females, education for children in grades one through eight, education through high school, education for all those desiring a college and university level opportunity, education for the blind and deaf, education for the handicapped, education for at-risk students, and education for the gifted and talented.

The simple principle, "Education for All American Youth" with its expanding realization is a unique feature and contribution of American education to the world. This universal education is what makes the "land of opportunity" different from the lands of the "haves and have nots."

Principals must resist trends, policies, and financial restrictions that produce elitism in education, restriction on students in curriculum choices, restrictions in post-high-school opportunities, non-participation in high school programs because of enlarging fee structures, and reduction in programs for handicapped or any established program that reduces the educational opportunities for all American youth.

Quantity vs. Quality

Quantity never was quality. These words are not the same; nor do they have the same use, except to confuse the issue; and that is what we have been doing in education, confusing the issue. For example, we keep increasing graduation requirements instead of asking, "How can we do it better in the same amount of time?" If students don't want to take math, the question to be answered is "Why?" not, "We need to require another class."

If students can't write well after 11 years of English, 1 more year of English is not the answer. *Writing* is the answer.

How do we get more writing? Assign it. Why isn't it assigned? Because teachers have too many students and soon decide they can't read all the papers, and so little writing is assigned.

The problems might better be solved by reducing the teacher's work load and/or by finding creative ways by which the writing can be read and students encouraged with appropriate feedback.

Attack the problem of quality! Do not assume that more quantity is a related skill will transfer into improved education in a specific skill. Increasing quantity should never be the first solution to improving quality.

Solving All Society's Problems

The schools must stop assuming the responsibility for solving all society's problems. The schools cannot be all things to all people. As school leaders, we must define the area of the school's responsibility.

Our curriculum continues to expand. As we take on new responsibilities, the time spent in the traditional assigned curriculum must decrease. For example, we added driver's education because society had a problem on the highway, and accidents became the responsibility of the school. We added sex education because society had become more promiscuous, and now we are responsible for the growing number of teenage pregnancies. Soon the schools will bear the responsibility for the increasing number of AIDS cases.

The critics are measuring school success by scores on national tests, but there are no points scored on the ACT test for winning ball games, combating drug use, and knowing how to manage in society as a single parent.

Is the school the proper agency in society to solve these problems? If we are that agency, we become accountable for performance success.

In the time allotted for instruction, we cannot be accountable for all things. There must be a definition. School leaders must help make this definition for the future. We must learn how to say "No, it is not our responsibility," or, if we say yes, we must negotiate a lower quality acceptance level for achievement in subjects traditionally assigned to the school and which are scored and related on national tests.

Promote the Successes of Our Schools

At the national and state levels, the image of the public school is severely tarnished. Morale is at an all-time low. People speak freely about our nation at risk because of the failure of our schools.

This writer does not believe the nation is at risk, nor does he believe the schools are failures. But, if the nation is at risk, it is

How to Develop Student Self-Esteem

Teachers and principals who participated in the Burger King Corporation 1989 In Honor of Excellence Symposium were asked how parents can help their children develop self-esteem and discover their hidden talents. The top tips were:

1. Communicate more effectively; ask and listen more carefully
2. Give your child a multitude of experiences—allow him or her to explore, expand, investigate, and share his or her talents with you
3. Be very observant—look for positive behaviors to reinforce
4. Let your child find his or her way after you have provided guidance and varied opportunities
5. Talk to your child as an equal (adult to adult) and show respect.

due to political decisions, not intellectual abilities. If the economy is faltering it is due to business and management decisions, not because of a lack of algebra.

In the future, our national, state, and local educational organizations must take stands against claims of school failure. We must establish a "non-responsibility statement." We must not be branded as failures when the fault is not ours. We can no longer passively take the blame for adolescent misbehavior. Protection of the name of a minor in a non-school act, at a non-school time, should not allow the reputation of a school to be smeared by association.

State education groups are constantly stating how "bad" our schools are so we can get more money to make the schools "good." To achieve one objective, we portray failure, not success. We must cooperate. No one wants to invest in a failing enterprise.

Conclusion

When the field gets muddy, someone must have vision and provide direction. Vision is not simply following the crowd, joining the popular trend of today. A leader is one who does the right thing for the right reasons. Values and principles are still fundamental in decision making.

We are living in a time when the public is interacting and making increased demands upon the school and school leaders. We must be careful in moving through the muddied field. Occasionally, we must walk on red-hot coals, but while crossing the pit of burning embers, we must still look beyond the crowds, the jeers, the doubters, and the underminers.

We must have vision that comes from meditation, a reliance on values, a knowledge that comes from building quality educational programs for all American youth so that each individual can progress and find self-fulfillment in a free society. Perhaps with such values and guidelines, based upon experience, the principal can have a vision of the future and "On a Clear Day, See Forever."

Article Review Form at end of book.

How are school leaders joining with teachers in sharing power and developing leadership teams? What are the obstacles to instructional leadership?

Collegiality

A new way to define instructional leadership

The demands on today's principals make it almost impossible to do the job alone. Mr. Hoerr suggests that the solution is to share the responsibility for instructional leadership with teachers, and he outlines the steps for building collegiality and supporting teachers in their new roles.

Thomas R. Hoerr

Thomas R. Hoerr is director of the New City School, St. Louis, Mo.

When a parent says, "My child's school is a wonderful school," what that parent really means is that his or her child has had a super teacher, followed by a great teacher, followed by a tremendous teacher. Sparkling facilities and state-of-the-art technology are important, and—to the degree that they enable teachers to do a better job of teaching—they are valuable. But the most important factor in a child's education remains what it has always been: the teacher. When children have wonderful teachers year after year, they flourish, and their parents are delighted with the school.

That's a simple premise, but it has important implications for principals. All principals know that teachers are the most important factor in the educational equation; we learned it in graduate school. We also learned that we are expected to provide the instructional leadership that enables teachers to grow professionally. But—like many of the important things in life—providing such leadership is easier said than done.

Obstacles to Instructional Leadership

During the last several decades, the role of the principal has become increasingly complex as society has made ever-greater demands on the schools. Today there are breakfasts to provide and after-school programs to oversee. There are special programs to coordinate for students at both ends of the academic spectrum. There are anti-gang and drug-awareness efforts, employee unions and neighborhood groups whose needs and interests must be attended to, IEPs and SATS—along with OBE, TQM, and the ADA. Indeed, the list is almost endless.

As schools have taken on a variety of new tasks, educators have come to understand much more about how children learn. And as knowledge of child development, curriculum, and instruction has burgeoned, the profession has become balkanized. Many of today's teachers have their own areas of expertise and their own professional language. One group of teachers may live and breathe thematic instruction, another group investigates student portfolios and other forms of alternative assessment, "the Reggio Approach" occupies the kindergarten crowd, and a committee considers putting in place a schoolwide program based on Howard Gardner's theory of multiple intelligences. It is simply not realistic to expect an administrator to

---

"Collegiality: A New Way to Define Instructional Leadership" by Thomas R. Hoerr. © 1996 Phi Delta Kappan. Reprinted with permission. Dr. Hoerr is the director of the New City School in St. Louis, MO.

serve as an intellectual resource or catalyst for all these (and countless other) efforts.

As Roland Barth said in his 1980 book, *Run School Run.* "The obstacles to the job are the job." But while we administrators can identify the constraints and the roadblocks that keep us from exercising instructional leadership, we cannot let those obstacles stop us. Our task is to find ways to remove or go around them.

The Teacher's Role

Although the principal bears ultimate responsibility for the quality of his or her school, it is both necessary and appropriate that teachers take on some of the responsibility for instructional leadership. This means that the principal will share power. It means leadership teams. It means that teachers will play a part in determining school procedures. It means that teachers will view their roles from a schoolwide, not just a classroom, perspective. It means that teachers, working together, will take responsibility for helping their peers learn and grow.

Like principals, however, teachers have obstacles that keep them from serving as instructional leaders. The greatest, of course, is their hectic and isolated workday. Most teachers spend 80% to 90% of their workday in direct contact with students. Planning periods, recesses, or lunch breaks are about their only times away from students. And many of these "free" periods are taken up by a child who needs extra attention or by a parent who can only be reached by telephone at work.

Another obstacle is the fact that most teachers are not trained to help peers grow professionally, and the vast majority of teachers find this new role uncomfortable at first. On those occasions when discussions in the teachers' lounge focus on education, they typically deal with the three C's: children, curriculum, and complaints. Rarely do teachers solicit feedback about their teaching performance from their peers; rarely do they offer help to one another that goes beyond sharing a ditto master or lending a pair of scissors. Teachers are often reluctant to view themselves as "teachers of teachers."

This mindset causes teachers to see themselves as figure skaters who are being scored individually on form and creativity. Instead, they ought to view themselves as hockey players, all playing on the same team and working toward the same goal: a better school.

However, empowering teachers to collaborate on schooled tasks and to work with one another on becoming more effective requires that a new relationship be forged between administrators and teachers. Implementing this kind of program is never easy. If collegiality has not existed before, resistance is likely to come from all quarters. To some extent, this is understandable: collegiality takes more time; it requires participants to play new roles, and it makes everyone accountable (since everyone is now part of the solution). Still, the benefits warrant the effort. The following factors should be considered in thinking about how to create a sense of collegiality in a school.

1. *Time is our most precious resource.* Sufficient time must be allocated for collegiality. Whether the time to talk comes during before-school or after-school meetings, at lunchtime, over dinner, at evening meetings, or on weekends depends on a given faculty's availability and preference. *When* is unimportant. The important thing is that teachers and administrators meet frequently enough and for sufficiently long periods to enable them to discuss their educational philosophies, long-term issues, and ways they can work together. Faculty meetings are too often perfunctory, covering information that could be disseminated in a school bulletin, or they are held in response to a crisis situation.

Once the time for collegiality has been carved out, someone—perhaps the principal, initially—needs to set an agenda and focus the discussion. Collegiality stems from discussions about students, instruction, and curriculum, and such discussions take significant chunks of time. Fifteen minutes won't suffice.

2. *An invitation is better than a command.* Change is best viewed as a series of concentric circles, starting small and expanding. Inviting everyone to participate at the start is important. From this beginning, a nucleus of interested teachers will no doubt emerge—people who are willing to take risks, to look at their roles differently, and to get involved with schoolwide issues. Complaints about favoritism can be avoided by continually sharing information with the entire faculty and by periodically opening membership in the group to everyone or by forming new groups to address

different topics. As participating teachers tell their peers that involvement has been rewarding, others will want to join in.

3. *Power shared is power multiplied.* But principals need to realize that, if teachers are going to invest their time and energy, they need to be heard and to make a difference on substantive issues. Inevitably, then, some things will be decided in ways that differ from the principal's preference.

   The key is thinking through ahead of time which issues are appropriate for collegial decisions and which issues should be resolved by the principal. The final say on teacher evaluation, for example, should probably reside with the principal. But there is no reason why teachers cannot provide the principal with input regarding the criteria used to evaluate them or regarding the evaluation process itself. Similarly, there is no reason why teachers cannot control a significant portion of their classroom budgets, set the agenda for faculty meetings, or provide input into the scheduling of specialist teachers and the use of teacher aides. Once such "administrivia" have been shared, the climate is established for teachers to work with one another on curriculum integration, on teaching higher-level thinking skills, or on observing one another's classes.

4. *We practice what we value.* When the principal actually takes part in the meetings, he or she demonstrates that collegiality is valued. Delegating responsibility to others is better than hoarding all the decisions, but actively participating in the group is better still. By his or her presence, the principal gives unequivocal testimony to the importance of the task.

   Teachers who engage in collegial activities can be supported in a number of ways. Hiring substitutes to free classroom teachers for planning sessions during the school day is one obvious means of showing that teachers' participation and input are valued. Even if substitutes are hired only a couple of times per year, the message is clear. A positive note about a teacher's participation in collegial efforts on end-of-year evaluation forms says too that such activities are valued.

5. *Focus on an important issue.* Make sure that the issue on which collegial efforts are focused is one that is meaningful to teachers. One way to find meaningful issues is through a reading group. Invite interested teachers to meet weekly to discuss articles or books that all participants have read in advance. Discussing such readings is a good way to begin talking about significant issues in a collegial setting. To keep the tone nonhierarchical and genuinely collegial, find a teacher to chair the meetings.

Teachers are often reluctant to view themselves as "teachers of teachers."

Another good way to find meaningful issues is simply to ask teachers what questions they would like to pursue, what frustrations they are experiencing, and how they would like to see their school change. This is a risky strategy for the principal, but if he or she cannot be vulnerable, the likelihood for sustained change is not strong.

Dramatic change is slow and difficult. But if schools are to excel, faculties must continue to learn and grow with their students. Clearly, a collegial approach that empowers teachers and lets them share the responsibility for instructional leadership holds promise for the future.

Article Review Form at end of book.

How can an instructional leader build a culture of lifelong learning through inquiry and collaboration? What are the six elements of effective staff development that are important for instructional leaders to implement?

In the Teachers' Own Words

Six powerful elements of effective staff development

Jo Blase and Joseph Blase

e-mail: jblase@coe.uga.edu
Department of Educational Leadership
University of Georgia

Recent efforts to democratize schools have included efforts to empower teachers and professionalize teaching, notably in the areas of instructional leadership and staff development. In particular, "supervision," the observation and evaluation of teachers by school leaders, has been increasingly viewed as the external imposition of bureaucratic, rational authority and has been challenged by many who work to professionalize teaching. As a result, many of today's successful schools are fast becoming centers of shared inquiry and decision making; teachers are moving toward a collective—not an individual—practice of teaching. They are collaborating with each other and with supervisors in a "kind of mutual nudging in the profoundly cooperative search for answers" to instructional problems (Dowling & Sheppard, 1976, p. 5). Instructional leadership is being shared with teachers, and in its best forms it is being cast as coaching, reflection, collegial investigation, study teams, explorations into intriguing and uncertain matters, and problem solving. Alternatives, not directives or criticism, are the focus, and administrators and teachers work together as a collaborative community of learners engaged in professional and moral (even noble) service to students.

Unfortunately, the relationships among leadership behavior, staff development, and classroom teaching remain relatively unexamined. Clearly, what exists about critical aspects of instructional leadership vis-a-vis teacher development is largely exploratory.

What We Know About Staff Development

For more than a quarter of a century, Bruce Joyce, director of Booksend Laboratories in Pauma Valley, California, has been studying teachers' repertoires and synthesizing research on teaching models. He and his colleagues have produced valuable resources to help educators enhance their skills and use varied, research-based strategies to help students learn. Joyce et al. have also reviewed the literature in the areas of curricula, teaching, learning,

---

Jo Blase and Joseph Blase (1998) Inquiry and Collaboration: Supporting the lifelong study of teaching and learning. International Electronic Journal for Leadership in Learning, v2, n7. URL: http://www.acs.ucalgary.ca/~iejll/

Jo and Joseph Blase are professors of educational leadership at the University of Georgia. Formerly a secondary school principal, Jo has published widely in the areas of administrator teacher interaction vis-a-vis school reform and supervisory discourse, leadership preparation, and instructional discourse among physicians. Joseph has published extensively in the areas of teacher stress, relationships between teachers, personal and professional lives, teacher socialization, principal-teacher relationships, school-level micropolitics, and democratic school leadership.

Reprinted with permission of the authors and the International Electronic Journal of Leadership in Learning.

training, and staff development; have conducted large-scale initiatives for school renewal; and have completed research involving thousands of teachers, administrators, agencies, districts, states, organizations, and countries.

From these sources, Joyce and his colleagues have produced solid evidence of the potential effects of instructional innovations such as teaching skills and technologies, and they have demonstrated these effects by using the most rigorous scientific methods, in the form of effect sizes (often measured as the difference between an experimental and a control group, computed in terms of standard deviations; see Glass, 1982, and Joyce & Calhoun, 1996, for more details).

Indeed, from volumes of data, extensive research, and many years of practice, Joyce and his colleagues produced a vision of an effective staff development system. His recent book with Beverly Showers, *Student Achievement Through Staff Development* (Joyce & Showers, 1995), deals with planning a comprehensive staff development system to support teaching and learning. This book also discusses the governance, design, and implementation of a system's elements and programs.

A Study Enhancing Joyce's Approach

Our study sought to broaden Joyce's approach, and we learned a great deal about instructional leaders' strategies, behaviors, attitudes, and goals vis-a-vis staff development. (Note that although in many cases instructional supervisors are, in fact, school principals, they may also be lead teachers, department chairpersons, curriculum directors, and staff developers). To accomplish this, we fashioned a large study of over 800 teachers who provided detailed reports of their leaders' instructionally-related actions.

The purpose of our study was to investigate the broad question, What characteristics (e.g., strategies, behaviors, attitudes, goals) of instructional leaders positively influence classroom teaching? (Adverse effects were also investigated and are reported in another article). We wanted to know the personal and professional effects of leader-teacher interactions and whether staff development emerged as a primary theme of effective instructional leadership.

Data Collection and Analysis

To encourage teachers' free expression and inclusion of details, we used a special protocol wherein data collection and analysis were consistent with symbolic interaction theory. Symbolic interaction, in contrast to some qualitative research approaches, stresses individual perception and interpretation. In this approach, data are analyzed to produce descriptive categories, themes, and conceptual and theoretical understandings (Bogdan & Biklen, 1982).

We gathered data by administering an inventory to a total of 809 teachers from southeastern, midwestern, and northwestern United States. Participants included men and women from rural, urban, and suburban locations; elementary and secondary schools; with a range of content areas and years of experience in teaching. Teachers were asked to provide detailed descriptions of their instructional leaders' characteristics that impacted their teaching, the areas of impact, the degree of effectiveness of the instructional leaders' actions, and their thoughts about such actions. We analyzed each reported characteristic to determine its impact on teachers' feelings, thinking, and behavior as related to classroom teaching.

Findings of the Study

Our findings suggest that instructional leaders' characteristics profoundly impact on teachers' classroom behavior; indeed, they lead to powerful cognitive, affective, and behavioral effects on teachers. Three primary themes define effective instructional leadership: talking with teachers, promoting teachers' professional growth, and fostering teacher reflection. We call this the TiGeR approach to instructional leadership (see Blase & Blase, 1998). We describe below some specifics of the second theme: promoting teachers' professional growth via staff development.

Along these lines, we found that effective instructional leaders frequently provided staff development opportunities that addressed emergent instructional needs; the meaningfulness of such sessions had substantial effects on teachers. Teacher input into the design and content of staff development, optional attendance, and active participation of the instructional leader also enhanced staff development. Broadly speaking, we learned that instructional leaders use staff development to provide the following conditions for teachers to learn about, synthesize, and enact various teaching strategies:

- Opportunities to study the professional literature and proven programs

- Demonstrations of new skills
- Practice of new skills
- Support from peer coaches
- Assistance in studying student learning through action research (i.e., gathering data about student achievement)
- Assistance in studying how new strategies are implemented and how they affect students

Six Powerful Elements of Staff Development

We found that the hallmark of effective staff development is a philosophy of and support for lifelong learning about teaching and learning. We also discovered that staff development, as a key aspect of effective instructional leadership, is consistently centered on six elements: the study of teaching and learning, collaboration, coaching, action research, resources, and adult development.

1. The Study of Teaching and Learning

To foster innovation in teaching (methods, materials, technology) and to increase student learning, principals who were effective instructional leaders helped faculty members stay informed about current trends and issues. This was accomplished by distributing professional literature and journal articles; inviting critical discussion of research and trends; supporting attendance at workshops, seminars, and conferences; and, most importantly, focusing professional development sessions and conversation squarely on teaching and learning issues.

The effects of sharing professional and research literature with teachers were very positive and included increases in teacher motivation, reflection on teaching and learning, and reflectively informed instructional behavior. For example, in terms of the latter, examination of the current literature helped teachers bring more instructional variety ("to get out of the rut") and innovation to the classroom.

In addition, teachers reported that their participation in workshops, seminars, and conferences positively affected their self-esteem and sense of being supported; and that their motivation, classroom reflection, and reflectively informed behavior were impacted most dramatically. For example, teachers discussed increases in innovation and variety of teaching methods in classrooms:

I want to learn new and more effective ways to engage students and increase learning by attending workshops. My principal is supportive of my natural need to learn new things. She cares enough about me to recognize my positive qualities and support me in fulfilling my need for growth. I think that it is very important to keep abreast of trends and issues in my field. Workshops do that for me. I have tried several of the teaching strategies I have learned. Some work for me and some don't enhance my teaching. I am very aware of all the resources teachers have. My principal recognizes that I do not want to be just an ordinary teacher. I feel proud and excited.

2. Building a Culture of Collaboration

Studies of innovation show that sustained improvement in teaching often hinges on the development of teachers-as-learners who collaborate with one another to study teaching and its effects (Joyce & Showers, 1995). Our data point out that effective instructional leadership was frequently based on related beliefs such as:

- We are all learners; thus school is a community of learners, including faculty, staff, students, parents, and administrators.
- We are all lifelong learners; thus, our goal is to prepare students for lifelong learning by teaching them (helping them learn) how to learn.
- We are all coaches; thus we learn from each other and help others learn.
- We are all colleagues and collaborators.
- We openly discuss our views and work toward consensus. This includes dialogue about curriculum, instruction, and program administration vis-a-vis students, teachers, administrators, supervisors, and parents. Such dialogue spans philosophy, belief, literature, and research. (Calhoun's [1994] matrix forms a good basis for such discussions.)

The myriad of formal and informal opportunities principals provided for teacher collaboration yielded vast positive results for teachers. Within teachers' enthusiastic comments about collaboration, we found strong impacts on teachers' motivation, self-esteem, confidence, and ownership of decisions. Also apparent were strong impacts on teacher reflection and reflectively informed instructional behavior (e.g., instructional variety, risk-taking, focus) and, of course, teacher-teacher collaborative interaction itself:

By observing other teachers, I have been able to think of my own teaching strengths and weaknesses from a new perspective. I have become more willing to ask for help from my principal and fellow teachers. We have all become more open to admitting difficulties and asking for help rather than closing ourselves off and complaining. I am very happy to be valued in that environment.

3. Promoting Coaching

We found substantial evidence that effective instructional leaders advocated coaching among teachers for purposes of teacher development. This happened in two ways. First, principals encouraged teachers to become models for each other. This served to improve teaching, to motivate teachers, to provide recognition of exemplary teachers. Specifically, principals actively encouraged teachers to visit the classrooms of exemplary teachers, asked exemplary teachers to serve as models to other teachers, and encouraged teachers to make presentations within their school and district and at professional conferences.

Teachers reported that modeling good teaching for their colleagues led to greater confidence, motivation, and self-esteem. Modeling for colleagues also increased a teacher's own reflection and reflectively informed behavior. One teacher noted,

He encourages me to share my teaching techniques with others; it makes me think that what I'm doing is working. Also, having another pair of eyes in my room, whether it be student teachers, recruits, or tenured teachers, makes me want to improve my teaching.

Second, for purposes of professional growth, effective instructional leaders encouraged teachers to visit other schools—to become the learner—to observe classrooms and programs.

Observing in other classrooms had positive effects on teacher self-esteem and risk-taking, and it yielded greater reflection and reflectively-informed behavior in the classroom. One teacher remarked:

Visiting other schools helped me keep an open mind when approaching new topics. I have felt validated as a professional by my principal. It has encouraged me to develop as a risk taker. I have been better able to make decision about curriculum, and I feel free to use professional judgment in how I implement new strategies.

4. Using Inquiry to Drive Staff Development

Our study showed that an essential part of good staff development was training in collection and analysis of data about student learning. The effective leaders described by teachers in our study attempted to plan and operate staff development as a large-scale action research project, although they admitted they failed to use action research on student progress to the degree they knew was necessary. One teacher noted:

The principal uses surveys to determine our needs and our educational background. Then we plan inservices to meet needs as indicated by the survey results.

5. Providing Resources to Support Growth and Improvement

The teachers we studied explained that effective leaders helped to develop faculty by providing essential resources and that this greatly enhanced teacher growth, classroom teaching, and student learning. They provided resources, sometimes in liberal amounts, to support teacher growth and to improve classroom instruction:

She will let our teachers buy anything within reason that is necessary for teaching effectively. She openly states that instruction of students is our chief priority, and any resource we might need to that end gets first priority.

Classroom materials were the most frequently described available resource (e.g., supplies, subject-matter texts including books and printed matter, manipulatives, games, and kits). Occasionally, instructional leaders gave teachers small amounts of money ($100–$200) to purchase classroom materials. Several teachers reported that such leaders also provided them with parent volunteers and paraprofessionals. Teachers said:

She does what she can to provide necessary instructional resources. Our school has a form that teachers can fill out listing the resources they need. The form goes to our teacher council. The teacher has a representative present a rationale for the need. Most often the request is approved and the material is bought immediately.

She is constantly asking us what resources she can find for us to improve our current teaching or classroom.

Our study produced no evidence that the availability of resources strongly affected teachers' positive feelings about teaching; however, having resources did yield major impacts on teacher reflection and reflectively informed behavior:

Extra classroom materials help me be creative in my lesson plans. I came up with different activities that students could work on. The extra money allows individual teachers the freedom to buy materials as they see fit.

Her help [in providing resources] encouraged me to be reflective, be on the cutting edge, and be a risk taker. She encouraged me to jump in. If I messed up, I would say "oops" and try again! I felt safe. Her emphases were always on personal growth and professionalism. My achievements were her achievements. She was not threatened by my success—she enjoyed it!

6. Applying Principles of Adult Development

Part and parcel of the design and implementation of staff development programs is an understanding of principles of adult development and the conditions that enhance adult learning. Phillips and Glickman (1991) have found that teachers who work in a stimulating and supportive environment can reach higher stages of development. Joyce and Showers (1995) have demonstrated that "virtually all teachers can learn the most powerful and complex teaching strategies, provided that staff development is designed properly" (p. 10). In contrast, the work of Glickman, Gordon, and Ross-Gordon (1995), which compares actual and optimal teacher development, shows that an oppressive school environment and traditional (e.g., bureaucratic, evaluation-oriented) approaches to supervision often hinder teacher development. As reflected in our findings, instructional leaders worked hard to:

- Adhere to the principles of adult learning
- Respond to and foster teachers' professional stage development
- Recognize and support different phases within teachers' life cycles
- Help teachers to understand, navigate, and learn from life transition events
- Recognize and accommodate teachers' various roles, and
- Enhance teacher motivation

Implications for Staff Developers

Based on the collective reports of over 800 teachers who participated in our study, we suggest that instructional leaders, including principals and all other staff developers, work to enhance teachers' professional development in the following ways:

1. Build an atmosphere and processes of democracy (shared decision making and collective responsibility) and a culture of learning (a belief that we are all life-long learners committed to creating a learning environment) among teachers and administrators.

2. Learn, with the faculty and parents, about school improvement and effective staff development (e.g., attend and participate in staff development sessions).

3. Provide training in action research. (For a basic understanding of action research, we recommend Calhoun's *How to Use Action Research in the Self-Renewing School* (1994.) This highly useful guide to action research is based on work with educators throughout the world. Among other things, Calhoun describes the phases of effective action research.)

4. Collectively assess the effects of instruction and the climate of the school.

5. Organize a staff development council to coordinate activities (see Wolf, 1994, for guidelines and resources).

6. Focus staff development programs on the areas of curriculum, instruction, and technology, as they are more likely to have effects on student learning.

7. Organize study groups and support their activities.

8. Develop peer coaching relationships and support their activities. (See Joyce & Showers, 1995 and Showers & Joyce, 1996, for more details on Nos. 7 and 8, study groups and peer coaching).

9. Provide time for collaboration for the study of teaching and learning. This will reduce the isolation, not the autonomy, that alienates teachers from each other.

10. Encourage a commitment to spend time studying outcomes, curriculum, and teaching practice rather than administrivia and technical/managerial matters. Put differently, increase time spent on items toward the top of the list below, and decrease time spent on items at the bottom (many educators have this backwards!):

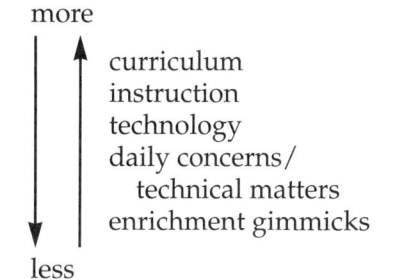

   more

   curriculum
   instruction
   technology
   daily concerns/
     technical matters
   enrichment gimmicks

   less

11. Provide time for study of implementation of innovations in curriculum, teaching, and instruction. (An

extensive discussion of teaching-learning models can be found in Joyce and Weil's *Models of Teaching* [1996]. For highlights of current research on effective teaching and its relationship to the improvement of learning, see Waxman and Walberg [1991].)

12. Encourage individual teachers to develop instructional goals and objectives and to meet with teachers to discuss their progress.

A Final Note

In this article we have described, at times in the words of teachers themselves, elements of an effective approach to staff development. Our findings about staff development programs in action confirm the importance of reflective professional growth for teachers. Broadly speaking, the fundamental challenge for instructional leaders, as we now see it, is one of building a culture of lifelong learning through inquiry and collaboration.

References

Blase, J. & Blase J. (1998). *Instructional leadership: How really good principals promote teaching and learning.* Thousand Oaks, CA: Corwin Press.

Bogdan, R. & Biklen, S. (1982). *Qualitative research for education: An introduction to theory and methods.* Boston: Allyn & Bacon.

Calhoun, E. (1994). *How to use action research in the self-renewing school.* Alexandria, VA: Association for Supervision and Curriculum Development.

Dowling, G. & Sheppard, K. (March, 1976). *Teacher training: A counseling focus.* Paper presented at the national convention of Teachers of English to Speakers of Other Languages, New York.

Glass, G.V. (1982). Meta-analysis: An approach to the synthesis of research results. *Journal of Research in Science Teaching,* 19 (2), 93–112.

Glickman, C.D., Gordon, S. P., & Ross-Gordon, J. M. (1995). *Supervision of instruction: A developmental approach* (3rd ed.). Boston: Allyn and Bacon.

Joyce, B.R. & Calhoun, E. F. (1996). *Creating learning experiences: The role of instructional theory and research.* Alexandria, VA: Association for Supervision and Curriculum Development.

Joyce, B. & Showers, B. (1995). *Student achievement through staff development* (2nd ed.). New York: Longman.

Joyce, B. & Weil, M. (1996). *Models of teaching* (5th ed.) Boston: Allyn & Bacon.

Phillips, M.D. & Glickman, C.D. (1991). Peer coaching: Developmental approach to enhance teacher thinking. *Journal of Staff Development,* 12 (2), 20–25.

Showers, B. & Joyce, B. (1996). The evolution of peer coaching. *Educational Leadership,* 53 (6), 12–16.

Waxman, H.C. & Walberg, H.J. (eds.). (1991). *Effective teaching: Current research.* Berkeley, CA: McCutchan.

Wolf, J. (1994). *BLT: A resource handbook for building leadership teams.* Minneapolis: The North Central Association of Schools and Colleges.

Article Review Form at end of book.

How do we create and sustain school programs that cultivate a wide range of human potential? What is the best guarantee for a broadly encompassing intelligence?

Schools for All Seasons

Schools for all our children and all our seasons must await the arrival of narratives designed to provide—if not the favoring circumstances of birth—the favoring circumstances of richly textured educational environments guided by caring, competent, and professional teachers, Mr. Goodlad points out.

John I. Goodlad

John I. Goodlad is a professor of education and co-director of the Center for Educational Renewal, University of Washington, and president of the Institute for Educational Inquiry, Seattle.

Over the centuries, several major narratives have dominated the human conversation: the narratives of salvation and everlasting life, of sectarian superiority, of gender privilege, of war and peace, of absolutism and relativism, of economic utility, of consumption and conservation. The struggle for dominance of ideology and belief has rarely been resolved on the basis of self-evident truth. More often, it has been resolved in the arenas of political and physical combat.

Schools too must face these fundamental issues of ideology. Schools are political entities charged with carrying out teaching functions designed to bring about specific student outcomes. These outcomes are determined through a political process by which an array of interests purporting to seek the common good compete for attention and for the right to determine both the means and the ends of schooling.

A major complaint of today's school-based educators is that there is no clear, agreed-upon mission for schooling: it changes with each election season. But these changes provide no greater clarity and stability than existed before. The narrative of developing responsible democratic character in the young does not enjoy any privileged status in today's educational marketplace. Moreover, there is little in the professional education of teachers and administrators to even suggest the possibility of such a prospect.[1] In its absence, a default narrative of economic utility has taken over, and, because it is appealing and straightforward, it has sought to push all others to the side.

In this situation, how are educators to prepare our schools and the children in them to meet the future? The school best prepared for tomorrow is the school best geared for today. It is a school for all seasons, engaging all of its students in as many domains of human experience as it can encompass. It is a school so committed to its comprehensive mission of preparing the young to participate broadly in the human conversation that democratic societies seek to sustain that it is not diverted into the narrowing of focus that devotion to some utilitarian narrative of schooling requires. This is not easy.

Creating and sustaining school programs that cultivate a wide range of human potential and simultaneously ensure the availability of the full range of abilities and dispositions that a robust democratic society requires is not easy because the supporting narrative is so weakly sustained in the surrounding environment. Parents want their children to have the opportunity to meet a very broad spectrum of educational goals. Nonetheless, the rhetoric of politically driven school reform teaches parents to settle for what they are told are reliable surrogates for that missing breadth—test scores. Though they weight the components somewhat differently, teachers, too, opt for a comprehensive set of personal, social, economic, and academic goals. And they, too, are told to

© 1998 Phi Delta Kappa. Reprinted with permission.

pay close attention to test scores. Those classroom activities that stress the intrapersonal and interpersonal are quite commonly regarded, as Neil Postman has pointed out, as frills or ornaments.[2] While it is difficult to come up with a domain of intelligence that is more significant to individual development and the common welfare than these personal intelligences, it is just as difficult to find a domain of intelligence less reflected in test scores.

In at least two significant ways, the losses suffered by the young as a result of the narrowing of school focus extend beyond merely being deprived of learning in the domains of intelligence that are left out of the school environment. First, the several intelligences are part of a functioning whole; the emotional, for example, profoundly affects the academic. The latter suffers in an atmosphere insensitive to the emotional states of the learners. The timeworn emphasis on teaching the whole child has depths of meaning that extend far beyond the platitudes so often attached to the concept.

The second loss to students is in the richness of teaching. The narrowing of school expectations to a limited array of easily tested outcomes tends to restrict teaching to relatively uniform procedures that simply leave out some modes of learning. For example, the range of teaching methods found in most kindergarten classrooms is commonly cut in half by fourth grade, when stress on testing increases significantly.

Accompanying this dual narrowing of curricula and teaching, there is very often an intensification of teacher interest in finding "the one best method"—an interest tirelessly fed by an education/business conglomerate peddling instructional "how-to-do-its." One such effort that carries considerable intellectual baggage has been particularly popular over the last two decades: brain science and its promise (not supported by neural scientists) of revolutionizing educational practice. In spite of the fact that "we do not know enough about brain development and neural function to link that understanding directly, in any meaningful, defensible way to instruction and educational practice,"[3] it is the rare conference for teachers that lacks an ardent speaker extolling the benefits of developing both the left and right hemispheres of the brain in daily classroom activities.

The necessary school for all seasons sustains a learning environment that is rich in sensory stimulation. As a teacher, one need not worry about what stimulates the right side of the brain or the left if the organizing centers selected by the teacher are broad and encompass the kinesthetic, the aesthetic, the social, the linguistic, the mathematical, and so on. But arranging for such organizing centers is exceedingly demanding and runs counter to the prevailing pedagogical view that emphasizes the selection of relatively small, sharply focused organizing centers for individual subjects and specific grade levels. The unit of selection designed to involve everyone in the class over a period of weeks, with accompanying teacher observation and diagnosis of individual learners, has largely disappeared from our schools, in part because it is associated in the public mind with "progressive education" and in part because it demands great pedagogical skill. Teacher education programs that intersperse over the four years of college a few courses in methods of teaching amid the demands of general education and a specific major simply do not suffice.

As a nation, we balk at ensuring for our teachers both the general and the professional education that fostering intelligence in the young requires. It should come as no surprise that the best guarantee of a broadly encompassing intelligence is to be born into a stimulating sensory environment and subsequently to attend a school in a community sufficiently affluent to provide the richest array of instructional resources and to attract and retain the teachers most favored in their own education. And, of course, there is a high correlation between these two sets of favoring circumstances, both little affected by proposals for school reform.[4]

Schools for all our children and all our seasons must await the arrival of narratives designed to provide—if not the favoring circumstances of birth—the favoring circumstances of richly textured educational environments guided by caring, competent, and professional teachers. Meanwhile, let us not be seduced by narratives that offer covenants to our children that limit their futures.

1. See John I. Goodlad, *Teachers for Our Nation's Schools* (San Francisco: Jossey-Bass. 1990).
2. Neil Postman, *The End of Education* (New York: Vintage, 1996), p. 28.
3. John T. Bruer, "Education and the Brain: A Bridge Too Far," *Educational Researcher*, November 1997, p. 4.
4. For a penetrating, data-based analysis, see Bruce J. Biddle, "Foolishness, Dangerous Nonsense, and Real Correlates of State Differences in Achievement," *Phi Delta Kappan*, September 1997, pp. 9–13.

Article Review Form at end of book.

What motivates teachers in teaching? What are the important criteria to consider in developing effective staff development for teachers?

Change and the School Administrator

Marlow Ediger

Change is all around us. It appears that changes do not stop, nor do we want complete stability to remain. Sometimes, we desire changes in certain areas, but not in others. Thus changes are wanted to promote longer, healthier lives. Perhaps, in the moral arenas, we desire more stability. Maybe, there is a trade off in that positively agreed upon changes such as better, safer medical practices as compared to traditional procedures in the healing arts are not the only areas affected when a changing society is in evidence. Values and moral standards also change.

With rapid changes in society, problems occur such as individuals engaged in drug abuse, an increased rate of crime occurs, a larger number of teenage pregnancies come about, and "war zones" are in evidence with heavy use of weapons and gang violence in poverty areas of large cities. I have wondered if all changes tend to represent Newton's third law of physics in that "to every positive action there is an opposite and equal reaction" such as joblessness, low income levels for many, and dysfunctional families.

George Friedrich Hegel (Strumph, 1971) in the 1800's developed a philosophy of dialectical reasoning in that there is a thesis (new idea), an antithesis (an opposite idea, traditional in nature), followed by a synthesis, a kind of harmony or midpoint between the thesis and antithesis. The synthesis could provide a moderating stance between the new and the old when thinking about changes in teaching and learning. Might selected changes be too different from what is now being emphasized so that a mediating influence, the synthesis, could be an end result? Later on, the synthesis could become the antithesis which is to be considered with an innovation or creative idea, a thesis. The thesis and the antithesis are again mediated to produce a synthesis. The dialect could be a continuous process in stressing change in an evolving curriculum.

Team teaching is praised by many educators and remains popular by writers and speakers in education. However, numerous public school teachers say that a nine month period of time in being a team member can be an eternity when bad human relations are in evidence. Thus there is an opposite reaction to the concept of team teaching being a good method of instruction. Team teaching certainly has its merits as well as its disadvantages when thinking about improving the curriculum.

I hope in this paper to present ways of implementing change whereby the results will be positive and not possess an opposite and equal reaction. This requires careful planning and implementing. Thus, for example, a carefully developed plan of team teaching might well eliminate the opposite and equal reaction.

Tenets of Change

Administrators, faculty, and staff need to perceive change as a process. Change then is ongoing and not an absolute. Change represents that which has movement and motion. That movement and motion emphasizes goal attainment in a direction. That direction should stress increased pupil achievement in all facets of development. The results indicate that the good, true, and the beautiful

"Change and the School Administrator" by Marlow Ediger. Copyright 1998 Project Innovation. Reprinted with permission.

will be an end result, meaning better learner achievement and progress. The vision for school personnel then is to perceive pupils in a special way and that way is the focal point of change. We cannot perceive of visions in education stressing less pupil achievement and progress. The latter would stress that there is an opposite and equal reaction to positive changes in the school curriculum. The focal point is on the learner in assisting him/her to grow, develop, and attain more optimally.

Change then should be viewed as guiding the pupil to achieve from the actual to the ideal. The actual is the present in terms of the goals of the school curriculum. There must be room for improvement or the faculty, staff, and school administrators would not wish to move in a new direction and that being to change to something better.

There needs to be quality processes used which assist in determining what should be changed. One procedure is to use a needs assessment procedure. Here a well developed, carefully prepared questionnaire may be sent to parents, teachers, administrators, pupils, and the general lay public to ascertain what is perceived as being vital in the school curriculum. The results from each of these categories of respondents may be tabulated and averaged for the different curriculum needs listed on the questionnaire. A category may be weighted so that an item responded to by parents receives more weight as compared to responses from teachers, administrators, pupils, and the larger lay public. I recommend giving the same weight from each category of individuals on the questionnaire. The questionnaire should also have a space for respondents to write in concerns that are not listed as curriculum concerns to be rated.

With clearly stated items on the questionnaire for respondents to respond to, the results should indicate to school personnel what is wanted in the school curriculum. Variations of the questionnaire might be an interview approach. A face to face situation here may guide interviewers to ask additional questions that are not thought of when preparing the questionnaire.

A second approach to use in determining what should be changed in the present school curriculum stresses surveying current literature in each curriculum area and drawing conclusions in terms of what needs to be changed. Perhaps, a committee of teachers desires to obtain information on a recommended updated mathematics curriculum. There should be parents, school personnel, and lay people on each committee that surveys educational literature using information from diverse reference sources as to what should be in a recommended curriculum area. The National Council Teachers of Mathematics (NCTM), the National Council for the Social Studies (NCSS), the National Science Teachers Association (NSTA), among other national study groups, have spent much time and money on developing objectives for pupil attainment. The different committees in a school district that are gathering information on improving a curriculum area may lean upon these national study groups for guidance and direction. Ultimately, conclusions should be reached on what to stress in updating a specific curriculum area. Each of the above named national organizations publishes a monthly periodical containing manuscripts useful in appraising a curriculum area. Comparisons might then be made of what is presently being emphasized as compared to what should be stressed in teaching and learning situations.

Proposed innovations need to be screened carefully so that an opposite and equal reaction is not possible when appraising the new approach being considered. New approaches may fail after adoption and the failure may come soon after implementation. There has then been much effort put forth that has been wasted.

Better use of school personnel efforts is needed. Greenfield (1995), in a research study, listed the following reasons why innovations fail in duration in the school setting.

1. Strength of leadership in the curriculum.

2. Lack of agreement of the need for making one or more changes.

3. Inadequate or no funding available to keep an innovation going.

4. The innovation falls apart due to rapid turnover of teachers in the school setting.

5. Schoolwide commitment and participation.

To each of the above reasons why innovations fail is an opposite and equal reaction such as in #1 whereby the strong leader is an antonym to a weak leader. Weaknesses need to be avoided so that a negative reaction may not occur.

Prior to attempting to restructure the school curriculum, school personnel need to look for strong leadership, be it the principal, supervisor, a teacher, or teaching team. The present curriculum needs to be studied thoroughly to determine what truly needs to be changed. Changes should not be made for the sake of doing so, but rather to guide pupils to attain more optimally in cognitive, affective, and psychomotor growth and development. Too frequently, innovations have been fads that have not had more of enduring values. Much time and money generally goes into the making of changes in the school curriculum. Should proposed changes then not be assessed carefully before their proposed consideration and implementation?

Each school building or district must study to ascertain the stability of faculty members' and administrators' tenure and commitment. What makes for a rapid turnover of personnel? Are there factors in the local school or school district that prevent innovations from being implemented due to a lack of stability in positions among faculty and staff in the school setting? If innovations are to have any degree of performance, they should be emphasized in a school unit that emphasizes stability among personnel. Educators then must attempt to weed out those situations that make for instability of positions in the school setting due to negative conditions. Teachers, administrators, and support personnel desire to improve their status and thus look for increased quality positions and salaries. This is to be looked upon positively. However, if conditions in a school are negative, there needs to be a comprehensive evaluation in terms of making the environmental conditions as positive as possible in the school setting for all school personnel. Numerous studies have been made as to what motivates teachers in teaching. From his research, Herzberg (1959) stressed the following as being motivators:

1. Achievement.
2. Recognition.
3. Work itself.
4. Responsibility.
5. Advancement.

It might well be true that all individuals desire to have the above enumerated items become a personal part of themselves and their responsibilities.

Guidelines to Follow in Teaching

There appears to be considerable agreement upon selected facets of teaching and learning, such as guidelines to follow by teachers in the instructional arena (Ediger, 1994). In the classroom, teachers need to stress the following:

1. **Meaningful lessons and units of study.** With meaning, pupils understand and comprehend that which was contained in ongoing learning opportunities.
2. **Interesting content and skills in the curriculum.** With interest, the pupil and the curriculum become one, not separate entities. Pupils attend to and achieve from ongoing lessons and units of study.
3. **Purpose in learning.** With purpose in learning, pupils accept reasons for attaining relevant facts, concepts, and generalizations presented.
4. **Sequence in learning.** With quality sequence, pupils relate newly acquired content with that previously achieved. Previous knowledge attained provides readiness for the new objectives to be achieved. Pupils need guidance to perceive relationship of knowledge in teaching-learning situations.
5. **Balance among objectives stressed.** Thus knowledge, skills, and attitudes—three kinds of objectives need to be achieved by students. These objectives interact and are not in isolation from each other. For example, if pupils possess positive attitudes, they should achieve needed knowledge and skills more readily.

Pertaining to item four above, too frequently a separate subjects curriculum predominates in teaching and learning. Thus a single academic discipline is emphasized largely or only in ongoing lessons and units of study. Emphasizing a single academic discipline in the curriculum area taught stresses a trend emphasized up to the latter 1800's. In the early 1900's, selected educators tended to emphasize the importance of the correlated curriculum. Here, pupils were taught to relate two curriculum areas. There were educators who believed that content should be further interrelated. Thus the fused curriculum was stressed such as the language arts, the social studies, science, or mathematics, among other curriculum areas to be related (Ragan and Shepard, 1982). For example, the social studies consists of history, geography, political science, economics, and sociology/anthropology. These academic areas may then be brought into a broader umbrella term such as social studies. Present curricular recommendations are that an interdisciplinary curriculum be in evidence. Here, the teacher may stress the social studies, for example, as the core and then relate mathematics, science, language and literature, art, music, and physical education around the core.

As an additional trend, cooperative learning is receiving much emphasis in educational literature. Pupils do need to learn to work together now in the home and school setting, as well as in the future such as in the family and in the work place. It is difficult for individuals if getting along is lacking. Harmonious relationships with others must be a definite goal in the school setting for pupils to realize at increasing levels of complexity. Schuncke (1988) lists the following criteria to use in forming committee or group work in the classroom:

1. **Interest.** Groups may be formed by allowing children to choose the topic they would like to pursue. At times, the children's choices may reflect factors other than interest—such as desire to be with one's friends—and you will need to determine if, indeed, being in a group based on the latter criterion is in the best interests of a given child.

2. **Sociometric.** You may wish to examine the social structure of your classroom by administering a sociometric test. The test will contain items such as "Name three pupils you'd like to have in your social studies group." The children's responses to this question (in the form of names) can be tabulated and illustrated graphically on a sociogram . . . Responses will indicate who, indeed, would like to work with whom. They will also indicate sociometric stars, individuals chosen quite frequently, and isolates, children for one reason or another are chosen infrequently, if at all. Groups can be constituted in a variety of ways using these data; you may wish to enlist the aid of a star in bringing an isolate more into the group.

3. **Capabilities.** Knowing the various capabilities of your students, you may wish to constitute your groups so that there is a balance of these. For example, you may want to ensure that a group is not composed of only nonreaders. Or perhaps, you'd like an artist or an individual who has certain map reading skills in each group. By constituting groups in this way you can insure that the groups' tasks can be approached effectively.

Teachers need to assist each pupil to become a member of a group and feel accepted with the status needs met. Being an isolate makes for feelings of rejection. Hardly can a person who feels rejected do well in school. Teachers need to experience quality inservice education programs in order to emphasize cooperative learning for pupils in the school and classroom setting.

It is recommendable to have appropriate balance in the curriculum between group and individual endeavors. Individuals, each day, spend time in groups as well as by themselves.

Evaluating Principal Effectiveness

School principals periodically should be evaluated by teachers. How well is the principal doing in his/her role as a school leader? This question needs to be answered by those involved under the principal's leadership. Relevant criteria need to be established for the evaluation. They should reflect the role of a quality school administrator. Care must be taken to ensure that each criterion is written clearly so that teacher respondents know what is wanted in terms of responses. A space on the questionnaire should be left so that teachers may write in comments not covered in the enumerated items of the questionnaire. A committee of teachers or an objective appraiser, disassociated from the school, may tabulate the responses from teachers as to the quality of work performed by the school principal. A conscientiously developed questionnaire might well provide principals with necessary knowledge to improve the quality of their work in the curriculum. Principals and teachers must desire to have an improved curriculum so that learners might attain more optimally.

Bickel (1995) lists the following criteria developed by teachers to evaluate principal effectiveness on a five point scale in Eau Claire, Wisconsin High Schools:

1. Follows up on student referrals in a punctual manner.

2. Performs effectively in stressful situations.

3. Informs staff about responsibilities, assignments, and/or changes.

4. Recognizes the achievements of individual staff members.

5. Uses authority in a firm, consistent, but compassionate manner.

6. Finds time to interact with faculty and staff.

7. Supports staff fairly in confrontations with students and parents.

8. Evaluates programs objectively.

9. Evaluates personnel objectively.

10. Encourages free and open flow of comments, suggestions, and recommendations.
11. Makes timely, cooperative evaluations of assigned staff members' performances.
12. Provides instructors, when appropriate, with positive/constructive feedback in regard to the teaching profession.
13. Prepares a budget for a fair, predetermined, and well-understood criteria that reflect the identified needs of the school.
14. Establishes a long range plan for expenditures.
15. Provides adequate time for setting/expanding the budget.
16. Attends extracurricular and other school sponsored activities.
17. Provides teachers with the support they need.
18. Maintains good working relationships and rapport with staff.
19. Evaluates staff fairly and effectively, constructively, and in a nonthreatening manner.
20. Admits mistakes and works toward a reasonable solution.
21. Encourages staff involvement in decision making.
22. Assists various departments in realizing their goals.
23. Carries out agreements with staff.
24. Reaches administrative decisions objectively.
25. Considers departmental recommendations in personal decisions.
26. Is a positive influence on staff behavior.
27. Understands my curriculum area.
28. Conducts supervision followup promptly.
29. Gives a high priority to curriculum development.
30. Conducts staff meetings that support the curriculum
31. Conducts staff meetings that support the classroom.
32. Creates a positive school environment.

There are numerous quality criteria listed above whereby principals may be evaluated on all levels of schooling be it elementary, middle school/junior high school, and high school. I believe more emphasis should be placed upon the principal's relationships with pupils. Here I have in mind such items as assisting pupils to have physiological needs met including food/nutrition, clothing, and safety. For nutritional needs, schools should serve breakfasts as well as the noon meal. Many schools, of course, serve noon meals, but more should go in the direction of serving breakfasts, as well as evening meals for latch key programs. With both parents or single parents working, it becomes a necessity to have an extended school program of excellent learning opportunities for latch key pupils after school.

Then too, there are an increased number of pupils from poverty level homes that need appropriate clothing for the different seasons of the year. The principal can be highly instrumental in obtaining quality used clothing from different donors. Pupils may then have appropriate attire for the different seasons of the year.

There are so many needs that today's pupils have. To obtain proper day care facilities for preschool age children is a great necessity. Those that do not exist are not properly licensed or the state has no requirements that need to be met to provide day care assistance. Day care assistance might be very costly and beyond the reach of many parents. Schuyler County Schools (central office located in Lancaster, Missouri 63548), adjacent to and directly north of my city of Kirksville, has a nursery school for three and four year olds as a part of the public school system. Parents still need to pay for the education of their offspring. The cost is moderate and parents have to realize that these young pupils will tend to have good care. All public schools should work in the direction of having free nursery schools for young children. Voluntary attendance of youngsters would provide opportunities for working parents to have a safe place for their offspring while at work. In addition to these recommendations to the above named list, principals should be more involved to see that pupils individually receive the kind of education whereby each achieves as much as possible. The education received will assist pupils ultimately to pursue jobs, vocations, and professions which remunerate adequately and provide for a satisfying life style.

Each level of schooling should possess proper articulation in that the sequence of learning opportunities among the different grade levels and building levels (elementary, middle school/junior high, and high school) provide appropriate relationships. Pupils might then experience as much success as possible with continuous progress, among and between the different levels of instruction. Principals and teachers from the different levels of instruction need to work together to have learners experience quality sequence in education.

There are numerous trends that principals should be aware of in teaching pupils, such as heterogeneous grouping, school and university collaboration in developing professional schools, clinical supervision, cluster schools, hands-on approaches in learning, open enrollment, working with disruptive pupils, safety in schools, at-risk instruction for pupils, multicultural education, prevention of pupils dropping out of school, and the increased responsibility of schools in educating pupils.

Staff Development

Staff development and continuous inservice education of all educators in the school setting is necessary. Ediger (1988) lists the following criteria, which he has used, in conducting staff development/workshop programs:

1. The theme should be decided upon cooperatively by involved persons.
2. The general session needs to work out problem areas that participants desire to solve.
3. Committees may be formed to solve problems identified in the general session.
4. Opportunities for individual projects and activities also need to be in the offing.
5. Consultant services should be available to all participants.
6. An adequate professional library needs to be available for participants to solve problems.
7. The number and duration of the sessions devoted to staff development should be decided by participants.
8. Appropriate and comfortable furniture should be available to further participant progress in staff development programs.

In Summary

There are numerous changes that have come about in the area of school administration. The administrator needs to stay informed of new developments and trends in education and in society. Inservice education of faculty and staff is necessary on a continuous basis. Pupils need a curriculum whereby individual differences are provided for and optimal achievement results.

References

Bickel, Lauri B. (1995). "Faculty and Administration: Collaborating on an Administrative Evaluation," *National Association of Secondary School Principals' Bulletin.* 79:75–80

Ediger Marlow (1994). "Early Field Experiences in Teacher Education," *College Student Journal* 28: 302–306.

Herzberg, Fredrick and others (1959). *The Motivation to Work*, 2nd Edition. New York: John Wiley.

Schuncke, George M. (1988). *Elementary Social Studies.* New York: Macmillan Company, 301302.

Shepard, Gene and William Ragan (1982). *Modern Elementary Curriculum.* New York: Holt Rinehart and Winston, pages 90–92.

Stumph, Samuel Enoch (1971). *Philosophy: History and Problems.* New York: McGraw-Hill Book Company, pages 304–326.

Article Review Form at end of book.

WiseGuide Wrap-Up

- Effective school research highlights the importance of the principal's role as instructional leader, demonstrating responsibilities as resource provider, communicator and visible presence.

- Implementing research-based reform programs requires leaders to be knowledgeable in both comprehensive and curricular efforts.

- Instructional leaders can profoundly impact teacher behavior by focusing on the themes of teacher-administrator communications, promoting teachers' professional growth, and fostering teacher reflection.

- Leaders should strive to create and sustain educational programs that cultivate a wide range of human potential and simultaneously ensure the availability of the full range of abilities that our democratic society requires.

- When teachers view themselves as learners, they can increase their teaching capacity by emphasizing a real-world context for learning, generative topics, innovation, bridging into practice, and the social dimensions of learning.

- Administrator effectiveness as an instructional leader can be assessed by reviewing key leadership behaviors, including supporting teachers' staff development.

R.E.A.L. Sites

This list provides a print preview of typical **Coursewise** R.E.A.L. sites. There are over 100 such sites at the **Courselinks**™ site. The danger in printing URLs is that web sites can change overnight. As we went to press, these sites were functional using the URLs provided. If you come across one that isn't, please let us know via email to: webmaster@coursewise.com. Use your Passport to access the most current list of R.E.A.L. sites at the **Courselinks**™ site.

Site name: Association for Supervision and Curriculum Development
URL: http://www.ascd.org/
Why is it R.E.A.L.? This well-developed and comprehensive web site contains a wealth and variety of information and resources, including "InfoBriefs"—synopses of key education issues, "Hot Topics"—excellent annotated bibliographic citations for educators, and articles and abstracts from ASCD's award-winning journal, *Educational Leadership*. There is also new distance learning opportunities at PD Online, as well as new initiatives/programs, such as Scoreboard for Schools and Classlink.
Key topics: change, collaboration, communication, community, cooperation, education, instructional leadership, management, reform, site-based management, team
Try this: Visit "InfoBriefs" for various areas, including class size, reading instruction, or teacher education to develop school programs or address research subjects in other classes.

Site name: Education Week
URL: http://www.edweek.org/
Why is it R.E.A.L.? This is an excellent resource for news and research in education that is published weekly. Calling itself "American Education's OnLine Newpaper of Record," it includes special reports, archives, daily news, *Teacher Magazine,* a job bank, and background papers on key education topics. There are also facts and information about each state in the nation, a glossary, and monitoring of the national education agenda.
Key Topics: accountability, change, community, diversity, education, entrepreneurs, goals, instructional leadership, leadership, management
Try this: Review the various resources at the web site. Visit the "Archives" section and search *Education Week's* database for subjects related to your professional development in the workplace or as a graduate student.

section 6

Change: To Understand, Respond, and Influence

WiseGuide Intro

Since the 1960s, major educational reform efforts have been initiated in the nation's schools. From Title I programs for the poor to major science initiatives, schools have felt the substantial pressure of change and reform for over thirty years. These change forces continue today. Social, economic, and political reform has transformed American society. Our lives at the end of this century are different than they were even ten years ago. Technology, diversity, communications, and globalization have all contributed to today's new society. Our world has changed, and we have changed.

Educational leaders struggle to understand these complexities and the impact of these forces on their profession. School leaders must seek new solutions for the new challenges in our schools. The solutions of yesterday will not work in building an educational system for tomorrow.

This section addresses the process of change. It is not a simple process, just as the challenges we face are not simple. The change process is a dynamic and complex one. This complexity inspired the section's title, "Change: To Understand, Respond, and Influence." Philosophers, poets, historians, and researchers have all contributed to our understanding of our complex world. Now, school leaders are faced with the challenges the world presents. One of the most significant responsibilities of school leaders is to face that challenge and respond with effective educational reform. This is no easy task, but our world depends on our schools' successful transition into the new millennium. This section addresses that challenge.

We begin with the view that educational organizations are part of a larger system's dynamic, just as nature is part of a larger ecosystem. This is the perspective presented by Kiuchi in "What I Learned in the Rainforest."

Sherrit and Basom's article, "A Good Case for Educational Change," supports this complex systems perspective. They begin the discussion of educational change as part of societal changes, including information technology, global knowledge, and cultural communications.

With an understanding of environmental dynamics, leaders are ready for the challenging process within their own organizations. In "Be a Model Leader of Change," Schneider and Goldwasser outline a set of actions for leaders, including a self-assessment of leadership readiness for change.

Fullan challenges leaders to review the appropriateness of their change efforts in "Breaking the Bonds of Dependency." He highlights the obstacles leaders face in mounting successful change initiatives, as well as the emotional intelligence they must possess.

Learning Objectives

- Compare and contrast the change forces in contemporary schools and the elements of environmental ecology, including evolutionary factors affecting life and work.

- Identify the effective leadership qualities, behaviors, and skills in successfully initiating and implementing change.

- Describe and analyze the conditions that create dependency. Detail the actions leaders can use to overcome dependency for effective organizational change.

- Summarize the concept of reflection and its purpose in the change process.

- Explain the interplay of important change factors in systematic reform efforts.

- Analyze the use of collaborative inquiry for change and as part of a constructivist methodology.

Organizational reflection and its usefulness in the change process are discussed in "The Power of Reflection" by Hammer and Stanton. The six steps of the process serve as a call to action for leaders embarking on systematic, comprehensive reform.

Extending the dialogue on comprehensive reform is McAdams's article "A Systems Approach to School Reform." McAdams provides five factors that serve as scaffolding for successful school change. Understanding these factors and integrating them into a systematic reform effort are important responsibilities for all leaders.

Finally, Wagner wraps up this section with his revealing and provocative discussion of change as a "constructivist" methodology in "Change as Collaborative Inquiry: A 'Constructivist' Methodology for Reinventing Schools." The use of collaboration, "genuine" dialogue, and discovery is Wagner's contribution to systematic school improvement.

Questions

Reading 34. What lessons can an organizational leader learn from the rainforest? What are the basic principles of ecology, and how do they apply to organizations?

Reading 35. How have the requirements for success in life and work changed? What are the forces that have come together to create change in our social institutions?

Reading 36. What specific actions should a leader take to ensure the success of a change initiative? As a general rule, how much time should the leader devote to the change process?

Reading 37. What are the four guidelines for succeeding at change and overcoming dependency? What are the two interrelated conditions that create overload?

Reading 38. What are the six tasks involved in the reflection process? Although successful organizations fail in many ways, all of these failures share one underlying cause. What is it?

Reading 39. What are the five factors that affect school reform? What propositions are suggested to improve school reform initiatives?

Reading 40. What are the four stages of the change process? What is a "constructivist" method for change?

What lessons can an organizational leader learn from the rainforest? What are the basic principles of ecology, and how do they apply to organizations?

What I Learned in the Rainforest

To grow and thrive, businesses should heed a few simple principles drawn from the globe's most diverse ecosystem.

Tachi Kiuchi

Tachi Kiuchi is managing director of Mitsubishi Electric Corp. and chair of the Future 500—a network of companies dedicated to sustainable industry based in Sacramento.

I have learned my most important lessons about business in the forest. My first lesson came 37 years ago, days after I graduated from the University of British Columbia. I was asleep. This was unfortunate, because I was driving through the Canadian Rockies at the time, headed toward a cliff. After waking up two days later in the hospital, with my jaws wired shut, I had plenty of time to reflect upon this incident.

Since then, I have come to believe that the global business community is driving quickly toward a cliff, with its eyes closed, and will soon suffer a similar fate. If we opened our eyes, we would see that 600 million of the earth's inhabitants in Europe, Japan, and the United States enjoy the material benefits of industrialism and that 2.5 billion more from China, India, and the former Soviet republics will join us. After them, the final 3 billion deserve the same. Yet to accomplish that goal today, we would need the resources of three planets. But we have only one. Thus our businesses need to begin creating affluence without effluence.

I am often told the needs of business and environment conflict—that the highest mission of a corporation is to maximize profits. But in the long term, there is no incompatibility. For example, a large market will arise for photovoltaic solar cells, especially in the developing world. Mitsubishi's work on such devices serves the company but also the global environment. Ultimately, profit is just money—a medium of exchange. You always trade it for something else. We don't run our business to earn profits. We earn profits to run our business.

And imagine how creative, how productive, how ecologically benign our businesses could be if we ran them according to the design principles of the rainforest. With thin soil, few nutrients, and almost no resources, rainforests could never qualify for a loan. Yet rainforests are more productive than any business in the world, home to millions of species of plants and animals, so perfectly mixed that they sustain one another and evolve into ever more complex forms. These environments excel by adapting to what they don't have.

Emulating the rainforest means following basic principles of ecology:

- **Get feedback.** In the rainforest, feedback leads to Darwinian evolution of a complex array of diverse organisms.

    Individual humans have excellent feedback systems—our eyes, our ears, our minds. But in our companies and communities, our collective feedback systems are not so well developed. My priority at Mitsubishi Electric is to create the world's best corporate feedback system so that we know the costs and benefits of every product—including the social and environmental needs we can help fulfill—better than any other

---

Reprinted with permission from *Technology Review*, published by the Association of Alumni and Alumnae of MIT, copyright 1998. *What I Learned in the Rainforest*, Tachi Kiuchi, Nov/Dec 1997. Reproduced by permission of the publisher via Copyright Clearance Center, Inc.

electronics company. In business, feedback indicates the potential for market demand. If consumers favor products and companies that avoid doing harm to the environment, then an alert company will profit by making such products. For example, Mitsubishi developed one of the first refrigerators that did not use chlorofluorocarbons—the chemical responsible for eating away the ozone layer—and is now a leader in that market.

- **Adapt and change.** It is not enough to see the cliff—the opportunities. We must turn. We all know that what gets measured gets done. Thus starting next year, Mitsubishi Electric will track not only quarterly profits but also our facilities' level of polluting emissions and how efficiently they use resources. We will also create incentives that reward people when they take steps to reduce damage to the environment. Such rewards might go, for example, to those at the company who develop a television picture tube that does not contain lead and that therefore can be disposed of in a landfill without poisoning the earth.

- **Fit a niche.** In the rainforest, conformity causes extinction. If two organisms have the same niche, only one survives. The other either adapts or dies. It is the same in many high-tech businesses. If two companies make exactly the same leading—edge product, only one survives. But in the rainforest, there are many winners. The same can be true in our economy. The question is not who is most fit, but where we best fit. If we fit—solve a social problem, fulfill a social need—we will survive and excel.

But what are most companies doing today? They are downsizing radically, desperately seeking the lowest cost. It is smarter to differentiate—to create distinctive products and fill unique niches. Mitsubishi learned this the hard way. We found we could not compete by always selling the cheapest TVs, stereos, and appliances. Rather than kill or be killed by our competitors, we must sidestep them by creating unique products that appeal to particular consumers.

- **Cooperate.** The rainforest's vitality and diversity stem from the fact that all the organisms together create a more efficient whole. Today, as companies grow different, we need each other to fill our gaps. Mitsubishi, for example, no longer expands simply by buying companies as subsidiaries. We profit more from cooperative joint ventures in which our partners retain their independence, specialty, and core competence. In one example of such a venture, Mitsubishi is working with an independent appliance dealer in Wisconsin to create a new company, Air Tech, to market a passive air exchanger and cooler that both lowers energy costs and helps prevent "sick building" syndrome. The product grew from collaboration between Mitsubishi Electric, which knew the technologies, and the dealer, who grasped the potential market for such a system among architects and builders. These cooperative relationships are now as vital to our future as are our products.

In Japan, we have two terms that help us understand why: omote and ura. Omote is the surface or front of an object—the external reality. Ura is the underlying reality. As business people, we have been looking at the rainforest all wrong. What is valuable about the rainforest is not omote —the trees, which we can take out. The real value of the forest lies in its ura—the design and the relationships among species. And the highest mission of business is to help fully develop the human ecosystem, sustainably like the rainforest, in all our diversity and complexity.

Article Review Form at end of book.

How have the requirements for success in life and work changed? What are the forces that have come together to create change in our social institutions?

A Good Case for Educational Change

Caroline A. Sherritt
Margaret Basom

Caroline A. Sherritt is an associate professor of adult education and Margaret Basom is an assistant professor of education leadership, both in the College of Education, University of Wyoming, Laramie.

A large contingent of citizens today, perplexed by perceived changes in education, long to go back to simpler times when schooling was a matter of acquiring basic academic and citizenship skills—reading, writing, computation, an orientation to Western culture, and the socialization necessary for getting and keeping a job. Such back-to-basics advocates mean well, but they miss a large part of the big picture. They correctly believe that schools were more effective at educating them than at educating their children and grandchildren. They are also right that schools are becoming ineffective at preparing people for life and work. What they fail to perceive is that the requirements for successful life and work have changed.

In the past, schools did a good job of educating citizens for an industrial age, something most schools continue to do well. However, we no longer live in an industrial age. The skills (the three Rs) that were needed and valued earlier are still important, but they are not sufficient for life in an information age. As the following discussion points out, perhaps the biggest challenge facing our educational institutions is turning out the right type of educated men and women for our present era.

Transition from Industrial to Information Age

Our mass educational system evolved at a time when workers were needed for a particular mission: perpetuating the industrial miracle. America took the lead in this phenomenon, mass producing vast quantities of consumer goods that could be found in most homes: toasters, washers and dryers, television sets, automobiles, radios, apparel. Huge businesses and industries grew up, their labor force requirements unique in the history of humankind. These requirements called for workers who could

- stay on task, often for years, in isolated jobs;
- follow directions;
- show up on time, punch a time clock, and ask few questions;
- draw on physical strength and stamina, in many cases; and
- acquire sufficient education, usually in twelve years, to last a lifetime.

These workers, who needed only basic skills sufficient for performing isolated tasks, did not necessarily have to

- cooperate with other workers, particularly those working in other areas;
- understand the company's "big picture" or contribute to its development; or
- take responsibility for the overall quality of the product or service.

The world in which most Americans were educated has changed, however. As Francese (1995) pointed out, there is no longer a typical American, an ordinary worker, an everyday wage, or a middle class as we knew them. The typical, middle-class American man who forty years ago went to work, performed his function, stayed loyal to the company, and was rewarded with a gold watch is gone. The milkman or appliance salesman who supported a wife and kids, bought a small house, had a car, and took yearly vacations on one salary is a distant memory. Managers who isolated themselves from workers ended up managing bankrupt corporations in the eighties. What seems difficult for many of us to accept is that stereotypical American roles are gone forever; there is no going back. Our viability as a nation, however, depends on learning how to navigate this strange and sometimes frightening new world.

Change in social institutions occurs when several forces come together, often violently, at a point in history. The extraordinary social forces colliding today include the following:

- Changing family structures, with more than half of women in the work force
- Global economic standards and interdependence
- Technology that has outpaced our human capacity, shrunk the world, and automated many tasks heretofore performed by people
- Economic and employment changes that are structural and lasting
- Major demographic changes, including an aging population, growing numbers of minorities and immigrants, a shrinking middle class, increased mobility, and more children living in poverty.

American institutions have been motivated by economic realities into addressing demographic change. When the United States could no longer deny the global economic mandate, creative businesses and industries responded. As Carnevale (1994) and others have noted, successful businesses learned to operate with small, high-performance work teams. Top-down management, always a cumbersome, inefficient method, became the newest dinosaur. Corporations were downsized and management was flattened. Unions lost ground because they could not successfully represent low-skilled workers in the face of third- and second-world competition. The greatest opportunity to realize the American dream was in a new arena: international trade. American consumers began to demand the type of quality, price, and choice they were getting from international producers. Businesses and industries that responded to these challenges prospered; those that did not expired or lost out. Who can deny, for instance, that Japanese automakers have changed the way American automobile manufacturers operate or that international competition in computer chips hit American computer manufacturers like guerrilla warfare? Some industries nearly died altogether and will never reach their former level of production.

American education, an entrenched, bureaucratic behemoth, is one of the last social institutions to respond to the new age. Most citizens know that our system of mass education is among the best in the world and has contributed to making the United States a world leader. They are understandably reluctant to support change in an institution that served them so well, even though it isn't serving them now. The problem, however, is not that educational institutions are deviating from earlier success; it is that they aren't deviating enough.

Even supporters of traditional education are shocked by data showing that our children are falling behind children in other industrialized countries in every school subject. Many believe that a solution to this dilemma is to go back to the good schools we had in the past. In other words, they believe that schools are failing precisely because they no longer demand what they used to demand. In fact, when schools fail today, it is more likely because they are demanding what they used to. They are still educating for the industrial age and doing a good job of it a lot of the time. There is nothing wrong with the three Rs. They simply aren't sufficient, however, for navigating this strange new landscape called the information age.

Education for the Information Age

A complex, technological, perpetually changing, interdependent world creates its own educational requirements. Throughout history, education has tried to turn out ideal citizens. In the golden age of Greece, for instance, educators developed good Greek citizen leaders. During the Renaissance, the purpose of education was to develop artists, poets, scientists, and other individuals with desirable humanistic qualities. During the Industrial Revolution, public schools turned out factory workers, farmers barely went to school at all, and universities presumed to educate an elite. Perhaps the biggest threat to education today is an inability or unwillingness to turn out the right type of citizens for an information age, citizens who have

- the group and interpersonal skills needed to work well in small, high-performance teams;
- flexibility;
- basic skills that can be applied to solve problems, to see the big picture, and to serve as a foundation for continuous learning;
- lifelong learning skills that allow a person to stay current with rapid change and retrain for new careers;
- the ability to use technology to access information and, even more important, sift through overwhelming amounts of information for relevance and truth;
- an investment in the whole service or product of the corporations for which they work;
- self direction;
- an internalized sense of social responsibility; and
- knowledge of the world and cross-cultural communication skills.

Unfortunately, many citizens, educators included, resist restructuring American schools. They know that our educational system is falling behind where it used to be but they don't know why. Some call for a return to the basics, but that plea is regressive, essentially calling for more of what doesn't work. Others call for vouchers and privatizing schools, but such proposals ignore basic educational problems. Visionary educators know the directions they need to take, but they lack wide support for their efforts. Innovations that do address the information age —for example, magnet schools, cooperative learning, site- or school-based management, empowerment of teachers, equity programs, global studies, programs that encourage development of problem solving and critical thinking, applied and experiential learning activities, and outcome-based curricula—are the very techniques and programs passionately resisted by traditionalists.

The changing paradigm requires conceptualizing education as a lifelong process, integrated with and responsive to demographic, technological, global, and employment changes. Clever higher education administrators, for example, are advancing relevant, user-friendly services and programs, recruiting returning adult learners, and rethinking the role of higher education in an information age. Not surprisingly, these are the very changes poorly funded by politicians, misunderstood by taxpayers, and sometimes rejected by faculty members.

Perhaps resistance to educational restructuring could be minimized if educators did a better job of communicating why changes are needed, particularly those changes that appear antithetical to cherished values of the past. Unfortunately, the heart is missing not only from such communication efforts but also from the restructuring programs themselves. Fundamental change in education will not occur without solid commitment from those responsible. Some public schools have changed their curriculum, for example, but not their mission. Some colleges and universities pretend to embrace nontraditional learning and learners while vehemently protecting the ideal of young students who live in dormitories, attend lecture classes, and are served by obsolete infrastructures.

The public perceives inconsistencies in education today, reflecting the inconsistencies of a world in transition. Some individuals and groups believe that consistency can be retrieved by going back to what used to be—the basics. However, the education imperative is, and always has been, to become consonant with the requirements of the historic moment, not to remain constant with the requirements of an earlier time. If, during the Industrial Revolution, American education had held fast to an earlier need to educate gentlemen farmers and an aristocratic ruling class as it did in the eighteenth century, the country would never have achieved world preeminence. If, during the information age, public education trains good factory workers and universities educate liberal scholars in the grand tradition, America will lose its preeminence. We are, in fact, beginning to see this trend now.

The United States is challenged to find a new model, to build on earlier successes, just as it did during the Industrial Revolution. Some promising new educational approaches are emerging, but powerful forces inhibit their application. Those individuals who impede educational change, although they may not realize it, are charting a dangerous course for the nation.

References

Carnevale, A. P. 1994. *Quality, education: School reform for the new American economy*. Washington, D.C.: Office of Educational Research and Improvement. ERIC Document Reproduction Service, ED 366 832.

Francese, P. 1995. America at mid-decade. *American Demographics* (Feb.): 23–28.

Article Review Form at end of book.

What specific actions should a leader take to ensure the success of a change initiative? As a general rule, how much time should the leader devote to the change process?

Be a Model Leader of Change

Here's how to get the results you want from the change you're leading.

David M. Schneider
Charles Goldwasser

David M. Schneider is partner-in-charge of Price Waterhouse's U.S. Organizational Change practice. Charles Goldwasser is a principal consultant leading Price Waterhouse's Organizational Change practice in the West Region. Both are based in the firm's Los Angeles office.

Ralph Waldo Emerson once said, "An institution is the lengthened shadow of one man." That is particularly true during a time of organizational transition, when strong sponsorship at the highest levels is critical to success. If you are leading change in your organization, you can rest assured that no single element will have a greater impact on the outcome than what you do, what you say and how you position the project.

People in your organization are sensitive to every nuance of your behavior. They will take cues from you and even mimic your conduct and actions. If you're upbeat, enthusiastic and engaged, they will be as well. If you expect difficulties and take them in stride, they will too. And if you show how important this initiative is to you personally, you can be sure that it will become a top priority for them as well.

Key Factors in Change

Before you can position a change initiative for success, you must be able to visualize the dynamics of the process. These dynamics play a key role in the management of change. In an early text on the subject, social scientist Kurt Lewin provided a useful model of planned change in which a company moves from the "current state" to a "target state."

As your company ventures from the former to the latter state, all employees must release their grasp on the present—a process sometimes disobeyed as "unfreezing"—and get a firm grasp on the scope and implications of the change at hand. This part of the process, called "refreezing," leads to the target state. Although refreezing involves an end goal, it is really a snapshot in time, a new baseline from which to measure continuous change.

During any transition, performance will inevitably decline before reaching the improved, desired state. The leader's goal is to keep the duration of this decline as short as possible. But that doesn't mean overlooking or avoiding it altogether. After all, you are conducting business as the change takes place, and transition issues affect performance and productivity both in the present and in the future. To create and maintain momentum, you'll want to create some early wins.

The transition consists of everything that occurs between the current and target states, and this period will make the most demands on the leader. It begins the moment you announce a change initiative, long before the future state is known. Nobody gets from here to there without the purgatory of transition. Indeed, managing change is about managing the transition. Most senior managers misjudge the amount of effort needed to get through the transition because they underestimate the impact of change on employees and on themselves.

A leader of change must anticipate employees' reactions, another key factor in the process. As shown in the chart on page 41,* these reactions occur along a

*Does not appear in this publication

Reprinted from *Management Review*, March 1998 © 1998. American Management Association International. Reprinted by permission of American Management Association International, New York, NY. All rights reserved. http://www.amanet.org.

"change curve." The blue line represents what is, unfortunately, typical: Unrealistically high expectations at the outset of a program lead to a relatively deep "valley of despair" when change doesn't come as quickly or easily as anticipated. Over time, employees do see a "light at the end of the tunnel" and the change eventually produces some positive results. The red line illustrates what is possible with effective change management: a less traumatic visit to the valley and greater results as the program reaches completion.

Can you avoid the "valley of despair" altogether? Probably not. All change programs involve some loss. The best approach is to acknowledge that employees will mourn the loss of business as usual, much as people experience stages of grieving when trauma invades their personal lives. During these transitions, employees move from immobilization to denial to anger. With the right types of information and motivation, however, they will return to a constructive path to change through bargaining, exploration and, finally, acceptance.

To manage the transition phase successfully, you must empathize with employees' experiences and concerns. These may include a loss of control, uncertainty about how to act, a suspicion that the balance of power is shifting, a fear of failure and a perception that the change threatens their careers. If not addressed, these issues fester and coalesce in that negative and harmful state known as resistance.

Employee resistance cannot be taken lightly. After all, change does not happen if employees don't want it to. In fact, in most studies of reengineering projects and other major change efforts, 70 percent of the initiatives are judged not to have met expectations. In many cases, senior management has consistently underestimated the amount of reinforcement needed to implement a successful change. While they've put a great deal of money into creating the plan, they've put relatively little into communication, training and reinforcement. Viewed as optional, these elements are the first to go when money gets tight. This is a fatal error.

As your organization moves from the known to the unknown, you need to clarify the criteria for success in the target state. The direct benefits of change must be explicitly stated for each individual. Otherwise employees will lapse back to their comfort zone: the status quo.

How Leaders Think

As noted, your words and actions will have a greater impact on the results of a change effort than any other element. You must think and act like a leader to guide employees to the new, targeted state.

What does it take to think like a leader? It's not as simple as it may seem. Employees, after all, are not the only ones who gravitate toward the familiar. Senior managers and their consultants often are most comfortable producing written reports and action plans. The problem is that plans amount to tangible, visible results of management efforts, while change often is intangible and invisible unless it is tied to measurable results.

Therefore, the leader must link change to key business processes and performance measures, set goals for the change effort using these measures and then track and report on progress against goals. To monitor your progress, you might measure specific change actions, such as the percentage of employees who understand the change, the percentage of new job procedures committed to writing and the percentage of employees trained on new systems and processes before a change is made.

The key is this: Don't just talk about change or draft reports. The "rubber meets the road" when you reach the implementation stage. Make change tangible and real. Use measures, targets and results to demonstrate your progress on a change path. This approach will get you where you want to go.

As a change leader, you also need to identify allies who will be key to driving the initiative and then develop the business case for change with these individuals. Ironically, this proves more difficult when business is good than when it's bad, but you're expected to have the vision to see farther down the road than others. Sometimes taking a close look at the competition can be very effective in creating a sense of urgency for change.

The allies you identify will play three key roles in the change process: sponsors, change agents and change targets. Sponsors and change agents are the primary advocates of change. Sponsors lead and sustain the change process, while change agents define and implement the change. The third group, change targets, consists of employees who must change some aspect of their work. Of course, in the strict sense, sponsors and change agents might also be change targets; they must recognize where they have this dual role and model new behaviors they want others to exhibit.

Usually, a company's earliest forays into change are primarily technical, dealing with systems and procedures that require only minor behavioral shifts. Broader, more impactful change focuses on organizational processes and behaviors. These cultural and behavioral changes require greater sophistication to successfully conceive, implement and lead.

A key leadership duty is to define the values and beliefs that can be used to shape behaviors and, ultimately, performance. It's up to you to create an environment that facilitates the open flow of ideas and information, which in turn will generate shared understanding, credibility, respect and trust. By aligning attitudes, you will build commitment to support project implementation efforts.

A variety of tactics will help to align attitudes. Certainly, your leadership actions make a strong impact because they communicate your beliefs, values and assumptions (see the "Self-Test for Leaders"). Performance measures also affect employees' attitudes. What does the company measure? Are the measures clear? Do they emphasize individual contributions or group goals? Do they value short- or long-term thinking? A third "shaper" of attitudes is vision, purpose and strategy. Employees must understand what the company's vision is and how the change initiative will help attain it. A muddled vision will cause employees to dissociate themselves from the program.

How Leaders Act

As a change leader, be prepared to provide the energy to sustain the new order. Always err on the side of anion. By setting your sights on win after win, you will avoid the "analysis paralysis" that cripples so many promising change campaigns. In your efforts to exude energy, you will:

- Set direction;
- Identify and address resistance;
- Secure commitment, using rewards and pressure to gain support;
- Provide visible support by committing adequate resources of the right level and type;
- Monitor and track progress;
- Create additional sponsors and develop change agents;
- Build teams;
- Transfer knowledge and skills; and
- Provide active communication.

Perhaps most importantly, you must set an example—and make sure it's noticed—to implement a change-management plan. Too often employees don't see anything new about the actions of those supposedly leading the initiative, so they assume that this, too, will pass. That's why symbolic acts are so powerful. Shredding the procedure manuals that guided behaviors in the past, for example, sends the loudest possible signal about the company's commitment to change.

A change leader must be very visible on the project from the first day to the last. Studies consistently show that people form opinions based on nonverbal cues much more readily than on verbal cues. Change is one project you just can't delegate. Because it directly impacts people's day-to-day roles and responsibilities, it requires real hands-on leadership to make it work effectively.

Even small gestures, such as putting the project first on your regular staff-meeting agenda, can demonstrate its importance. Reinforce your interest by requesting frequent status updates. And make it your business to have lunch periodically with different project team members.

A key indicator of your commitment—some would say the key indicator—is how generously you reward desired behaviors and results. To catch employees' attention, you can offer a bonus for reaching a stated progress goal, recognize significant contributors in the employee newsletter, treat them to lunch or award gift certificates. You get the idea.

Nothing provides more potent reinforcement than recognition. Be sure to reward people as you go, instead of waiting until the very end. To use a track-and-field metaphor, think of your change program more as a series of sprints, each with a set of recognized winners, than as a marathon, with one set of winners at the very end of a long course.

How much time should you spend "leading the charge"? There's no one answer; it all depends on the magnitude and complexity of the change, the risks that must be managed, the level of resistance, etc. But as a general rule, it will take between 20 percent and 50 percent of your time to make the effort succeed. This time commitment usually overlaps with preexisting duties. Sometimes, for example, it just means bringing a different focus to meetings, asking frequent questions about the initiative and providing some visible support to hardworking team members. It all boils down to a strategic approach to communication.

A Self-Test for Leaders

Take this test to determine how you rate as a sponsor of change. Circle the number that describes your response and add up the total. An interpretation of your score can be found below.

	Not really	Almost	Absolutely
Am I fully committed to the success of the projects?	0	1	2
Do my verbal and nonverbal messages demonstrate my commitment?	0	1	2
Can I clearly articulate the business case for change?			
Have I cleared my plate enough to be an effective sponsor?	0	1	2
Have I dedicated the necessary resources to the effort?	0	1	2
Have I ensured that change management activities are built into the project plan?	0	1	2
Am I participating in a campaign to reach all stakeholders?	0	1	2
Do I look for and address signs of resistance among key stakeholders?	0	1	2
Have I empowered the project team to think "outside the box"?	0	1	2
Have I motivated change agents to remain committed?	0	1	2
Am I sure that managers and supervisors understand their role in the change process?	0	1	2
Do I understand how this change relates to other company initiatives?	0	1	2

What Your Score Means

0–6 You are not yet a change-ready sponsor. Reassess your commitment level and role.

7–15 You are doing some things right. Seek improvement in areas where you scored low.

16–24 You are a change dynamo. Keep up the good work and celebrate your successes!

Communication

Companies traditionally have viewed stakeholders as a captive audience. But today's workplace requires a different approach. If you want to change employees' attitudes and behavior, you need to woo them as you would any other customer.

That's why your strategy must be more advertising campaign, less corporate edict. Rather than making general announcements to broad audiences, issue specific messages to specific groups. Rather than relying on words alone add actions and processes. In lieu of standard communication vehicles, use creative new formats to deliver messages continuously, not just occasionally. And in place of one-way, formal pronouncements, introduce two-way, more informal dialogues.

Be aware that everything you say has to sell the project to stakeholders. Intellectual buy-in alone will not change behavior, but self-interest definitely helps it along. As you build the business case for change, create a "burning platform" that the status quo is no longer acceptable or even safe in today's highly competitive marketplace. Don't allow resisters to think that all they have to do is wait it out, as they've done before, and things will return to business as usual.

To overcome inertia, your case for change must be strong and weighted toward opportunities. Include the history of the change process, the motivation for change, the implementation plan and the progress to date. Above all, be honest and straightforward; if you're bluffing or being evasive, employees will respond unenthusiastically. Lay out realistic expectations for the future while making them relevant to employees.

Making the Case

You'll need to work with multiple salespeople to reach all stakeholders with your "ad campaign." These key individuals will be delivering your base message and subsequent communications throughout the organization. Equip them with an "elevator speech" of no more than 30 seconds that encapsulates what the project is about and why it is important. Then augment their efforts with the whole arsenal of electronic, printed and face-to-face communications vehicles at your disposal.

You're in the position to effect successful change within your company. However, it won't come easily because change challenges the comfort of the status quo. You've got to persuade people about the necessity for change.

If you were an advertising executive, you'd face this sort of challenge everyday. Ads have to get people's attention and prompt them to change their behavior in some discernible way. The effective ones gain a "share of mind" by breaking through the clutter of information—from the radio, TV, billboards, newspapers, magazines, Internet, e-mail voice mail, etc.—that confronts people throughout the day. This is a huge communications challenge that requires a high degree of creativity. There is a definite parallel in the process of leading a change program.

If you personally demonstrate great enthusiasm for the project, reward desired behaviors and transmit a steady stream of honest communications, you'll make it happen. Bear in mind that many people can lead your troops in the present, but only you can lead them into the future. Are your ready?

Article Review Form at end of book.

What are the four guidelines for succeeding at change and overcoming dependency? What are the two interrelated conditions that create overload?

Breaking the Bonds of Dependency

Overload and vulnerability make it difficult for reform-minded principals to think outside the box. But a new mindset and four guidelines for action can help them truly lead.

Michael Fullan

Michael Fullan is Dean of the Ontario Institute for Studies in Education, University of Toronto, 252 Bloor St. W., Toronto, ON, Canada M5S 1V6.

Wanted: A miracle worker who can do more with less, pacify rival groups, endure chronic second-guessing, tolerate low levels of support, process large volumes of paper and work double shifts (75 nights a year out). He or she will have carte blanche to innovate, but cannot spend much money, replace any personnel, or upset any constituency.[1]

The job of the principal or any educational leader has become increasingly complex and constrained. Principals find themselves locked in with less and less room to maneuver. They have become more and more dependent on context. At the very time that proactive leadership is essential, principals are in the least favorable position to provide it. They need a new mindset and guidelines for action to break through the bonds of dependency that have entrapped those who want to make a difference in their schools.

The Context for Dependency

Dependency is created by two interrelated conditions: overload and corresponding vulnerability to packaged solutions. First, the system fosters dependency on the part of principals. The role of principals in implementing innovations more often than not consists of being on the receiving end of externally initiated changes. The constant bombardment of new tasks and the continual interruptions keep principals off balance. Not only are the demands fragmented and incoherent, but even good ideas have a short shelf life as initiatives are dropped in favor of the latest new policy. Overload in the form of a barrage of disjointed demands fosters dependency.

These demands have recently taken on an even more intrusive quality as school boundaries become more permeable and transparent. In the third book in our trilogy, *What's Worth Fighting For Out There,* Andy Hargreaves and I document how very different the school environment is today compared to even five years ago (1998; see also Fullan 1997 and Fullan and Hargreaves 1996). The walls of the school have come tumbling down, metaphorically speaking. "Out there" is now "in here" as government policy, parent and community demands, corporate interests, and ubiquitous technology have all stormed the walls of the school. The relentless pressures of today's complex environments have intensified overload.

[1] Evans, R. (April 12, 1995). "Getting Real About Leadership." *Education Week.* 14, 29: 36.

The situation just described makes principals and other leaders especially vulnerable to the latest recipe for success—the second aspect of dependency. Providers of management theories and strategies are only too happy to oblige the demand for instant solutions. Management techniques, like so many fads, have a terrible track record. Part of the problem lies in the nature of the advice. As Micklethwait and Wooldridge (1996) say about the "guru business": "it is constitutionally incapable of self-criticism; its terminology usually confuses rather than educates; it rarely rises above basic common sense; and it is faddish and bedeviled by contradictions" (p. 12).

Where does that leave the modern boss? ask Micklethwait and Wooldridge:

The simple answer is, overworked. He [or she] faces a far more complex challenge than his [or her] predecessors: today's boss is expected to give power away while keeping some form of control, and to tap the creative talents of . . . employees while creating a common culture within the company (p. 172).

The most serious problem, however, is not that the advice is wrong, but that there is no answer out there. Mintzberg (1994), who wrote the definitive critique, *The Rise and Fall of Strategic Planning,* observes only half-facetiously, "Never adopt a [management] technique by its usual name" (p. 27). Farson (1997), the author of *Management of the Absurd,* advises, "Once you find a management technique that works, give it up" (p. 35). These authors drew these odd conclusions because they wanted to stress that there is no external answer that will substitute for the complex work of changing one's own situation.

Contrary to what management books would have us believe, organizations did not become effective by directly following their advice. Evans (1996) notes:

It is one thing to say in most successful organizations members share a clear, common vision, which is true, but quite another to suggest that this stems primarily from direct vision-building, which is not. Vision-building is the result of a whole range of activities (pp. 208–209).

Educators and business leaders have wasted precious time and resources looking for external solutions. Times of uncertainty and relentless pressure prompt an understandable tendency to want to know what to do. The first insight is that there is no definitive answer to the "how" question. Take, for example, the very clear research finding that student achievement increases substantially in schools with collaborative work cultures that foster a professional learning community among teachers and others, focus continuously on improving instructional practices in light of student performance data, and link to external standards and staff development support (Newmann and Wehlage 1995). To know and believe this does not tell educators *how* to change their own situation to produce greater collaboration. They can get ideas, directions, insights, but they can never know exactly how to go about it because such a path is exceedingly complex, and it changes as they work with their organization's unique personalities and cultural conditions.

Realizing that there is no answer, that we will never arrive in any formal sense, can be quite liberating. Instead of hoping that the latest technique will at last provide the answer, we approach the situation differently. Leaders for change get involved as learners in real reform situations. They craft their own theories of change, consistently testing them against new situations. They become critical consumers of management theories, able to sort out promising ideas from empty ones. They become less vulnerable to and less dependent on external answers. They stop looking for solutions in the wrong places.

Giving up the futile search for the silver bullet is the basic precondition for overcoming dependency and for beginning to take actions that do matter. It frees educational leaders to gain truly new insights that can inform and guide their actions toward greater success, mobilizing resources for teaching and learning with children as the beneficiaries. We formulated four such novel guidelines in *What's Worth Fighting For Out There* (1998):

1. Respect those you want to silence.
2. Move toward the danger in forming new alliances.
3. Manage emotionally as well as rationally.
4. Fight for lost causes.

Respect Those You Want to Silence

Reform often misfires because we fail to learn from those who disagree with us. "Resistance" to a new initiative can actually be highly instructive. Conflict and differences can make a constructive contribution in dealing with complex problems. As Maurer (1996) observes:

Often those who resist have something important to tell us. People resist for what they view as good reasons. They may see alternatives we never dreamed of. They may understand problems about the minutiae of implementation that we never see from our lofty perch atop Mount Olympus (p. 49).

Thus, for example, it is a mistake for principals to go only with like-minded innovators. Elmore (1995) puts it this way: "Small groups of self-selected reformers apparently seldom influence their peers" (p. 20). They just create an even greater gap between themselves and others that eventually becomes impossible to bridge. In turbulent times the key task of leadership is not to arrive at early consensus, but to create opportunities for learning from dissonance. Mobilizing people to tackle tough problems is the key skill needed these days: "Instead of looking for saviors we should be calling for leadership that will challenge us to face problems for which there are no simple painless solutions—problems that require us to learn in new ways" (Heifitz 1994, p. 2).

Move Toward the Danger in Forming New Alliances

I have said that the boundaries of the school have been permanently penetrated. I also conclude that this is a good and necessary development because school reform cannot succeed without community reform. Healthy neighborhoods and healthy schools go hand in hand (Schorr 1997), and school-community relationships are key. The problem is, What do you do if you do not have a strong relationship with the community? Here leaders have to do the opposite of what they feel like doing. Instead of withdrawing and putting up barricades, they must "move toward the danger." Today's environment is dangerous, but it is also laced with opportunities:

In a school, where mistrust between the community and the administration is the major issue, you must begin to deal with it by making sure that parents are present at every major event, every meeting, every challenge. *Within the discomfort of that presence* the learning and healing could begin (Dolan 1994, p. 60, emphasis added).

The same is true with other dimensions of the new environment. For example, educational leaders must directly address state policy that results in student performance data being generated and published. The way to deal with potential misuses of student performance data is to become assessment-literate. Schools put themselves in the driver's seat when they invest in professional development and collaborative cultures that focus on student learning and associated improvements in instructional practices.

In all cases, the new leadership requires principals to take their school's accountability to the public. Successful schools are not only collaborative internally, but they also have the confidence, capacity, and political wisdom to reach out, constantly forming new alliances.

Manage Emotionally as Well as Rationally

Leaders moving their staff toward external dangers in a world of diversity cannot invite disagreement without attending to their own emotional health.

As Maurer (1996) says, "Dealing with resistance can be very stressful. People attack you and your precious ideas. Sometimes they seem to show no respect for you" (p. 59). Someone will always be dissatisfied with the leader's performance. Relaxation exercises, physical fitness, recalling a higher purpose, teaming up with a supportive peer, separating self from role, and ignoring the temptation to get even are some of the remedies Maurer suggests.

The emotionally intelligent leader also helps teachers, students, parents, and others create an environment of support, one in which people see problems not as weaknesses but as issues to be solved. Managing emotionally means putting a high priority on *reculturing*, not merely *restructuring*. Restructuring refers to changes in the formal structure of schooling in terms of organization, timetables, roles, and the like. Restructuring bears no direct relationship to improvements in teaching and learning. Reculturing, by contrast, involves changing the norms, values, incentives, skills, and relationships in the organization to foster a different way of working together. Reculturing makes a difference in teaching and learning.

Reculturing, because it is based on relationships, requires strong emotional involvement from principals and others. It also pays emotional dividends. It contributes to personal and collective resilience in the face of change. It helps people persist as they encounter the implementation dip when things go wrong. Principals who manage emotionally as well as rationally have a strong task focus, expect anxiety to be endemic in school reform, but invest in structures and norms that help contain anxiety. Collaborative cultures promote support, but they also elevate expectations.

Fight for Lost Causes (Be Hopeful When It Counts)

In *What's Worth Fighting For Out There* Andy Hargreaves and I carefully examine the fascinating concept of "hope." It turns out that the best definition of *hope* is "unwarranted optimism." Vaclav Havel, president of the Czech Republic, captures this best:

> Hope is definitely not the same as optimism. It is not the conviction that something will turn out well, but the certainty that something makes sense, regardless of how it turns out. It is hope, above all, that gives us strength to live and to continually try new things, even in conditions that seem hopeless (1993, p. 68).

Principals with hope are much less likely to succumb to the daily stresses of the job. They place their problems in a loftier perspective than enables them to rebound from bad days. Once leaders realize that having hope is not a prediction, that it is independent of knowing how things might turn out, it becomes a deeper resource. Leaders with hope are less likely to panic when faced with immediate and pressing problems.

It is especially important that leaders have and display hope, that they show they are prepared to fight for lost causes, because they set the tone for so many others. Teachers are desperate for lifelines of hope. They understand that hope is not a promise, but they need to be reminded that they are connected to a larger purpose and to others who are struggling to make progress. Articulating and discussing hope when the going gets rough re-energizes teachers, reduces stress, and can point to new directions. Principals will be much more effective (and healthier) if they develop and pursue high hopes as they reculture their schools and their relationships to the outside.

Scale Up

As we approach the next century, the big question preoccupying policymakers and others is how to scale up. We have witnessed pockets of innovation, but little that could be characterized as large-scale patterns of success. The main problem, I would say, is not the spread of good ideas. Making reform widespread is related to replicating the *conditions* of successful change, not to transferring products (Healey and DeStefano 1997). These conditions involve scores of principals and other educational leaders breaking the bonds of dependency that the current system fosters. The societal context for educational reform has radically changed. To be successful, future leaders of the school, district, or other levels will require very different characteristics than those expected of leaders in the last decade.

Dependency is a function of insecurity, which can never be resolved under conditions of uncertainty. The education leader of the 21st century, paradoxically, will find greater peace of mind by looking for answers close at hand and reaching out, knowing that there is no clear solution.

"Life is a path you beat while you walk it," wrote the poet Antonio Machado, and DuGues (1997) calls this line of poetry "the most profound lesson in planning and strategy that I have ever learned." Breaking the bonds of dependency involves grasping this basic truth: "It is the walking that beats the path. It is not the path that makes the walk" (p. 155).

References

DeGues, A. (1997). *The Living Company.* Boston: Harvard School Business Program.

Dolan, P. (1994). *Restructuring Our Schools.* Kansas City, Mo.: Systems and Organizations.

Elmore, R. (1995). "Getting to Scale with Good Educational Practice." *Harvard Education Review* 66, 1: 1–26.

Evans, R. (1996). *The Human Side of School Change.* San Francisco: Jossey-Bass.

Farson, R. (1997). *Management of the Absurd.* New York: Simon and Schuster.

Fullan, M. (1997). *What's Worth Fighting For in the Principalship?* 2nd ed. New York: Teachers College Press.

Fullan, M., and A. Hargreaves. (1996). *What's Worth Fighting For In Your School.* New York: Teachers College Press.

Hargreaves, A., and M. Fullan. (1998). *What's Worth Fighting For Out There.* New York: Teachers College Press.

Havel, V. (October 1993). "Never Against Hope." *Esquire.* 65–69.

Healey, H., and J. DeStefano. (1997). *Education Reform Support: A Framework for Scaling up School Reform.* Washington, D.C.: Abel 2 Clearinghouse for Basic Education.

Heifitz, R. (1994). *Leadership Without Easy Answers.* Cambridge, Mass.: Harvard University Press.

Maurer, R. (1996). *Beyond the Wall of Resistance.* Austin: Bard Books.

Micklethwait, J., and A. Wooldridge. (1996). *The Witch Doctors: Making Sense of Management Gurus.* New York: Time Books, Random House.

Mintzberg, H. (1994). *The Rise and Fall of Strategic Planning.* New York: Free Press.

Newmann, F., and G. Wehlage. (1995). *Successful School Restructuring.* Madison, Wisc.: Center on Organization and Restructuring of Schools.

Schorr, L. (1997). *Common Purpose: Strengthening Families and Neighborhoods to Rebuild America.* New York: Doubleday.

Article Review Form at end of book.

What are the six tasks involved in the reflection process? Although successful organizations fail in many ways, all of these failures share one underlying cause. What is it?

The Power of Reflection

Michael Hammer
Steven A. Stanton

If you were asked to identify the major U.S. companies best positioned for success, you'd probably list Microsoft, Intel, Procter & Gamble, Hewlett-Packard, Merck, GE, and the like. Ask yourself then to construct a scenario that leads each of these companies to the brink of extinction ten years from now. Despite the apparent vigor of the companies on the list, you would no doubt have little difficulty in developing these scenarios—probably with great glee. Some of your scenarios might stretch the bounds of credulity, but most would be frighteningly plausible: a new technology that is ignored until it is too late; a fundamental market shift whose reality is denied; a breakthrough competitor innovation in marketing or service that takes the company unawares; a growing sluggishness and bureaucracy that dampen the fervor that helped create the position of leadership and success.

Now, a third question: If you were an executive at one of the companies in question, what would you do today to prevent such calamitous scenarios from coming to pass? Don't return to the list of nightmares you've just created and identify a set of specific steps to ensure that those outcomes remain fantasy rather than reality: an early investment in the threatening technology, a preemptive strike against the competitor, anticipation of the new market trend. All those measures are predicated on accurate foreknowledge of the disasters lying in wait. Real disasters are not so considerate; they do not telegraph their arrival in advance and allow us to prepare for them.

Nothing Fails Like Success

What we are discussing here is one of the most perplexing problems facing successful organizations: Why is it that they are frequently unable to maintain their success over time? How could Sears have possibly let Wal-Mart steal a march on it? Why is Pan Am, which dominated air travel 50 years ago, today just a memory? Why didn't Howard Johnson's, which in 1965 had sales greater than those of McDonald's, Burger King, and Kentucky Fried Chicken put together, come to dominate the fast-food business? It is not terribly helpful to reply that Sears dismissed everyday low pricing or that Howard Johnson's was too entrenched in its ways to catch on to the new trends in restaurants. The real questions is, why?

The Reflection Imperative

The answer is that, although successful organizations fail in many different ways, all these failures share one underlying cause: a failure to reflect. Organizations, particularly successful ones, are so caught up in carrying out their day-to-day work that they rarely, if ever, stop to think objectively about themselves and their businesses. They do not ask the probing questions that might lead them to call into question their basic assumptions, to refresh their strategies, to reengineer their processes.

Reflection entails awareness of self, of competitors, of customers. It means thinking without preconception. It means questioning cherished assumptions and replacing them with

Reprinted from the November 24, 1997, issue of FORTUNE by special permission; copyright 1997, Time Inc.

new approaches. It is the only way in which a winning company can maintain its leadership position, by which a company with great assets can ensure that they continue to be well deployed.

Why do so many organizations fail to reflect? One mundane reason is time—or rather, the lack of it. The daily concerns of managing an enterprise can easily soak up all of management's time and energy, leaving none for the effort that reflection requires. Voice mail, electronic mail, meetings, performance reviews, and all the other paraphernalia of modern business so sap managers' time that there is none left over for real thinking. Reflection must be deeply rooted in a company's day-to-day operations. In short, reflection must be institutionalized as a business process.

Reflection as a Process

Over the past decade, in the aftermath of the quality movement and reengineering, companies have come to recognize the value of managing work as process. A process is a group of activities that together create a desired result: Order fulfillment is a process whose constituent activities include inventory allocation, picking and packing, traffic planning, and shipping. Companies now realize that merely concentrating on individual tasks does not ensure that the desired results will be achieved.

By identifying and managing key business processes—such as product development, order fulfillment, and demand generation —companies can ensure that these are well performed on a sustained basis. When the organization recognizes work as a process and manages it as such, achieving its goals becomes deliberate, rather than the accidental by-product of performing its various constituent tasks.

There are four parts of managing work as a process. The first is clearly articulating the goals of the process; the second is designing the work in such a way that achieving the goals is not left to chance but is a dependable outcome; the third is measuring process performance continually; and the fourth is assigning end-to-end responsibility for the process to a key senior manager. When business processes are managed in this way, they perform well and do so reliably. Processes from order fulfillment to product development have benefited from this discipline; reflection must also be managed as a process if it is to deliver its results reliably. The whole reflection process, not just its individual tasks and components, must be performed regularly and carefully.

There are six tasks involved in the reflection process: developing deep customer insight; conducting broad environmental monitoring; developing competitor intelligence; performing honest self-assessment; engaging in ongoing mind expansion; and questioning fundamental assumptions. The first four of these are information-gathering activities, the fifth entails changing the dynamics of the company's thinking, and the last integrates all the others. All six need to be accomplished for the reflection process to perform effectively. While many of these activities may sound familiar, combining them into a process produces results that go beyond what they individually achieve.

Customer Insight

In order to avoid being surprised by shifts in customer behavior, it is necessary to understand your customers better than they understand themselves. This goes far beyond reviewing customer-satisfaction surveys. It means appreciating your customers' unstated and unmet needs, knowing their businesses or lifestyles in ways that extend beyond their use of your current product or service.

The calculator division of Texas Instruments, for example, focuses on making TI calculators the de facto standard in high schools. To this end, managers work closely with mathematics teachers to see how they incorporate calculations into their teaching. TI creates simulated classrooms to understand both how mathematics teachers teach and how people learn mathematics—and how improved calculators could help them do so.

When Tom Kasten, a vice president at Levi Strauss, was a merchandiser responsible for developing Levi's Jeans products for the teenagers of America, he used to drive down weekly to the Fillmore Auditorium in San Francisco, where every Saturday kids would line up early in the morning to buy tickets for that night's rock concert. Tom would get out of his car, talk to the kids in line to determine what they were looking for in a pair of jeans, and observe what they were doing to their own jeans to customize them. Even now Tom takes more than his share of carpool turns each week driving his son and his friends to high school. This extra duty affords him additional opportunities to study the latest in teenage thinking and fashion. "The kids love to talk about where they shop, what they like, and what they hate," he says. "This is where it all begins, so that is what I do to learn, by watching consumers in their natural habitat."

Developing insight entails meeting with customers' customers in order to recognize opportunities to add more value; modeling and analyzing your customers' operations to identify opportunities for cross-company integration; engaging customers in your own improvement programs and becoming engaged in theirs; and having a broad cross-section of your organization establish relationships with their counterparts in various customer organizations.

Environmental Monitoring

Major shifts in a company's environment rarely (if ever) happen overnight—nor do they happen very often. The signs of fundamental shifts are always there for those who care to look for them. Even such seemingly dramatic changes as the end of the Cold War or the emergence of the Internet were many years in the making. There is no excuse for being caught unawares by new technologies, geopolitical shifts, regulatory changes, demographic trends, and the like. The trick is to notice a phenomenon while it is still emerging and to begin to prepare for it before it is upon you. Shell's scenario planning, which helped it deal with the "unanticipatable" oil shock of 1973, is a well-known case in point.

The great danger in this context is to look for signs that things are changing in all the familiar places. This is rarely if ever effective; by definition, "surprises" come from unexpected directions. Those involved in environmental monitoring need to avoid this mistake. To that end, for example, an effort to identify new directions in information technology should not be left to the information systems personnel. They are usually so close to the existing order that they will not look at what is truly new or recognize it as important; the only people who understood the significance of the PC later than mainframe vendors were their best customers, corporate information departments.

Competitor Intelligence

To prevent being blindsided by competitors (old or new), it is not sufficient to know what they are doing today; it is necessary to surmise what they might be intending to do tomorrow. At Oxford Health Plans, one of the country's fastest-growing managed-care companies, members of the senior management team spend a full day each quarter in an intensive competitive review. They analyze the bids submitted by Oxford and its competitors at key accounts in the preceding quarter. Their goal is to read between the lines of competitor actions to understand their strategies and plans. As Bob Smoler, CEO of Oxford Health Plans New York, says, "It all comes down to watching the chess moves they are using to drive their top line—whether it's product, price, or broker commissions." By analyzing these bids, Oxford can divine who is commoditizing their business and who is specializing their offerings, who is underpricing to buy share and who is underpricing because they are in trouble, who is raising broker fees to sweeten a deal and who is introducing what new products. Oxford uses these reviews to quickly identify new entrants into its markets and to assess how well the merger of its major competitors (US Healthcare and Aetna) is going. In this way it avoids being caught flat-footed by new developments.

To be effective, it is not sufficient to apply this discipline to one's existing competitors; nascent and potential competitors deserve the same kind of attention. A suitably broad definition of competitors is a prerequisite for success at this endeavor. At the very least, your competitor list must include everyone who might be able to solve the same customer problems that you do. Current industry boundaries are increasingly transient in nature and can be more harmful than helpful. To a customer, distinctions between a discounter and a department store and between a PC and a minicomputer are not nearly as significant as they are to players in those industries.

Self-Assessment

Internal decay, unabetted by external change or competitor depredations, is a common form of failure. Companies can simply start operating on autopilot and thereby lose the edge that propelled them into success in the first place. This rot often sets in without executives' noticing: first, because they are too far from the day-to-day operations of the business to sense it, and second, because their attention is preoccupied on those notorious lagging indicators, financial results. By the time "the numbers" start to decline, it is often very hard or even too late to deal with the underlying causes.

The beginning of the answer is to listen very carefully to the sounds of operating performance. How well is the company doing at the blocking and tackling level? What is the cycle time of order fulfillment? What fraction of customer inquiries are being resolved on the first call? Managers need to know whether the company is still performing at least as well as it has in the past relative to customer expectations and competitor capabilities.

A second area to which attention must be paid is that of cultural alignment. An important leading indicator of future failure is a weakening of the cultural values that root employees in their company and inspire them to extraordinary performance. Cynicism, indifference, and defensiveness are attitudes that eventually and inevitably destroy even the strongest organization. Company leaders often seem to think that merely repeating pious homilies or printing noble slogans on laminated wallet cards will maintain a strong company culture. Close observation of actual behavior, confidential interviews, and "cultural audits" can all help determine the real spirit of a company. For instance, Consumers Power, a large Michigan utility, retained a cultural anthropologist to develop an objective assessment of the real values and attitudes that governed employees' behavior. They discovered that people obeyed such rules as "good news goes up, bad news gets managed," rules that would lead to problems if allowed to persist.

Mind Expansion

The activities we have described so far all center on acquiring various kinds of information. But information does not carry its own interpretation; that must be supplied by those who evaluate it. The danger is that the real meaning of potentially significant information will be missed because those looking at it will view it through traditional lenses. To prevent this, company leadership must ensure that people throughout the company are able to perceive information from a fresh perspective rather than filtered through their current mental models.

There are no cut-and-dried procedures for expanding managers' minds; the best advice is that practice makes perfect. People need experience at "getting out of the box" if they are to do so when it matters. One interesting approach is that practiced by CEO Lou Gerstner at IBM. Every six weeks he takes his top 40 managers off-site for a two-day retreat. But these are not typical operating reviews. Rather, they are dedicated to management learning in nontraditional areas. Each session features an outside speaker who addresses a topic that is peripheral to the immediate concerns of IBM's leadership. These speakers may be academics, executives from other industries, or even representatives of the art world. Gerstner personally leads these sessions; his objective is to give his executives practice in stretching their thinking and developing new perspectives on IBM's business.

Assumption Breaking

The last of the components of the reflection process, this one brings all the others together. The seeds have been gathered by the four information-gathering activities, and the ground has been turned over by mind expansion. What remains is to plant and harvest the crop, to turn information into ideas for action. The goal is to surface real insights—like the ones we tried to imagine in the exercise at the beginning of this article—to prevent future disaster: investing in a new technology, shifting the company's direction, addressing new markets, redesigning modes of operation, and all the rest.

The hardest part of undertaking radical steps like these is reaching the conclusion that they must be taken and summoning up the fortitude to carry them out. This is done by identifying and questioning the business' underlying assumptions. Every business floats on a sea of assumptions that shape its view of the market, its strategy, and how it operates. We compete with other manufacturers on the basis of price; every new product we develop must be unique; our people are the best and most highly motivated in the industry—these are but samples of such assumptions. It is natural and necessary for companies to have them. They provide the basis on which a company designs its operations and makes a broad range of decisions. When change causes assumptions to lose their validity, while the company persists in its old ways of doing business, disaster is inevitable.

Assumption breaking is the most arduous of all the steps in the reflection process, because identifying and questioning assumptions goes against the organizational grain. Many people in the organization have strong interests in the status quo, and asking unsettling questions causes them anxiety. Yet, without this step, all the others are purposeless. Collecting new information by itself leads nowhere; it is in the nontraditional thinking of assumption breaking that its value is realized.

Business disasters are not considerate—they don't telegraph their arrival in advance.

Understand customers better than they understand themselves—know unmet needs.

The trick is to prepare for a phenomenon while it's still emerging, before it's upon you.

Rot sets in because executives are involved with lagging indicators—financial results.

Article Review Form at end of book.

What are the five factors that affect school reform? What propositions are suggested to improve school reform initiatives?

A Systems Approach to School Reform

Is significant school reform possible? The answer is clearly yes, Mr. McAdams says, but successful reform requires an understanding of the interplay of five factors and the ability to integrate this knowledge into a systemic reform effort.

Richard P. McAdams

Richard P. McAdams is an assistant professor in the Department of Educational Leadership at Lehigh University, Bethlehem, Pa.

Is large-scale school reform possible? The accumulated evidence of the past 40 years of reform efforts is not encouraging. While hundreds of individual schools and a few school districts have created and sustained successful reforms, the vast majority of America's school districts have remained impervious to substantive reform. Why is this so and what can be done about it? Repeated failed attempts at reform suggest that our standard approach to reform is fundamentally flawed.

Substantive reform in a complex social system such as a school district requires a level of intellectual sophistication and unity of purpose that is seldom attainable under our prevailing model of school governance. Moreover, leading educational researchers and theorists typically focus on narrow slices of the reality of school systems and ignore the relationships between phenomena in school and other relevant phenomena in school system operations.

Below I summarize the findings of leading scholars in the fields of leadership theory, local politics and governance, state and national school politics, organizational theory, and change theory. For the purpose of my summary, I will consider each of these areas as an independent phenomenon, though it is the interactions of these factors within a school system that are seldom analyzed and often doom our efforts at reform. I conclude by discussing what can be done in light of these interrelationships and by outlining the characteristics of a school system that would be more amenable to reform.

Leadership Theory

How do leaders put themselves in a position to make significant changes in an organization? Peter Senge develops the concepts of personal mastery, shared vision, mental models, and team learning as necessary precursors for mastering what he calls the "fifth discipline" or "systems thinking."[1]

A careful reading of Senge's work portrays a leader of an organization involved in systemic change as both a reflective and highly moral individual. He describes such a leader as having been in a position of leadership for a sufficient time to inspire trust and respect from the staff and to build a culture of teamwork.

Stephen Covey's views parallel Senge's insights concerning the need for a leader to reflect on his or her own personal core beliefs and to develop the trust and

Copyright © 1997. Reprinted with permission from Phi Delta Kappan and the author.

skills necessary to work for change collaboratively. Covey's notion of a "character ethic" rather than a "personality ethic" is akin to Senge's notion of personal mastery.[2]

Howard Gardner distinguishes between indirect and direct leadership. Indirect leadership is exercised by a person within his or her sphere of specialized knowledge. Gardner is referring mainly to academics and other recognized experts. Direct leadership, on the other hand, is exercised in a general political sense and is not restricted to a given area of knowledge. By virtue of position, a school superintendent must be able to exercise indirect (specialized) leadership as the instructional leader of the district. But a superintendent must also exercise direct, more generalized leadership with the school board and community. The ability to do both effectively is an uncommon gift that is nonetheless critical in leading a significant reform effort in a school district.

Local Politics and Governance

The politics of local school districts and the tendency toward micromanagement by many boards can seriously inhibit a board's policy-making function and weaken a superintendent's ability to sustain reform. Indeed, American school boards spend 24% of their time dealing with the problems of their own children or the problems of the children of relatives and close friends.[3]

The political imperatives of local school board governance militate against the development and implementation of long-range plans. The tenure of a typical school board member in the U.S. is about four years.[4] Coupled with the adversarial nature of many board elections, this short tenure both erases institutional memory and undermines the consistency of mission needed to achieve substantive reform. Successful school reform requires that board members "recognize that continuity of purpose, vision, and structure depends on the board's ability to maintain a steady course despite change in superintendencies and even changes in the membership of the board."[5]

Visionary leadership on the part of a superintendent and a board, which is required to produce systemic change, presupposes sufficient time to develop a shared vision. To develop a cohesive team with a commitment to a common mission requires a level of trust and mutual respect that is one of the fruits of longer-term professional relationships. The time required to form such trusting relationships is simply not available to many school superintendents and boards. Indeed, the average tenure of superintendents in a recent national sample was only about five years.[6]

The relatively short tenure of board members and superintendents is to some extent a function of political controversies within a school community. A 20-year review of property tax changes in 55 Pennsylvania school districts indicated that districts with the highest rates of tax increases had a significantly higher rate of turnover among school board members than did districts with the lowest rates of tax increases. This same study revealed a statistically significant correlation between the turnover rates for school board members and the turnover rates for superintendents in the same districts.[7]

For the sake of simplicity, let us assume that the average tenure for both superintendents and school board members is five years. Assume further that these school officials are serving in a state, such as Pennsylvania, in which there are nine board members. A typical superintendent who began his or her five years on 1 July 1997 will find that the entire nine-member board will have turned over by the end of his or her tenure in 2002. During this five-year period, the superintendent will have dealt with 18 different individuals.

Power struggles between the board and the superintendent, rather than mutual trust, often emerge from this swirling mix of personalities. In a national sample of school board members and superintendents in the mid-1980s, Donald Alvey found significant differences in the perceptions of both groups regarding their appropriate roles in addressing 27 issues common to school district governance.[8] A similar study of Pennsylvania school officials a decade later yielded similar results.[9] The political infighting that such conflicts often engender can be fatal to the spirit of collaboration and common purpose that is required to sustain school reform.

Superintendents are clearly vulnerable to the political shifts on their school boards and can become the victims of the often whimsical priorities and enthusiasms of ever-changing boards. Superintendents must be nimble enough to change with the turnover in board priorities—or comfortable with frequent relocations. In either event, bold leadership by a superintendent over the long term is the exception rather than the rule.

180   Educational Leadership

State and National Politics

So far I have dealt with local politics. But the vagaries of the local political winds could be somewhat lessened if cohesive education policy initiatives existed at the state and national levels. However, the interplay of governmental bodies, of special interest groups, and of the knowledge industry has repeatedly stymied efforts at systemic education reform.[10]

Conflicts among competing interests are exacerbated in large urban districts, where there is great diversity among constituencies. Even the traditional homogeneity and stability of most suburban and rural communities are rapidly giving way to the increasing diversity and mobility of the American citizenry.

John Chubb and Terry Moe have argued that the political nature of American public schools is a fatal impediment to significant school reform.[11] The heart of their argument is that conflict, rapidly changing priorities, a tendency toward micromanagement, and cumbersome controls are essential characteristics of the political process. Chubb and Moe found that the most effective schools were characterized by a high level of professional autonomy at the individual building level, a condition that seldom exists in a highly politicized environment. Their conclusion is that privatization represents the only way to achieve substantive school reform.

A similarly somber prognosis for public schools is offered by Seymour Sarason. After decades of studying school reform, he has concluded that there is virtually no chance that it will come from within the system. He believes that the stakeholders simply have too much to lose and warns that, if the governance issue is not faced, schools will get worse, and public schools will ultimately be abandoned.[12]

At the state level, the normal machinations of the political process have a major impact on education policy and practice. The terms of governors essentially bracket the time frame for change on educational issues. The dynamics of the political process dictate that each new governor will develop a plan for improving, if not radically reforming, public education. The initiatives of the previous administration are always downplayed, and in many cases they are flatly repudiated. Meanwhile, battle-weary local school officials frequently adopt a "this too shall pass" attitude. We have already seen that a four- to five-year period is not long enough to make systemic change at the local level. How much more constraining is the arbitrary time limitation that terms of office impose on statewide change initiatives?

The experience with school reform in Texas in the 1980s is instructive. At the beginning of the decade, Texas enacted its "no pass/no play" rule for school athletes. Dramatic changes in the areas of curriculum and assessment were undertaken as well. The legislature adopted statewide goals and standards. Initiatives to improve teacher quality and develop more equitable school funding were launched.

After a decade of effort, the results were minimal. The assessment program changed four or five times during the 10-year period. Few teachers elected to participate in the career-ladder program. Staff development was mandated—but never funded. Little progress was made on funding equity, despite the involvement of the courts. Only 45% of students taking the statewide assessments in 1991 passed all three sections of the test. By 1992 half of Texas school districts still failed to meet state educational standards.[13]

A study of six southeastern states reveals the same dynamics at work in Alabama, Florida, Georgia, Mississippi, North Carolina, and South Carolina.[14] Only two of the top 36 education policy makers in these six states were still in office after 10 years. The normal turnover in seats in the six state legislatures and in the governors' mansions during this 10-year period ensured that there would be little institutional memory regarding the successes and failures of education policy.

This same study reported that on-again, off-again reform initiatives were a direct result of political instability and budget shortfalls. The authors concluded that the time necessary to initiate positive change in schools is longer than the tenure of political officials. Teachers in the trenches, they said, had grown "improvement weary."

Organizational Theory

Leadership and political issues aside, significant organizational characteristics of schools also impede reform efforts. Because of the major influence of the external environment on the operation of school districts, the schools are an excellent example of an "open system." The community powerfully influences education policy and practice, because it provides the students and because parents and the general public are strongly interested in taxes and property values—if not in high-quality education directly. Indeed, many staff members play dual roles as employees and parents or community members.

To be successful, a major school reform must enjoy a community consensus that extends well beyond the requirements for internal team building and shared vision of private organizations. Action by consensus slows down the change process and often dilutes the magnitude of the changes attempted. American schools, by design, feature much more community involvement than do schools in other industrialized nations.[15]

Even when we restrict our attention to internal organization, schools can be thought of as "loosely coupled systems."[16] As such, each school can be considered a semi-autonomous unit. The concept of site-based management is based on the assumption that decentralizing decision making will lead to better decisions and more effective schools. Such educational reformers as Theodore Sizer, Robert Slavin, James Comer, and Henry Levin are attempting to change education one school at a time. Sizer's concept of a good superintendent and school board, for example, is that they should be supportive but nonintrusive where site-based reforms are concerned.

This loosely coupled model may well be best for an educational enterprise. However, it is a serious obstacle for those who would initiate statewide or even district-level reforms. The very culture of schooling is highly resistant to such top-down reforms.

Even if the resistance to top-down reforms could be overcome at the building level, there would still be major resistance by individual teachers. In an analysis of organizational structure, Henry Mintzberg identified five basic types of organizations. His model of the "professional bureaucracy" closely fits the mode of operation in many school buildings, which features a large core of classroom teachers who perform the critical activities of the organization. "Mintzberg's Professional Bureaucracy is characterized by autonomy at the operational level. The autonomy of the professional makes it very hard to make systematic change."[17]

Teachers see principals and central office administrators as middle managers who ideally play a supportive and subordinate role in the actual instructional process. Teachers jealously guard their professional prerogative to determine the actual content of instruction. Convincing a critical mass of teachers to adopt a major reform project, especially one directly affecting instruction, is a time-consuming process fraught with practical and political difficulties.

The recent concept of the "agile organization" dramatically reveals the impediments to change that schools face. Agility is seen as a fundamental requirement for an organization to succeed in a rapidly changing world. There are four major characteristics of an agile organization: 1) enriching the customer, 2) cooperating to enhance competitiveness, 3) organizing to master change and uncertainty, and 4) leveraging the impact of people and information.[18]

If such organizational characteristics are necessary for success in the post-industrial world, American school systems are at a distinct disadvantage. Based on an industrial and bureaucratic model, school systems are ill-suited to respond rapidly to a changing environment. Teachers and school officials are inclined by temperament and experience to adopt an incremental rather than a radical approach to reform. A commitment to the principles of agility listed above is quite unusual in the publicly financed and protected world of the public schools.

Change Theory

Michael Fullan carefully analyzed the major school reform efforts of the past 30 years and reached some compelling conclusions about the nature of the change process. Not surprisingly, he found that substantive change is both a time-consuming and an energy-intensive process. He concluded that "the total time frame from initiation to institutionalization is lengthy, [and] even moderately complex changes take from three to five years, while major restructuring efforts can take five to ten years."[19]

I have already discussed how the short tenure of board members and superintendents and the influence of politics work against the institutionalization of a school reform. A third phenomenon, which Fullan calls the "implementation dip," further undermines the reform of public schools.

The implementation dip is the period of time, early in the implementation process, during which productivity and morale both decline because of the tensions and anxieties generated as educators, parents, and students attempt to deal with unanticipated problems.[20] Political demands for accountability and expectations for quick results often assert themselves at just this stage of the change process. Many promising reforms have been discarded during this period.

Thus far I have discussed change as if it were primarily a rational process. In reality, organizations change only when the people in them are willing and able to do so. In addition to strictly structural and political considerations, the prospective change agent must draw on motivational theories in planning for meaningful change.[21] Moving from the individual to the organizational level, we find that the assumptions, values, and norms of the organization itself are powerful influences on the change process. All these phenomena can be considered as constituting the culture of an organization.

Just as the character of a person is deep-seated and resistant to change, so the culture of an organization is difficult to influence. Indeed, many proposed changes are viewed as threats to the existing culture and may be resisted for that reason alone.

Phillip Schlechty affirms that "to change an organization's structure . . . one must attend not only to rules, roles, and relationships, but to systems of belief, values, and knowledge as well. Structural change requires cultural change."[22] Thus one can say that an organization needs to be "recultured" before it can be restructured.

Unfortunately, many would-be change agents seem unaware of the impact of school culture on the process of change. The history of education reform is littered with examples of interventions that failed or had adverse effects because those involved had only the most superficial and distorted conception of the culture of the school they sought to change.[23]

Meaningful education reform implies a significant change in the interaction between teachers and students. To achieve such change requires major changes in curriculum, instruction, and standards of achievement. All three of these areas are viewed by classroom teachers as the technical core of their work. And teachers strongly resist efforts by outside forces—be they superintendents, school boards, or state agencies—to influence their control within the classroom. Few school districts are willing to devote the time and staff development resources needed to build trust between leaders and staff members sufficient to overcome the teachers' fear of losing autonomy.

What Can Be Done

The negative impact of any one of the five factors outlined above would be a serious handicap to effective school reform. If there are malfunctions in several of these areas at once—an all too common occurrence—then school reform will almost certainly be blocked. A consideration of the complex variables that affect school reform offers a new perspective for reformers to consider. The question changes from why school reform has been so difficult to achieve to whether significant school reform is even possible.

The answer is clearly yes. But successful school reform requires an understanding of the interplay of the five factors described above, as well as the ability to integrate this knowledge into a systemic reform effort. The knowledge needed can be summarized in the following series of propositions.

1. An effective superintendent must have a sense of personal integrity, an articulated vision and mission, and the ability to inspire the staff and school board to share that vision. Such a leader must also have the time and opportunity to develop mutual trust and respect among members of the leadership team. The leader must be able to practice the skills of team learning and systems thinking with the leadership group. Finally, the leader must be able to assert indirect leadership within the educational community while exercising direct political leadership in the wider community.

2. Political stability within a school district is an essential condition for the flourishing of reform. Both school board members and superintendents must be able to count on being around long enough to shepherd the reforms through until they become institutionalized. Longer tenure for school board members and superintendents would allow time for such officials to gain a more thorough understanding of their particular school district and a more sophisticated appreciation for the nature of the change process itself. In addition, stability at the top would raise the comfort level of teachers and administrators, making them more open to the risk-taking that school reform requires.

3. The political nature of many superintendencies precludes the type of strong leadership practiced by effective chief executive officers in the private sector. The crisis mentality of many boards and communities inclines superintendents to think tactically rather than

strategically and to avoid major change rather than to embrace it. A superintendent who is secure in his or her position with the school board and the community and who anticipates a long tenure will be much more likely to tackle the risks and challenges that significant school reform requires. Long-term working relationships between a superintendent and school board also tend to diminish the role conflicts that so often characterize their relationships.

4. The nature of state-level educational politics offer little hope that many states will be able to sustain the 10 years or more of consistent effort required to achieve lasting statewide school reform. The Kentucky school reforms of recent years offer perhaps the best model of long-term commitment to statewide change. However, even this initiative might have unraveled quickly had the opposing political party won the Kentucky gubernatorial race in 1995. A convincing argument can be made that substantive school reform is easiest to achieve at the individual school level. While school reform at the district level is possible, it is difficult to achieve, and lasting school reform initiated at the state level is highly unlikely to occur under existing political conditions.

5. The presence of the positive elements in leadership, school governance, and board/superintendent interactions is necessary but not sufficient for successful school reform. Board members and superintendents need a sophisticated understanding of their districts as systems that are open and loosely coupled. Organizational agility and a subtle understanding of the nature of professional bureaucracies and the principles of system thinking are also imperative if an ambitious reform agenda is to be successfully implemented.

6. A deep understanding of change theory is necessary for a superintendent to guide a proposed school reform from inception to institutionalization. Everyone involved in the change process, including the school board, should anticipate an implementation dip early in the process. The superintendent must also apply knowledge of motivational theory and an understanding of school culture to the reform initiative.

Insightful school leaders recognize that nothing is as practical as good theory. And there are superintendents, principals, and school board members in some districts who possess these understandings. There are communities in which political stability in school governance is the rule. Such happy alignments of the right people at the right place and time provide a fertile soil for creating those examples of positive school reform that do exist.

Peter Senge presents a powerful concept called "creative tension" to describe the gap between a vision for an organization and the current reality in that organization. Policy makers, politicians, and educational researchers often possess a strong vision of reform but are blind to the interconnecting variables that make up current organizational reality. Frontline educators, on the other hand, are often so focused on the challenges of dealing with their current reality that they become wary—and weary—of repeated calls for ambitious reforms from the educational and political elites.

The confluence of outstanding leadership and fortunate circumstances has catalyzed substantive systemic reform in a small minority of American school districts. Unfortunately, neither outstanding leadership nor fortunate organizational circumstances are the norm in America's schools. The "scaling up" of successful reforms cannot occur until the prevailing realities of school governance, superintendent/board relationships, the change process, and the nature of school system operations are substantially altered.

A systems approach to school reform offers the best hope for implementing proven reforms on a large scale. Researchers need to take a systemic view in identifying why reforms are successful in some school districts. I believe that such investigations will demonstrate that the political, cultural, and social dynamics in these districts are significantly different from the norm. Demonstrating that the political, organizational, and cultural characteristics of most school districts are major impediments to school reform is a necessary but not sufficient first step. The harder task of convincing Americans to alter fundamentally some of their cherished traditions for governing and organizing their schools might require a decade, if not a generation, of commitment and effort. Let us begin!

1. Peter M. Senge, *The Fifth Discipline: The Art and Practice of the Learning Organization* (New York: Doubleday Currency, 1991).
2. Stephen Covey, *The Seven Habits of Highly Effective People* (New York: Simon & Schuster, 1991).
3. Marilyn L. Grady and Miles T. Bryant, "School Board Turmoil and Superintendent Turnover," *School Administrator*, February 1991, pp. 68–72.
4. Thomas Glass, *The Study of the American School Superintendency* (Arlington, Va.: American Association of School Administrators, 1992).
5. Phillip C. Schlechty, *Schools for the 21st Century* (San Francisco: Jossey-Bass, 1990), p. 12.
6. Glass, op. Cit.
7. Richard P. McAdams, "Interrelationships Among Property Tax Rate Changes, School Board Member Turnover, and Superintendent Turnover in Selected Pennsylvania School Districts," *Planning and Change*, vol. 26, 1996, pp. 57–70.
8. Donald Alvey, "A National Survey of the Separation of Responsibilities Between School Boards and Superintendents" (Doctoral dissertation, Virginia Polytechnic Institute and State University, 1985).
9. Brad Cressman, "The Roles of Pennsylvania Superintendents and School Board Members as Perceived by Superintendents and School Board Members" (Doctoral dissertation, Lehigh University, 1995).
10. Joel Spring, *Conflict of Interests: The Politics of American Education*, 2nd ed. (New York: Doubleday Currency, 1993).
11. John Chubb and Terry Moe, *Politics, Markets, and America's Schools* (Washington, D.C.: Brookings Institution, 1991).
12. Seymour Sarason, *The Predictable Failure of School Reform* (San Francisco: Jossey-Bass, 1990); and idem, *Parental Involvement and the Political Principle* (San Francisco: Jossey-Bass, 1995).
13. Texas Center for Educational Research, *A Decade of Change: Public Education in Texas* (Austin: Lyndon B. Johnson School of Public Affairs, University of Texas, 1993).
14. Southeast Regional Vision for Education, *Overcoming Barriers to School Reform in the Southeast* (Washington, D.C.: U.S. Department of Education, 1994).
15. Delbert C. Hausman and William L. Boyd, "School Administration in the Federal Republic of Germany and Its Implications for the United States," paper presented at the annual meeting of the University Council for Educational Administration, Philadelphia, October 1994; and Richard P. McAdams, *Lessons from Abroad: How Other Countries Educate Their Children* (Lancaster, Pa.: Technomic, 1993).
16. Karl E. Weick, "Administering Education in Loosely Coupled Schools," *Phi Delta Kappan*, June 1982, pp. 673–76.
17. Lee G. Bolman and Terrence E. Deal, *Reframing Organizations: Artistry, Choice, and Leadership* (San Francisco: Jossey-Bass, 1991), p. 88.
18. Steven L. Goldman, Roger N. Nagel, and Kenneth Preiss, *Agile Competitors and Virtual Organizations: Strategies for Enriching the Customer* (New York: Van Nostrand Reinhold, 1995).
19. Michael Fullan, *The New Meaning of Educational Change* (New York: Teachers College Press, 1991), p. 49.
20. *Managing Change: The Dynamics of Change* (videotape), *Video Journal of Educational Change*, vol. 2.
21. Wayne K. Hoy and Cecil G. Miskel, *Educational Administration: Theory, Research, Practice*, 5th ed. (New York: McGraw-Hill, 1996).
22. Schlechty, p. xvi.
23. Sarason, *The Predictable Failure*.

Article Review Form at end of book.

What are the four stages of the change process? What is a "constructivist" method for change?

Change as Collaborative Inquiry

A "constructivist" methodology for reinventing schools

To make the implementation of higher standards a reality for most children, we must develop a new practice of "whole-school" change that is consistent with our understanding of how learning takes place and how organizations change, Mr. Wagner asserts.

Tony Wagner

Tony Wagner is director of Consulting Services, Harvard Graduate School of Education. His book, How Schools Change: Lessons from Three Communities, *with a foreword by Theodore Sizer, was recently released in paperback by Beacon Press. ©1998, Tony Wagner.*

For the last several years, the big push in education reform has been to develop new, more rigorous state and district standards for learning. While the debate continues to rage in many communities over the exact nature and extent of these standards, as well as over how they will be assessed, it seems that we may have reached some kind of national consensus that there will be standards. For now, at least, many educational leaders have come to believe that the need to monitor progress toward genuine equality of educational opportunity and achievement outweighs the danger that the standards movement will simply lead to more of the same: more "coverage" of the same stale Carnegie-unit curriculum and more use of the same standardized tests for accountability purposes.

So much for the easy part. The development of new learning standards was a fairly simple matter in comparison to what it will take to actually implement them. The adoption of new standards does not answer the question of how we make the necessary changes that will enable all students to achieve at higher levels and meet the new learning standards.

Most approaches to systemic education reform are rooted in obsolete, top-down or expert-driven management beliefs and practices that reflect neither what we know about how people learn nor what we have come to understand about how organizations change.[1] To make the implementation of higher standards a reality for most children, we must develop a new practice of "whole-school" change that is consistent

Reprinted from Phi Delta Kappan. © 1998 Tony Wagner. Reprinted with permission.

with our understanding of how learning takes place and how organizations change. We must connect our means and our ends. We need to create a methodology for a more collaborative, "constructivist" process of change in schools and districts, if we are to develop what Peter Senge calls a "learning organization."

Since 1988 I have been studying and helping with the change process in K–12 public and independent schools in the U.S. and Brazil. Initially, I worked as a researcher and an independent consultant, but since 1994 I have headed a team from the Institute for Responsive Education that is working on whole-school change with clusters of K–12 schools in seven low-income communities around the country. In our work with our partner schools, we are developing new, "constructivist" approaches to whole-school change.

Our methodology contrasts sharply with more conventional practices in each of the four stages of the change process, as I have outlined them in earlier work: 1) defining the problem, 2) developing the goals of change, 3) implementing change strategies, and 4) assessing results.[2] We are also coming to understand the new kind of leadership required in a successful school change process.

Defining the Problem: 'Failure' Versus Obsolescence

Since the publication of *A Nation at Risk* in 1983, a growing and increasingly shrill chorus of business and political leaders (Democrats and Republicans alike) and of national and local media has reached virtual consensus on one thing: U.S. schools are failing. You read it or hear it nearly every day in the media. This analysis of the problem, while lending itself to dramatic pronouncements, is fundamentally wrong and is a serious impediment to change in schools.

By most objective criteria, American public schools are doing a better job than they were 25 years ago: a greater number of students—both white and minority—are graduating from high school, taking the SAT, and attending college.[3] Our schools are not failing. They continue to do exactly what they were designed to do nearly a hundred years ago: they sort out a small percentage of students to be prepared for further learning and for professional and managerial jobs, while giving the remaining students the minimal skills needed for manual labor or assembly-line work.

The problem is that our "assembly-line" forms of schooling no longer fit the needs of the new economy. The same thing occurred in the late 19th century when the one-room schools of the agrarian era no longer fit the needs of an increasingly industrial and urban society. Those schools were not "failing" any more than today's schools are failing. They were obsolete, as are today's schools—and that is a very different problem, requiring a different solution.

What's the difference between saying that schools are failing and saying that they are obsolete? In a word, blame. The problem with the notion of failure in school reform is exactly the same as in a "non-constructivist" classroom except that, in this case, the adults, rather than the students, suffer most from the stigma of having "failed." The label of failure creates a paralyzing sense of shame and defensiveness, which translates for many adults into blame.

A majority of adults in schools feel blamed for having helped to create bad schools. Scapegoating and a victim's mentality are widespread in American public schools today—especially those in low-income communities. High schools blame middle schools; middle schools blame elementary schools; teachers blame parents; parents blame the teachers or the students.

In such a climate, it is impossible to develop the sense of self-confidence and professionalism required to undertake any serious changes. It is equally difficult to foster responsible risk-taking, collaboration, and the formation of new partnerships with parents and community members. Yet we know that all three are needed in order to fundamentally improve our schools. In short, the way we have defined the problem in American education seriously limits the likelihood of motivating the "frontline workers" to search for a solution.

In addition to fostering the blame game and strengthening the culture of victimization, a diagnosis of failure encourages simplistic and even punitive rhetoric about the "solutions" to the problem. What's the stated goal of change? It is to send more people to "reform(ed)" schools! "Make teachers accountable" is another example of a popular punitive slogan that ignores the reality of how change—or learning—happens. Pressure in the form of increased emphasis on test scores may get the attention of some teachers, but it will not create the organizational learning required to obtain significantly better results. As in a good "constructivist" classroom, the challenge in the change process is to create significantly higher expectations without the crippling anxiety that thwarts risk-taking and learning.

By contrast, framing the problem as "obsolete" systems of schooling that must be "reinvented"—not merely reformed —makes the dimensions and complexity of the challenge clearer. Moreover, it suggests that the solution must be a shared responsibility. No one group is to blame or has all the answers. We must decide collectively what our high school graduates should know and be able to do and how we can best support them in achieving these educational goals.

Developing Goals: 'Buy-In' Versus Ownership

In most school or district change efforts with which I am familiar, a single individual—the principal or the superintendent—or perhaps a small committee determines the goals of change. Whether it is districtwide standards and curriculum frameworks or a new form of block scheduling for a high school, there is rarely any discussion of the need for the change or what its goals should be among the groups most directly affected— teachers, parents, and students. Sadly, the change process looks much like a teacher-dominated classroom on a large scale. A few people do all the talking, while the passive majority is expected to sit still, be quiet, and then go do the assigned "homework."

Recently, some educational leaders have begun to realize that the lack of broad support for the goals of change can be a significant impediment to change. A growing number of superintendents now give at least some lip service to the goal of "public engagement." The language they use to describe the goal, however, reveals the shallowness of their thinking. Most often, what these leaders say they want is simply "buy-in" from parents and community members—as if they were selling a product and the only problem was to line up the requisite number of customers. By contrast, the language of "investment" and "ownership" suggests a far more generative endeavor and a long-term relationship involving equal partners.

Another problem with the "buy-in" mentality is that teachers are rarely considered a part of the "public" to be engaged. The thinking must be that, since teachers "make" the product, they are not the primary consumers. It is most telling that union cosponsorship of new initiatives is almost never sought. Teacher resentment and union resistance are the almost inevitable results of treating educators as if they were assembly-line workers rather than partners in a collaborative endeavor.

On the other hand, when a change process begins with discussions of the need for and goals of change with teachers and then with parents and the community, it can be dramatically accelerated. Although inclusive discussions take time, once there is a real consensus among diverse groups on goals and priorities, we have observed that the nature and pace of the change process is faster and that the changes are deeper and longer lasting.

But the conversation has to be genuine. In one large urban school district where I consulted, a talented, committed superintendent quickly passed new learning standards and curriculum frameworks in his first year on the job with no discussion with teachers or parents, other than a few focus groups. He justified this action by saying that the documents were just drafts, "works in progress."

However, the senior personnel in the district who used this phrase would add that the new standards and frameworks were "nonnegotiable" and not subject to change. For all practical purposes, the documents were so long and apparently "complete" that there was nothing left to talk about anyway. Thus the invitation for further teacher and parent input seemed a sham.

The result in this particular school district was that many teachers became more passive than ever—in much the same way that students shut down when a class "discussion" is really only a game of "guess what's on the teacher's mind." For example, when I tried to engage a middle school faculty in a discussion of the important things they thought all graduating eighth-graders need to know and be able to do, the response was "Why should we bother talking about that? The superintendent's already decided what we should teach."

More significantly, the lack of a genuine dialogue leaves unaddressed the deepest concerns of many students, parents, and community members. While education reformers talk about skills and standards, 71% of Americans believe it is more important to teach values than academics, according to a recent study by the Public Agenda Foundation.[4] Business leaders worry understandably about having a skilled labor pool that will help maintain a competitive advantage in the global economy, but the vast majority of Americans are much more worried about the apparent disintegration of social norms. Public Agenda's newest study of student attitudes toward school found that, while many high school students feel academically unchallenged, they are equally concerned about the lack of respect and civility in their schools. Sixty-nine percent of the students surveyed said that they would learn "a lot more" from teachers who respected them.[5]

The development of both workplace skills and civil values can and must be addressed in a genuine school improvement effort, but there must first be real understanding and agreement on the need for and goals of change. Such understanding does not happen when "public engagement" is no more than good "public relations." It must be "constructed" through a process of genuine dialogue and discovery—in exactly the same way as "deep understanding" happens for students in a classroom in which there is active learning.

Implementation Strategies: 'Answers' Versus Inquiry

Thus far I have described how the conventional approach to school improvement begins with a "deficit" model (failing schools/students) and then tries to address the problem with a "teacher-dominated" approach to instruction ("buy-in" for the reform program). Unfortunately, the assembly-line methodology for school change also extends to typical implementation strategies that attempt to "cover" everything and are "answer-driven."

Go into a typical "reforming" public school in a progressive urban district and ask to see the "school improvement plan." You will be handed a large, heavy, impressive-looking three-ring binder overflowing with the school's strategic plan for change. It will, of course, include the requisite school vision and mission statement, "target" population profiles, recent test scores, and dozens of goals, time lines, organizational charts, and team leader designations. Once a year, it is updated by the principal, with a few minor additions or deletions, and then submitted to the district as a "progress report." It is the school's "improvement curriculum." And like most other coverage-based curricula, it has little or no long-term impact on its intended audiences.

There are a number of reasons for the failure of these so-called school improvement plans, which are not unlike the reasons for the failure of most conventional textbook-driven approaches to teaching. First, the plan resides almost wholly in the hands of the principal. Few in the school have seen the plan before it is formally issued, and fewer still have contributed to its creation. The plan rarely reflects the concerns, interests, or expressed needs of teachers and parents.

Second, the plan, like a typical American history textbook, attempts to cover everything with no clear sense of what's important. Tell a teacher or a student that everything must be covered, and the result is that almost nothing of consequence will be accomplished or learned. Even more than in a classroom, the success of a genuine school improvement effort requires selecting and maintaining a clear, long-term focus on a few important priorities.

Anthony Alvarado became superintendent of New York City's District 2 in 1989. At the time, the district's reading scores placed it in about the 30th percentile of districts in the city. The vast majority of students were reading two to four years below grade level. After studying the problem and consulting with teachers and parents, Alvarado decided to make literacy—reading and writing—the single focus of all efforts to improve teaching and learning. All professional development was focused on developing teaching skills in these areas. School principals were no longer evaluated on impressiveness of their school improvement plans or plant management skills, but rather on the improvement of teaching and learning related to literacy in their buildings.[6]

Alvarado has maintained this districtwide focus not for six months or a year but for nine years. He reasons that, if students cannot read and write, then they will fail at math and science. Only now that all students are close to reading at or above grade level is the district considering a different focus.

Another common trait of conventional school improvement plans is that, like most curricula, they are answer-driven, rather than inquiry-based. Consider the hot new trend in high school restructuring, flexible time or so-called block scheduling. At the moment, it is the innovation of greatest interest to American high school principals. Yet teacher resistance in most schools presents a serious obstacle. Many high school teachers see significantly longer classes as a threat to their tried-and-true methods of instruction and suspect that block scheduling is a fad—akin to the "open classrooms" and "new math" of days gone by. They resent being coerced or cajoled into adopting the latest thing.

The teachers' skepticism is understandable. The problem is that, like so many other promising innovations, block scheduling is presented as an answer to a problem that has never been discussed. Ask high school principals why they want block scheduling in their schools (as I have done), and many will tell you that they just want to shake things up. "Teachers are too stuck in their ways. They need to try new things," I've been told by a number of principals. A few may say that the goal is to "improve student learning," but rarely can a principal explain how block scheduling—or any other "innovation of the month"—will contribute to improved student outcomes or how or when the new initiative will be assessed.

If these principals had started not with an answer but with a question to teachers—"What are some of the greatest obstacles to improving teaching and learning that you face?"—the results would be very different. Most high school teachers will tell you that their number-one problem is not with the organization of time but with the lack of time: time to meet with students, time to research and plan new lessons, and time to meet with colleagues.

Suppose that a principal who heard this complaint from his teachers created a committee and gave it access to the Internet, a little released time, and some travel money. Suppose then that the principal met with the committee and asked it to interview all the teachers in the building to get a clearer picture of the problem, to go off and study some different scheduling models that would give teachers more of the time they need, and to create a written report with recommendations for presentation to the full faculty for consideration. Suppose the final step was a broader discussion of the proposed changes with parents, students, and community members.

In fact, I have worked with high schools that have pursued such a "constructivist" strategy for change, and the results are very different from the usual resigned compliance with a change project. When presented with questions rather than answers, teachers are challenged to take their own work issues and schoolwide problems more seriously and to consider alternatives. Similarly, teachers can and should be asked to look at real data about poor student achievement and to compare their students' test scores with those from other schools—and with their own inflated grades. When such an effort is a genuine inquiry, most teachers become engaged and are challenged much more deeply than if they had been merely presented with an analysis of the problem and a set of prescriptive solutions designed by the central office.

The same answer-driven approach is often the fatal flaw in the various civics or character education efforts that are now so popular in elementary and middle schools. A principal—and sometimes even a majority of teachers, as well—decides that students are lacking in morals. The answer is to buy a curriculum—such as the Character Counts Program now used in many schools—and teach young people a new value every month through literature, songs, and so on. The result may be more pretty slogans and rosy pictures for the classroom walls, but behaviors rarely change.

An alternative, inquiry-based approach that I have used successfully in a number of schools and communities begins with a set of questions and does not leave out the adults. We begin by asking, "What behaviors are of concern to us here, adults as well as students?" Then we consider the questions "What behaviors do we want to see more of, what kinds of changes might be required to foster these behaviors, and what might we, as adults, need to do differently?"

In sum, a successful strategy for implementing school improvement is focused and prioritized. Rather than take on everything at once, the strategy attempts to identify the most significant problems. Second, it is inquiry-based. It begins with real questions or problems that all relevant groups have discussed and agree are important. Finally, understanding of the problem is augmented by a careful analysis of all relevant data—both quantitative and qualitative—and of research into best practice. In short, the process allows the participants to construct their understanding of important problems and potential solutions.

Assessing Results: Summative Versus Formative

If schools are seen as failing, then all too often standardized test scores are the "report card" that delivers the failing grade. Politicians, the media, school boards, and superintendents rely almost exclusively on standardized test scores to determine whether schools are good or bad—passing or failing. Like other traditional summative judgments in education—letter grades, for example—standardized tests may have their uses, but they have no real educational value.

The public does not understand and the media have not attempted to explain that there are good and bad tests and that most forms of standardized testing are as obsolete as the factory model of schooling for which they were developed. Bad tests of the common multiple-choice, norm-referenced variety do not require problem solving and do not assess real competencies. They were designed for one major purpose: to sort students into tracks or groups. And they have only one virtue: they are cheap to buy and to score.

Many stories have appeared in the media recently about some of the ill effects on teachers and schools of a heavy emphasis on improving standardized test scores. Some of the more bizarre stories tell of tests being stolen in advance of the test date and school test scores being falsified. Much more common and less widely known are the cases of teachers who spend weeks drilling students with sample tests and principals who discourage certain students (or whole groups of students) from coming to school on the day the tests are given. In a recent study conducted by William Zlatos, the percentage of students taking standardized tests in 14 urban districts ranged from 66% to 93%.[7]

There have been very few reports about the impact on students of the increased emphasis on standardized tests. But many teachers can tell you. More time spent going over multiple-choice questions and test-taking strategies means less time for real learning and fewer interesting things being done in school. Sadly, such a "tougher" approach to increasing teacher and school accountability for improving test scores is likely to increase student passivity, diminish motivation for learning, lessen the amount of class time spent on challenging and interesting material, and undermine the development of real academic competencies.

Traditional standardized tests of reading comprehension have some value as diagnostic tools for schools. They give at a glance a picture of the severity of the problem—the percentage of students reading below grade level. But they don't say anything about what the students really can do; they don't say anything about their intellectual competencies. As one fourth-grade teacher recently explained, "My kids do okay on the citywide reading tests, but if I give them a book to read at their level and then ask them to talk or write about it, they're totally lost." It is interesting to note that European countries, whose education systems are often touted as superior to ours, have not historically relied on standardized tests at all. Their exams have always been essay-based.

Some districts and states are moving to develop "criterion-referenced" tests that are better able to assess students' real competencies, but progress has been slow. Many districts are holding back because the reliability of these tests has not yet been demonstrated. Moreover, they are expensive. Given the increased emphasis on test-based accountability and the damage that teaching to a bad test can do, it is hard to understand why developing better tests isn't our highest priority. I wonder if many educational leaders are resisting the widespread use of competency-based tests because they fear that student performance on such tests will be even worse than on existing tests and thus put their jobs at risk.

Not waiting for the development of better tests, a growing number of schools are creating their own forms of "authentic assessment" of student work. Inspired by Theodore Sizer and other educators who discuss the value of "exhibitions of mastery," some members of the Coalition of Essential Schools have pioneered the development of portfolios and exhibitions as high school graduation requirements.[8] Such an emphasis on public performances and written documentation of student work provides a very different and more "formative" kind of accountability. Attending a math and science night or an assembly at which students discuss their research or present projects, parents and community members can see for themselves how much students really know and can do. An emphasis on examining students' actual work, as opposed to letter grades or some numbers on a piece of paper, also makes teachers more accountable to one another, and the data from such assessments can be a powerful tool in the process of school improvement.

It is interesting to note that at Central Park East Secondary School, which has moved to graduation by exhibitions of mastery—what I like to call the "merit badge" approach to examinations—students are much more motivated to learn. Ninety percent of the students graduate, and almost all go on to four-year colleges. Meanwhile, the graduation rate for other high schools serving the same kinds of students in New York City is under 50%. It is less widely known that this school's standardized test scores are at best mediocre. Clearly, the more authentic assessments are both a positive incentive for learning and tell us more about students' real abilities.

Formative schoolwide assessments also include two other practices generally not discussed in more conventional approaches to schoolwide accountability: peer review and upward coaching. As a writing teacher in a constructivist classroom more than 20 years ago, I learned that my high school students cared far more about what their peers thought of their work than about what I thought. I have had much greater success with a "writers' workshop" approach than with any amount of time and red ink I have ever expended on reviewing their work. Surprisingly, this constructivist lesson has rarely been applied to the task of school improvement.

Much like the products of a writers' workshop, all school improvement plans should be public documents and should be widely read and discussed both within and beyond the schools. Such discussion will inevitably raise important questions about what a good plan is and how a school will know if it is succeeding. Teams of principals, teachers, and parents should also be involved in reviewing one another's improvement plans. Peer reviews, in the form of periodic school visits to assess progress toward the written goals, can be informative both for the visitors and for the school being visited.

A few schools in Boston took some first steps toward peer review during the 1996–97 school year when all schools were required to write a comprehensive school improvement plan. With some coaching from a talented district specialist, a group of principals agreed to have their peers read and critique their draft improvement plans. The final drafts of these plans were consistently of higher quality than those that had been reviewed only by central office personnel. One principal told me that the exercise had been the most helpful professional development experience of his administrative career.

In a serious systemic school improvement effort, formative reviews should be done not just by peers or top-down by supervisors. They should also be done "bottom up." Superintendents expect principals to use data to assess their schools' strengths and weaknesses, to be accountable, and to be rigorously evaluated on the basis of results. But very rarely do they ask principals to evaluate district-level personnel and services. District-level change should also be data-driven. Principals and members of school site councils need regular opportunities to assess the quality of the help they are receiving from the district, and data from these assessments should drive improvement efforts at the district level. My colleagues and I at the Institute for Responsive Education in Boston and the staff of New Visions for Public Schools in New York are beginning to gather such data, but it is too soon to know whether senior district personnel in these cities will use the information for districtwide restructuring.

Leadership for Change: Dictating Versus Coaching

To be successful, reinventing schools with a truly constructivist methodology requires a kind of leadership that is very different from what one finds in most education systems today. Ronald Heifitz has described the importance of new styles of leadership in corporate change efforts, but thus far there has been very little discussion in our schools and districts of the new roles and skills educational leaders must learn.[9]

Most educators suffer from what I call "answeritis." They like having all the answers, and they are usually very quick to share them with others. Indeed, winning the conventional school "game" requires one to have lots of right answers. As students, many educators excelled at the game. Principals and superintendents are no different. Indeed, many feel their jobs depend on their having all the "right" answers for their schools or districts. Too many school boards hire new superintendents because they have a master plan for the district.

But leading a real change or reinvention process requires very different skills. Like a good teacher in a constructivist classroom, a leader of a change effort must pose engaging challenges, help people understand the importance of the challenges, ask tough questions, monitor progress, and give constant feedback—both praise and criticism. In the classroom Theodore Sizer calls this role "teacher as coach." And the lesson applies at all levels. Rather than provide the right answers, principals, superintendents, and other educational leaders must also become coaches—helping educators, parents, and others to develop their own understanding of the issues in reform and helping them work together to find solutions.

Such leadership requires a different kind of "emotional intelligence"[10] and a different set of intellectual skills. Too many school boards and superintendents I have observed create adversarial relationships with both colleagues and constituents. One of the deepest concerns of many teachers, parents, and students is how poorly people treat one another in their schools. I find it is often impossible to begin real work on issues related to academic standards without having first addressed the problems of lack of trust and respect among the adults in schools. Without trust and respect, there is no safe ground for dialogue, and without dialogue and rigorous inquiry, there will be no change.

To be both credible and effective, leaders in a change process must model what they preach and develop genuine collaborative relationships with teachers, parents, union leaders, and other based on openness to constructive criticism, mutual trust, and respect. High standards aren't just for the intellect or just for students; standards must also be high for the heart and must apply to everyone in the organization.

Compliance Versus Collaboration

The obsolete strategy for achieving high standards, whether in a classroom or an organization, is that someone at the top sets the goal and everyone else does the minimum required to comply. From what I have observed, this is still too often the model for implementing new teaming standards in school districts around the country.

A constructivist approach to change, by contrast, is based on collaboration rather than compliance. It is a process of action research and development in which everyone works to understand the problem, engages in discussion to reach agreement on the goal, and shares in the responsibility for implementing change, assessing progress, and achieving results. Ultimately, a constructivist change process helps to create and become embedded in a new school and district culture that values continuous learning and improvement both for adults and for students.

Over time, the constant interaction in such a collaborative change process creates a different set of work incentives—just as it does in a constructivist classroom. As people begin to share ideas and develop common aspirations, the goal is no longer simply to do only what is necessary to comply with the demands of the boss. Rather, people begin to work to earn the respect of their colleagues and to create something truly worthwhile together.

I have never met a teacher or a parent who wanted students to fail, and only a few seek to do just the minimum. Most of us who work with young people want to be part of an effort that makes a real difference for students—that helps to prepare them for future work, citizenship, lifelong learning, and responsible family life. We need to reinvent school systems together if they are to have a realistic chance of accomplishing this goal for all students, and we need a methodology for change that involves all adults in a collaborative process of learning and reinvention.

1. See, for example, the many books and articles by W. Edwards Deming, the founder of the quality movement in business; and Peter Senge, *The Fifth Discipline* (New York: Doubleday, 1990).
2. See Tony Wagner, "Systemic Change: Rethinking the Purpose of School." *Educational Leadership*, September 1993, pp. 24–28.
3. See David C. Berliner and Bruce J. Biddle, *The Manufactured Crisis: Myths, Fraud, and the Attack on America's Public Schools* (Boston: Addison-Wesley-Longman, 1995).
4. Jean Johnson and John Immerwahr, *First Things First: What Americans Expect from Public Schools* (New York: Public Agenda Foundation, 1994), p. 23.
5. Jean Johnson and Steve Farkas, *Getting By: What American Teenagers Really Think About Their Schools* (New York: Public Agenda Foundation, 1997).
6. See Richard Elmore, "Staff Development and Instructional Improvement, Community District 2, New York City," unpublished paper, Graduate School of Education, Harvard University, Cambridge, Mass., 1996.
7. William Zlatos, "Scores That Don't Add Up," Education Life, special supplement, *New York Times*, 6 November 1994, p. 22.
8. See Theodore R. Sizer, *Horace's School: Redesigning the American High School* (Boston: Houghton Mifflin, 1992).
9. See Ronald Heifitz and Donald L. Laurie, "The Work of Leadership," *Harvard Business Review*, January/February 1997, pp. 124–34, which describes principles of leadership for rapid "adaptive" change in corporations and is an especially useful work for educators.
10. Daniel Goleman, *Emotional Intelligence: Why It Can Matter More Than IQ for Character, Health, and Lifelong Achievement* (New York: Bantam Doubleday, 1995).

Article Review Form at end of book.

WiseGuide Wrap-Up

- Political, cultural, demographic, and organizational factors require schools to initiate change programs for survival and success.

- Issues requiring educational focus for change include preparing the citizenry for the information age, developing interpersonal skills, and addressing changing demographics.

- Successful change requires leaders to demonstrate specific behaviors, model change practices, devote personal energy, and commit leadership time to the process.

- Restructuring schools also requires reculturing—changing the norms, values, incentives, skills, and relationships in the organization to foster a different working relationship.

- A systems approach to change, whole-school change, and a constructivist model of change are all complex and dynamic perspectives of the process.

R.E.A.L. Sites

This list provides a print preview of typical **Coursewise** R.E.A.L. sites. There are over 100 such sites at the **Courselinks**™ site. The danger in printing URLs is that web sites can change overnight. As we went to press, these sites were functional using the URLs provided. If you come across one that isn't, please let us know via email to: webmaster@coursewise.com. Use your Passport to access the most current list of R.E.A.L. sites at the **Courselinks**™ site.

Site name: School Change
URL: http://www.sedl.org/change/
Why is it R.E.A.L.? This comprehensive web site, hosted by the Southwest Educational Development Laboratory, is a treasure of resources on change literature. This web site draws on more than three decades of research, expertise, and experience in effective school change. It provides school leaders with assistance and training to help them learn about new practices, initiate planning for their improvement efforts, redesign their schools to support serious teaching and learning, implement their plans for change, and realize improved results for students.
Key topics: accountability, behavior, change, collaboration, communication, community, culture, empowerment, power, reform, shared leadership, values, vision
Try this: Visit the web site and select "Leadership Characteristics That Facilitate School Change." Describe the "characteristics of leaders of change."

Site name: Parent Engagement as a School Reform Strategy
URL: http://www.ed.gov/databases/ERIC_Digests/ed419031.html
Why is it R.E.A.L.? This ERIC Digest serves as a comprehensive literature review on parental involvement in school reform. Topics include viewing the school and community as an ecology, building relationships based on common concerns, and acknowledging the role of power in school-community partnerships.
Key topics: accountability, behavior, beliefs, change, collaboration, communication, diversity, empowerment, honesty, human relations, politics, power, reform, shared leadership, success, team, trust
Try this: Review this digest and provide strategies for fostering the collaborative leadership skills of principals. Use information from this site as a catalyst for discussions with school-site councils on joint school-community change initiatives.

Index

References in boldface type are authors of readings.

A

Accessibility of leader, 80
Accountability of leader
　assessment quiz, 22
　improvement guidelines, 23
　of workplace leader, 21–23
Addams, Jane, 101
Adjective Checklist, 39
Adolescents, family, importance of, 67
Adult development, 147
African Americans, in leadership positions, 26
Alexander, W., 119
AlliedSignal, 53
Alvarado, Anthony, 189
Alvey, Donald, 180
American companies, best companies, 53–57
Amundsen, Roald, 33
Andrews, R.L., 134
Archetypes, of modern leader, 7
Arco, 65
Aristotle, values and business, 75–78
Arnau, J., 31
Asea Brown Boveri, 113
Ash, Mary Kay, 54
Asian Americans, in leadership positions, 25, 26–27
Avolio, B.J., 39

B

Banks, J.A., 29, 30, 31
Barron, F., 41
Barth, Roland, 141
Basom, Margaret, 162
Bass, B.M., 32, 34, 35, 39, 71
Bauer, S.S., 18
Bedrosian, M., 30
Behr, Thomas E., 58
Bellah, R.N., 13
Bell, S.R., 30
Benjamin, Susan, 124
Bennis, Warren, 6, 32, 34–35, 63–65, 81
Benson, J.K., 8
Bentz, V.J., 39
Berliner, David, 187
Bhaskar, R., 10
Bickel, Lauri B., 156
Blase, Jo, 143, 144
Blase, Joseph, 143
Bogdan, R., 144
Bolman, L.G., 18
Boltes, H.W., 47
Borman, W.C., 33

Bossidy, Larry, 53
BP Norge, 113, 114
Bray, D.W., 35, 37, 39
Bruer, John T., 150
Bureaucracy, professional bureaucracy, 182
Bureaucratic-managerial leadership, 5–6
　elements of, 6
Burns, J.M., 3, 4, 11

C

Calhoun, E., 145, 147
Campbell, D., 49
Campbell, J.P., 32
Candor, of leader, 80
Capps, Ian, 61
Carrow-Moffett, Patricia A., 68
Change
　approaches to, 151–153
　culture, changes to, 183
　cycles in change process, 108–111, 186–196
　from industrial to information age, 162–163
　leader of change concept, 165–169
　leader self-test, 168
　leadership and change, 167–169
　overcoming dependency, 170–173
　resistance to, 70–71
　transition, elements of, 165–166
Character, and leadership, 64
Charismatic leadership
　elements of, 39
　personality traits, 39
Chattergy, V., 31
Chidester, T.R., 33, 35, 39
Children, Youth, and Families Initiative, 99
Chubb, John, 181
Churchill, Winston, 4, 5
Citicorp, 63
Clinton, Bill, 64
Coaching
　versus dictating, 192–193
　teacher as, 192
　of teachers, 146
Collins, Art, 55
Comer, James, 182
Communication, effective, aspects of, 125
Communitarianism, 101
Community
　community coalition building, example of, 102–104
　community development, 95–96
　community-oriented teaching/learning, 96–97
　education community forums, 90–92
　elements of, 95

　Japanese concept of, 29–30
　and leadership, 8–9
　narratives of, 11
　school governance structures, changes to, 97–99
　and school reform, 96
　school-to-work programs, 97
Community education, benefits of, 126
Compass Program, 60
Competitor intelligence, 176
Conger, J.A., 39
Constructivist leadership, 127–130
　meaning of, 127–128
Consumers Power, 177
Cooper, G.E., 39
Corey, S., 70
Covey, Stephen, 179
Cronback, L.J., 41, 42
Cultural competence, meaning of, 30
Cultural differences
　bicultural adaptation, 31
　bicultural leader, 31
　pluralistic integration, 30
　views of, 28–29
Cummings, T., 118, 119
Cunningham, W.G., 18
Curphy, Gordon J., 32, 33, 35

D

Davis, Thom, 84
Dawkins,, 32
DeGues, A., 173
Democracy, and leadership, 14
Democracy in America (Tocqueville), 28
Dependency, 170–173
　context of, 170–171
　overcoming, guidelines for, 171–173
DeVries, D.L., 34
Dewey, John, 96, 101
Digman, J.M., 37
Direct leadership, 180
Districts
　and local politics, 180
　school board governance, 180
　and school restructuring, 98–99
Dixon, N.F., 33. 34
Dolan, P., 172
Domhoff, G. William, 24
Donaldson, Gordon A., Jr., 108
Donohue-Clyne, I., 28
Dowling, G., 143
Drury, W.R., 19
Duden, N., 19
Duffield, Dave, 53–54
Duke, D.L., 18

195

E

Ecology, basic principles of, 160–161
Ediger, Marlow, 151, 153
Edmonds, R., 134
Educational leadership
    constructivist leadership, 127–130
    development of, 68–69
    educational policy/practice, 30–31
    encouraging leadership, 129
    entrepreneurial leader, 47–49
    guidelines for leaders, 138–139
    instructional leadership, 29–30, 134–136, 140–142
    leader profile, 10–11, 48
    leaders as change agents, 69–71
    school board governance, 180
    skills of leader, 48–49
Educational level, and power position, 24–25
Education community forums, 90–92
    aims of, 91
    recommendations for future, 91–92
Education. *See* Schools and education
Effective Schools era, 110
Eibl-Eibesfeld, I., 32
Eisner, Michael, 26, 63
Ellis, R.J., 37
Elmore, Richard, 172, 193
Emancipatory leadership, 8–9
Emergent leadership, 37–38
Emotional intelligence, leaders, 172–173, 192–193
Empowerment, 69–70
    criteria for, 117
    by leaders, 70
    meaning of, 69, 117
    of school staff, 116–117
    self-managed teams study, 117–123
    of teachers, 141
Entrepreneurial leadership, 46–49
    in schools, 47–49
    vision in, 48
Escalante, J., 31
Estabrook, R., 19
Ethics
    importance of, 76–77
    of leadership, 11–12
    virtues of successful leaders, 56–57
Evans, R., 171
Evil leaders, 4, 11, 33–34

F

Faidly, R., 68
Family, importance of, 67
Farson, R., 171
Fay, B., 10, 11, 13
Federal agencies, and school restructuring, 99
Fiedler, R., 5
Fiske, D.W., 37
Flanigan, Jackson L., 18
Fleishman, E.A., 41
Flymier, J., 116, 117

Foster, William, 3
Foushee, H.C., 39
Fowler, W.J., Jr., 18, 19
Frase, L.E., 18
Fukuyama, F., 79
Fullan, Michael, 108, **170,** 182
Future, view of management, 41–42

G

Gandhi, Mahatma, 4, 5
Garcia, O., 30
Gard, Jane, 124
Gardner, Howard, 179
Gates, Bill, 53
Gatewood, T.E., 123
Geffen, David, 28
General Electric Co., 114, 174
George, Bill, 55
Gerstner, Lou, 177
Giddens, A., 8,9
Gillespie, John, 59
Gilmour, Allan, 27
Glaser, Robert, 82
Glasman, N.S., 18
Glass, G.V., 19
Glatthorn, A., 135
Glaxo, 65
Glickman, C.D., 147
Goals 2000, 99
Goizueta, Robert, 27
Goldberg, L.R., 37
Goldwasser, Charles, 165
Goleman, Daniel, 192
Goodlad, John I., 149
Gough, H.G., 37, 39
Gramm, Wendy Lee, 26
Grant, Ulysses S., 33
Gretzky, Wayne, 65
Grob, L., 9
Groups
    classroom work groups, 154
    Japanese concept of, 29–30
    self-managed teams, 113–123
    team building and leaders, 40–41, 80–81
    team performance and leaders, 39–40
    team teaching, 151
Grove, Andy, 53, 115
Gruber, J., 118

H

Haas, Robert, 113
Hackman, J.R., 117
Hallam, G.L., 40
Hamilton, M.H., 41
Hammer, Michael, 174
Hansen, J.H., 18
Hargreaves, Andrew, 108, 173
Harris, M.M., 35
Hattiesburg Area Education Foundation, community evaluation by, 87–89
Hayes, Cassandra, 21
Hazucha, J.F., 35, 40
Hegel, George Friedrich, 151

Heifitz, Ronald, 172, 193
Hewlett-Packard, 174
Hitler, Adolph, 4, 33
Hjelmas, Thor A., 113
Hoerr, Thomas R., 140
Hogan, Joyce, 32, 34, 41
Hogan, Robert, 32
Holland, J.L., 41
Holsti, D.R., 120
Homosexuals, in leadership positions, 27–28
Hopper, Grace, 64
Hough, L.M., 42
House, R.J., 33, 35, 39
Howard, A., 34, 39
Howard Johnson, 174
Hsu, F.L.K., 29
Hughes, R.L., 34

I

Identity management, of new power elite, 25
Indirect leadership, 179–180
Information age, transition to, 162–163
Innovation Luggage, 59–60
Institute for Responsive Education, 192
Instructional leadership, 29–30, 134–136, 140–142
    activities of, 135
    barriers to, 140–141
    characteristics of, 134–135
    coaching, promotion of, 146
    differences among leaders, 29–30
    leader as model, 135
    and staff development, 144–145
    TiGeR approach to, 144–145
Intel, 53, 174

J

Japan
    ecological approach to management, 160–161
    group and community in, 29–30
Jennings, John F., 90
Jews, in leadership positions, 26
Johannessen, Odd Jan, 113
Johnson, Jean, 188
Johnston, W.B., 41
Joiner, C.W., 48
Jordan, Vernon, 26
Joyce, B., 143–144, 145, 147

K

Kaizen, 60
Kanter, R.M., 32, 47, 48
Kaplan, R.E., 40
Kasten, K.L., 117, 119
Kasten, Tom, 175
Katz, R.F., 117
Kelleher, Herb, 53
Kenny, D.A., 37

Kerfoot, Karlene, 79
Khazzaka, Joseph, 29
Kimbrough, R.B., 18
King, Martin Luther, 5
Kissinger, Henry, 63
Kiuchi, Tachi, 160
Kouzes, J.M., 19, 48
Kowalski, T.J., 19

L

Laabs, Jennifer J., 75
Laguna, J., 68
Lambert, Linda, 127
Lane, Kenneth E., 18
Latinos, in leadership positions, 27
Lawler, E.E., 118, 119
Leaders
    accountability of, 21–23
    activities of leaders, 33, 48
    and change process, 166–169
    coaching of, 40
    emotional intelligence, 172–173, 192–193
    evaluation of, 35–36
    executives, selection of, 34–35
    failure, reasons for, 39–40, 64
    personality traits, 37, 39–41, 63–64, 67
    selection of, 34–36
    thinking process of, 166–167
    values of, 56–62
    working smarter leader, 111
Leadership
    of best American companies, 53–57
    bureaucratic-managerial model, 5–6
    charismatic leadership, 39
    as critical practice, 9–10
    direct leadership, 180
    educators. *See* Educational leadership
    emancipatory leadership, 8–9
    emergent leadership, 37–38
    ethical commitment of, 11–12
    indirect leadership, 179–180
    leaders as educators, 10–11
    versus management, 6, 17, 64–65
    modern archetypes of, 7
    political-historical model, 3–5
    versus power, 4, 11
    significance of, 33–34
    transactional leadership, 4
    transformational leadership, 4, 6–8, 10
    value-based leadership, 59–62
Leadership (Burns), 4
Lear Corp., 60, 61
Levin, Henry, 182
Levi Strauss, 113, 175
Lieber, Ronald B., 53
Lightfoot, S.L., 116
Lincoln, Abraham, 33
Lincoln, Y., 8
Liontos, L.B., 19
Loeb, Marshall, 63
Lombardo, M.M., 40
Lord, R.G., 37
Lowe, Jack, 55
Lubetkin, Martie Thleen, 102

M

MacIntyre, A., 7, 11
Mackay, John, 55
Mackwood, G., 28
Makie, Don, 60, 61
Management
    definition of, 16
    ecological approach to, 160–161
    evaluation of, 36–37
    incompetence of, 34
    versus leadership, 6, 17, 64–65
    middle management, 34
    of Workforce 2000, 41–42
Manager
    leadership characteristics of, 19
    role of leader as, 7
    subservient manager concept, 84–85
Mann, R.D., 37
Manz, C.C., 118, 119, 122
Mao Tse Tung, 4
March, J.G., 7
Mariotti, John, 16
Mary Kay Inc., 54
Masland Industries, 60, 61
Massey, M., 70
Matthews, David, 90
Maurer, R., 172
McAdams, Richard P., 179
McCall, M.W., 40
McConnell, D., 68
McCrae, R.R., 37
Medtronic, 55
Merenbloom, E.Y., 119
Merriam, S., 119, 120
Micklewaith, J., 171
Microsoft, 53, 174
Miles, M.B., 120
Mills, C. Wright, 24
Mintzberg, Henry, 171, 182
Model, leader as model, 135
Moe, Terry, 181
Moorthy, D., 18
Moravec, Milan, 113
Morgan, G., 68, 69
Morris Institute for Human Values, 75
Morris, Tom, interview with, 75–78
Motivation
    Aristotle's view of, 76
    and self-managed teams, 113
Murphy, J.D., 35

N

Naisbitt, J., 47
Narrative
    of community, 11
    of leader, 13
Newmann, F., 171
New Visions initiative, 98, 192
New Youth Connections, 96
Niche, importance of, 161
Nicoll, David, 14
Niece, R., 134
Nilsen, D., 35, 42

O

Occupations, occupational
    types/categories, 41
O'Leary, Hazel, 25
Omote, 161
Open systems, 181
Organizational theory, 181–182
Ovard, Glen F., 137

P

Patrick, J.J., 30
Peabody, D., 37
Peck, Kyle L., 46
PeopleSoft, 54
Personality of leaders, 37, 63–65, 67
    of charismatic leaders, 39
    dark side traits, 39–40
Peterson, D.B., 40
Peters, Tom, 32, 117
Phillips, M.D., 147
Pigford, Aretha B., 66
Plato, values and business, 75–78
Political-historical leadership, 3–5
    forms of, 4
    views of, 4–5
Powell, Colin, 25
Power
    versus leadership, 4, 11
    sharing of, 142
Power Elite, The (Mills), 24
Prestine, N.A., 18
Principal
    challenges to, 18
    effectiveness, evaluation of, 154–155
    expectations of, 137
    leadership characteristics of, 19
    staff development, 143–147
    teachers' perceptions of, 18–19
    See also Educational leadership
PR Newswire, 61
Procter & Gamble, 174
Professional bureaucracy, 182
Pulskos, E.D., 42

R

Race and ethnicity, and power position, 25
Rashford, N.S., 18
R.E.A.L. sites
    American Association of School
        Administrators, 50
    Association for Supervision and
        Curriculum Development, 157
    Centrality of Character Education, 72
    Compact for Learning: An Action
        Handbook for Family-School-
        Community Partnerships, 105
    Critical Issue: Building a Committed
        Team, 131
    Education Week, 157
    Ethical Leadership, 72
    Mistakes Educational Leaders Make, 50

School-Based Reform, 131
Schools as Communities–ERIC Digest, 105
Test Your Ethics Quotient, 72
Work Teams in Schools, 131
Reflection process, 174–178
    elements of, 175–178
    importance of, 175
Reich, Rob, 93
Resistance to change, 70–71
    change-back phenomenon, 71
    environmental barriers, 70
    personal barriers, 70
Restructuring of schools, 95–126
    and community development, 95–97
    and culture of school, 124–126
    district level changes, 98–99
    redefinition concept, 100
    school/community readiness for, 100–101
    school level changes, 97–98
    school reform guidelines, 183–184
    self-managed teams study, 117–123
    shared leadership, 126
    and societal commitment, 99
    state/federal levels, 99
Richardson, Michael D., 18
Rinehart, J.S., 118
Rohlen, T., 29
Roosevelt, Franklin D., 4, 5
Rose, Lowell, 90
Rost, J., 6
Rueb, J.D., 37
Rynn, M., 29, 30

S

Santos, S.L., 28
Sarason, Seymore, 181
Sashkin, M., 48
Schein, E.H., 28, 29, 68
Schneider, B., 41
Schneider, David M., 165
School district. *See* Districts
Schools and education
    categories of schools, 128–129
    educational change guidelines, 162–163
    entrepreneurial leadership in, 46–49
    for human potential development, 149–150
    leadership, effects of, 13–14
    and organizational theory, 181–182
    school restructuring. *See* Restructuring of schools
    transactional leadership in, 4
    vision in, 11
    working smarter process, 108–112
School-to-work programs, 97
Schorr, L., 172
Schuncke, George M., 154
Scientific management, 8
Scott, Robert Falcon, 33
Selby, Cecily Cannan, 25

Self-criticism, of leaders, 13
Self-esteem, developing in students, 139
Self-managed teams, 113–123
    applied to schools, study of, 116–123
    challenges to, 115
    and empowerment, 117–122
    examples of, 114–115
    and motivation, 113
    operation of, 118–119
    self-management, meaning of, 114
    successful teams, elements of, 122–123
    teaching teams, 119
Senge, Peter, 61, 69, 70, 179, 186
Shannon, C., 42
Shaver, J., 29
Sheive, L.T., 48
Sherritt, Caroline A., 162
Short, Paula M., 116, 122
Silins, H.C., 18
Situational leadership, 5
Sizer, Theodore, 108, 182, 191, 193
Slavin, Robert, 182
Slyke, Sue van, 86
Smircich, L., 8
Smith, W., 134
Smyth, W.J., 47
Social change
    societal commitment, 99
    and transformational leader, 4
Socioeconomic status, and power position, 24
Staff development, 143–147
    elements of, 145–147
    guidelines for, 147, 156
    study of, 143–145
Stalin, Joseph, 33
Stanton, Steven A., 174
States
    politics of, 180–181
    and school restructuring, 99
Stein, R., 18
Strike, K.A., 14
Stumph, S.E., 151
Sullivan, Leon, 26
Sullivan, W.M., 12
Superintendent. *See* Educational leadership
Sweetland, J., 35

T

Taylor, R.L., 47, 48
TDIndustries, 55
Teachers
    as coach, 192
    coaching of, 146
    collegiality, creation of, 141–142
    as learners, 145–146
    obstacles to, 141
    role of, 141–142
    staff development, 143–147
    teaching guidelines, 153
    See also Instructional leadership
Teams. *See* Groups

Tellegen, A., 37
Tett, R.P., 42
Texas Instruments, 175
Therapist, role of leader as, 7
Thomas, G. Scott, 86
Thomson, D.D., 18, 19
3M, 113, 115
Tichy, N., 6
Timpane, Michael, 93
Toch, Thomas, 112
Tocqueville, Alexis de, 28
Transactional leadership, 4
    meaning of, 4
    in schools, 4
Transformational leadership, 4, 6–8
    meaning of, 4
    in organizations, 6–7
    transformation process, 10
Trust, 79–83
    elements of, 79–81
    low level, signs of, 82
    trust building tips, 82–83
Truthfulness
    of leaders, 76
    in workplace, 76
Tucker, R.C., 4

U

Unity, of workers, 77
Ura, 161
USAA, 54

V

Values
    nature of, 70
    public and private, 14
    putting into practice, 125
Values of leaders, 56–62
    Aristotle/Plato on, 75–78
    character, importance of, 64
    commitment, 57
    compassion, 57
    competence, 56
    differing from work group, 70
    embodied by company, 60
    integrity, 56
    truth, 56
    value-based leadership, elements of, 59–62
Vanikar, R., 30
Vemmestad, John, 114
Vision
    in education, 11
    of educational leaders, 48
    of leaders, 63, 67, 69

W

Wachner, Linda, 25
Wadsworth, Deborah, 90

Wagner, Tony, 186, 187
Waxman, H.C., 148
Web sites. *See* R.E.A.L. sites
Weick, K., 7, 8
Welch, Jack, 64, 114
Whitaker, Beth, 134
Whitford, B.L., 119
Whole Foods Market, 55
William of Ockham, 77
Wilson, B., 68
Wolf, J., 147

Women, in leadership positions, 25–26
Workplace
    beauty in, 76
    extraordinary facilities, importance of, 54
Wriston, Walter, 63

Y

Yates, Albert C., 56
Yukl, G.A., 33, 34, 40

Z

Zaccaro, S.J., 37
Zimmerman, M.A., 117
Zlatos, William, 191
Zweigenhaft, Richard L., 24

Putting it in *Perspectives*
-Review Form-

Your name:_____   Date: _____

Reading title: _____

Summarize: Provide a one-sentence summary of this reading: _____
_____
_____
_____

Follow the Thinking: How does the author back the main premise of the reading? Are the facts/opinions appropriately supported by research or available data? Is the author's thinking logical?
_____
_____
_____
_____
_____
_____

Develop a Context (answer one or both questions): How does this reading contrast or compliment your professor's lecture treatment of the subject matter? How does this reading compare to your textbook's coverage?
_____
_____
_____
_____
_____
_____

Question Authority: Explain why you agree/disagree with the author's main premise.
_____
_____
_____
_____
_____
_____

COPY ME! Copy this form as needed. This form is also available at http://www.coursewise.com
Click on: *Perspectives*.